THE MAGICAL TAROT OF THE GOLDEN DAWN

THE MAGICAL TAROT OF THE GOLDEN DAWN
Divination, Meditation and High Magical Teachings

Revised Edition

Pat Zalewski and Chris Zalewski

AEON

Originally published in 2008. This new revised edition published in 2019 by
Aeon Books Ltd
12 New College Parade
Finchley Road
London NW3 5EP

British Library Cataloguing in Publication Data

A C.I.P. for this book is available from the British Library

ISBN-13: 978-1-91159-729-2

Typeset by Medlar Publishing Solutions Pvt Ltd, India

Printed in Great Britain by TJ International Ltd, Padstow, Cornwall

www.aeonbooks.co.uk

Dedication

To

Babs and Ian Nairn,
late of Whare Ra,
who helped us in our early years
of Golden Dawn work

CONTENTS

INTRODUCTION

In this present volume on the Tarot of the Golden Dawn, you will find many new innovations and directions that were never part of the original Golden Dawn manuscripts, but have been adopted by our own Thoth-Hermes temple.

One of the original problems we had to deal with, when preparing this volume, was that the original manuscripts we worked from were extremely sparse, possibly so students would do their own research. The early Tarot manuscripts of the Golden Dawn were written in such a way that they fell in line with the Golden Dawn rituals and knowledge lectures and unless one knows the rituals and papers of the Order they are no more than barely adequate. The Golden Dawn Tarot was created in the late 1880s and by today's standards suffers somewhat from a certain amount of stagnation. Since the last century many new innovations of New Age systems to the Tarot have greatly increased its meaning and direction. At the Whare Ra temple in New Zealand, this was understood, with many members making their own notes that included much of these additional teachings, which to us was a basic evolutionary approach. We mention this because Whare Ra temple lasted longest of the Golden Dawn temples, sixty-six years (1912–1978) and gave us a guideline on how the Golden Dawn stood up under the avalanche of new Tarot material that is now making itself available to the general public. We found that it would be stupidity to ignore additional teachings and simply stop at what was in the original papers, as one would then have a very thin Tarot book indeed. What is presented, in this volume, is both the traditional material and the additional New Age awareness, all utilised in our own Thoth-Hermes Temple and some of that utilised at Whare Ra Temple as well. We have not changed anything but simply added where there was a need.

It has always intrigued both of us that the Golden Dawn did not do more work on understanding the Tarot. At Whare Ra temple, the situation was so bad that many of the Whare Ra adepts did the BOTA course and used it for their Tarot studies. One of the last Chiefs of Whare

Ra actually used a couple of BOTA lectures on the Tarot and gave them out under the Golden Dawn banner. When we were studying with some of these people and they mentioned this, both of us felt very disappointed that they did not try to explore the Golden Dawn Tarot system more fully. All it would have taken was dedication, time and research.

In this practical volume on 'Book T' we have tried to present where possible a new corpus of material that relates particularly to the Golden Dawn cards, so that others who love the system as much as we do will be able to build further on it. In many respects the word 'new' is misleading since much of the information is expanded from the Golden Dawn manuscript 'Book of General Correspondences'. This was a series of tabulations by Golden Dawn members on a variety of subjects such as colour, mythology, gems, plants, astrology and angelic hierarchies, to name but a few. Since these tabulations were first written up, well over one hundred years ago, there has been a wealth of published material available that allows newer and deeper insights. As a result of this, many of the old tabulations of the Golden Dawn have been changed to fit in with the abundance of information now available.

A study of these Kabbalistic associations of the cards brings in a wealth of additional knowledge which is not generally associated with the Tarot. It gives the reader a chance to go deeper into the mysteries of the Tarot and gain an overall picture. When all of these associations are placed together they comprise a formidable book on the Kabbalah as a tool for more research into the Golden Dawn perspective. For to study the Tarot of the Golden Dawn is to study the Kabbalah as well.

Concerning the colouring of the Golden Dawn cards, the Trumps in particular, oral traditions of Whare Ra tell us that when the Trumps were originally shown to the postulants during rituals, they were not coloured. At Whare Ra this changed, mainly due to a lecture Mrs Felkin wrote where she had all the Trumps with specific colours on them.

The colouring of the original Golden Dawn cards was taken from the four colour scales, which were not shown to students until they reached the 5 = 6 level. If you study the Crowley deck, you will see how they were supposed to be coloured. However, the Golden Dawn kept adding additional colouring to the original instructions. We have included very detailed sections on colour, the Kabbalah and how specific colours can be applied, the colouring of the Trumps being but one example. Some of this fits in with the original associations, while some does not. As an example, the Golden Dawn later used the seven prismatic colours for the rainbow in the Trump Judgement. To his credit, Crowley rejected these 'ad hoc' aspects and concentrated solely on the four colour scales, which is what we have also done.

We have included the full use of ritual with meditation and the Tarot. Meditation and the Tarot have never been new to the Golden Dawn. A rudimentary attempt at what today is called a Path working was given out in Flying Roll Knowledge Lecture Four, in 1892 by Elaine Simpson and Florence Farr. Information on the methodology of the technique was scattered through various Golden Dawn documents. We have placed this material in some sort of order. We have also blended other sub-systems of the Order in so that an entirely new level of approach can be achieved when studying the cards, especially with the use of angelology associations.

The theme of the Tarot is the theme of creation itself, which is why it was sometimes referred to as the Book of Life. A good example of this is found in the text of the 'Emerald Tablet' utilised in the Golden Dawn and other Hermetic Orders. Its thirteen steps define an abstract structure that can be applied to almost any branch of Hermetic thought. We have applied it in this instance, here directly to the structure of the Tarot in light of its theoretical and practical uses:

1. *I speak not fictitious things, but what is true and most certain.*
   This is the first spark of divine manifestation. The author here states that he speaks with personal knowledge. It is the Spirit revealed in all its truth and glory. It is Thoth the Enterer speaking, in his form of 'Hermes', author of the Emerald Tablet.
2. *What is below is like that which is above and what is above is like that which is below, to accomplish the miracles of one thing.*
   This is really the first fundamental principle of the Tarot and embodies the duality of the Macrocosm and the Microcosm. It shows that even the smallest change in the heavens will have an effect on the earth. The premise is that change on a grand scale (astrology being one such example) will have a similar effect on the Microcosm (man). The Tarot in its Golden Dawn format has heavy astrological and Kabbalistic ties, so that when an event happens in man the Microcosm it can also be expanded upwards so that the Microcosm effects the Macrocosm as well, chaos mathematics being one such example. The *one thing* referred to is both the Microcosm and Macrocosm. The Major and Minor Arcana being one such example.
3. *And all things were produced by the meditation of one being, so that all things were produced from this one thing by adaptation.*
   A good example of this is the numbering system of the Tarot, both Major and Minor Arcana. The application of the Tarot to astrology and the Kabbalah is yet another aspect.
4. 'Its father is the Sun, its mother the Moon; the wind carries it in its belly, its nurse is the earth'.
   This is the breaking up of the Tarot into various divisions, the creating of the Four suits.

Sun	=	Wands	= Fire
Mother (Moon)	=	Cups	= Water
Wind	=	Swords	= Air
Earth	=	Disks	= Earth

5. *It is the cause of all perfection throughout the whole world.*
   The Tarot, taking into consideration all its associations, represents a perfection of abstract thought and design which is unlimited in concept.
6. *Its power be perfect if it be changed into earth.*
   This is analogous to bringing the abstract thought of the Tarot into practical applications.
7. *Separate the earth from the Fire, the subtle from the gross, acting prudently and with judgement.*
   This is a study of all the major and minor divisions of the Tarot.
8. *Ascend with the greatest sagacity from the earth to the heaven and then again descend to the earth and unite together the powers of things superior and things inferior. Thus you obtain the glory of the whole world and all obscurity will fly far away from you.*
   This is the use or invocation of the Higher Powers and the uniting of the Major and Minor Arcana into a complete Golden Dawn system of correspondences. This is the story of the Tarot as applied in the heavens and its fundamental plan, which is universal in scope and direction. It is also the asking of a divinatory question, using all of these principles.

9. *This thing is the fortitude of all fortitude, because it overcomes all subtle things and penetrates every solid thing.*
   This tells us that all is revealed to those who wish to use the Tarot, especially for divination and nothing can be hidden from its subtle probing when questions are asked.
10. *Thus were all things created.*
    The end result. The knowledge obtained from the divinatory question.
11. *Thence proceed wonderful adaptations, which are produced in this way.*
    The transmutation of the knowledge gained into action, proceeding in some useful direction.
12. *Therefore I am called Hermes Trismegistus, possessing the three parts of the philosophy of the whole world.*
    The mind, soul and body parts of the Tarot and its relationship to the story of creation and the Book of Life.
13. *That which I had to say concerning the operation of the Sun is completed.*

The completion of the work and function of the Tarot.

While reviewing some notes made on the Tarot by Mathers for the Alpha et Omega, in the 'Brazen Candlestick of the Star of the Heptagram' paper, we found yet another set of designs for the Trumps associated to the planets. These purported to give the true design of the Tarot.

Apparently, Mathers never did complete a Golden Dawn deck. Felkin did and his deck was used in the A.O. We mention all this because very little remains the same in matters of occult teachings such as the Tarot, especially in original branches of the Golden Dawn where members were constantly striving to push new limits on some explanations.

The artwork on 'The Magical Tarot of the Golden Dawn' deck was done by Skip Duschus. Our original Whare Ra decks were so badly drawn that over half of the cards had to be re-done. Also, in a few instances in the Minor Arcana, the original Golden Dawn descriptions did not match the Stella Matutina decks, so these had to be redrawn as well. Skip also re-drew the Court Cards to incorporate the original Westcott drawings which, though good, were not good enough for publication. As a result of this collaborative effort between Skip and ourselves it is hoped that a colour and a black-and-white Golden Dawn Tarot pack of these drawings will be brought onto the market.

Pat Zalewski and Chris Zalewski
1993/2007

Historical

The first general reference to modern European Tarot cards is in the writings of the Abbe de la Rive who made the statement that the Tarot cards originated from Spain in 1267. They were brought to Italy by Castilian princes who came to Scilly and Calabria then extended into Italy. Another early reference to the Tarot comes from the fifteenth century, chronicler Giovanni Covelluzo, who stated:

> *There were encamped about Viterbo paid troops of the opposing factions of Clement VII and Urban VI, who did commit depredations of all kinds and robberies in the Roman states. In this year (1379) of such great tribulations the game of cards was introduced into Viterbo, which came from the Saracens and was called Niab.*

An ancient fragment of paper from the Museum of Islamic Art is said to represent an early Egyptian Court Card (see Richard Ettinghausen 'Further Comments on Mamluk Playing Cards') but to attempt to say what this fragment actually represented would be pure speculation. It does show a possible connection to the theory that the origins of the Tarot were in Egypt. In China, earlier editions of playing cards are recorded in a Chinese dictionary called the 'Ching-tse-tung' which states that card games were invented in 1120 for the Emperor and his wives. Since no evidence exists of these early packs there is, unfortunately, no way to connect the Chinese cards and the European ones, unless they were brought to the Middle East by Arab traders.

One of the greatest misconceptions about Tarot cards is their reputed Gypsy origin, which stems mainly from late nineteenth century writings, such as those of J.A. Vaillant. In fact, the available evidence indicates that the cards arrived in Europe well before the migration of the Gypsies to Europe from India.

The modern occult revival of the Tarot was apparently started by the Frenchman Alliette, or 'Etteilla' as he was publicly known, who wrote a series of books on the Tarot. These books relate the occult origin of the Tarot and expound the theories of de Gebelin, who viewed the Tarot as a book of learning and occult wisdom. In 1853 Julia Orsina wrote eight volumes called 'Le Grand Etteila, ou l'Art de Tirer les Cartes' which bridged the gap with occultism even further. In 1854 Eliphas Levi's 'Dogma and Ritual of Transcendental Magic' firmly linked the Tarot and Hebrew mysticism together by associating the twenty-two Tarot Trumps with the letters of the Hebrew alphabet. This association of tarot cards and the Hebrew letters, when applied to an aspect of Hebrew mysticism called the Kabbalah, entrenched the Tarot as a very high form of occult learning. In England, in 1888, the Society for the Hermetic Order of the Golden Dawn was founded. This immensely influential magical group concentrated its teachings on applying the Tarot to the Kabbalah and, when expanded to the Macrocosm, would also take in the various constellations themselves. The esoteric genius behind this society was Samuel Liddel Mathers who utilised the Tarot as a part of Golden Dawn ritual by having the hidden esoteric explanation of the Trumps explained at pertinent points of the ceremony.

This hidden tradition of the Tarot takes the Hebrew name of God, YOD HEH VAU HEH (Jehovah) and equates each letter to an element, being Fire, Water, Air and Earth respectively. Since the Tarot Trumps relate to the four elements, as well as the seven planets and the twelve Zodiac Signs (the final Tarot Trump has a dual association of both a planet and an element) the Tarot was further equated with symbolism contained within a very early book on Hebrew cosmology called the 'Sepher Yetzirah' which purports to give the formation of the universe and of creation itself.

The Tarot is in reality not one but two different packs. The first is the Major Arcana which contains the twenty-two Trumps and the second is the Minor Arcana which consists of sixteen Court Cards and forty Pip Cards as they are sometimes called. The division of the Minor Arcana is in Four Suits of Wands, Cups, Swords and Disks and which have elemental associations analogous to the letters of YOD HEH VAU HEH, thus:

Yod = Fire = Wands
Heh = Water = Cups
Vau = Air = Swords
Heh = Earth = Disks

Mathers maintained that the word Tarot was a metatheses of the letters TARO: TORA (Hebrew) = Law; TROA (Hebrew) = Gate; ROTA (Latin) = Wheel; ORAT (Latin) = it speaks argues or entreats; TAOR (Egyptian) = Taur, the Goddess of Darkness; ATOR (Egyptian) = Athor, the Egyptian Venus. The Tarot deck of the Golden Dawn was not revealed to the public until 1977 when a version was published by Robert Wang under the direction of Israel Regardie, a former initiate of the Stella Matutina, a name given to the Golden Dawn after 1903. Regardie was a member of the Bristol-Hermes Temple in England for a few years in the 1930s and demitted from it after he decided to publish its teachings and rituals. Regardie's original Tarot cards were stolen some years ago and Wang worked on colour photocopies of this deck that Regardie had previously given to a friend. Since some of the cards in the deck Regardie had were changed from the original Golden Dawn designs by the Stella Matutina, Wang actually altered the Bristol-Temple deck to what he believed was the correct Golden Dawn symbolism and colour scheme, which it was not.

In 1983, when Regardie came to New Zealand to visit members of the Thoth-Hermes Temple, which had descended from Whare Ra Temple established in 1912 by Dr R. Felkin, we had the opportunity of showing him the original Tarot colouring scheme. This scheme, for the main part, was used in the Thoth deck by Aleister Crowley. Further to this, I had access to part of a deck that was painted by Moina Mathers, wife of Golden Dawn founder MacGregor Mathers, which was given to Felkin by Brodie Innes, another member of that Order around 1911–12. This consisted of the Minor Arcana, about three Trumps and one Court Card. The Trumps were from the elemental rituals.

The first noticeable difference between our deck and Wang's is the colour scheme, which is based on the Four Colour scales of the Golden Dawn–The King, Queen, Prince and Princess Scales. The next main point of difference is in the Court Cards, for these are taken from copies of the deck belonging to Wynn Westcott and sent to us by Mr Bob Gilbert. Although Westcott had these cards among his possessions, we do not think he drew them. His small cramped writing style does not show in the sketches. Neither of us are experts in these matters and the point in question as to who painted the Westcott Court Cards is worth considering. For the purpose of this book we have worked on the premise that the Court Cards were Westcott's (until it is proved either one way or the other).

The original Golden Dawn Tarot papers were actually more descriptive than informative, especially of the Court Cards and we have rewritten these as the descriptions are not really necessary when the reader is able to study the card itself. The backing of the cards is also different to the Wang version and the original for this was in fact published many years ago in Crowley's periodical known as The Equinox, Vol. 1, No. 8.

All in all, the Tarot deck as it is presented here to the general public is, in fact, an entirely new deck. Due to many changes the original Golden Dawn deck underwent in the Order since its inception in 1880s to the present day and we have tried to present the deck as it was originally. It should be noted that the Court Cards involve by far the greatest changes. It should be noted Dr Wynn Westcott also in fact assisted Dr Felkin with some of the changes made to the Stella Matutina deck which were done nearly twenty years after the original deck was conceived. What we wanted to present here was the original deck, thereby avoiding possible arguments as to what actually constitutes a Golden Dawn deck, depending on which temple and what period it came from. According to Jack Taylor, Mathers created some of the Trump Cards and the Pip Cards from the Marsellies Tarot designs, while Westcott contributed the Court Cards, which Mathers altered at a later date.

To fully understand some of the differences between this deck and that of Wang's take, for example, the card 'Magician' in which the Four Talismans of Ireland are placed on the altar and not the elemental weapons (used by advanced members who belonged to the Second or Inner Order). When Wang studied Regardie's version of this card he changed it to incorporate the elemental weapons by simply following the instructions of Mrs Felkin's Stella Matutina lecture on the Trumps. Copies of Regardie's cards, which appear in 'The Complete Golden Dawn System of Magic', show that they are almost identical to our own Whare Ra deck, given to us by Taylor to paint some years ago.

A careful study of the Golden Dawn Trumps shows a very peculiar change in theme. The first Trumps have heavy Celtic symbology with 'The Fool' for the main part, associated with Sir Parzival of the Round Table and his upbringing in the almost enchanted forest along with the story of him and the dog on the leash. Sir Parzival was often referred to as the 'Divine Fool'. 'The High Priestess' is another aspect of the Grail legend. This Celtic tendency however seems to stop abruptly at this point and Felkin seems to have embraced more of the Marseille line of thinking, although endowing it with heavy Kabbalistic symbology. The Grail legend, as written by Wolfram Von Eschbach, was considered by many of those within the Golden Dawn to be the central point of origin of the Tarot and oral tradition has it that this was studied very carefully by Mathers and Westcott, and that Westcott, took the symbology of the Court Cards from this text.

The Golden Dawn Tarot is not an easy pack to work with because of its strong esoteric significance and therefore is not one for the beginner. When studying this book, the reader would do well to consult other various books on the Order's teachings and rituals, especially 'The Golden Dawn' by Regardie and our own work on the rituals, so that many of the esoteric terminologies are understood.

By personalising each card, that is, by painting it, one starts a very intricate internal process involving the acceptance of the card on a very deep level. This is a type of meditation that is, possibly, closely allied with states of Zen, for it not only helps the mind attune itself to the task in hand but has a number of therapeutic values too numerous to mention. It could be said that by painting this deck, using the Four Colour Scales, one goes through a very advanced state of internal reaction that, in many instances, supersedes the necessity of committing to memory various occult tabulations. It is the vital act of doing that is important here and not simply theorising. What we have tried to present here is the Golden Dawn deck as it was originally done. It would be impossible to give updated versions because these varied so much in the later years. Today, there is a great disappointment in the Wang version of the Golden Dawn deck and it is very obvious that he went his own way on a number of the cards he drew. The deck was published while the New Zealand Temple, Whare Ra, was still functioning (and which incidentally, held the copyright on the Stella Matutina version of the Golden Dawn deck) and therefore it was not very favourably received, still less so by some other Golden Dawn students. This new edition gives the student a chance to personalise one's nature into the deck by colouring it the way each student thinks will work best for him or her, yet still utilising the Golden Dawn colour allocations and leaving a great deal of room for experimentation. In our own New Zealand Temple, Thoth-Hermes, this type of colour personalisation is considered mandatory as part of one's training and I cannot overstate its value enough.

The Golden Dawn deck as we know it today, was originally conceived by Westcott, improved on by Mathers (who drew only half the Trumps) and completed by Felkin in collaboration with Westcott, in or around 1910. A number of years ago when I was studying various mandalas in India, under my teacher the late Vivandatta, he would have me paint numerous designs of certain colours to help integrate me with the work in hand. In many instances that was all we did with some startling results that were only intellectualised at a later date. This is how, I feel, one should approach painting the Golden Dawn.

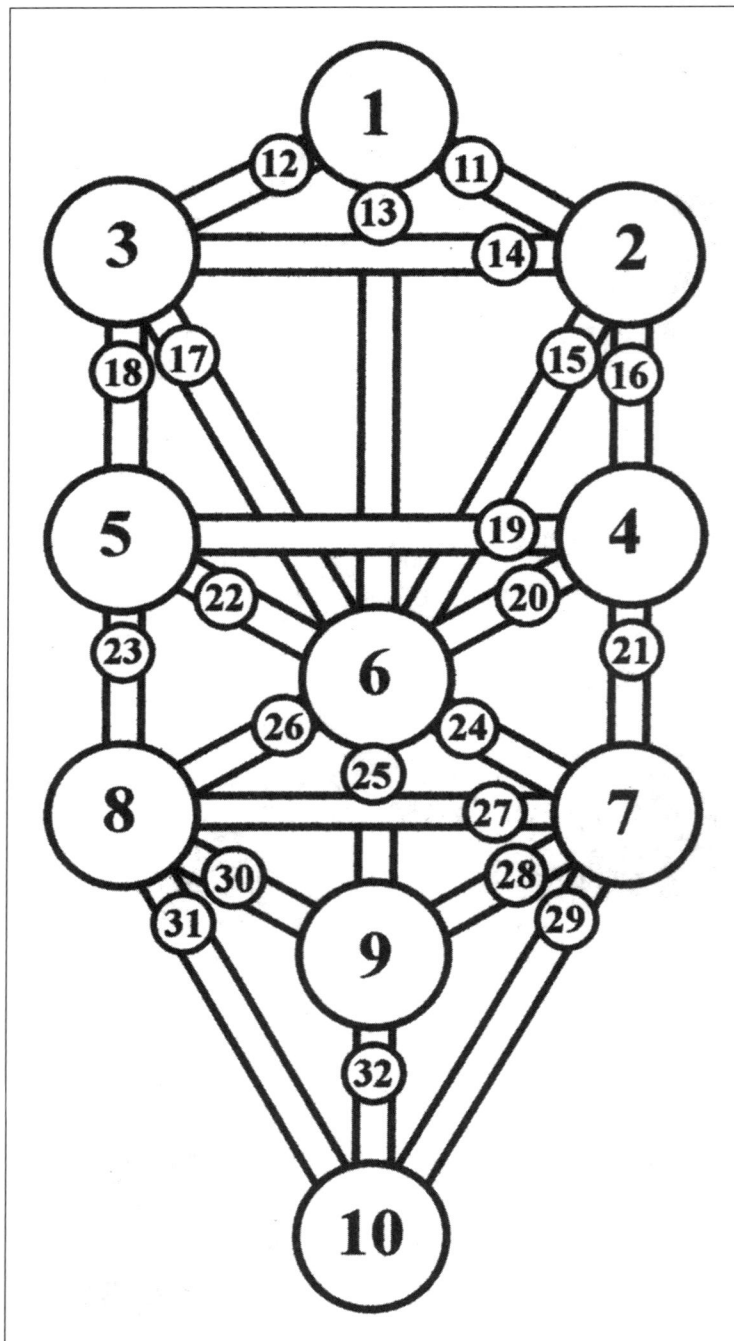

The Tarot and the Kabbalah

The Kabbalah was originally an obscure sectarian teaching from Hebrew mysticism that gradually was adopted by many of the greatest philosophers of Europe throughout the ages to the present day. It is presented as a form of thinking in ten stages, that is connected by various paths, each attributed to letters of the Hebrew alphabet. With this form of metaphysics many other philosophies of both Eastern and Western thought appendaged themselves to its core so that its boundaries grew with every coming age. One of the best descriptions of the Kabbalah that I have ever seen was given in a nineteenth century book called the 'Canon' by William Stirling: 'The Cabbalistic theology, representing the endless reasoning of countless generations of ingenious men, is the epitome of man's first efforts to grasp the problems connected with the cause and continuance of life, the inscrutable mystery which baffled the understanding of all inquiries alike. They reasoned concerning all phenomena of existence by their analogy to human creation and it was supposed that the universal creation took place after the manner of human creation and the generative attributes of a man and a woman were those of God and the universe and finally that all bodily functions of a human being and their counterpart in the Macrocosm or Greater World'.

It was not until the mid-nineteenth century that it was revealed by occultists such as Eliphas Levi in his 'Dogma and Ritual of Transcendental Magic' and also in his numerous books after that, that the Kabbalah and the Tarot were in fact related to each in form and concept.

The Kabbalah on the Tree of Life — the Minor Arcana

Kabbalistic theology informs us that light, spirit or influence actually came into being in this universe in three stages before it was sufficiently manifested enough in form. The stages were called the Three Veils of Negative Existence and were called in Hebrew, the Ain = Negatively,

Ain Soph = The Limitless and Ain Soph Aur = Limitless Light. The Hebrew letters of the last name are nine in number and they constitute the unmanifested steps or spheres, which the Kabbalists called Sephiroth, so that at the number nine we cannot progress further without returning to unity.

The First of the Sephirah is called Kether, the Crown and shows the first manifested form which many have associated with the Hebrew name of God as shown in the letters AHIH (or Eheieh). It is the incomprehensible deity and Kether is often referred to the Godhead as the primal source of manifestation. The very ancient Kabbalistic Book, the 'Sepher Yetzirah' states that Kether is called 'The Admirable, or Hidden Intelligence' for it shows the Light giving the power of comprehension to the first principle which has no beginning or end. Aligned with the Tarot we have the initial card of the four suits of the Minor Arcana linked here. The Ace of Wands, Cups, Swords and Pentacles. Each of these cards shows the manifested state of something just born through their respective framework of the Four Elements. They exist but are still extremely pliable in nature and are very much the essential nature of the Aces.

The second Sephirah is called Chokmah, Wisdom and it shows the establishment of polarity in a balanced and harmonious disposition. Its Yetziratic title is 'Illuminating Intelligence' and refers to implanting of intelligence and wisdom. The ability to discern things has now come about and to a certain extent it shows the result of exaltation or spirit in matter through intelligence, the prime aspect that separates man from the animals. It is also very much the concept of reflected glory of Kether as well. The Tarot association here are the four Twos of the four suits, all of which are extremely positive in outlook.

The third Sephirah is Binah, Understanding and it shows the establishment of the Triad. It is the next step after Wisdom for while Wisdom gives us the ability to discern things, Understanding shows us the way to do it. The name Binah, in fact, comes from the Hebrew BYNH, Ben-a Son and YH from Chokmah, showing the Son of Chokmah. The Yetziratic title of this Sephirah is 'Sanctifying Intelligence' and signifies being the first order of development of Intelligence (sometimes called Primordial Intelligence), since the establishment of polarity in Chokmah, though it is ever mindful of its roots in Kether. The Tarot association here relates to the four Threes and shows the realisation of action.

The fourth Sephirah is Chesed, Mercy and the establishment of the Quaternary. This shows Mercy being expressed from Wisdom and Understanding. While we are investigating the formation of the Kabbalah, it must always be considered that it can be used like a ladder for those ascending it and trying to unite with the Godhead in Kether. The Yetziratic title is 'Cohesive or Receptive Intelligence' because it is a Sephirah that contains all the newly manifested emanations from the Supernal and is, to a certain extent, not tainted with negativeness at this point. The Tarot associations are the four Fours and show the perfection of matter, its realisation or completion.

The fifth Sephirah is Geburah, Severity. This is the polar opposite of Mercy and shows that an extremity has been reached through harsh action and thus it is very applicable to the number five. This is not an easy Sephirah and deals with victory after trial and tribulation. It shows that nothing in its area of influence will come easy. The Yetziratic Title here is 'Radical Intelligence' and after seeing the makeup of this Sephirah it is not really surprising it is called that. It is closely linked to Binah which is directly above it. Geburah is the Sephirah of rule and retribution, trial and tribulation and is the extreme of these actions. The Tarot association here is the four Fives which are associated with opposition, strife, struggle, obstacles and war.

The sixth Sephirah is Tiphareth, Beauty. This Sephirah stands directly below Kether on the Middle Pillar. The emanations that flow from it are mixed with those of Geburah and Chesed so that a perfectly balanced radiant polarity for the whole Tree of Life is found. Its title is directly related to the emanations of Kether that bind it to harmonising those of Geburah and Chesed and this perfection is often called beautiful. The Yetziratic Title of this is called 'Mediating Intelligence' as, being in the Central position of the Tree, it not only receives the emanations from both the Pillars of Severity and Mercy but from the Middle Pillar also, making it quite unique to receive the varying degrees of emanations and combining them into a single neutral force. The Tarot association here is the four Sixes which relate to a definite accomplishment and carrying out of matter.

The seventh Sephirah is Netzach, Victory, which relates to the end of the emanations from the Pillar of Mercy which has successfully won through. Its Yetziratic Title is 'Occult Intelligence' and shows the combination of both Faith and Virtue through the perception of the former with the impetus of the latter. The term 'Occult' simply means Hidden Knowledge and thus relates to the secret side of our nature in its expression. The Tarot association here is the four Sevens which generally associate with a force, transcending the material plane, much like a crown which is powerful but relative to the personality of those who wear it. The Sevens show a possible result which is dependent on the action taken.

The eighth Sephirah is Hod, Splendour. This Sephirah, is the last in the Pillar of Severity showing that the energy of this dynamic Pillar is now at its strongest. The Yetziratic title is 'Absolute or Perfect Intelligence' showing the martial aspect of Geburah. Geburah is directly above Hod and influences it strongly, for being absolute can only mean total power or control. The Tarot association is the four Eights which generally show solitary success or success on a minor level, limited to a certain structure or framework.

The ninth Sephirah is Yesod, Foundation. This is the Sephirah on the Middle path that now tapers the two completed forces of Splendour and Victory into Foundation which is a basic building block on which further developments can be built. In many respects this Sephirah is much like the foetus in the Womb, fully formed but not yet grown to full maturity. The Yetziratic Title applied here is 'Pure Intelligence' because here the Intelligence has not been tampered with in any way before it is exposed to a new world where the various impressions it will form will put this pure form through many experiences so that the individual will have a chance to grow. The Tarot association here is the four Nines. Generally they show a very great fundamental force, or an executive power, because they rest on a firm basis, powerful for good or evil.

The tenth Sephirah is Malkuth, Kingdom. Malkuth is of course the final Sephirah where an emergence of a complete cycle has been completed. Apart from the emanations of Yesod placed above, it is now time for the emanations from Hod and Netzach to blend in together and give additional impetus to the form. It shows the stabilisation of matter through the influence of the Spirit in Kether which Malkuth is a reflection of, although in a much deeper form. The Yetziratic Title of this Sephirah is 'Resplendent Intelligence' and shows that the direct emanations through the Middle Pillar from Kether are still very strong. The Tarot association here is the four Tens which generally show fixed and culminated completed forces, whether for good or evil. Thus matter is thoroughly and definitely determined. It is similar to the force of Nines.

The Kabbalah and the Macroprosopus — Court Cards

In the previous section we have dealt with the ten Sephiroth of the Kabbalah applied to the Tree of Life. In this formation we are dealing with what is called the 'Symbolical Deific Form'. In this instance the entire concept of the Kabbalah is applied to the Greater Universe. The ancient Kabbalists applied this concept to the framework of man, though somewhat expanded it to take in the Macrocosm. In essence this is merely another form of Kabbalistic teaching that has strong roots in the Zohar, which some see as a later and more traditional teaching of the Kabbalah. Instead of having Ten Sephiroth as in the previous section, we now are going to be dealing with four emanations. All of these originate from a Kether-like source, but on an entirely different level than the previous one. In the past a number of people have found that these Four emanations, when placed over the Tree, resemble the Sephiroth of Chokmah, Binah, Tiphareth and Malkuth and as such, have associated the Tarot Court Cards to these Sephiroth as well, for the sake of convenience. However, in the Golden Dawn Tarot papers written by Mathers that I have in my possession, the Court Cards are firmly applied to this formulation of the Kabbalah and not the previous one. The first visible emanation is called the ABBA and is called the Supernal Father and this is analogous to some of the energy displayed by Chokmah. This comes under the Yod force of the Divine Name of Yod Heh Vau Heh (or YHVH). The Tarot association here is that of the four Knights, or figures mounted on horses, showing the primary or Yod force of the Divine name in each Suit, the radix, Father and commencement of Material Forces. This is a force in which all others are implied and of which they form the development and completion. A swift force which is violent in action, but whose effect soon passes away and is therefore symbolised by a figure on a horse riding swiftly and clothed in complete armour.

The Second emanation is called AIMA, the Supernal Mother and is analogous to Binah. This is representative of the Heh force of the Divine Name, applied to each suit of the Tarot and shows the four Queens seated on Thrones. This symbolism reveals the Mother and bringer forth of Material Force, a force which develops and realises the force of the Knight. A steady force which is unshaken, but not rapid though enduring. It is therefore symbolised by a figure seated upon a Throne but also clothed in armour.

The Third emanation is called the Zaur Anpin or Lesser Countenance and is represented by the Son or Vau force in the Divine Name. This emanation is, in fact, analogous to the six Sephiroth from Chesed to Yesod. The four Kings (sometimes called Princes) are seated in chariots and constitute the Son of the Knight and Queen who realises the influence of both scales of force. This is an Emperor whose effect is rapid but not as swift as the Knight, but enduring though not as steady as that of the Queen. It is therefore symbolised by a figure borne in a chariot and clothed with armour. Yet his power is illusionary, unless set in motion by his Mother and Father.

The Fourth emanation is Malkah the Queen or Kallah, the Bride, the wife of the Son or Zaur Anpin. This represents the Heh Final force of the Divine Name and is analogous to the Sephiroth of Malkuth. The four Princesses are associated here and they are representative of Amazons standing firmly by themselves, neither riding upon horses nor seated on Thrones, nor borne in

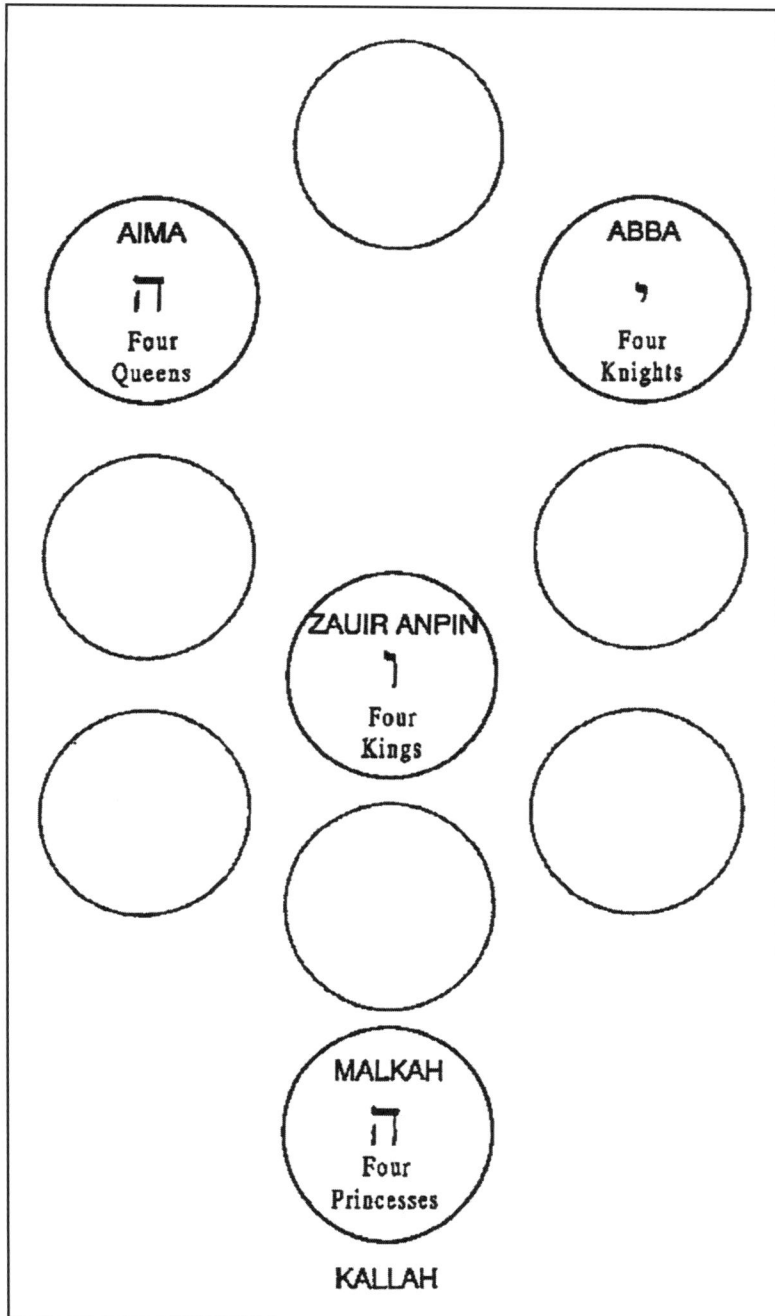

AIMA

ה

Four
Queens

ABBA

י

Four
Knights

ZAUIR ANPIN

ו

Four
Kings

MALKAH

ה

Four
Princesses

KALLAH

chariots. The Princess is the daughter of the King and Queen and who has married the Son to become the Empress and whose effect is a combination of the Knight, Queen and King/Prince. Her power is strong but she exists because of her marriage to the Son and is the woman warrior who can fight for what she wants and dominates all opposition.

The Four Worlds and the Four Suits

In Kabbalistic doctrine there are Four Worlds or levels of existence, each becoming more definitive than the one before it. The worlds are said to represent the Four Suits of the Tarot and the Four Letters of the Divine Name. Generally they can be applied to Four separate versions of the Tree of Life, or also divide one Tree into four separate divisions.

The First World is that of Atziluth and is linked to the Yod Force of the Divine Name and the Tarot Suit of Wands. This is often called the Archetypal or World of the Spirit for here we have the first impetus of an idea that works on the broad outline of a concept of a plan.

The Second World is that of Briah and relates to the Heh force and the Suit of Cups. This is the Creative World and shows that the idea or concept as formulated in Atziluth has now taken root in some sort of large framework and is being developed into a workable structure.

The Third World is that of Yetzirah and concerns the Vau force and relates to the Suit of Swords. This is the World of Formation showing the actual development of the ideas through the framework of Briah. This is very much the mental World where things have been brought through and are now down on paper, so to speak.

The Fourth World is that of Assiah and is the Heh (Final) Force relating to the Suit of Disks, or Pentacles as they are sometimes called. This is the world of the Material or Physical World. Now that the whole mental process of the idea has been assimilated this World now works on the physical action of it, the end result of the lofty concepts as first formulated in Atziluth.

The Sepher Yetzirah and the Four Suits

The 'Sepher Yetzira' is considered the first real Kabbalistic Book. Its written origin dates back to about the sixth century though its oral traditions are said to be much earlier. The book itself shows the formation or creation of all things by using the analogy of the formation of the twenty-two letters of the Hebrew alphabet. These letters were, in turn, adopted by some modern Kabbalists to coincide with the meanings of the twenty-two Trumps of the Major Arcana. On studying the meaning of each Trump and letter of the Hebrew alphabet one can see a remarkable similarity between them. In the 'Sepher Yetzirah' there is a tract called thirty-two paths of Wisdom which contain what we have referred to as the 'Yetziratic Titles'. These relate to the title of each of the Ten Sephiroth and twenty-two paths. This part of the book is actually an appendage to the original 'Sepher Yetzirah' but hangs together so well with the original that most modern day Kabbalists tend to accept it as part of the 'Sepher Yetzirah' itself. The first three Hebrew letters of the 'Sepher Yetzirah' are called the Three Mother letters and are Aleph, Mem and Shin. In the Golden Dawn these were related to the Elements of Air, Water and Fire. The Seven Double letters were said to represent the Seven planets and the Twelve Simple letters the Twelve Zodiac Signs. Each set was said to give birth to the one below it. It is a remarkable book on Cosmology.

Gematria and the Tarot

In the descriptions of the Tarot cards, or Keys as they are known, there are a number of references to matching words of the same numerical value in order to aid the descriptions of the Key. According to Mathers, this matching of words of the same numerical value is called Gematria and it is a metathesis of the Greek word 'Grammateia' meaning 'secretariat'. The concept behind this is that Hebrew is a language that has a numerical value for each letter. Generally speaking, words of similar value are related in the concept of expression. By comparing these words which have the same value a more detailed analysis of the original Hebrew letter or word can be undertaken. One of the best books available today, which lists the value of Hebrew words and letters, is the 'Cabalistic Encyclopedia', by David Godwin, published by Llewellyn Publications. There are other systems closely allied with Gematria worthy of further exploration (such as Notariqon and Temurah), but for the purposes of this book will not be discussed. Since the discovery of Pluto modern day Golden Dawn temples tend to attribute the three slower planets to the corresponding Tarot cards 'Fool', 'Hanged Man' and 'Judgement' with the elements associated to the Court Cards.

The Four Colour Scales of the Golden Dawn as applied to the Tarot

One of the most intriguing set of teachings within the Golden Dawn is the application and use of the Four Colour Scales as placed on the Four Trees of Life. When Mathers created this system he took it from twenty-two systems of colour theory with no two colours being exactly identical and sometimes the separation being only a slight taint of a lighter or darker colour. This subject was indeed the most complex among the Order's teachings and due to the difficulty of painting them many adopted their own set of scales. What we have tried to present here is what was given out originally in the Golden Dawn. The following set of colour scales is taken from a very early manuscript that was later altered a number of times by various temples over the years. This manuscript also had a set of very well preserved scales and we had the advantage of making the comparison and found that the colour description was the area that caused most of the confusion. It was surprising how many people could not tell the difference between purple and violet or confused the two.

There are some interesting differences when compared with Crowley's 777 and we note that Binah in the Queen Scale is given the correct colouring of Blackish Red where Crowley gives it as Black, altogether ignoring its Red Root. Since the Crowley Scales are readily available we have decided to give this version which was obtained from the papers of a former Chief of Whare Ra Temple. What we have done here is to give the colours a modern name, using the 'Methune Handbook of Colour' as a basis of matching colours with the modern descriptions to try and bring in some degree of uniformity. The colours were patiently generated by Chris to give what we have listed below. The truth of the matter is that there are so many versions of the Colour Scales, even Mathers altered his on a number of occasions, that to give the original version is nigh on impossible though we can but try.

The two versions published by Regardie are inaccurate in the Princess Scale and have been tampered with considerably. We suggest that the reader ignore the Regardie Scales and follows

19

the version given below. The scales are numbered from one to thirty-two. The first ten Numbers relate to the Sephiroth while the rest are associated with the Paths. The association of the twenty-two Trumps to the scales actually starts at No. 11, the first Path after the Ten Sephiroth.

Colouring the Trumps

When colouring the Trumps the Golden Dawn applied four colours and the complimentaries so a total of eight colours could be used. The four colours originate from each of the four Scales, being the King, Queen, Prince and Princess scale. These are associated with the Paths. For example, the card 'The Fool' is placed on Path 11 (see following table). Therefore, the colours on paths 11 from all four colour scales are the four main colours used in this card. The complementary colours to these four are then the additional colours used in the colouring of the Fool. The correct method for obtaining the complementary colours then, was to place a colour against a white background, then gaze at the colour for a short time while maintaining your whole focus there. Then shift your focus to viewing around the edges of the colour, until you see a shimmer of another colour coming off the original over the white background. Next, shift your gaze completely to the white paper. One interesting error that has crept into these scales over the years is the association of Black to Binah in the Queen Scale. It was originally Blackish Red but Black to look at with the naked eye. Not only were a number of people in the Order confused but also others who demitted from it such as Crowley and Case who both used Black in their respective organisations. If Black is used the other colours cannot be generated correctly and this can only be done with Blackish Red. It also shows a number of people simply copied the colours without trying to generate them.

As it turns out there is more than one generating process for the colour scales, hence the confusion with the Golden Dawn papers.

You will see the new colour form in exactly the same shape and proportions as the coloured paper previously gazed upon. This is the complementary colour. Because shading disrupts the use of a pure colour process, the Adept would then make his colour translucent, if it was too dark and this substituted for shadings, though we must admit that this rule was bent a few times for the sake of artistic license. No flesh colours were to be used as this disrupted from the overall colour flow, the flesh usually being a translucent colour of one of the eight colours applied. The general rule of thumb was that, wherever possible, complementary colours were kept to a minimum and not to overshadow the four main colours in comparison. As to what colour went exactly where on each Trump was left for the individual to decide, as originally fixed colours for the Trumps were frowned upon. Only in later years when members started copying each others Tarot was this system abandoned as it was too complex and time wasting, when a deck could be copied with very little effort. The use of white and black to obtain better shaping and shading in the colouring of a card, is permissible.

Colouring the Court Cards

Elemental Colours were applied to the Court Cards. These are Primary Red for Wands, Primary Blue for Cups, Primary Yellow for Swords and for Disks a mixture of Citrine, Olive, Russet and Black Satin (the complementary colours for the first three are the Sephiroth of Netzach, Hod and

Yesod in the Queen Scale). Unlike the colouring of the Trumps there was a certain amount of restriction placed on the Court Cards as these were considered the first cards of the Minor Arcana and more for divination than for meditation. Black and White can also be used to form shapes as these are neutral colours.

What follows is a basic guide to painting your Court Cards, however, you will see a certain amount of artistic licence is still left to the adept.

Knight of Wands

Yod of Yod. This card is the Fiery part of Fire, therefore the colours used will be Primary Red with its complementary Green, both in varying shades. The Knight has Red-Gold hair, Hazel Eyes, Black horse, Red club and Scarlet cloak. His crest is also Black. The colour of his skin is translucent Red. The remainder of the card is to be coloured in varying shades of Red and complementary Green.

Queen of Wands

Heh of Yod. This card is the Watery part of Fire, therefore the colours used will be Primary Blue and splashes of its complementary Orange and Primary Red and splashes of its complementary Green. The Queen of Wands has Red-Gold hair and Blue eyes, Orange winged leopard's head as her crest. Translucent Red for the skin. The rest of the card is painted predominately Red with a little Green and at least a quarter Blue, in varying shadings.

King (Prince) of Wands

Vau of Yod. This card is the Airy part of Fire, therefore the colours used will be Primary Yellow with splashes of its complementary Violet and Primary Red and splashes of its complementary Green. The King (Prince) of Wands has Golden Hair, Blue-Grey eyes, a winged Lion's Head as a crest. His skin is translucent Red and the chariot has Yellow, Violet and Green shadings. The Lion is Red and Yellow and the remainder of the Card is coloured Red with at least a quarter Yellow and complementary colours.

Princess of Wands

Heh final of Yod. This card is the Earthy part of Fire, therefore the main colours used will be Primary Green and Primary Red, each being the complementary colour of the other. Elements of Gold, Russet, Citrine and Olive can also be used sparingly in painting this card. The Princess has Red-Gold hair and Blue eyes, Gold altar and translucent Red Skin. This card is made up of Red with a quarter Green for her earthy influence along with complementary Green.

Knight of Cups

Yod of Heh. This card is the Fiery part of Water, therefore the main colours used will be Primary Blue and Primary Red and their complementary colours Orange and Green used to a lesser degree. The Knight of Cups has fair hair and Blue eyes and sits astride a White horse while his crest is that of a peacock opening its wings. His skin is translucent Blue. The card is one quarter Red and three quarters Blue with shadings of the complementaries.

Queen of Cups

Heh of Heh. This card is the Watery part of Water. The main colour used is Primary Blue, along with its complementary colour Orange/Gold. The Queen of Cups has Gold Brown hair and Blue eyes and translucent Blue skin. An Ibis is her crest which is Orange. The rest of the card is Blue with complementary Orange.

King (Prince) of Cups

Vau of Heh. This card is the Airy part of Water and the main colours used are Primary Yellow and Primary Blue with their complementary colours Violet and Orange used to a lesser degree. The King of Cups has Brown hair and Grey or Brown eyes and translucent blue skin. An Eagle is his crest. One quarter of the card is Yellow and the rest Blue with a small amount coloured in the complementaries.

Princess of Cups

Heh (final) of Heh. This card is the Earthy part of Water, therefore the main colours used are Green and Blue and their complementary colours Red/Russett and Orange are used to a lesser degree. The Princess has Brown hair and Blue Brown eyes with a swan as her crest. Her skin is translucent Blue. One quarter of the card is Green and the rest is Blue with splashes of the complementaries. Russett, Olive, Citrine and Gold can also be used in this card.

Knight of Swords

Yod of Vau. The Knight of Swords is the Fiery part of Air, therefore the main colours will be Red and Yellow and their complementary colours Green and Violet used to a lesser degree. The Knight has dark Brown hair and dark eyes and translucent Yellow skin with a winged hexagram as his crest. His horse is Brown. One quarter of the card is Red with the rest Yellow with splashes of the complementaries.

Queen of Swords

Heh of Vau. The Queen of Swords is the watery part of water, therefore the main colours will be Blue and Yellow, the complementaries Orange and Violet used to a lesser degree. She has Grey hair and light Brown eyes and translucent Yellow skin. As a crest she has a winged child's head. One quarter of the card is Blue while the rest is Yellow with complementaries.

Knight (Prince) of Swords

Vau of Vau. The Prince of Swords is the Airy part of Air. The main colour used is Yellow with its complementary Violet. He has dark hair and dark eyes. His skin is translucent

Yellow and a winged angel's head is his crest. The remaining colours are varying shades of Yellow and its complementary. White and Black is applicable here for shaping and shading.

Princess of Swords

Heh final of Vau. The Princess of Swords is the Earthy part of Air, therefore her main colours will be Green and Yellow. The complementaries Red and Violet are used sparingly. She has light Brown hair and Blue eyes, a Silver altar and a Medusa's head as her crest and her skin is translucent Yellow. One quarter of the card is Green and the rest is Yellow with complementaries. Olive, Citrine, Russett, Black and White can also be used.

Knight of Disks

Yod of Heh (final). The Knight of Disks is the Fiery part of Earth, therefore the main colours used will be Red and Green and to a lesser degree Citrine, Olive, Russett, Black and White. He has dark hair and eyes and translucent Green skin and sits upon a light Brown horse. A winged stag's head is his crest. One quarter of the card is Red while the rest is Green with the other colours of Malkuth.

Queen of Disks

Heh of Heh (final). The Queen of Disks is the Watery part of Earth. The main colours used will be Blue and Green and a smaller percentage of the complementaries Orange and Red, with splashes of the other colours of Malkuth, Citrine, Olive, Russett and Black. She has dark hair and eyes and translucent Yellow skin with a winged goat's head as her crest. One quarter of the card is Blue and the rest is Green with complementaries etc.

Knight (Prince) of Disks

Vau of Heh (final). The Prince of Disks is the Airy part of Earth. The colours used here are Yellow and Green, with a smaller percentage of their complementaries Violet and Red and the colours of Malkuth.

He has dark Brown hair and dark eyes and translucent Green skin with a winged bull's head as his crest. One quarter of the card is Yellow and the rest Green with complementaries.

Princess of Disks

Heh final of Heh final. The Princess of Disks is the Earthy part of Earth, therefore her colours are Green with a little of its complementary Red and those of Malkuth. She has rich Brown hair and dark eyes, translucent Green skin and a winged ram's head as her crest. The rest of the card is a varying shade of Green with complementaries.

L·I·F·E·   ·V·I·TA·

T   A

O   P

B·I·O·S·

Colouring of the Minor Arcana

All the Minor Arcana have definite colours placed on them. Each suit will draw its colours from the Scale its suit applies to. For example Wands will be associated to the King Scale, Cups to the Queen Scale, Swords to the Prince Scale and Disks to the Princess Scale. The background colour of each card relates to the Paths on the Tree which represent the Zodiac Signs, while the implement (wand, sword, cup, disk) is the colour of the Path of the planet. The Clouds are coloured either white or the same as the Sephiroth that the cards relate to. For example taking the Three of Wands, the background colour would be from the Path of Aries in the King scale, while the wands would be the colour of the Path of the Sun from the King Scale. The clouds would be the Crimson, or white with crimson aura, from Binah in the King Scale, as all threes are allocated to this Sephirah. The hand holding the wands is white. When colouring the Three of Cups, one should paint the background the colour of the Path of Cancer in the Queen Scale and the Cups the colour of the Path of Mercury, while the clouds are Blackish Red of Binah (or white with a blackish red aura) in the Queen scale and the hands white. The Lotus bush from which the white water flows is the complementary colour of the background or sign.

The Three of Swords would then work with the Prince Scale. The Three of Disks the Princess Scale. The bushes in the Disks are the complementary colour of the backgrounds of each card. In the Princess scale there are flecks for the Planets and the Disks will be a combination of these two colours. The roses in this scale are white as are the hands with the clouds relating to the Sephiroth of the Princess Scale. The roses used in the swords and disks will be painted white.

There are, however, some exceptions to the rule where deliberate colours are used in the Pip Cards. Take for example, the Two of Cups, where the two dolphins are Silver and Gold and the water coming from them has the same colours. In the Two of Swords the rose emits five white rays from its petals. The Two of Disks has a green and gold serpent uniting them.

The Aces

These are in the colours of the elements with the background being the complementary. The hands holding them are all brilliant white. For example the Ace of Wands has primary red wand and yods, green background with white hand and clouds. The Ace of Disks is a combination of Green and Black with a complementary red and white for the main background. The Earth colours here are dual, but it is not the four divisions of Malkuth as applied to the Queen Scale, as we are dealing with primary elements and their complementaries only.

The backing diagram of the card

Placed on the back of every card is the following diagram of the Crux Ansata. The background of this card is black and the writing on it is white and relates to Light and Life coming into the Darkness of Chaos. The letters T.A.O.P may be read as the word ROTA or TAROT. The word is formed from the Latin R being replaced with a Greek P because it is found between the Alpha et Omega of the Apocalypse. The Tau cross is the starting point for it means LIFE as do the letters VITA which is its Latin counterpart. The word B.I.O.S is from the Greek which also means Life. The two Pentagrams are Gold (for the Sun) and Silver (for the Moon) which also relate to the Alpha et Omega. The Crux Ansata is in the form of a Rose Cross. One arm is Scarlet with the symbols of Leo and the Wand in Emerald Green. Another arm is Blue with the Eagle and Cup in Orange. A third is Yellow with Aquarius and Dagger in Violet. The last arm is in the four colours of Malkuth (in the Queen Scale), with Pentacle and Taurus in Black. The outer rim is white with the Name of the Great Angel HRU written in black lettering of the Theban script as given by Agrippa. In the centre is the White circle and Red Kerubic Cross. The colours in the head of the Ankh-like figure show the formation of the letters of the Sepher Yetzirah or Book of Formation. The whole backing of each card is designed to show the formation of Life through a given framework so that everything will be evenly distributed and there will be no distortions.

The Four Colour Scales

(This paper compiled by Sr. L.Z.T.M. 7 = 4 of the Thoth-Hermes Temple, Wellington New Zealand, 1991.)

The colour Scales of the four Kabbalistic Trees of Life as taken from a Whare Ra document on the Golden Dawn Colour Scales. These colour scales below have been generated and renamed in some cases with names that more suitably name each colour. This is because the colours given on the Whare Ra document were more colour descriptions rather than colour names and their accuracy in colour description confusing when comparing with colour descriptions of the Trees of Life. For example, whoever recorded the paper I am working from, did not know the difference between violet and purple. From my work with these scales I found that the colours described as purple, were actually various shades of violet. No colour should be the same, therefore more accurate naming became necessary to show the differences between the colours. Therefore, in one column below the Whare Ra (Golden Dawn) description will be listed and in the other a more suitable name has been given.

These new names were taken from the Methuen Handbook of Colour, reprint 1981, Eyre Methuen, London. To the best of my ability I have kept these colours as close as possible to the descriptions of the Whare Ra document. As you will see, some colours are generated and some placed. Those generated might show a difference to the Golden Dawn description. This may be due to the type of paints I was using (student's acrylics) or due to the colour described not fitting into the pattern of generation. These colours are not the colours published by I. Regardie and A. Crowley whose charts were based on the original Golden Dawn scales.

Accuracy in the use of the colours is necessary for painting of your Tarot cards and the painting of the Vault.

World of Atziluth—King Scale.

Path	Whare Ra	Recent name/description
1	White	Very Brilliant White
2	Pure Soft Blue	Bluish White
3	Crimson	Crimson
4	Deep Violet	Deep Violet
5	Orange	Deep Orange
6	Clear Rose Pink	Rose Pinkish White
7	Amber	Amber Yellow
8	Violet Purple	Deep Violet Purple
9	Indigo	Dark Indigo Blue
10	Yellow	Vivid Yellow
11	Pale Yellow	Pale Yellow
12	Primrose Yellow	Primrose Yellow
13	Pale Silvery Blue	Pale Silvery Blue
14	Emerald Green	Emerald Green
15	Blood Red	Lake Red
16	Red Orange	Fire Red or Flame Scarlet
17	Marigold	Marigold
18	Dark Amber	Carrot Red
19	Greenish Yellow	Sun Yellow
20	Yellow Green	Yellowish Green
21	Violet	Violet
22	Grass Green	Sap Green
23	Deep Blue	Prussian Blue
24	Blue Green	Bluish Green
25	Deep blue with hidden Red	(same)
26	Indigo	Indigo Blue-green
27	Poppy Red	Poppy Red
28	Amethyst	True Purple
29	Crimson	Deep Crimson
30	Golden Yellow	Clear Orange
31	Orange Red	Orange Red
32	Dark Indigo	Darkest Indigo
Daath	–	Blue Lavender White

World of Briah—Queen Scale.

Path	Whare Ra	Recent name/description
1	White	Brilliant White
2	Grey	Soft Bluish Grey
3	Blackish Red	Blackish Red (not reddish black)
4	Blue	Vivid Blue
5	Scarlet	Vivid Red
6	Daffodil Yellow	Pastel Yellow
7	Green	Deep Green
8	Persimmon	Tawny Orange
9	Dark Petunia	Dark Petunia (a clear deep violet)
10	Tertiaries Red	Tertiaries (Oxide Citrine, Deep Blue Green and Black)
11	Pale Blue	Baby Blue
12	Violet	Soft Lavender
13	Silvery White	Silvery White
14	Sky Blue	Light Sky Blue
15	Dark Rose Red	Dark Rose Red
16	Maroon	Light Maroon
17	Violet	Violaceous (an amethyst-mauve)
18	Deep blue-purple	Heliotrope
19	Black	Blackish Purple
20	Indigo	Clear Indigo Blue
21	Blue	Princess Blue
22	Blue	Blue
23	Olive Green	Olive Green
24	Sky Blue	Sky Blue
25	Pale Slate Grey	Pale Slate Grey
26	Yellow	Yellow
27	Red	Primary Red
28	Dove Colour	Dove Colour (soft blue white)
29	Warm Golden Brown	Warm Golden Brown
30	Golden Yellow	Golden Sunflower Yellow
31	Scarlet	Vermilion
32	Black	Soft Black
Daath	–	Very light Lavender Grey

World of Yetzerah—Prince Scale.

Path	Whare Ra	Recent name/description
1	White	White
2	Pearl Grey	Bluish Grey
3	Crimson, with black edge and rays	(same)
4	Deep Purple	Lapis Lazuli
5	Bright Scarlet	Bright Scarlet
6	Rich Salmon (Pink)	Shell Pink
7	Bright Yellow-green	Grapefruit
8	Red-Russet	Garnet Red
9	Very Dark Purple	Very Dark Violet Blue
10	Tertiaries, flecked into glowing gold	(same)
11	Greenish Grey	Turquoise White
12	Grey	Soft Reddish Grey
13	Very cold pale Blue	(same)
14	Pale Blue-Green	Turquoise Green
15	Rich Red	Claret
16	Red-Grey-Brown	Tomato Red not dark
17	Red-Grey-Violet	Cinnamon Brown
18	Silver Grey (neutral)	(same)
19	Yellowish Grey	Greyish Yellow
20	Grey-Blue-Green	Greyish Green
21	Blue Purple	Blue Violet
22	Blue-Green	Bottle Green
23	Greenish-Lemon	Greenish-Lemon
24	Pale Greenish Blue	Azure Blue
25	Pale Grey Blue	Pale Grey Blue
26	Pale Grey	Pale Bluish Grey
27	Rich Scarlet	Scarlet
28	Mauvish Grey	Soft Lilac Grey
29	Brownish Crimson	Oxide Red
30	Rich Amber	Deep Melon Yellow
31	Red	Red
32	Blue Black	Blue Black
Daath	–	Very light Lavender Grey

World of Assiah—Princess Scale.

Path	Whare Ra	Recent name/description
1	White rayed with Gold	(same)
2	White flecked with red, blue and Yellow	(same)
3	Grey flecked Pink	(same)
4	Deep Azure, flecked Yellow	(same)
5	Red, flecked with Black	(same)
6	Golden Amber	Straw Yellow
7	Olive, flecked Light Green	Green flecked Amber Gold
8	Yellow-Brown	Reddish Golden flecked White
9	Citrine flecked Azure	(same)
10	Black, rayed with Yellow	(same)
11	Yellow-Green	Pastel Green flecked Yellow
12	Indigo rayed Violet	Grey Indigo rayed Violet
13	Silver rayed Sky-Blue	(same)
14	Cerise rayed pale	Cerise rayed Turquoise Green
15	Crimson	Fraise (deep red)
16	Rich Brown	Rich Red Brown
17	Very pale Grey	Purplish Grey White tinged Purple
18	Dark Blue-Grey	(same)
19	Reddish Amber Brown	(same)
20	Livid Indigo	(like back of live lobster)
21	Bright Blue	Cool Blue rayed Yellow
22	Light pale Green	Pastel Turquoise
23	White flecked with Black	(same)
24	Dark Vivid Blue	Aqua-Sapphire Blue
25	Red-Grey to Mauve	Mauve Grey
26	Dark Greenish Brown	(same)
27	Scarlet rayed Amber	Poppy Scarlet rayed Amber
28	Buff, flecked White	(same)
29	Violet or plum	English Red (brown)
30	Amber rayed Red	Amber Yellow rayed Red
31	Red flecked Green	Paprika Red flecked Green
32	Black rayed blue	(same)
Daath	–	Pale Grey Lavender

The Meaning of Colour

Ponder now on why the Golden Dawn adepts put such emphasis on colour and using specific colours for each card. To increase your understanding on the power of colour, we advise books like 'Colour Healing' published by Health Research, Mokelumme Hill, California; 'The Aura and What It Means to You', also published by Health Research and other books on colour healing, of which you will find many, published to date.

To summarise, however, colour instigates a change in the human, emotional, physical and psychological responses. In fact, all life forms respond to colour. The Universe may very well have been created by Light and Sound. Colour is Light and colour has a vibration which is Sound. In fact, all things vibrate Light and Sound.

As people we wear colours, decorate our environments with colour and use colour to our commercial advantage. To the healer and adept, colour is used to heal physical, emotional and psychological complaints, which is in harmony with the meaning and use with the esoteric philosophies and symbology of colour. It is these two latter studies of colour (philosophy and symbology) which are used in the Tarot.

Colour is LIFE. When you, as the student, study colour, you will find yourself studying LIFE, or, the Cosmic Force and its immeasurable power. As colour enters into consciousness, it will also spring into form. It penetrates into the subconsciousness and exerts a powerful influence on an individual's mind and emotions, not forgetting physiological response. Hence, the importance of having the right colours on each Tarot Card.

In line with the teachings of the Sepher Yetzirah and of creation, colour comes through as Light and Sound. At each stage of manifestation it becomes denser. At this stage, mankind measures Light in two systems, the spectrochrome and the colour visible to the naked eye. The first is the translucent light in all its subtle shades, not detectable to the naked eye except under certain circumstances. The second is the dense visible form in manifestation. However, in either case the following is how it is formed.

From White (Light) come the three primaries, Blue, Yellow and Red, which generate the seven rays: Violet, Indigo, Blue, Green, Yellow, Orange and Red. These, when mixed with each other generate twelve rays of colour, which in turn on further mixing generate more colours, each level more denser than the other, finally arriving at Black.

As colour is the result of etheric vibrations of different wave lengths (active, vital radiation), you will find that your very feelings and thoughts will vibrate to colour. This is evidenced by the very colours our auras vibrate. The following is an example of the type of energy and psychological states some colours can vibrate.

Violet   – Spirituality, meditation, wisdom
Indigo   – Intuition, devotion, universality
Blue   – Religious inspiration, spiritual power, emotions
Green   – Harmony, growth, sympathy
Yellow   – Intellect, the Will
Orange   – Energy, unifies body and mind
Red   – Life, energizing, physical existence

Each of the above colours can, of course, be divided through mixing to many sub-hues, e.g., violet can mix to heliotrope, amethyst, royal purple, orchid and lavender.

The general rule is that bright clear colours represent positive or good qualities and dull, dark, cloudy, mottled shades represent negative or bad qualities. High-ethereal states of consciousness are represented by pale misty pastel tints.

The Tarot Major Arcana

The Tarot Major Arcana is twenty-two in number starting from 0 to 21. Another term used for the Major Arcana is the Keys of the Tarot, also known as the Trumps.

The following twenty-two chapters are explanations of each card of the Major Arcana. We have written the explanations on the Tarot cards in such a way that a divinative meaning can be perceived from the whole text, rather than just the last paragraph, as is often given in many books. Divination is in the whole of the card together with the symbology, myths, colour, numerology, alchemy, kabbalistic symbolism, etc. We urge, therefore, the reader to read the text with this understanding in mind.

In any study of the Tarot, the twenty-two Trumps or Keys, represent THE TOTAL KNOWL-EDGE. Any limitation anyone experiences from these cards would be only by one of association. What we have presented here is, in effect, the skeletonic framework of the Trumps. The astrological, numerological and kabbalistic associations given to each Trump represent only certain doorways. These associations are in fact what could be considered the main ones, though as one progresses with a study of the Trumps, many other associations will open up.

The Trumps are the main backbone of the Tarot and represent huge dimensions of associations of which the Court Cards and Minor Arcana are but a part. The Golden Dawn associations to the Trumps do not always fall into line with other published associations to other Tarot decks, even though at first sight they may appear to do so. What they do cover, however, is a holistic perspective of symbology and meaning. After all, the Tarot is a Book of Life from a universal perspective and not a single culture or individual's perceptions.

Study of the Tarot Trumps is best handled by building up a file reference. Spend a few minutes meditation on each Trump and write down your impressions. A few weeks later come back and repeat the process. Any time you come across something different in your divination readings, make a note of it in your file. After a while you will have quite a collection of worthwhile notes.

Study also the cards and all their associations and symbology. Do further research as well. One of the traps many fall for is sticking to the published text and accepting everything written, but looking no further. There is always room for improvement. For example, if you are accurate in divining health problems of your clients, or can give an accurate account of a person's psychological makeup, or predict stock market trends, then do so. Don't leave your discoveries unrecorded.

The Tarot Keys used in Golden Dawn ritual, both Inner and Outer Orders, were constructed in such a way that they incorporated the whole teachings of the Paths of the Tree of Life and were entirely compatible with many of the ritual diagrams and speeches that were given on a Path (during the Grade Rituals) that related to that particular Tarot key in question. We have not concentrated on this aspect of the Tarot associations as this will be catered for adequately enough in the Z5 and Z4 series of books on the Golden Dawn rituals. We mention this first because this aspect of Tarot associations is of primary importance and tends too often to be either overlooked or ignored.

The methodology in our approach to describing the actions of the Trumps, or Keys as they are sometimes called, is to take various associations of the Kabbalistic Path which the Trumps are connected to and then apply these to the meaning of the specific Trump.

In the following explanation of the Trumps, there are four areas that will be new to some Golden Dawn students. The first is numerology. There are three main numerological systems utilised simultaneously to explain the hidden symbolism of each Key or Trump.

Secondly, the student will be introduced to the new alchemical meaning and symbolism of each Trump. In the past, there has been very little done on this. In presenting a meaning for each Trump we have tied in an entire alchemical structure which works in juxtaposition to other Trumps. Granted there are additional alchemical meanings that could be interpreted by some Trumps but they fall down badly when placed in with the structure of the Trumps as a whole. The basis for this analysis is the Hebrew manuscript 'Sepher Yetzirah'. Some of the steps and associations given by us have not been what one would call 'standard' but they do work from a practical viewpoint and have been put to the test by both authors. So what we talk about happening alchemically in a Trump can also be used to describe part of a practical laboratory step. We have done this because we feel that too much has been made of the psychological aspect of alchemy with none of the practical considerations being taken into account. We would also point out that the Alchemical steps work in three stages which incorporate a seven stage system within them and which in turn incorporates the twelve stage system. It fits in identically with the Astrological association of the Three Elements (not including earth) and slower planets, the seven esoteric planets and Twelve Zodiac Signs.

The third new aspect is the application of the Colour Scales from the four Trees to the Keys. Each Key (Trump) will be a composite of the path it represents in the four Worlds, analogous to the Colour Scales. Though the Scales have been given before in previous Golden Dawn publications their association to the colouring of the Golden Dawn Tarot has not.

The fourth new application is the association of the Eastern Chakra system to certain Trumps. Though Mathers never did any lectures (that we are aware of) on the Chakras, a number of those in the Stella Matutina and the Alpha et Omega Temples did. Alpha et Omega Temple Chief Langford Garstin apparently discussed them at length with other members and also wrote of them in a Kabbalistic context in his 1932 book 'Secret Fire'. At Whare Ra Temple in New Zealand and in Bristol Temple in England they were also studied. The Planetary/Chakra association has always been a difficult one to understand and the associations given in the Trumps are based on our own work with them.

To avoid confusion with the colours of the new scales, the colours applied to each card are given in the old scale name, using earlier Golden Dawn colour scales. We have done this so the traditionalists will find the colour reference a lot easier.

O

FOOL

The Fool

Title : The Spirit of Ether
Number : 0 (Zero)
Astrological : Uranus
Element : Air—Sylphs
Kabbalistic : Eleventh Path of Scintillating Intelligence
Hebrew Letter : Aleph
Alchemical : Separation
Mythology : Nu; Divine child myths; Green Man
Sound : E—Natural
Colour : Pale Yellow; Baby Blue; Turquoise White; Pastel Green flecked Yellow:
Complementaries
Chakra : Crown

Equilibriating points

A strong esoteric association of the Fool, in its Golden Dawn format, is the Hebrew letter Aleph or A. This is the first letter of the Hebrew alphabet and its association with this Key is by virtue of its shape and its symbolical and numerological associations. The shape of Aleph is said to resemble that of a plough shears and as such, it stands for the potential growth factor. When applied directly to the child pictured, it shows the tremendous potentiality that he is about to give the world in which he is abandoned. Symbolically, Aleph also relates to mankind in general. The numerological value of the Hebrew spelling of ALPh is 831 (using Ph final), which, in turn, relates directly to 'teaching' and shows yet another hidden aspect of the Fool. For even though the Fool is a child abandoned, he is considered a teacher in the wilderness around him and, as such, controls his environment, shown by the docile wolf he holds in check beside him.

The English meaning of Aleph is 'an Ox' which, in turn, is related not to the astrological sign of Taurus but to the Age he represents. The Taurean Age is one in which the Bull was worshipped as the most prominent god of its time by various cultures. The Bull is also a symbol of Air for it has been shown in Egyptian drawings as carrying the body of Osiris and has been interpreted as the area between Fire and Water.

The Elemental Association of this card is dual, for it not only relates to the Element of Air but to the planet of Uranus as well. One of the Golden Dawn titles of this card was 'Spirit of Air' which directly related to the Kabbalistic Association to that part of the Kabbalistic Soul called the Ruach. Ruach literally means 'breath' and has the Latin equivalent of spiritus or 'spirit' as it is known in English, making Spirit and breath an almost indistinguishable entity.

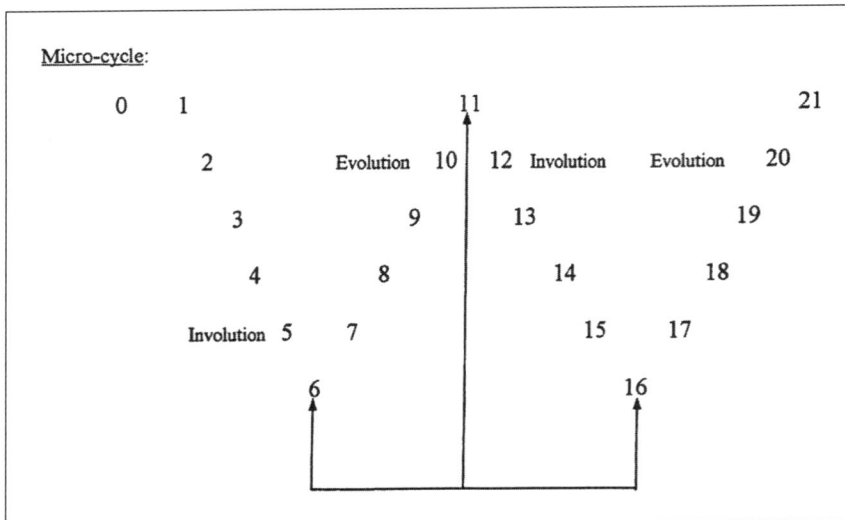

Micro-cycle:

0	1			11		21
	2	Evolution 10	12 Involution	Evolution	20	
	3	9	13		19	
	4	8	14		18	
Involution 5	7		15	17		
	6		16			

Another of the associations to this card is that of the Sylphs, or the Elemental Spirits of Air, who are led by their King, Paralda. It is no coincidence that the origin of the word 'Fool' comes from the Latin 'follus' or 'follis' which relates to a 'bellows' or puffed cheeks' which in turn represents Air. The Sylphs are winged beings, who appear in just about every civilization and are said to bestow the virtues of Intellect and Wisdom to all who offer devotion to them. Eastern equivalents of the Sylphs are the Maruts, sons of the Goddess of Monsoons. In this respect they are classed in relation to gods of the energies of the atmosphere: wind, rain and storm. By using this analogy we have in fact two ends of the spectrum to associate with the Element of Air. The basic principle behind this is that these Elemental beings are said to provide nourishment to those who ask for their help and send an overabundance of force to pressure those who displease them.

The psychological mode of expression that this card represents is very much the Uranian concept of the 'awakening'. This is more than a new beginning, it is a complete shattering of old values, with the individual finding that a whole new era of development has begun. Some have considered that awareness becomes so acute that one enters a state of Super-consciousness, which many have termed 'Illumination'. Where others see the old concept of the Fool, the new approach is based on a perception that attaining the awakening is so far advanced that new levels of development are then perceived within the self. Speed in achieving understanding is one of the key characteristics that this level of consciousness attains. With such an attainment one can sum up a situation, in some instances, in what could almost be described as a blink of an eye. The negative expression of this state of awareness is when blockages occur and the power emanating through cannot be expressed. Thus, the individual finds himself going round in circles with no outlet for such energies.

The Kabbalistic association of the Fool relates to the Eleventh Path of Scintillating Intelligence (taken from the 'Sepher Yetzirah') which is said to relate to the 'curtain' or 'veil' placed before the Godhead of the spirit. No man has looked upon this because this is the truth or totality of man's existence at his innermost point and as such, can never be revealed fully, as no one would be able to perceive or grasp its meaning. The use of the term 'Scintillating' relates back to the principle of the divine spark of the first essence of life itself. Its direct application to the card shows the raw essence, the child, not being able to comprehend where it is but having Divine Innocence. Through its pure state it is able to control the surrounding environment. This purity acts as an energy, or force, which can be controlled and manipulated through the auric vibration which the child emits.

Though this Key reflects the energies of the eleventh Path it is also associated with the Kabbalistic Sephirah of Chokmah because they are both associated with the Planet Uranus. Chokmah, which has the title of 'Illuminating Intelligence', relates to Wisdom and shows many of the characteristics inherent and latent in the Fool. The 'Sepher Yetzirah' states that Chokmah is 'exalted above every other head' which shows yet another relation to the state of Superconsciousness ascribed to the Fool.

The Alchemical stage that this card represents is Separation. This is the process where the three vital components of the Animal, Vegetable and Mineral kingdoms are individualised and isolated from each other. The first of the three divisions is Mercury, which represents the Spirit. The Separation Process actually involves numerous other steps and is the concept of identifying and controlling each of the three vital component parts of alchemy.

In mythology, one of the associations of the Fool is the God form of Nu, one of the eight Gods of Khemennu. Nu is referred to in the 'Egyptian Book of the Dead' in a form of an Invocation: I am the great god self created, Nu, that is to say, who made his name in a company of the Gods as God.

By analogy one can refer directly to the child that is in Man. This shows Man, self-created through evolution suddenly finding him with godlike powers. Analogies of this are depicted in the ancient myths depicting that Man starts to accept that he is coming into the level of a new dawn, a complete new area of development.

The Divine Child myths apply here as well. Take, for example, Hermes of Greek mythology who was born in a cave and rose to become one of the favoured Olympian Gods. Dionysus is another Greek association and was said to have been nurtured in Jupiter's thigh after being prematurely born. Thus he was protected by the greatest God of them all. Paul Foster Case, in his book on the Tarot, quotes from the Mystical Theology of Dionysus which is worth repeating: 'He has neither imagination nor reason, nor does He know anything as it is, nor does anything know Him as He is.' The next stage after Separation is Purification and then finally Cohobation. Each of these stages represents the Three Elements and the Three Slower moving planets.

The numbering of the Fool is zero (0) which is the intangible, the unmanifested Monad. Zero is considered boundless and infinitely potential and to some, the empty circle of the zero is considered to be space from which the Source of all manifestation enters through. A circle encloses space, hence the association to Air, but with space do we have emptiness, or an enclosed universe of all possibilities? Another number for this card is number 22. Following the Fool's path and experiences through the Major Arcana, it eventually manifests again through the World, Key 21, the twenty-second and last Key. Key 21 is the manifested completion of one cycle, while twenty-one is the numerical value for the title Fool, using the English Kabbalah. The Fool then becomes infinite potential again. 22 is a hidden number as no Major Arcana card is numbered thus and yet there are twenty-two Keys in total. To reach the purified state of zero, a state of chaos is passed through, which is depicted by the number twenty-two. It is a number of folly and error, something so uncontrollable that madness can occur; the fool and imbecile with a mind that is 'no mind'. All structure is torn away, dissolved and purified before the Source can be reached and then return to repeat the cycle of manifestation once again—Involution.

This also works in the reverse where the manifested goes through the process of evolution to return to the Source in a super-conscious and illumined state. Thus Key 22 becomes Key 0 via Key 21.

Using basic numerology and the numerology of Pythagoras, the name of the Fool produces hidden numbers which can be matched with Tarot Keys. Interestingly enough this name also brings forth the number of the Beast:

FOOL: 6 + 6 + 6 + 3 = 21 (World—an old title for Key 21)

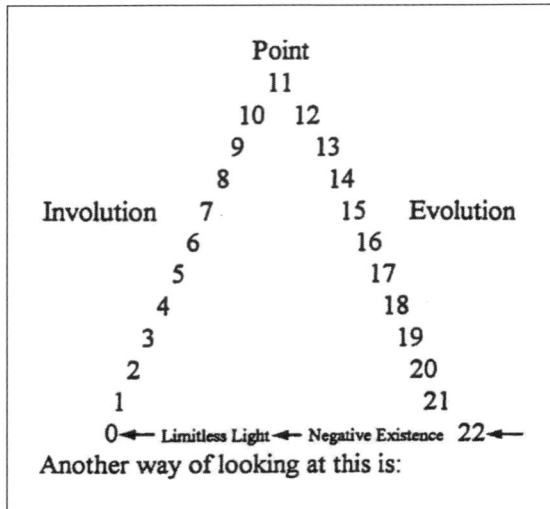

```
                        Point
                         11
                      10    12
                   9           13
                8                14
   Involution   7                15   Evolution
              6                    16
            5                       17
          4                          18
        3                             19
      2                                20
    1                                   21
   0◄— Limitless Light ◄— Negative Existence  22◄—
   Another way of looking at this is:
```

FOOL, the hidden factor of the abyss or man climbing the ladder to pass through the abyss to illumination: 6 + 6 + 6 (666) = 18 = 1 + 8 = 9 (Hermit). The 'L' which sounds very much like the name of God in Hebrew, EL, is represented by the number three, which is a number associated to the Holy Trinity. So, the three sixes multiplied by the three: 3 × 6 = 18 (The Moon), which reduces to 9. Pythagoras's numerology also gives number nine as the numerical evaluation of this card's name. Hence we have three keys as hidden meanings in Key 0, just as Key 0 is a hidden meaning in these three Keys. As discussed before, Key 21 is the final passage of the end before the beginning and the Hermit is the wise aged man which the foolish youth, in his journey, becomes. The Moon is the dangerous path by which The Fool and Hermit walk.

In this system of numerology no number goes beyond a single digit of 9. The hidden association is the number reduced to a single digit. For example, Key 12 comprises of numbers 1 + 2 which = 3, its hidden numerological meaning.

Evolutionary cycles

As a cycle: Following the Keys from 0 to 21 is an Involutionary phase, to manifest. Following then the return journey from Key 21 to Key 0 is the Evolutionary phase, to return to the source.

Involution is the first half of any cyclic process and is dominated by 'life' or necessity. It is the karmic need to be born and grow, to become manifest and aware. In this is the struggle to overcome dissolution.

Evolution is the second half of any cyclic process and is dominated by death, but is the continuation of the life process where an assimilation and deconditioning follows. This is also an evolving process where awareness was experienced at the peak of the involutionary phase and the desire to return to the source is very strong. So Evolution requires a growth in consciousness to full awakening.

On the face of it, one has what at first glance appears to be a madman, hence the analogy of the Fool. Despite this superficial appearance, there is more depth here when examined more closely. Because of the state of awareness of super-consciousness which the Fool has attained, he works to a plan not perceived by others. In fact, he is far above others in both thought and action. They see things at their own level of perception while he sees things from his and who is to say which is right.

The Crown Chakra which in itself is almost indescribable, is like the archetype of the Fool and is the doorway that opens to totally new dimensions of thought. Its physical seat is in the Pineal Gland and its association to the spiritual body is the point of Spirit, the highest of the subtle bodies and the point hardest to reach on any conscious level as we know it. Looking closely at the figure in this Key, one will see that he reaches for the lowest blossom, which in reality is the Crown chakra. Above him are five more blossoms which show the additional five chakras above the head. These five centres work at aligning the subtle bodies with each other so that the Spiritual Source (Higher Self) can transmit to us accurately what it requires us to accomplish at varying times in our life.

The child stands in the shape of the letter Aleph showing the new beginning of his reign. He faces upwards and to the left, towards his Kabbalistic point of origin, the ELOHIM, the name of God in Kether. When the Golden Dawn Tarot pack was first drafted in the late 1880s, the shape of the child was also associated with the Fylfot or Swastika. This involves another analogy of his shape which had the centre of the Fylfot as the Sun and each branch of the bent cross associated with the three Zodiac signs and the element that ruled each branch. This force showed that the child was the initiator of the Gasgillum or wheels, an association with Chokmah before Uranus was placed there. The geometric shape of the blossoms on the Tree relate directly to the main stars of the Constellation of Lepus the Hare. The magical influence of this constellation is that it was said to bring madness. Some of the primal stars had titles such as 'Nibal the Mad', 'Rakis the Bound' and 'Sugia the Deceiver'. The nakedness of the child shows his exposure and his Inner Robe of Glory, a title referred to Chokmah and in this instance relates to the Life Force within the Child which is now exposed in its raw and innocent State.

This symbology involves the concept that the child, as man, must learn to understand and relate to his growth structure, which is further enforced by the thirty-six leaves on the Tree, relating to the Zodiacal Decans. The wolf shows that the negative area or shadow area of the unconscious is under control, as the docile attitude of the wolf towards the child implies. The Sky is the unmapped region of the Intellect to which the child raises its hand to try and grasp. The older concept of the Fool showed a wandering vagabond or, imbecile, which many have associated with the ancient Celtic festivals of the coming of Spring processions, in which the Fool was portrayed as the Green man who heralds the beginning of Spring. It showed a man or youth in this world with his mind in another level of existence, totally unaware of the hidden energies of nature that guided his travels. The Golden Dawn took this concept to its optimum point and applied the symbology as the new-born babe amidst the approaching dawn of a new era. The main difference between these two modes of interpretation is (while they do overlap in some areas), the position the Fool takes in the present reality. As a Youth or Man he is doomed never to improve his lot but as a babe or child he has the opportunity to grow and learn while still keeping the high State of Divine Innocence.

In Divination, under the old design, the Fool used to mean good fortune for spiritual matters but folly for material things. In this Golden Dawn version of the Card, the Fool promises hope and great potentiality for both the day-to-day world, as well as the spiritual one. All changes that occur to the Fool will be done so very quickly. In that brief flash of insight he has summed up the situation. It shows a mind far above the normal levels of comprehension. Naming this card the Fool after the old versions, is something of an overkill, for it really does not apply here. A better title for the card would be the 'Awakening', for this is exactly what it is. The title of the Fool really only applies to the judgement of his peers, but only in the short term, for the Fool works to a universal plan. He is Man coming to perfection, knocking on the door of the Godhead in Kether.

Divination

Idea, thought, spirituality, that which endeavours to rise above the material (that is, if the subject inquired about being spiritual). But if the divination concerns a material event of ordinary life, this card is not good and shows folly, stupidity, eccentricity and even mania, unless accompanied with very good cards indeed. On its own it is too unstable to be generally good in material things. The Crown of Wisdom, the Primum Mobile acting through Uranus on the Zodiac.

How often have you cut or dealt the cards to answer a question for a querent and received the 'Fool' as an answer, then not known how to answer the person? This card does not answer 'Yes' or 'No'. In fact, it is rather neutral and is pure potential as to the outcome of the question. What you say, however, depends also on the type of question asked. In a lot of cases this card is telling you that the question is either a foolish one, or the querent should already know the answer, or the question is premature, as the outcome has not been defined as yet. When turned up on matters of home/accommodation the Fool depicts a state of limbo, or instability as to permanency. In other matters it may show the querent taking matters from day to day and not planning each day as it comes—spontaneity. In travel issues, it is wandering, sudden trips unplanned, travelling with no specific direction in mind. In financial matters a person may be depicted as being the fool with money, not caring or saving. Or, it may be just meaning that no money is coming in. It can represent young children, or an 'air-head' youth. However, in all things it is a card pertaining to the unexpected or an awakening. A new step, but what is to come is pure potential—at least you are ready.

I move by impulse. I follow my soul my soul guides me.

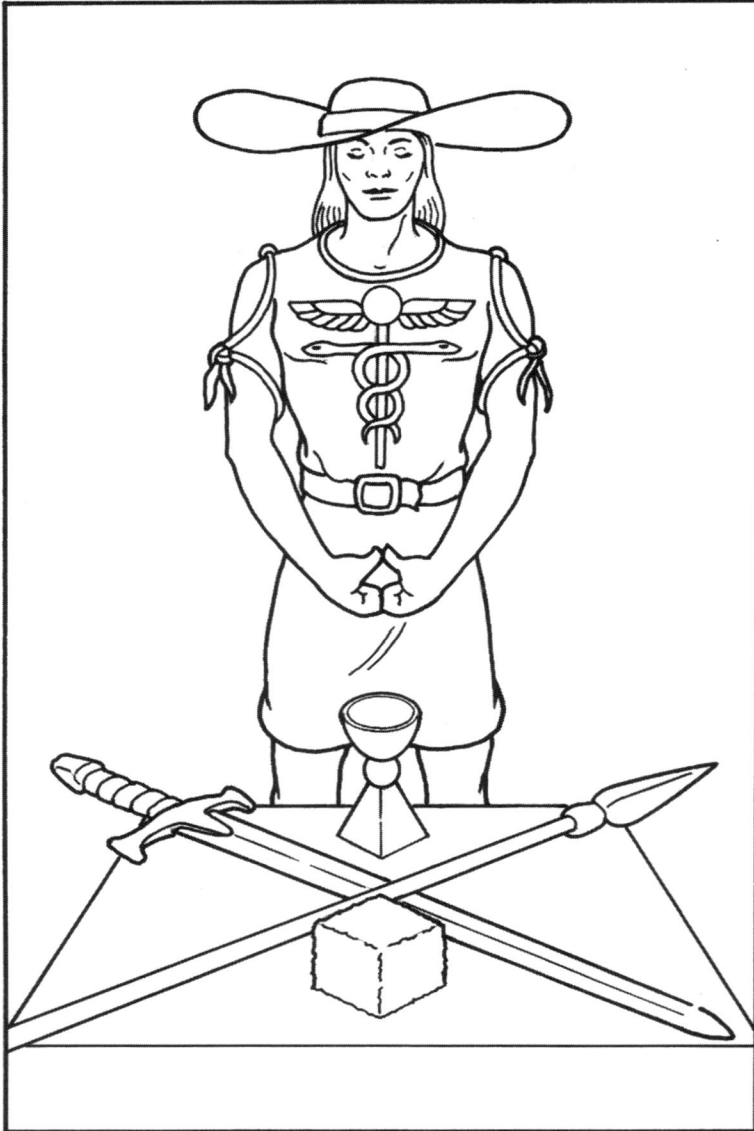

I

MAGICIAN

Key 1—The Magician

Title	:	Magus of Power
Number	:	One
Astrological	:	Mercury
Kabbalistic	:	Twelfth Path—Intelligence of Transparency
Hebrew Letter	:	Beth
Alchemical	:	Distillation
Mythology	:	Thoth: Hermes: Four Talismans of Ireland
Sound	:	E—Natural
Colour	:	Primrose Yellow; Soft Lavender; Soft Reddish Grey; Grey Indigo rayed Violet
Chakra	:	Throat

The number of this Key is 'I' which is the father of numbers, as it is the manifested Monad after Zero. By its addition to itself and the numbers manifested from it, it generates all numbers. For example: 1 + 1 = 2, 2 + 1 = 3, 3 + 1 = 4 and so on. It always returns to itself, for once you obtain the number 10 it reduces to 1; 100 reduces to 1; 1000 = 1; 1 × 1 = 1 × 1 = 1 × 1 = 1. It is complete and so is the symbolic meaning of the Magician in the evolutionary scale as the Completed Being. A composite of all skills and knowledge, the Mage. 'One' is the number of Will, the Ego-conscious, 'I am' and is a masculine number, the male principle (Yang). On the involutionary journey number one seeks experiences which will establish identity, selfhood and yearning for full manifestation.

Using the English Kabbalah, the hidden numbers within the name Magician are: 39 which reduces to 3 + 9 = 12 (Hanged Man) and 12 reduces to 1 + 2 = 3 (Empress). Key 1 plus itself: 1 + 1 = 2, Two being the feminine, the mother number which must produce a third. In basic terms, male + female = child. The Empress often represents the pregnant woman, but in more spiritual terms number three alludes to the Trinity within Key 1, which shows it is complete within itself. Key 3 is also Key 1's counterpart, emotions versus mind.

The other number generated from the Magician, using the Pythagorean system is one, hence it returns to itself and becomes its own counterpart and is in harmony with all things and ONE with the Universe. On the involutionary path the Magician is the maturing Fool, who has gained intellectuality, skill and dexterity where he can be a juggler, trickster or use his skills more positively. On the evolutionary path he is the Adept.

The Hebrew letter associated with this card is Beth which, through abstract imagery, is linked to the concept of a 'house' or 'dwelling place', or 'interior', through the mouth of man. Applied directly to the Magician we have the use of invocation (through the actions of the mouth), to bring out the inner energy from the self, which is within all of us. The basic concept of a house, as applied to Beth, is that of a structure, whether it be for shelter, or an abstract concept to study. This also includes the formula of the Macrocosm and the Microcosm, for the true Magician must study them both through the faculty of nature.

The Alchemical stage that this Key represents is Distillation, which incorporates other steps as well. This relates to the separation of the Spirit, through vapour from the matter through a Distillation apparatus, with a receptacle at the end catching the liquid. It is the separation of the Volatile from the non-volatile. It differs from the previous step of Sublimation because the vapour is not returned to the matter, which in effect has also changed composition. Here the Magician draws forth energy from Spirit Mercurius and transmutes its essence from Chaos (Volatile) into the non-volatile.

The astrological association of the Magician is the planet Mercury which governs the intellect and communication. As a planet, Mercury opens up higher forms of communication and learning and enables the intellect to come to grasp with newer ideals and concepts in pursuit of the higher aspirations of the Higher Self. Mercury is also, sometimes, called the 'Seeker' for it is relentless in its pursuit of the ideal and is nearly always stimulating and rarely satisfied.

The psychological mode of expression represented by the Magician is 'Initiation', for from this, a certain amount of freedom and independence is born in a new area, or structure, for the psyche to adapt to. Reason and rationalisation occur on a scale never before utilised. His conscious expression is to learn the way or the 'why' of things and he has an insatiable appetite to learn and adapt. Through initiation he has to look deeper at his beliefs and structures and quickly amend these when they do not suit his purpose in understanding what is happening on the Inner Planes.

The Chakra associated here is the throat centre with its physical counterpart in the thyroid gland. This chakra is one of creativity and is somewhat of a bridging chakra with its higher and lower counterparts. It is the centre of the Creative Word, initiated by the higher self to fulfil part of an individual's destiny. It is a moderator of the entire physical function of a person, for when this centre is out of alignment it throws the other chakra centres out as well.

As an individual, the Magician must have mastered his environment. If he is weak in any of the elements, then they will control him and produce the opposite effect of what he is trying to accomplish. This is where initiation into a structured area of magical philosophy helps break down this barrier through the process of dynamic ritual. The internal mechanism of the Magician is the unification of consciousness through, what could be simply called, the Higher and Lower Wills of the individual. An example of this is taken from a Golden Dawn paper, 'Task Undertaken by the Adeptus Minor', which describes the fledgling magician and his work:

> *This then is the task to be undertaken by the Adeptus Minor. To expel from the Sephiroth of the Nephesch the usurpation by the evil Sephiroth; to balance the action of the Sephiroth of the Ruach in those of the Nephesch. To prevent the Lower Will and Human Consciousness from falling into and usurping the place of the Automatic Consciousness. To render the King of the Body, the Lower Will, obedient to and anxious to execute the commands of the Higher Will, that he be neither a usurper of the faculties of the Higher, nor a sensual despot—but an Initiated Ruler and anointed King, the viceroy and representative of the Higher Will, because inspired thereby, in his Kingdom which is man. Then shall it happen that the Higher Will, i.e., the Lower Genius, shall descend into the Royal habitation, so that the Higher Will and the Lower Will shall be as one and the Higher Genius shall descend into the Kether of the Man, bringing with him the tremendous illumination of his Angelic Nature. And the man shall become what is said of Enoch. 'And Chanokh (Enoch) made himself walk with God and he was not, for God took him'.*

The association here, from the 'Sepher Yetzirah' to the twelfth Path, is 'Intelligence of Transparency' because one sees beyond the normal dimensions of sight, into the Astral Plane through the development of the Lower Will in linking with the Higher. Since the twelfth Path, like the one before it, leads to Kether the rays of this Sephirah are, through reflection only, subjected to the archetypal interpretation of the structure one is working with. The Higher Self has allowed a glimpse of the power from the Godhead in Kether and instils in the Magician the 'Kavanah' or 'intention' of what he seeks. He is being guided through these emanations to try and tune in on the correct vibrations that he has to work with, through the faculty of reason, while also trying to come to grips with the distortions of this reflected light on the path.

The energy of the Sephiroth are also expressed here, as well, through Hod which has the title 'Splendour'. Hod is the Sephirah of the Intellect and 'Splendour' relates to its shining light that bathes in its glory. Since the Magician works a great deal in the Astral Planes he must be very careful that the imagery he encounters is not false. Here, his sense perception must be brought to a very fine point due to the Etheric energies he works with. His vision of Splendour one relates to the vision of Ezekiel; Chapter 1:

> *And I looked and, behold, a whirlwind came out of the North, a great cloud and a fire unfolding itself and brightness was about it and out of the midst therefore was the colour of Amber …*

The Egyptian God-form associated with this card is 'Thoth' who was considered the scribe of the Gods and the teacher of all the Arts and Sciences, including magical speech. To a certain extent Thoth was very neutral and sided with no one and only recorded what was said and done. In many respects the Magician should emulate this aspect of Thoth, for he is but only a tool of the higher forces to make themselves manifest. The Greek concept of Thoth was, of course, Hermes the messenger of the Gods and this also applies very well to the petitions of the Magician, as does his Roman counterpart, Mercury.

The Magician stands and meditates before his Altar on which are four implements. These equate with the Axiom from the Emerald Tablet of Hermes, so often misquoted, which says:

> *In truth and without doubt, whatever is below is like that which is above and whatever is above is like that which is below, to accomplish the miracles of one thing. Just as all things proceed from One alone by meditation on One alone, so also they are born from this one thing by adaptation.*

From this statement it is evident that the Magician must use the Macrocosm, or Greater Universe and reduce it to the Microcosm or Lesser Universe, through adaptation by the process of meditation, which is evident by his closed eyes.

On the Altar placed in front of the Magician are a Spear, Sword, Chalice and Stone. These, in fact, were the Four Magical Talismans of Ireland in its pre-Christian period, with a strong Celtic heritage. It is thought, however, by some historians, that the Four Grail Hallows were, in fact, descended from the Four Talismans, or Treasures of Ireland, which also seems to link to this card and its origins.

The Cauldron relates to Dagda, the 'Father of All'. It was said that this Cauldron could never be emptied and as such Dagda took the role of providing spiritual nourishment for his people, for anyone who partook from this cauldron never came away unsatisfied. There is also a strong element of fertility associated here as well. The Spear is associated to Lug 'of the Long Arm' whose aim was deadly and by penetration of the spirit and control he attained mastery over all arts and crafts. The Sword is related to Nuada 'of the Silver hand', which, once unsheathed, one could never escape. The square stone related to Fal, which showed the concept of Ruling by Divine right and which would cry out when stepped on by an unlawful King. These were the Gods of the 'Tautha De Danann' who called upon their powers through the aid of each of their four magical weapons. There is a strong relationship here to the Four Magical Weapons of the Inner Order. Of the Four Elemental weapons Mathers has this to say:

> *These are the Tarot Symbols of the letters of the Divine name YHVH and of the Elements and have a certain bond and sympathy between them. So even if only one is to be used the others should be also present, even as each of the Four Elemental Tablets is divided in itself unto Four Lesser Angles representing the other three Elements bound together therewith in the same Tablet. Therefore also let the ZAM remember that when he works with these forces he is as it were dealing with the forces of the Letters of the Divine Name.*

The Four Talismans are arranged in the form of the Pentagram which, in itself, forms yet another power base to work from a subtle level. Of this Pentagram Mathers states:

> *The Pentagram is a powerful symbol representing the operation of the Eternal Spirit and the Four Elements under the Divine Presidency of the letters of the Name YEHESHUAH. The Elements themselves in the symbol of the Cross are governed by YHVH, but the letter SHIN, representing the Ruach Elohim, the Divine Spirit, being added thereto, the Name becometh YEHESHUAH or*

YEHOVASHAH—the latter when the letter SHIN is placed between ruling Earth and the three other letters of TETRAGRAMMATON.

The introduction of Shin or Spirit is done through the Will of the Magician and the Astral Links that he has formed.

The Altar of the Magician, on which the Talismans are placed, is described in the Neophyte Ritual of the Golden Dawn by the officiating Officer, the Hierophant:

The double Cubical altar in the centre of the hall, is an emblem of visible nature, or material universe, concealing within herself the mysteries of all dimensions, while revealing her surface to the exterior senses. It is a double cube because the Emerald Tablet says that the things that are below are a reflection of the things that are above. It is described in the Sepher Yetzirah or Book of Formation, as an Abyss of height and as an Abyss of Depth and an Abyss of the East and as an Abyss of the West, an Abyss of the North and an Abyss of the South.

The figure of the Magician himself has an abundance of hidden symbolism. His hat has in itself layers of meanings. The first and most obvious, is that the brim of the hat represents a figure 8 seen sideways. This of course will be familiar to many as the snake eating its own tail. It shows infinity, with a crossover effect symbolising dual worlds functioning side by side, in both this and the next world. A modern Magician would class this as a basic blueprint for a parallel universe theory, all of which the Magician has at his disposal. The conical centre of the hat represents Kether, the Crown and analogous to the Yechidah, the highest part of the Kabbalistic Soul. They both represent the innermost kernel of the individual and his Spiritual centre. The hands of the Magician are in the grip that was used in the 2 = 9 Grade. An emblem of the Caduceus on his chest, as well as his figure being the subtle outline for the Caduceus, with the hat representing the wings and the tunic the serpent outline. The small Caduceus together with the larger one, show the dual nature of the Macrocosm and the Microcosm, both of which the Magician must become. This is sometimes done through the method of God-form assumption within the plane or structure of the Kabbalah as shown in the 2 = 9 grade of Theoricus, which gives the following explanation:

The tree of Life and the three Mother letters are the keys wherein to unlock the meaning of the Caduceus of Hermes. The upper point of the wand rests in Kether, the wings stretch out to Chokmah and Binah, the Three Supernal Sephiroth. The lower seven are embraced by the serpents whose heads fall upon Chesed and Geburah. They are the twin Serpents of Egypt and the currents of the Astral Light. Furthermore, the wings and the top of the wand form the letter Shin, the symbol of Fire. The heads and the upper halves form Aleph, the symbol of Air, while their tails enclose Mem, the symbol of Water. The Fire Above, the Waters of Creation below.

Mathers described this Key so that it represented the Adeptus Minor invoking with a Lotus Wand. The magician wears the Rose Cross and a magical Sword hanging from the 5 = 6 white sash around the waist is a purple belt with the word 'Mikael' in gold. On his head is a winged cap of Mercury.

Divination

Skill, wisdom, adaptation, manipulation, communication and travel; depending on its dignity. Other significant symbols are the Crown of Understanding, the beginning of material production, the Primum Mobile, Uranus acting through the Philosophic Mercury on Saturn—The Magus of Power. He denotes a person manipulating the affairs of life, one of his many skills and adaptability; the adepts; linguists; counsellors; study and knowledge. Usually shows a situation needing clear handling and communication, which is to be put under control. Sometimes, a person too clever to trust, a trickster or manipulator, however, the Golden Dawn version is usually interpreted on the positive side, unless adverse conditions are connected, in the reading. This card represents ideas, projects, achievement.

The Magician is a card both singular and dual in nature, therefore although in matters such as relationships, it could refer to a monogamous partnership, but it can also show a person remaining single and 'playing the field'. Quite often a querent has admitted after this card turns up, that she is dating two people and is quite happy not to make a choice. The Magician can also depict someone who is developing further skills or knowledge. This can be almost in any field, however, the main theme is communicating. Do not identify communication with just verbal or business skills, for it can be communicating through music, art or craft. In business matters he can range in meaning from high skill and achievement to being a manipulator. It will depend entirely on the surrounding cards or the querent's question. Under matters of property etc., the magician shows negotiations and legal matters. In spiritual matters, you would interpret this card according to its true essence. Under yes/no questions this card could usually be interpreted as a yes. The Magician is one with skills and talent and a full creative potential.

I am capable, talented and skilled. I believe in myself.

Ⅱ

☽ PRIESTESS ☽

Key 2—High Priestess

Title	:	The Priestess of the Silver Star
Number	:	Two
Astrological	:	Moon
Kabbalistic	:	Thirteenth Path—Uniting Intelligence
Hebrew Letter	:	Gimel
Alchemical	:	Putrefaction
Mythology	:	Hathor; Soma; Aah-Tehuti; Artemis; Diana
Sound	:	G Sharp
Colour	:	Pale Silvery Blue; Silvery White; Very cold pale Blue; Silver Rayed Sky-Blue; plus complementaries
Chakra	:	Ida (channel of the Kundaline)
Stone	:	Moonstone

The number two is awakening of Soul awareness; the consciousness of the receptive feminine unconscious energy which is able to receive the positive masculine archetypal energy of the number one. In so doing, form is moulded as a vehicle for the Soul and Spirit to inhabit. A pre-birth state. Being a number of duplication and reproduction, this number must reproduce and become three, which is the numerical analysis and hidden number of the name 'High Priestess' in Hebraic and Pythagorean numerology. Key 2, as the pure essence is the virgin source of universal consciousness manifesting through human personality in Key 3 (Empress) as the inner principle of nature of conscious energy. Hence the Empress is the development from the High Priestess.

Using the English Kabbalah, another numerical evaluation and hidden Key of this name comes to 9, which is the Sephirah of Yesod and is associated with the planetary number of the

Moon. The Moon is also the astrological association of this card. Key 9, the Hermit, acts as a counterpart by virtue of the Triple Goddess. The Hermit in this case does not necessarily represent a male figure. It can also be the Wise Woman which is the feminine version of the Sage:

Triple Goddess High Priestess = Maiden
Empress   = Mother
Hermit   = Crone (Wise woman)

The High Priestess is the Maiden and her potential is the Mother who then becomes the Crone. These three are purely archetypal and symbolic explanations of the three female mythological aspects. Number 9 also is the last single digit from numbers 1 to 10. Therefore, the hidden purpose within Key 2 is to complete, to manifest. On the involutionary path she is the young, fickle, inexperienced woman with latent powers—the virgin, the intuitive and psychic. On the evolutionary path she becomes the true High Priestess, the feminine form of the Adept.

The Hebrew letter Gimel (meaning a Camel) is associated with this card. The hieroglyphic meaning of this letter relates to the throat of man, or any such conduit or canal. The key factor behind this is the receptivity of the cavity of Gimel to receive input which would be fundamentally liquid in concept. Since the name itself means Camel then it is considered analogous to a water receptacle. The numerical value of the Hebrew word GML (Gimel) is 73 which also equates with the value of Chokmah (Wisdom) and the Hebrew word ChSh, which has a similar meaning of 'taking shelter and trusting in'.

Mathers' description of this key seems to fit in with that of the Hegemone. Her headdress is the Triple Crown. She wears a belt of orange, with the word 'Gabriel' in scarlet. In her right hand is the sceptre of Hegemone—in her left hand are the bows and arrows of Luna.

The Golden Dawn concept of this card is a radical departure form the previous European designs, which were for the most part called the *Papesse* (Female Pope) which was linked to the legendary Pope Joan. By assuming the title of the High Priestess instead of the *Papesse* one would immediately think the Golden Dawn have played with the meaning or influence of the card. The *Papesse* however was title based on deception and that is a key to its utilisation. The title High Priestess, is far more personal and ethereal, rather than dogmatic and is based on purity and innocence. It is the quality of the virginal—which the *Papesse* was not.

Another hidden aspect of the High Priestess is that she is veiled and offers up a cup. The presumption here is that she is the bride who offers up her virginity. The lunar crescent above her head shows both the waxing and waning side of her very fluidic nature and her energy is related to the Moon's strengths and weaknesses. Within the Golden Dawn and later the Stella Matutina, the High priestess was taught as representing the SHEKINAH, the feminine counterpart of the masculine YEHOVAH, who resides in Kether which links to the thirteenth Path of Gimel directly. The Shekinah is of course heavily shrouded in kabbalistic symbolism. One of the best explanations here is from A.E. Waite, in his book 'Holy Kabbalah', who says:

It must be remembered in the first place that Elohim is a title of Shekinah and also is Adoni, in which sense—but presumably for us in manifestation—she is called Mirror of Jehovah. Like the First matter of the Great Work in Alchemy, Shekinah is almost myrionymous in respect of her designations, but almost without exception, the ascriptions are feminine. She is now the Daughter of the King; she is now betrothed, the Bride and Mother and again she is the sister in relation to the world of man at large. There is a sense also in which this daughter of God is—or becomes—the Mother of Man. In respect of the manifest universe, she is the architect of worlds, acting in virtue of the Word uttered by God in creation. In respect of the myth of Paradise, the Shekinah is the Eden which is above, whence the river of life flows forth that waters the garden below and this is also the Shekinah as she is conceived in external things–or Bride, Daughter and Sister in the world below.

Considered in her Divine Womanhood, in the world of transcendence, she is the beloved who ascends towards the Heavenly Spouse and she is Matrona who unites with the King, for perfection of the Diviner male is in the Divine Female.

The literal translation of the High Priestess is 'Feminine Elder', an individual who takes charge of the spiritual aspirations of those around her while still retaining the elusive virginal quality. She is linked firmly with the Moon which also relates to many of her actions attributed to mood swings, shifts, changes and fluctuations.

Early representations of this card show a woman seated between two pillars, thus showing the stability and structure within the bounds of chaos, for the opening portal or safe haven is indicated by the cup. This relates to a form of regression through the womb and is one of its vital meanings. By taking the offered cup, one comes to the path of the true adept, the person who can open and close the portal and draw from it when needed. This is, in part, shown by its position on the Tree linking Tiphareth to Kether showing that structure previously utilised is no longer necessary.

The Kabbalistic Path associate here is 'United Intelligence' and is so called because it is the Essence of Glory. It is the consummation of the truth of individual spiritual things. Because this path links or unites Kether with Tiphareth, the head with the heart, it takes the course of the middle action and offers no restriction; hence the relationship with Truth.

The Alchemical stage this key refers to is Putrefaction. To a certain extent this is still part of the Dissolution Process where great care must be taken so that the matter being dissolved (under moist heat) must be stopped at a certain point in the experiment. This is when complete separation has occurred, for at this critical level an entirely new substance has been formed or transmuted. It is one of the most important steps in any alchemical operation. Its separation process is of the Celestial Essences from the Elements. The Cup of the High Priestess is being offered to be drunk—which action is both the Dissolution and Separation process. It is like the Holy Grail in the sense that all who drink from it will have immortality—Transmutation at its best.

While there is no chakra associated with the High Priestess she does represent the current or channel that Indian mystics call the Ida. It is a channel that starts on the left (negative) side of the main channel in the spine, which is called the sushumna and rises to the left nostril. Its function is to pacify and cool the Kundaline current when rising up the sushumna and in effect is a vital part of a stabilising influence on the Kundaline itself.

The Psychological Mode of Expression represented by the High Priestess is responsiveness to outside stimuli through dreaming. Since we are dealing with an ever changing process, the dream criterion is the one which helps the Ego Consciousness change and adapt, through various plays that occur in dreaming. There are two areas here that the High Priestess is closely linked to. The first is that of 'dream clairvoyance', when the conscious joining of varying degrees of the psyche is not possible and has to be on the unconscious level and expressed the same way. The second method is that of dream control, which is done on a conscious level, but can only be expressed subconsciously. This is a method by which many of the important means of occult symbolism can be accessed. It is a vital step in the conscious controlling the unconscious, the ultimate goal of psychology. The High Priestess has a very strong link to the Sephirah of Yesod, but this link is a passive one. Yesod is called 'Pure Intelligence' simply because it purifies. Purification is part of the function of the High Priestess and also by virtue of this card's central position on the Tree, it cannot be affected by energies that are either too positive or too negative.

The cup, which she holds in her hands, is linked to that of Solstices who acts the role of purifier in the grade rituals. Of this position, Mathers says in the 3 = 8 ritual:

> The Cup of Solstices partakes in part of the Symbolism of the Laver of Moses and the Sea of Solomon. On the Tree of Life, it embraces nine of the Sephiroth, exclusive of Kether. Yesod and Malkuth form the triangle below, the former the Apex, the latter the base. Like the Caduceus, it further represents the Three Elements of Water, Air and Fire. The Crescent is Water which is above the firmament, the circle is the Firmament and the Triangle the consuming Fire below, which is opposed to the celestial Fire symbolised by the upper part of the Caduceus.

Around the rim of the cup are five visible Moonstones and five not visible by the hidden rim of the cup. These relate to the tenth month of Virgo, showing a virginal approach which is synonymous with the High Priestess. The Moonstone affects the emotions and draws people together for spiritual purposes. It deeply tunes a person in with the subconscious and as a result the individual may experience waves of emotions which are released from the mind, making their way to consciousness. As a healing stone it is ideal for female disorders and spinal re-adjustments. Its powers can tap into the depths of the subtle bodies and bring into control deep emotional problems. It works on both the Solar Plexus chakra and the Brow chakra. On the base of the cup one stone is visible and this is Pearl. Pearl stabilises emotional imbalances and helps augment the Solar Plexus and Spleen chakras. It is no accident that the Pearl was placed on the support base of the Cup of the High Priestess for it helps to stabilise the Base chakra in its sexual nature.

On her brow she wears a silver Luna crescent which lies on its back. Silver not only relates to the Moon but has the effect of stimulating neurological responses. The feminine part of our nature becomes balanced and Pineal and Pituitary glands are strengthened. Silver causes an alignment with our Physical and Astral subtle bodies so that there is no danger to possession or over stimulation of deep emotional issues. The Luna crescent also is linked to the bull's head of Hathor, who was also linked with Isis. Hathor was a guide to the Underworld, a realm the High Priestess must be familiar with, for she, as the High Priestess, is chosen to guide the spirits of the dead to advise the living. Around the waist of the High Priestess is a belt with diagrams showing the twenty-eight phases of the Moon. Each phase is known to the High Priestess and utilised for her Will. She uses this belt to instruct her pupils and to keep count of the phase of the moon in which she will work her rituals. It is also used as a guide to the menstrual cycle for this is the time that a woman becomes the most psychically aware.

An additional mythological association is the Egyptian Aah-Tehuti (a variation of Thoth), the Moon God. It normally is shown with two faces which both symbolise the waxing and waning Moon. At one point he was considered King of the Gods and was related to procreation as an agricultural God. The Greek Goddess linked to this path is Artemis who is also an agricultural goddess (the virgin huntress). Her Roman counterpart was Diana, the Goddess of Light and Swiftness.

Divination

Change, alteration, decrease and increase—fluctuation. Other meanings are the Crown of Beauty, the Beginning of Sovereignty and Beauty, the Primum Mobile acting through the Moon on the Sun, The Priestess of the Silver Star.

This is a card showing that a decision is necessary and one must listen to inner truth and act and not vacillate, as it is also a card of indecisiveness. In spiritual matters and matters of study, learning, the card is beneficent. In matters material, the card depicts a lack of substance or concentration for any positive outcome. It shows a need to nourish the spirit as well as the physical body. Listen to your inner voice and centre and listen. Then an answer will be forthcoming. Trust your intuition. On health matters it is suggested that more concentration be placed on good nutrition. On relationship questions the High Priestess signifies a single state and remaining free. Sometimes one can be too free however and lose values; in other cases being pure of value and of correct conduct. Asian and eastern cultured countries are often represented by this card.

Listen to my intuition–I trust myself–my higher self is with me.

Key 3—The Empress

Title	:	Daughter of the Mighty Ones
Number	:	Three
Astrological	:	Venus
Kabbalistic	:	Path fourteen—Illuminating Intelligence
Hebrew Letter	:	Daleth
Alchemical	:	Solution
Mythology	:	Hathor; Aphrodite; Venus; Macha
Sound	:	F Sharp
Colour	:	Emerald Green; Light Sky Blue; Turquoise Green; Cerise rayed Green; plus complementaries
Chakra	:	Heart
Stone	:	Beryl

The number three is a Holy number of creations depicting Trinity. The Soul now encompasses an embodiment of both the Spirit realm and Material realm. Here a triangular balance is sought to bring Spirit and Matter together. It works on a conscious level to bring forth life and creative expression, as it reflects through the working principles of numbers one and two. We have now a manifestation of self expression. The hidden Keys to this card obtained by analysis of the name 'Empress' are 9 (Hermit) and 5 (Hierophant) and as said, when discussing number two in the High Priestess, 9 is the number of the Moon and the Triple Goddess. The Empress is an aspect of Motherhood in this archetype. Also, 9 is the last single digit of single numbers and hence is the purpose in the number three to 'manifest'.

One could assume the High Priestess would be the counterpart of the Hierophant by virtue of her old name La Papesse. However, if you look at the hidden symbolism of the trinity in the Hierophant, the Empress more accurately expresses the trinity than would the High Priestess, which is duality. The Empress then, is the High Priestess in a more complete, matured form. In Chaldean numerology the name Empress, reduces back to the number three—a reflection of itself.

On the involutionary path she is the pregnant woman, mother of virtue or vice, the nurturer and matured female archetype. On the evolutionary path she is the woman of Power, Authority and Wisdom.

The title 'Empress', means 'She who rules'. She represents the fourth letter of the Hebrew alphabet, Daleth, meaning door or entranceway. As a symbolic image Daleth represents the breast, a source of nourishment, though it is also considered as an abundance born of division, showing a separation is imminent and as such, a divided nature. There is a strong relationship here with both the uterus and the Womb, for these are the hidden parts through the doorway of Daleth.

In Alchemy this Key is the stage of Solution. Solution is when Matter is dissolved in a liquid as a result of the previous step of Sublimation. The pregnant lady, the Empress, is about to give birth to the Green Lion, which is a solvent. This will be a twin birth, with the Green Lion dissolving its twin when he appears. This process will elevate the raising of the matter to the upper part of the vessel. This is shown in this card by the dove flying above the Empress.

The astrological association here is to the planet Venus, who in turn, represents Love, harmony and fertility. The Goddess Venus is one who is related to the strongest of all cults; Mathers described the figure as being the 'Talismanic figure of Ariel'. In the left hand she carries three lilies like a sceptre; a crux ansata hangs from her left wrist (coloured bluish green). She wears a yellowish green robe with a square golden lamen on the breast of the robe. The whole figure is a feminine counterpart of Adoni Ha Aretz. The whole card dominates the Heptagon.

The original Celtic meaning of this card relates to the Goddess Macha, a fertility Goddess who died giving birth to twins and who also was a warrior Goddess. There is a very strong link here to the previous card of the High Priestess and in many respects, the Empress is still also the Priestess, but a Priestess who has fulfilled her role. In the previous Key she shows untapped depths. Being placed on the Kabbalistic Path of Daleth between the Great Mother and Father (Binah and Chokmah), she shows her own birth was due to extremities of each parent and the duad giving birth to the triad.

The psychological mode of expression the Empress represents is Motherhood and relates to the individual being in empathy with all around her. Here she is sharing her love and affection, which is of a universal nature, showing a reverence for all living things. It is a time of inner harmony and communication before the period of division occurs within and before she gives birth to a new state of awareness. This is the state of awareness of the group working and relates to the emanations of the Collective Unconscious being tapped for the benefit of many. Her emotive response is one of sharing though she also has the tendency to over do things by going from one extreme to another.

The Association with the 'Sepher Yetzirah' is that of the fourteenth Path of Illuminating Intelligence. It is so called because, fundamentally, it deals with concealment of a Holy nature. On this Path we are told that the Scintillating Flame brings illumination. The first concept here is analogous to some states of Zen, for this illumination is not sudden but is nurtured along and is concealed in its nature until it is ready to manifest itself. This not only applies to knowledge, but also to the physical act of conception and pregnancy which, followed by the birth itself, is something linked very strongly with this card. It is the concept of the idea, that has to be nurtured so that it can grow and develop. By the time it is born it appears to have come suddenly, breaking away the shackles of ignorance.

In the Introduction to his Book 'Kabbalah Unveiled', MacGregor Mathers said of the ALMA, that part of the Kabbalah that is analogous to the Empress and is the archetype of the Mother: 'Aima, the great productive Mother, who is eternally conjoined with AB, the Father, for the maintenance of the universe in order. Therefore is she the most evident form in whom we can know the Father and therefore is she worthy of all honour. She is the supernal Mother, co-equal with Chokmah and the great feminine form of God, the Elohim, in whose image man and woman are created, according to the teaching of the Kabbalah, equal before God. Woman is equal with man and certainly not inferior to him, as it has been the persistent endeavour of so-called Christians to make her. Aima is the woman described in the Apocalypse (ch. XII). This third Sephirah is sometimes called the great sea. To her are attributed the Divine names, ALHIM, ELOHIM and IHVH ALHIM; and the angelic order, ARALIM, the Thrones. She is the Supernal Mother, as distinguished from Malkuth, the inferior Mother, Bride and Queen'.

The Empress is also associated with the Heart Chakra. It is the centre of love and harmony, the love of fellow man as well as the love of a man and woman. Its functions are to unite all people together in harmony, in belief and action. Its physical function is the thymus gland, the centre which helps us with work with humanity as a whole for the key word utilised here by this centre is 'fusion'. It is the doorway to the Rays of initiation.

The energy of the Sephirah of Netzach is also expressed here as well and is fundamental to the meaning of this card. The Title of Netzach is Victory, which shows struggle and competition before accomplishment. The influence of the Sephirah is more subtle and underlying than that of the path, but it is just as important and it shows the deep emotional base. A very different approach to the energy of this Sephirah is noted in a French book called *L'homme et l'absolu selon la Kabbale* (Editions Buchet–Chastel, Correa, 'Paris 1958' by Leo Schaya) and which masterfully explains the Netzach function:

> *The emanation of Grace is in the Sephirah of Netzach, divine 'Victory'. This is the 'male', active positive power of the Creator, which produces all the manifested worlds in giving life to all beings and objects by 'extensions, multiplication and force'. Thanks to Netzach, the transcendent beauty of God, in Tiphareth, is spread over the whole of creation. Netzach issues from Tiphareth as an infinite flow of pure essence of Life, made of Light and bliss with which it fills everything born from the illusory or cosmic 'multiplication of the Monad'.*

Many of the old versions of the Empress are taken from Biblical descriptions as these were always considered by those in the Golden Dawn to constitute one of the Secret Keys of the Tarot.

However in the Golden Dawn proper, a lot of this symbolism was used on a much subtler level.

The jewels on the crown are beryls. They help align the base and Brow Chakra. This blends sexuality with spiritual growth. Psychics have maintained that beryl aids as a type of protection to the wearer and develops increased receptivity, which is something the Empress cannot do without, in her reign. On the crown of the Empress only six gems are visible, relating to six months following the Spring Equinox. The remaining six unseen are analogous to the Autumnal Equinox and the six months following. A time of change. Here the Empress is mother nature herself, which is also shown by the curtain behind her, held by seven clips to the rail. The clips represent the number of the Sephirah of Netzach.

In her left hand she holds the Ankh of Life, a symbol of the Zelator Adeptus Minor (which is identical to the symbol of Venus and generally worn on the left wrist) which is placed directly over her womb. This not only shows fertility but hints at pregnancy and relates to Venus being the door to the Vault of the Adepti, which some consider the womb. To enter the vault one must wear the ankh as a symbol of power and direction. Within the ankh is included the symbology of the Ten Sephiroth. In this Key, the ankh is gripped by Yesod and Malkuth, therefore the Empress is herself directing the energy of the Foundation and Kingdom to within herself. She is both giving and creating life. This is further amplified by the five-pointed crown she wears with each point relating to a letter in the Holy Name of YHShVH. By implication, YHShVH relates to the hidden power of the spirit within.

The dove beside her is strongly related to the 'Doves of Venus' but also shows the impregnation of spirit entering matter and is also a universal symbol of motherhood. The arms of the throne are shaped as lion's paws. Alchemically, her throne is the green lion, the sceptre held by her right hand shows her authority but it also represents the womb of the world and her power being universal by nature and also relates to her impartiality. It is also the staff of the Kerux and as such shows that she is instructing as she directs. As Mother Nature she is a symbol of learning.

The girdle she wears is in fact the girdle of Venus, which is called 'Zone' by the Greeks and 'Cestus' by the Romans. This girdle was the seat of her magical power for it gave all those who wore it a sense of beauty and elegance, no matter what their physical appearance. She wears an emerald broach, a symbol of Venus, depicting many of her traits of giving love and prosperity. Its psychic meanings are that it helps the heart chakra and aligns various subtle bodies, resulting in a stabilisation of the wearer. The symbolism of the curtain behind her is also important for it represents a hidden, or unrevealed side, of her nature. Its greenness suggests Spring, a time of growth and fertilisation. Its green colour also suggests a stage of transmutation and is about to give birth to yet another stage which is generally in two parts—fixed and solvent, with the solvent devouring the fixed.

The Empress is also associated with Aphrodite who, apart from being a mother, was also a woman warrior. Her symbolism of power, though, must not be overlooked. She is also Hathor, the cow-headed Goddess of pleasure and Het-Hert which means 'House above the Heavens'.

Divination

Beauty, happiness, pleasure, success, also luxury and sometimes dissipation, but only with very evil cards. Other important meanings are the Wisdom of Understanding, the Union of the Powers of Origination and Production; Motherhood; the Sphere of the Zodiac acting upon Venus through Saturn—Daughter of the Mighty Ones.

The Empress plays many roles from the sexually free modern woman, to the mother or pregnant lady, to a quiet, retiring nature of high moral conduct. She is wisdom in a feminine form. Whichever aspect she plays in a reading, will depend on the surrounding cards, the querent's question and your own clairvoyant interpretation. When enquiring on relationships, unless adversely affected, the Empress will show a fulfilled and happy person. By virtue of her office, in more material or business matters, the Empress shows one taking control, being in harmony and happy with what is being developed. Often this card has represented European/ Mediterranean or South American cultured countries.

I am strong, I am beautiful, I am Woman. I accept myself and Love myself for what I am.

IV

EMPEROR

Key 4—The Emperor

Title	:	Son of the Morning, Chief among the Mighty
Number	:	Four
Astrological	:	Aries
Kabbalistic	:	Fifteenth Path—Constituting Intelligence
Tribe	:	Gad
Hebrew Letter	:	Heh
Alchemical	:	Reverberation (2nd stage Calcination)
Mythology	:	Men Thu; Arthur
Sound	:	C Natural
Colour	:	Lake Red; Dark Rose Red; Claret; Fraise; plus complementaries

Number four represents manifestation in a solid form and is the 'root and foundation' of the rest of the numbers. It is a number containing the threefold consciousness which takes form in concrete reality as four. Therefore, in Assiah, the Material World, the fourfold division manifests itself in the four elements, with the potential of all trials and tribulations that await man in this world, from his unfoldment from the three Kabbalistic worlds above him into Assiah, the World of Matter. Four is a number depicting law and order, authority, endurance, purpose of Will and is the concreting phase of one, two and three, hence complete in itself. So, again, like the High Priestess and the Empress who are the same in each and have the number of completion as their hidden symbol and purpose, the Emperor's name, using the English Kabbalah reduces to 9 (Hermit). In this case, however, the purpose is not just 'to manifest', for he 'Manifests'; brings forth existence with the help of the generation of Keys 1, 2 and 3. In the number nine he reproduces himself over and over again, as the number nine in multiplication and addition always reduces to nine again. This concept is repeated again in the numerology of Pythagoras where the name 'Emperor' reduces back to 4, a mirror of himself—he is 'life power'. Another analogy can be given here. Consider the young conqueror that in the aging process gains wisdom and loses the sense of importance in ruling. He focuses his life on a more spiritual path of meditation and retreat, leaving the throne to a younger man. The Emperor becomes the Hermit, the wise sage or counsellor shining his lamp for others to follow. On the involutionary path he is the warrior, conqueror, the destroyer in order to re-build and he is 'Mankind' finding power. On the evolutionary path he rules with compassion and wisdom. He is the teacher of life and is the Father to all.

The actual title 'Emperor' is similar to that of the Empress, with the exception of gender and it means 'He who Rules'. The Hebrew letter associated here is Heh which relates to a window, or some such opening. Heh is considered the symbol of universal life, the breath. It may be translated into English as either E or H and is closely allied to the Hebrew letter Cheth in meaning as well as form. It is frequently used as an article and may be translated as 'the', 'this', 'that'. In this respect it is used as a prefix or an affix. It forms, when united with a vowel sound, the principle Deity names and in this aspect indicates an abstraction that no modern language can render adequately. Thus YH (Yod Heh) is Absolute Life which is Eternal and Immutable. AHIH can only be adumbrated as 'that which is-was-will be'. It is the root of the verb 'to be', to exist and is used to denote the source of human life in the name of HVH which we translate as EVE, but which also may be given as HUA, the third-person singular of the verb 'to be, or simply as HEH. When the significant Yod is added it becomes Tetragrammaton–Yhvh, the Inviolable name which must not be taken in vain and which was only intoned by the High Priest, upon entering the Holy of Holies. All of this, related back to the figure of the Emperor, shows his Divine origins of rule and relates very strongly to the concept of the Emperor/Priest.

The Kabbalistic association of this card with the 'Sepher Yetzirah' and with the fifteenth Path, is 'Constituting Intelligence' and 'is so called because it constitutes the substance of creation in pure darkness and men have spoken of the contemplations'. What this relates to is the creation of life out of Chaos, the development of life, where before there was none, through Light and Heat in the gestation period. The actual meaning of Constituting Intelligence 'is composed or elected Intelligence' which also relates closely with the meaning of the Emperor, for the word 'Constitute' is very closely allied with 'originate', 'setup and establish', make distinctions. All of this pertains to the establishment of Law and Order and good government.

Another important Kabbalistic association given here is with the Sephirah of Chokmah, for MacGregor Mathers says of this:

> *The name of the second Sephirah is ChKMH, Chokmah, Wisdom, a masculine potency reflected from Kether … This Sephirah is the active and evident Father, to whom the Mother is united, who is the number 3. This second Sephirah is represented by the Divine Names, IH, YAH and IHVH; and among the angelic hosts by AWNIM, Auphanim, the Wheels (Ezek. i.). It is so called AB, the Father.*

The Alchemical association here is Reverberation, which is Calcination in its second stage. This is where the previous stage (shown in the Tower) leaves off. The initial burning has now finished and a more refined process of direct heat alternating with Reverberation and Repercussion of the salts into a fine calx. This is needed to take the experiment to the Yellowing and then to the final Reddening stage of the process. When applied directly to this Key, one will find the consistency shows power (heat) that gives strength and durability to transmute the matter to a form of Soluble purified and exalted Salt.

The Astrological association here is to the Sign of Aries, having a ram's head as its symbol. This relates very strongly to the ram's nature of being headstrong and possessing head butting aggressiveness along with strong procreative abilities. Dynamism is a very strong characteristic of an Aries nature. The Aries nature shows the need to win, almost at any cost. Since Aries is the first of the Astrological signs it is the beginning, which closely allies itself to the Sepher Yetziratic principle of Constituting Intelligence and its ramifications.

The Psychological Mode of Consciousness that the Emperor represents is: All forms of action occur through the power of the Will. This is, of course, also related to the concept of self motivation, which the Emperor exemplifies both inwardly and outwardly. He is an individual who loves a challenge and anything that is difficult is exciting and is part of his integral makeup. When going to extremes the Emperor can become tyrannical and bowl over the opposition, caring for no one except those who help him get his way and they may be discarded when his task is completed. At this level he can be pushy and arrogant but he will succeed. There is also much of the bravado of youth in him which also helps him obtain the goal he has set for himself.

The Golden Dawn version of the card differs from most decks which show a bearded monarch in profile with his legs crossed, the outline of which many occultists have associated with the symbol of Sulphur. This is sometimes linked with the Sephirah Chokmah which, in itself, is but a reflection of Kether above it. The ram at the Emperor's feet shows creative energy, solar power with the horns representing thunder. Also, considering the Christian viewpoint, it is spiritual direction under the guidance of the leader of the flock. The orb gripped by his left hand not only represents royalty, but a Christ-like ruler at his peak. The sceptre, which his right hand grips, is mounted with a ram's head. It is the masculine generative power, the phallus; transmission of energies from beyond. The concept of the two different types of implements represents the energy of the Pillars of Solomon and the Tree of Life, the Pillar of Mercy and the Pillar of Severity; the two main attributes of power wielded by a ruler. The clasp of his cloak is the figure eight side on and is the symbol of infinity showing no limitations to his power over those he governs.

The Emperor holds an Orb directly to the centre of his body and there are two other orbs on the throne. These three Orbs form a triangle of Fire with the Cross on top. This is the symbol of the Golden Dawn in the Outer. The five points on his crown depict the energy of the planet Mars acting through the Sephirah Geburah.

Men Thu, the Egyptian god of War and an extension of the Sun God, Amen Ra, is also associated to this card. He was Ra's favourite, though they were rivals, and Men Thu was once King of Upper Egypt. The Arthurian concept must also be looked at. Here we have Arthur, King of the Britons, who ascended to the throne through Divine help.

A very interesting association here is with the Hebrew Tribe of Gad which is associated to Aries. For Jacob says, *Gad, a troop shall overcome him, but he shall overcome at the last.* Moses says, *Blessed be he that enlargeth Gad; he dwelleth as a lion and teareth the arm with the crown of the head and he provideth the first part himself because there, in a portion of the law-giver, was he sealed: And he came with the heads of the people, he executed the justice of the Lord and his judgements with Israel.* This entire concept is in accord with the Emperor and his functions.

Divination

Conquest, victory, control, power and stability, reason and ambition; challenge seized, won over and new goals set; help given whether asked for or not; one who will not rest and must continue to create, build, rule. This is the Wisdom of Sovereignty and Beauty and the originator of them. It also stands for Uranus acting through Aries upon the Sun—Son of the Morning, Chief among the Mighty.

Quite often when this card turns up in a reading it will represent a Commonwealth country like England, or Canada. In most matters however, it shows power over a situation, where control and achievement can be obtained. A catalyst is provided for one to move forward rather than back. At times the Emperor is the teacher or father figure of authority. Other times it represents a person in the armed forces. He can be the business man, manager, dictator, etc.

I empower myself I motivate myself for I am dynamic.

HIEROPHANT

Key 5—The Hierophant

.

Title	:	Magus of the Eternal Gods
Number	:	Five
Astrological	:	Taurus
Kabbalistic	:	Sixteenth Path—Triumphal/Eternal Intelligence
Tribe	:	Ephraim
Hebrew Letter	:	Vau
Alchemical	:	Fixation
Mythology	:	Apis
Sound	:	C Sharp
Colour	:	Fire Red; Light Maroon; Tomato Red; Rich Red Brown; plus complementaries

The number five seems to hold a powerful meaning which in most interpretations draws upon the concept of severity, fear, worry, loss, etc. But perhaps this is because it is a number of power that is drawn on in times of adversity. Take for example the invocative and protecting force of the pentagram (five points). Five, drives out negativity, expels poisons etc., liberating the good from bondage. It is a number of the four elements and spirit; experience gained through the lessons of the lower vehicle, the body and mind which must lead to awakening. Five is the number of mankind. It is considered a holy number hence its association to the Hierophant who depicts the spiritual teacher. But this can also go too far in expressing the letter of the law and spiritual beliefs as laid down by the Emperor as Key 4. It becomes dogma and too much rigid force applied until something breaks or gives. Then it cleans up the trouble and brings union and harmony as shown in the next Key 6.

In the Hebraic and the English Kabbalah numerology, the name 'Hierophant' reduces to the number six. His potential and purpose then is to bring a marriage of the higher and lower to form harmony and balance in existence. Using another variation of the Pythagorean theme of numerology, by counting the number of letters in a word then reducing them to a single digit, applying this to the name 'Hierophant' reduces to one, the number of the 'Magician'. In the involutionary phase the Hierophant is the maturing Being, bringing his new flashes of insight and visions as teachings to others. In the evolutionary path the Hierophant is the spiritual/religious Being on the path to Adepthood even though he has attained a form of adeptship.

According to the Golden Dawn papers, the Hierophant in the ancient mysteries, was an officer who taught the rites of sacrifice and worship and was chief initiating Priest at Eleusis. He was the equivalent of the Roman Pontifes Maximus or High Priest. The word Hierophantos is derived from 'Hieros' and 'Phaino' which means to show forth, expound or teach. He was the head of the ancient Eleusinian cult and was chosen from the hieratic family of the Eumolpidae. As expounder of the mysteries a deep resonance of voice was an important attribute and being seen by the uninitiated in his ceremonial robes meant death as a penalty for the indiscretion. One of the old titles for this card is the 'Pope', which related to the dogma of Catholicism, but with this change in name the emphasis of what he stands for shifts to a more esoteric consideration and not to the doctrine of ex cathedra. Within the Golden Dawn's document Z3, we are told of the Hierophant that he is a member of the Second Order and therefore initiated into the secret knowledge of esoteric symbolism.

The Hebrew letter associated with this card is Vau. The English association with this letter is O, U or V and associated to a pinhook. It must be pointed out though that its symbolism differs considerably with the mode of pronunciation of the letter. As a V it is used as a conjunction and is placed at the beginning of a word. It also may be translated as 'and, also, thus, afterwards' but it links words together more intimately than any of these. When it is utilised as a vowel it is a sign of movement or action in any tense, though when this aspect of Vau is applied, as an eye, it is a symbol of light. As an ear it is a symbol of wind and air all of which are applicable to sound. The whole process is one of transmutation.

The Kabbalistic association with the sixteenth Path is Triumphal or Eternal Intelligence. This is 'so called because it is the pleasure of the Glory beyond where there is no other Glory like it and which is also called the Paradise prepared for the Righteous'. Basically this shows the way one must take to enter the concept of Paradise that adheres to one's belief structure. Because this Path joins the Sephiroth of Wisdom and Mercy it is harmony, but hints at strong religious overtones with Spiritual Happiness as the end result.

The Alchemical Stage that this step represents is a Fixation state of the experiment, the stabilising or fixating of a volatile substance until it is no longer volatile and remains permanent in the fire, to which it is gradually accustomed. This can happen through Calcination, Sublimation and Coagulation, or by adding a fixed substance. This key, then, shows the stabilisation process through the dogma of religious ideals; the fixing of laws, ideals, society, beliefs etc., through its Taurean nature.

The Astrological association here is the sign of Taurus the Bull. This sign is an Earth one and a fixed zodiac sign. It relates strongly to the actions of a Bull, strong and almost unstoppable if aroused, but slow and lumbering to reach its goal. In many ways this is reflected by the Hierophant which also shows concerns for the materialistic side of life, though, in this instance, this is well-framed within the spiritual confines of one's beliefs. The Bull also shows restriction and impeded progress. Some of the Stars in the constellation of Taurus bear this out as well with Aldebaran (the follower) and Pleiades (congregation of the ruler) which also means Kimah (CUMH) in Hebrew, relating to accumulation.

The Association with the Tribe of Israel is that of Ephraim. 'The first of his Bullock-majesty is his. And his horns are the horns of the wild ox. With them he shall push the peoples, all of them, even to the ends of the Earth. And they are the ten thousand of Ephraim …' (Deuteronomy 33: 17).

The Psychological Mode of Expression that the Hierophant represents is the establishment, or the conservative side of one's nature. The main action here is that, due to the slowness of things around us, nothing appears to be moving the way we want it, whereas in reality, a lot is going on beneath the surface and this part is not yet visible to us at present. The Hierophant represents very much the solid citizen and not the activist, or reactionary. To others he may appear dull and boring on the outside but, if he performs his function correctly, he produces results in his own good time. In dealing with the Hierophant one will discover that he will filter out all that he thinks is superfluous to us and simply give us the bare facts. In many ways the Hierophant would make the ideal public servant. His impatience and stubbornness, if aroused, show his negative side and he can cause many problems to those he opposes.

Behind the Hierophant is a curtain. It is the Veil of the mysteries that is yet unrevealed to us. What we only see is the visible head, or manifestation of its representative, in the figure of the Hierophant. There are nine rings holding the curtain. These relate to the number of Yesod and its lunar association, the Moon, which is exalted in Taurus. The crown, or Tiara, worn by the Hierophant at first is similar to the Papal crown, but, since it is the Hierophant and not the Pope, the meanings alter. The triple crown, in fact, shows the descending cross into the triangle formed by the brooch which represents the sun and the two bulls' heads on the throne. This is spirit descending into matter shown by the altar diagrams in the Outer Order rituals. Since the Bull alludes to strength the throne supporting their weight is of even greater strength and stability. The crown represents the Supernal Triad which emanates power down to the lower Sephiroth of the Tree. The tassels hanging from each side of the crown are eight in number, four on each side and are the elements in their corporeal and incorporeal forms which the powers of the Supernal can manifest through.

He holds a scroll that is a warrant to govern. This is the warrant that is given from the Second Order and is his power and authority. His ring on the left hand further enforces this. It appears to have a hexagram on it and though this is too small to be visible in detail, it is the symbol of the Second Order. It shows a hexagram with the symbol of the Sun and the Moon on either side of it with the letters R.C., which stand for Christian Rosenkreutz. The crowned Christ-like figure in the centre of the ring is man as both the Macrocosm and the Microcosm, with a circle around this in the elemental colours. The Hebrew letters on the figure are the names of the Sephiroth.

The scroll is in the shape of a square and when placed in the centre of the Hierophant's chest the hidden geometrical symbolism is the Square within the Triangle. This shows the septenary giving birth to the quaternary the forces of the higher echelon manifesting through the lower. The staff he holds is, at first glance, identical with that of a Bishop of the Catholic church which represented the Crook of the Shepherd and also that of the letter Vau and its meaning of a hook and symbolic of Osiris. However, the top part of the crook actually coils with three ribs emitting from it. This represents the Wheels or Chakras held in check and controlled through religious or spiritual ideals. The cloak of the Hierophant shows the authority of his office.

The Egyptian God form related to this Path is Apis (also called Asar-Hapi and Serapis). Apis was often shown with the head of a bull wearing the solar disk and plumes while holding a crook and scourge. This deity was made a God of the Underworld and was considered a close link with Osiris and also he has a certain link with Ptah. Apis was born when he sprang from a virgin heifer (which was impregnated by Ptah). There are many close links here with the New Testament and the impregnation of the Virgin Mary by God the Father, so that his son Jesus could be born, who was in fact part of himself.

Divination

Teaching, intuition, marriage, inspiration, material success, occult power, restriction, boredom, results slow in coming, toil, large organisations, those in authority, government, churches, institution of marriage in a stable form, social welfare, beneficiaries, counselling, institutions, stability. Other meanings are Wisdom the fountain of Mercy, Uranus acting through Taurus upon Jupiter—Magus of the Eternal Gods.

On matters of love the Hierophant can show a marriage. But, in general relationship enquiries, it will show the intended being more a friend, or spiritual lesson, to the querent rather than a lover. On deeper matters the Hierophant is the spiritual teacher; higher wisdom and learning in a structured form. Under home and property issues this card shows stability and long-term residency. If surrounding cards show a catalyst and movement, the Hierophant may show purchase of a property. In business matters there is stability and long-term employment. Nothing is earned quickly, as everything must be worked for.

I listen to the higher wisdom of my soul and accept the greater purpose of my existence which is beyond the mundane.

VI

LOVERS

Key 6—The Lovers

Title	:	Children of the Voice Divine, The Oracles of the Mighty Gods
Number	:	Six
Astrological	:	Gemini
Kabbalistic	:	Seventeenth Path—Disposing Intelligence
Tribe	:	Manasseh
Hebrew Letter	:	Zain
Alchemical	:	Separation
Mythology	:	Perseus and Andromeda; Castor/Pollux; Romulus/Remus; Horus/Set
Sound	:	D Natural
Colour	:	Marigold; Violaceous; Cinnamon Brown; Purplish Grey White; plus complementaries

The number six, in some teachings, has been considered a perfect number. Key 6 is one of the three equilibrators in the Tarot Major Arcana. Six, is a number of beauty and love, harmony and equilibration; a mediating number of co-operation and marriage; a number of realization of experiences which reveal purpose in life. Here mankind begins to take responsibility for its actions and the higher self is sought.

The hidden numerical symbolism in the name 'Lovers' concerns the numbers ten (Wheel of Fortune) and nine (Hermit). The Hermit is the card of enlightenment, its path is off Tiphareth which is the sacrificial point of the tree—a place of rebirth. Looking at the symbology of the Lovers, Andromeda is sacrificed to the sea monster but is saved through the spirit which is Perseus. 9 cannot go any further as a single digit and as soon as it becomes 10 the Wheel of life turns back to 1. The lovers in the card represent a marriage of opposite forces, positive and negative, higher and lower; whereas the Hermit is alone. But, isn't the 'marriage' what the archetype of the Hermit has already achieved? He may appear to walk alone, but he is complete in himself where he has unified his higher and lower selves.

In the involutionary path the Lovers, Key 6, is archetypically the union of man and woman in a marriage of the flesh, a sacrifice of the self to another. It is also the beginning of an awakening of the higher self into consciousness. In the evolutionary path the Lovers can be the alchemical union (chymical wedding) of the masculine and feminine in the one being and/or of the higher and lower natures of the self.

The Golden Dawn version of this Trump is a vast departure from the previous line which followed the Marseilles tarot pack. The main theme, here, is concentration of the unification of opposites, which is of course the conjunction. A main difference between the Golden Dawn version of this card and the old concept of tarot symbology, is that the Golden Dawn version takes into account the catalyst which causes the conjunction. In other words, the Golden Dawn version of this card is wider in scope and meaning than in the old tarot versions.

The Hebrew letter associated here is Zain, which means Sword and is equivalent to the English letter Z. The original Hieroglyph of this letter was a sword, arrow, javelin or spear as not only its shape attests but also the hissing sound it made when launched. As an abstract sign its feature is that of a link which unites. Also, it suggests a dazzling ray of light on a polished metallic object which gives greater lamination. Since Zain has a numerical value of 7, another word it associates with is ABD which means 'perish or destroy'.

The Kabbalistic association to the seventeenth Path of the Sepher Yetzirah is Disposing Intelligence. This provides faith to the Righteous and they are clothed with the Holy Spirit by it. It is called the Foundation of Excellence in the state of higher things. This entire concept shows that faith and hope come only when they have been earned. The Holy spirit referred to is, in fact, the emanations of Binah uniting the Son in Tiphareth. Tiphareth is the Sephirah of the Righteous and the Foundation of Excellence, for it receives the emanations from Binah through this Path in the state of higher things.

The Tribe of Israel associated here is Manasseh. For Jacob said 'Joseph is a fruitful bough, even a fruitful bough by a well, whose branches run over the wall: The archers have sorely grieved him and shot at him and hated him: But his bow abode in strength and the arms of his hands were made strong by the hands in the mighty God of Jacob (from thence is the Shepherd the stone of Israel). Even by the God of thy Father, who shall help thee and by the Almighty who shall bless thee with blessing of Heaven above, blessing of the deep that lieth under …' The reference here, yet again, turns to war and turmoil to achieve one's aims as stated in the other Kabbalistic associations which gives a basic understanding of the reason why Mathers redrew this card to fall in line with the Kabbalistic interpretations.

The Alchemical representation of this Key is that of a Separation process (in which the Soul is freed from its chains to the physical senses). The processes within this are Filtration and Distribution, precursors to Separation and Distillation. Separation is the dividing and separating of the pure from the impure. Looking at this Key one will find the Lovers 'to be' are separated and not united (as in some decks). The impurity, which in this instance is the sea monster, must be removed before Andromeda can have her chains released and the Conjunction with Perseus can occur. The astrological association with this card is the Sign of Gemini, the twins. Gemini represents enormous versatility, especially in the field of communications. Gemini people hate routines, are very quick on the uptake and are individuals who are constantly moving around and never settling in one place, are intellectuals but also have an artistic temperament. The constellation of Gemini relates to the legend of Castor and Pollux, with a number of the stars relating to war and wounding.

The psychological mode of expression of the card the Lovers is unification of the separate natures of the Self; giving way to one's impulses and a lack of stability, possibly due to immaturity; a tendency for some form of schizophrenic condition to occur, possibly due to the complexity of the character, but this is more a condition of the extreme end of the scale. Conditions like this can produce an atheist. In addition this card's level of consciousness is one of the prime mover, or frontier state, a pioneer in one's own field; setting standards where there are none and bringing change to disorder.

The whole concept of this trump can be described by the story of Perseus rescuing Andromeda from Cetus the sea monster. Andromeda, the daughter of King Cepheus and Queen Cassiopeia of Ethiopia, was so beautiful that Neptune became jealous and wanted Andromeda to be offered up into sacrifice to him by her Father and, as an incentive he sent Cetus the sea monster to destroy his kingdom if he refused. Cepheus reluctantly gave in and chained Andromeda to a rock to await Cetus. She was, in fact, rescued by Perseus, who happened to be flying by and slew the sea monster by turning it into stone with the Medusa's head and then proceeded to carry off Andromeda. The whole concept shows the trials and tribulations of true love winning in the end against a fair degree of opposition.

When looking at the Hebrew associations of war and fighting associated with the Hebrew letter Zain and the seventeenth path, it is no wonder that Mathers chose a legend such as this to expound the principles of the conjunction. This conjunction has a certain degree of turmoil before perfection can be reached and this representation does not show in any of the standard tarot decks. The emblem of the Sun on Perseus's shield depicts brightness or purity of thought and deed and a high form of spirituality. This was the shield that reflected the image of Medusa whom he killed in a previous confrontation where he managed to behead her. The twelve points on the shield stand for the twelve lettered name of God, HIH-HVVH-VIHIH, which means 'He was, is, will be' and relates to the shield's brightness and corresponding with Kether and the letter Zain. In this instance Perseus is fighting in God's name and the principle that divine help is available to those who need it when all appears lost.

One Golden Dawn Adept wrote of this card:

> *The sword held here by Perseus is highly significant, for it relates very closely with the Hebrew letter Zain, the sword, for the object of Perseus is that of penetration resulting in the release of Andromeda. The maiden chained to the rock shows a struggle for freedom, which is obtained only after considerable anguish and effort before the nightmare is finished. The rock to which she is chained represents a prison that has held her which, in turn, represents her lifestyle tied to her royal duties.*

While we have concentrated on the struggle that has lead up to the union of Perseus and Andromeda we must now look at the result, for this is total and immortal by virtue of being placed in the Heavens as constellations. This type of bondage is one that is unbreakable and one of total commitment.

The alchemical consideration is very important as well, for here we have the liquid stone which Andromeda, as the spirit, is released from by Perseus, through his aerial nature. This is never so more apparent than in the alchemical text of the 'Circulatum Minus of Urbigerus' where, when the liquid stone is actually made, the reader will find it goes through the actions that are very applicable to this Key. Alchemically, the principle of the Conjunction also applies, together with the Separation.

Divination

Attraction though not without initial problems; love and affection; impulsiveness in affection; unions; eventual harmony at someone else's expense and commitment. Other crucial meanings are: the Understanding of Beauty and the Production of Beauty and Sovereignty; Saturn acting through Gemini on the Sun—Children of the Voice Divine, Oracles of the Mighty Gods.

In many readings it is separation from a situation or relationship before a better union can be found, for only true love will win out against opposition. The Lovers card does not always represent love and marriage. If for example, the 3 of Swords or 8 of Cups is laid with Key 6, the story would be of separation and love lost. The lesson of this card is that before you can accept a happy relationship, you must accept the dual male and female within yourself. However, unions, love and marriage are also shown with the right surrounding cards to back this up. In most other matters the theme is, difficulty in the beginning, then something or someone comes along to free up a situation and bring happiness. On business levels there would be a merger, or a freeing of hard times.

As I accept and love myself I also accept a partner into my life and willingly receive and give love.

VII

CHARIOT

Key 7—The Chariot

Title	:	Child of the Power of the Waters, Lord of the Triumph of Light
Number	:	Seven
Astrological	:	Cancer
Kabbalistic	:	Eighteenth Path—Intelligence of the House of Influence
Tribe	:	Issachar
Hebrew Letter	:	Cheth
Alchemical	:	Circulation
Mythology	:	Apollo; Laeg; Khepra
Sound	:	D Sharp
Colour	:	Carrot Red; Heliotrope; Silver Grey; Dark Blue Grey; plus complementaries

Number seven is one of Mastery over all things earthly and has both masculine and feminine energies within. Seven shows now that wisdom has been obtained, direction developed and is a vehicle for human life and spirit. It is a number of royalty, fame, triumph, inspiration, travel and honour. The Hebrews consider it a number of oath, blessedness and rest. However, seven is not a number of balance and must be on the move, travelling on and seeking knowledge, seeking answers to mind, body and soul. As a number of conflict, an awareness of an imperfect state of being stimulates a purification process.

The Pythagorean numerical analysis of the name 'Chariot' reduces to 9 (the Hermit), therefore its purpose is to seek completion and as discussed in previous cards, illumination of consciousness. Another hidden aspect is Key 11 (Justice). Here the Charioteer seeks justice and balance of the forces of Light. On an involutionary path Key 7 is the aspiration of man's need to gain victory over matter and search for a deeper understanding of self and the world, on an intellectual level. On an evolutionary path Key 7 is the path to 'know thyself—communication with the universal mind and to gain victory in a more non-earthly state'.

Since Levi published his version of the Chariot (given below) in his 'Ritual of Transcendental Magic' the main emphasis has been placed on stationary or fixed chariots:

> *A Cubic Chariot, with four pillars and an azure and starry drapery. In this chariot, between the four pillars, a victor crowned with sacrifice adorned with three radiant gold pentagrams. Upon his breast are three superimposed squares, on his shoulders the Urim and Thummim of the sovereign sacrifice, represented by the two crescents of the Moon in Gedulah and Geburah; in his hand a sceptre surmounted by a globe, square and triangle: His attitude is proud and tranquil. A double Sphinx or two sphinxes joined at the haunches are harnessed to the chariot; they are pulling in the opposite directions, but are looking the same way. They are respectively black and white. On the square which forms the fore part of the chariot is the Indian Lingham surrounded by the flying sphere of the Egyptians.*

Traditional positioning of the Chariot, however, was usually a vehicle of movement, which is what the Golden Dawn adopted. The Chariot is a Key of both simplicity and complexity, depending on the level one is working on. In his 'Qabalistic Tarot', Robert Wang has the chariot descending from the sky. This is his own interpretation and certainly not that of the Golden Dawn or the Stella Matutina, or from Regardie's pack. The latter is identical to the one I was given, where the approach of the chariot is horizontal in movement like the sun crossing the sky.

The Hebrew letter associated here is Cheth which means 'fence' or 'enclosure' and relates strongly to the concept of the boundary. Indirectly it hints at safety and a refuge. The numerical one Using the English Kabbalah 'Chariot' has a total of 38. (3 + 8 = 11) value of Cheth is 8 and relates to other words of the same value, such as AGD, meaning 'to bind together' and GH, meaning to 'restore to its former state' and DAG meaning 'agitated'. One former head of the Stella Matutina says of this:

> *Cheth is a letter closely allied with Heh both in form and significance. Although as it is a more closed form it is more guttural in sound and of a material connotation. It signifies life, but on a lower plane. It implies effort, labour and care. Thus in concrete example it indicates a field, an enclosure upon which labour must be expended.*

The Tribe of Israel associated is Issachar, for Jacob says: 'Issachar is a strong ass crouching down between two burdens: and he saw that rest was good and the land that it was pleasant and he bowed his shoulder to bear and became a servant under tribute'. Moses says: 'Rejoice Issachar, in thy tents … and they shall suck of the abundance of the seas'.

The Chariot relates to the 'eighteenth Path of the Intelligence of the House of influence (by the greatness of whose abundance the influx of good things upon created beings is increased) and from its midst the arcana and hidden senses are drawn forth, which dwell in its shade and which cling to it from the cause of causes'. Since this Path connects Binah and Geburah it shows the abundance of the Mother, in Binah, giving her energy to Geburah beneath. Reference to the

Hidden senses is of course the Abyss which this path passes through, though it is held in place by the cause of causes—Kether.

The Alchemical stage that this Key represents is the Circulation process. This is when heat is applied to an alchemical apparatus containing liquid. The liquid is then circulated continuously until a state of Exaltation occurs. This Circulation is a process of Sublimation also, where liquid is heated to a gaseous state. It then cools at the top of the Circulation vessel and returns to liquid once again. This key shows the rising Chariot through the vapour clouds like the rising Spirit.

The astrological association is the Sign of Cancer, which is ruled by the Moon and in which Jupiter is exalted. It shows that 'one's home is one's castle' and the Cancerians' concerns are about trying to protect that aspect of their environment, which is most important to them. Also, Cancerians often like change and have a certain wanderlust about them. Though this may contradict the 'home body' aspect it merely shows that some Cancerians transfer their affections to their possessions which are not always stationary objects. Or, on a higher level, to their own centre and soul. As a constellation symbol, Cancer was originally a beetle in both Hindu and Egyptian zodiacs. The concept of Cancer as a Crab actually came from the Greeks who related this sign to Juno who bit the heel of Hercules when he fought Hydra. An Arabic title for this constellation is 'Al Sartan', which means 'holding' or 'binding' and which relates very closely to the Hebrew letter associated here.

The Psychological Concept of this card relates to the protective nature in the individual. This aspect in turn relates to the patrol of the Charioteer who is constant in protecting his realm. His actions are territorial and instinctive by nature. As he is a warrior and responsible for any intrusion into his territory, he has an in-built defence mechanism that, at first glance, is threatening and to some he can be the extreme meaning of the word 'threat', though he also can be very protective and loving to those around him. As such his mood swings can be great but still work within the given framework. The Chariot was considered by Mathers to represent the Macrocosm and the Microcosm. These are brought together when it is used like that of the Merkabah (which related to both ascent and descent) the ancient form of what could now be described as Astral Travelling using the chariot as the vehicle and which is closely allied with the visions of Ezekiel and Elijah. This early Biblical visionary work has prompted numerous authors of tarot packs to use the four sphinxes (analogous to the four Cherubim), to draw the chariot forward (though they are unmoving), as Levi, Crowley and Case have done. Basically, this description is an internal one where Mathers concentrated partially on it, but also for the external Solar influence, for the Golden Dawn is a solar orientated Order. This was further amplified by the twin suns shown on the front of the chariot and the two horses drawing it, movement being a definite prerequisite for the figure of the card.

Jack Taylor, from Whare Ra Temple, had this to say about the Chariot:

The Driver is of course the Astral Body of the Adept which can be taken and directed by the forces of Light and Darkness, shown by the two horses, the Eagle's head between them being the guiding force because of its keen eyesight and being representative of the true spiritual nature. The driver must balance the work equally between the two opposing forces and this is where the keen eyesight of the eagle comes into it. Though this is a one dimensional viewpoint of the card it is the dimension I choose to work from in this instance.

The Greek mythology of Apollo as the Charioteer here, in this instance, is a very apt one and strongly relates the Solar theory and the coming of summer, as his journey took him from Delphi to Boreas. This is analogous to the influx of Light into Darkness or order into chaos. The Chariot must also be shown as the Conqueror, for Light conquers Darkness. This is shown by the attire of the charioteer in armour which in turn is analogous to the outer shell of Cancer the Crab, for this is the framework which binds him.

The Golden Dawn version of the Chariot also heavily relates to the Irish Celtic myth of Laeg, who was 'King of the Charioteers' and driver for Cuchulainin. In this instance the two horses relate the grey of Macha and the black of Sainglead. The raven, eagle or crow between the horses is the Morrigan, the goddess of war and Conquest.

The horned helmet he wears is linked to Hathor, the Moon-Goddess, who rules Cancer. The crow or raven shows the Spiritual Path of man in the surrounding heavens and is able to lead man on a clear path through the cloudy mists of confusion. The raven also depicts his journey through the seven heavens—withdrawal of the outer senses. His wings depict that he has reached a very high spiritual level, while the eight spokes of the wheel represent the numerical value of the Hebrew letter.

Divination

Triumph, victory, travel, promotion, new opportunities, general improvement, occult study, travel of the spirit. Expansion of horizons and opening up new boundaries are often foretold by the Chariot. Boldly going where you haven't gone before. Groups, gatherings, happiness, a Victory. Other meanings include understanding acting on Severity, Saturn acting through Cancer on Mars—Child of the Powers of Water, Lord of the Triumph of Light.

The Chariot is constant movement, a journey. In relationship matters it is more likely to show people travelling off in their own directions rather than towards each other. It is not a card of concretely manifesting one's desires. It is instead the travel of one's mind and spirit towards 'making manifest'. For straight yes/no questions, however, this card states a strong yes.

I allow my mind and soul to soar from my body and experience the exaltation of the heights, as I know there is more in life than my earthly perceptions.

Key 8—Strength

Title	:	Daughter of the Flaming Sword, 'Leader of the Lion'.
Number	:	Eight
Astrological	:	Leo
Kabbalistic	:	Ninteenth Path—Intelligence of the Secret of all activities
Tribe	:	Judah
Hebrew Letter	:	Teth
Alchemical	:	Exaltation/Solution
Mythology	:	Bast; Hercules
Sound	:	E Natural
Colour	:	Sun Yellow; Blackish Purple; Greyish Yellow; Reddish Amber Brown; plus complementaries

In the number eight there is the rhythm of eternity and alternating cycles of involution and evolution. Although a number of justice, this is the justice of the Law of Nature and not of man. This supports the case for leaving this Key where it is on the Tree of Life (Key 8 and Key 11 used to be interchanged). It is a number of power, strength, control and responsibility and shows the alternating play of positive and negative forces, attraction and repulsion.

The numerical analysis of the name Strength is the number seven (Chariot) in the Pythagorean system. Key 7 is mastery of the lower realms, while Key 8 is mastery of the higher realms and speaks of the Law of Spirit embodied in Nature. Attunement and cyclic forces of nature and spirit are ever interacting. Using the English Kabbalah, a numerical analysis of the name 'Strength' (39 = 3 + 9 = 12) brings forth Key 12 (Hanged Man), which is illumination through sacrifice. In Key 8 the Lion sacrifices his power to the young woman and in so doing the lion looses its animal consciousness and is illumined. So does the woman who sacrifices her flesh by being positioned where she could be attacked and harmed, to release the power of her Spirit. In so doing she is actually unharmed and becomes illuminated, thereby experiencing strength and power.

On an involutionary path, Key 8 shows increased influence on life through self control—seeking of power over matter. As an evolutionary path, Key 8 brings a clearer integration between Spirit, Soul and body.

This card, at first glance, appears traditional, but on a closer inspection it shows that it departs from the basic Marseilles theme in the sense that there is no direct confrontation between the woman and the lion. In many respects the basic theme of Crowley's card 'Lust' is much closer to the Golden Dawn concept than any of the others, though he takes what could be called the extreme viewpoint and applies it specifically to sexuality. Nevertheless the framework from which Crowley's version operates is closely allied with the Golden Dawn principle of 'absorption through manipulation' and not 'confrontation'. This can be easily seen if one views both cards abstractly. Both used the concept of Chesed acting on Geburah which is passive resistance winning through over superior strength, through the actions of the Path that joins them.

The Hebrew letter associated to this card is Teth, meaning 'snake', and has a numerical value of 9. The coiled serpent is generally regarded as the hieroglyph of the serpent guarding her eggs and from this the concept of shelter or protection is given. The Hebrew word NChSh, meaning serpent, is worthwhile looking at as well, as its numerical value is the same as that of the word Messiach, or Messiah. This is associated to a transformative process of moving from aggressiveness towards love and protection, which also relates very strongly to Strength. Using the Biblical analogy of Genesis and the Serpent as the tempter, we find that it represents illusion. An Indian concept of serpent power is also worth considering for here we are linked directly to sexual energy and Crowleyan ideology. This brings yet another approach, giving the Biblical version of Genesis a narrative with very heavy sexual overtones.

The Tribe of Israel associated here is Judah for Jacob says: 'Judah, thou art he whom thy brethren shall praise: Thy hand shall be in the neck of thine enemies; thy father's children bow down before thee. Judah is a Lion's whelp: From the prey, my son, thou art gone up; he stooped down, he couched as a lion and as an old lion; who shall rouse him up? The sceptre shall not depart from Judah, nor a law giver from between his feet, until Shiloh come; and unto him shall the gathering of the people be…'

The nineteenth Path of the 'Sepher Yetzirah' is related here for it is 'the Intelligence of the secret of all activities of the spiritual beings and is so called because of all the influence diffused by it from the most high and exalted sublime glory'. The first part of this description shows that the joining of Chesed and Geburah work on highly spiritual principles and the secret works are the modifications one Sephirah has on the other. The final part of the quotation relates to the horizontal paths being a diffusion of the light from Kether, which works the secret influence through the influence of the Serpent on the Tree of Life and who shows the order of the paths.

The Alchemical stage represented here is Exaltation. This is the raising of the vitality and virtue of the Matter to a higher Spiritual level through a transmutation process which involves dissolving it to a higher degree. This, to a certain extent is part of the Sublimation and Circulation process. Mathers directly referred to this card as representing the 'Green Lion', which is a solvent that dissolves stronger substances into it. This is shown in this Key by the weaker Green

Lion as the woman, apparently controlling the stronger Red Lion beside her. Here superior strength will not work through any method of confrontation, for the Green Lion wears down that superior strength and gradually absorbs it.

The astrological association of this card is Leo. It relates to great shows of strength, along with pride and influence that one would attribute to an autocratic leader. The most prominent star in this constellation is Regulus which means 'standing' or 'treading'. Other stars in this constellation are: Denebola, meaning 'judge', Al Gibha, meaning 'exaltation' and Zosma meaning 'shining forth'. The Star of Regulus has particular importance in Golden Dawn astrological theology as it is considered the Star from which the Zodiac is measured and not that of 0 degrees Aries. The mode of psychological expression linked with this card shows the will to succeed, as achievement is of paramount importance. Now, unlike the actions of the Sign of Leo where success is usually by way of direct confrontation, the mode of expression here is one of passive manipulation of the circumstance directly opposing one. This does not mean capitulation, but simply shifting one's viewpoint so that survival is ensured. There is a constant shifting and adjusting of energy to meet an external and superior influence, until the individual finds himself averting defeat. Within this card there is very much the nature of opposite polarity, which could possibly be best explained in alchemical terms. The Lion is in this instance the alchemical Red Lion while the woman is considered the Green Lion. Because the Green Lion is a solvent, she saps the red lion's vitality by manipulation through desire, depicted by the roses. You have here the King of beasts beside a woman who, at first, appears defenceless. The Lion, in fact, stands for the rampant masculine force but he has been conquered by the woman through her feminine nature.

In the Golden Dawn version of the card the Lion is docile and the woman holds four roses. One New Zealand Golden Dawn Adept says of this card:

> *The four roses she holds symbolises the four animals of the Cherubim as shown on the altar of the vault. These are of course our lower natures which can be attributed to the four lower charkas. The female controls these centres. Though this card shows manipulation by a weaker force and also relates to transmutation as the weaker force controls the stronger. In fact the lion has given its essence to the woman who absorbs it, so that he can survive in another form. This is also explained in the grade of 7 = 4 when we are told that the passion must be transmuted to patience. If you look at this Trump in terms of the path where Dr Felkin considered the Lion as Guardian, you will find a basic change in attitude is required, for to circumvent a force you have to bend with it rather go directly against it. This is the action of this card and the lesson of the Path.*

In her left hand the woman holds the Lion's mane, thus showing her power. In her right hand she holds the four roses which control her lower nature. The shawl around her resembles a figure 8, which relates to a complete cycle of change or transmutation which has been made before the cycle can begin again. For this is the cycle of infinity and karmic patterns that have to be learned.

The Egyptian mythological figure associated to this card is Bast, the cat-lion headed goddess. She is a goddess of fire, a title she shared with Sekhet. But she represented heat in the sun in a more milder form than her sister goddess. There is a strong link to the Moon because of her association to fertility and child-birth. The Greek association relates to Hercules and the Nemean Lion. This was part of his twelve Labours and in this particular legend he fought the lion without weapons and killed it with his own strength.

Divination

Success over adverse conditions through quietness or passiveness, courage, transformation of attitudes to win, sexuality in all its forms, control and manipulation, Fortitude, Mercy tempering Severity, inner power and contemplation. The Glory of Strength, Jupiter acting through Leo on Mars—Daughter of the flaming Sword and leader of the Lion.

In peace and harmony and quiet repose is strength. In centring oneself and creatively visualising your needs, are such things attracted to you. In matters of relationships this card can show lust, wantonness—having fun. However, depending on the surrounding cards this card can show a building of a strong relationship, or the reverse and a focus on individuality. In material matters it shows a lack of movement, a time of waiting and strength in such.

In stilling my mind and body I touch my centre—there I experience life to the fullest.

HERMIT

Key 9—The Hermit

Title	:	The Magus of the Voice of Light, 'The Prophet of the Gods'
Number	:	Nine
Astrological	:	Virgo
Kabbalistic	:	Twentieth Path—Intelligence of Will
Tribe	:	Naphthali
Hebrew Letter	:	Yod
Alchemical	:	Dissolution/Subtilizing
Mythology	:	Treverizent; Britomartis; Virginia; Isis;
Sound	:	F Natural
Colour	:	Yellowish Green; Clear Indigo Blue; Greyish Green; Livid Indigo; plus complementaries

With number nine the directives of super consciousness now flow to matter as the sojourn of the numbers are perfecting and completing one cycle. Therefore nine is an end of a cycle with attainment and also the foundation of a new cycle. It is a number of the intellect and spiritual knowledge, wisdom and mystery. A number complete in itself which continuously reproduces itself. If you multiply it with any number, or add 9 to itself on a continuous basis, the reductions of the resulting numerical evaluations will always come to 9.

Through alphabetical numerical analysis of English Kabbalah, from the name 'Hermit' we get 10 (Wheel of Fortune), which is also the natural next cyclic generation of 9. 10 becomes 1, the Magician and as you see by the Title of the Hermit, he is a Magus. With 10, number 9 is the finishing point of cycles where 10 is the turning point so that another level can be reached on the path to fulfilment or illumination. In Key 7 (Chariot) one of the hidden numbers is 9, which is the Pythagorean numerical evaluation of the name 'Hermit', which indicates travel of the spirit and aspirations of the Hermit. This is evolutionary, to have his spirit lifted out of the earth element to fly across the heavens in his chariot. On an involutionary cycle the number 9 represents the vigilance of purifying mind, body and spirit.

This card is very much in the traditional mould of the Tarot. For here we have the outcast, whether self-imposed or not, seeking solace through the act of self-discipline of the senses and communion with his maker through his particular belief structure. In many ways the Golden Dawn concept of the Hermit is applied to the Temple Officer called the Kerux which, in fact, is a Greek word meaning 'Herald' or 'Messenger' and is linked to the Latin word 'Caduceator' or 'bearer of the Caduceus'. This is exactly what the Hermit is and does. In ancient Greece the function of the Heralds was to summon the political assembly (which later became religious) and to keep order. They made the arrangements for sacrifices to the Gods and often interpreted the omens of these sacrifices. Their persons were considered sacred by both law and religion. Their wands of office were called the 'Skeptron' which, in turn, became 'Sceptre' or 'Kerukeion' and was originally shaped like a Caduceus. The verb 'Kerusso' meant 'to officiate as a herald', which in turn meant reading proclamations and summoning forth people to appear before the councils to be judged. Overall the function of the Kerux or Herald was that of the proclaimed.

The Hebrew letter associated here is Yod which means 'hand' and has a numerical value of 10. As a symbol Yod is a deeply significant one. To simply say that Yod is a hand is a mistake as it is what the hand is used for, which is the main point of consideration. It is a symbol of the initial impetus of action and as such, is incorporated in some form or another in every Hebrew letter. Yod is the first letter of the Holy Name YOD HEH VAU HEH and is the first contact. Its shape is like a drop or seed and that is in many ways its function, for from this larger things will develop. It is the pathfinder of the Hebrew letters and as such fits in very easily with the concept of the Hermit as the herald of the dawn of a new era. In Zohar we are told:

> … and all things are included in IVD, Yod and therefore is the Father called all, the Father of Fathers.

This, of course, relates to the Divine essence in Yod and its application to the Supernal Father as ABBA and its relationship to Chokmah.

The association to the 'Sepher Yetzirah' with the twentieth Path is the Intelligence of Will and is called this because it is the means of preparation of all and each created being. By this Intelligence the existence of the Primordial Wisdom becomes known. This refers to the true Will or Karmic direction each man must take in his life, being not made manifest until now. In many respects it is a very acute inner awareness of communion with the Higher Self. Once this link has been established, if the destiny one wishes to fulfil is understood, then more information will flow down to man from his spiritual self so that it can guide his actions.

The Tribe of Israel linked with this card is Naphtali for Jacob says: 'Naphtali is a hind let loose, he giveth goodly words'. Moses says, 'O Naphtali, satisfied with favour and full with the blessings of the Lord, possesses thou the West and South'.

The alchemical stage represented here is the Dissolution process. This is part of the Putrefaction stage where a solid substance is reduced to a liquid, but stops at the first phase of the operation. This is also Dissolution which changes the gross to the subtle, fixed to the volatile.

In relation to this Key we have the Hermit who has 'dissolved' himself of worldly possession and seeks the volatile nature of his spirit.

The astrological sign for this Trump is Virgo. In this sign Mercury both rules and is exalted, showing a very strong communicative factor and is linked by this planet to the card, the Magician. The influence of Virgo is very prominently in the Hermit. The Hermit is preoccupied with the central matter or influence to which he is subjected, to the exclusion of everything else, including personal possessions. The main constellation of this Sign is Bethulah, meaning 'Virgin' and its Arabic counterpart is Sunbul, meaning 'an ear of corn', hence the formation of the figure associated to Virgo.

The Psychological Mode of Expression associated here is best described by Carl Jung. Jung considered that isolation, by any form or secret or hidden agenda, results in the activation of a psychic atmosphere which is manifested from within the Self due to loss of contact with others. This of course reacts in both delusions and illusions. Good examples of this are shown in the Bible, such as the experiences of both Moses and John the Baptist. It is not that these experiences are not real enough but they are extremely personal. Jung was, perhaps, a little harsh in his descriptions which altogether left out the truthfulness of the visionary experience, but the framework in which he cites that they manifest, indirectly relates to that of the Hermit.

The Hermit by nature is very much a guide and must be treated as such for he shows us we must join him and commence a journey through the Path chosen by us and that now is the time to do it. It is his function to guide us and not the other way round, a point often confused with this card. His influence is the Light or Lux of the Spirit that drives and guides us through areas that will be completely alien to us.

The Greek myth associated here is that of Britomartis while the Roman one is Virginia. Both of these talk of purity and untapped resources of the Inner-Self of all humans being held back before these resources are destroyed by negativeness. The Hermit is also Treverizent in the Grail mysteries who instructed Parzival, the Divine Fool, after his journey into the castle where the Grail was held. Since the Hermit is analogous by nature to the Kerux, the Staff of the Hermit is like a beam of light originating from Hidden Wisdom which is from the three Mother Letters of the Sepher Yetzirah—Aleph, Mem and Shin. From these three letters all things come and to which all things return. The Lamp he holds is, in fact, a symbol of the ever burning mysteries for these lamps are knowledge that burns and will burn forever and can only be extinguished when coming into contact with impurities of the Air. The geometrical location of the lamp is, in fact, at the centre of the card and held against the chest (Tiphareth centre) of the Hermit, who is guided through his Ruach and from which six beams emanate. The Hermit is not seeking followers here and is, in fact, waiting for them to come to him. Hence his stationary position and in many ways, his lamp, is a beacon in the darkness of night.

The rope around his waist shows both the binding of his oath and loyalties to the Hermetic mysteries. From it hangs the Cross of the Four Elements which show his mortality. The Hermit faces his right, the direction of the Pillar of Severity. This is the direction from which those who will come to him, come, for his road is not the road of comfort and ease. His long beard shows Wisdom and is likened to the Beard of Adam Kadmon, the archetypal man. The top of his cowl is shaped like the letter YOD while the closed hand drawn on it also signifies the action he is taking. The cloak he wears is the hidden or mysterious side of his nature and covers all of his teachings as well as his mantle of office.

Divination

Divine Wisdom sought, a journey taken, sacrificing luxury for conscience, unshakable beliefs; searching for something, the path of learning, walking alone, inner retreat. The Mercy of Beauty, the Magnificence of Sovereignty. Jupiter acting through Virgo on the Sun—the Magus of the Voice of the Light, the Prophet of the Gods.

How lonely can loneliness get, or are we just alone? Either way, you have to tread your path alone without support. You will have a clear picture of where you are heading with full awareness of where you have been and the lessons learned therefrom. In property matters the Hermit invariably shows looking for another place to live. In education matters it is long-term commitment to studies. Developing knowledge through life is more likely, however, than through academic studies, but it can mean either and/or both. In relationships it often shows one being alone either emotionally and/or physically. However, 'alone' is not always 'loneliness'. This is also inner retreat, allowing time in one's life for meditation and spiritual development.

I like being alone. I have peace; I achieve the most clarity when I am alone.

X

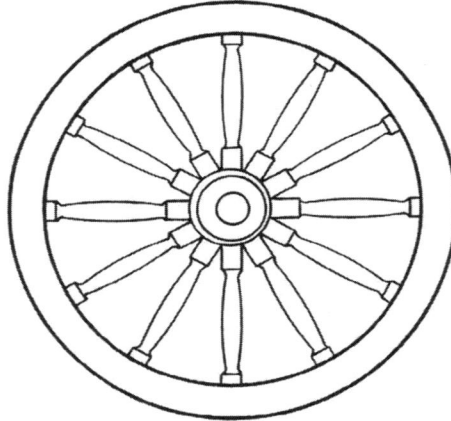

Ↄ FORTUNE 4

Key 10—Wheel of Fortune

Title	:	The Lord of the Forces of Life
Number	:	Ten
Astrological	:	Jupiter
Kabbalistic	:	Twenty-first Path—Intelligence of Conciliation and Reward
Hebrew Letter	:	Kaph
Alchemical	:	Sublimation
Mythology	:	Atum/Temu; Zeus/Cronus; Jupiter
Sound	:	A Sharp
Colour	:	Violet; Princess Blue; Blue Violet; Cool Blue rayed Yellow; plus complementaries
Chakra	:	Sacral

Key 10 reduces to 1, the Magician and 0, the Fool. In 1 is the father of numbers which carries the divine spark in 0, thus giving the outpouring of life. Ten, is a number of Karma, just as the Wheel of Fortune is in some decks the Wheel of Fate. By numerical analysis of the English Kabbalah, the name 'Wheel of Fortune' reduces to 11 (Justice). In this is the next generation of the number. It is strength and wisdom bridged by sacrifice and suffering. Pythagorean Kabbalistic numerology reduces this name to 222 which is a counterpart to the previous reduction, the Fool as the imbecile. So you can see the dual nature of 10 through these reductions. The turn of the wheel can be a turn to the positive or negative.

The number ten is also a number of the tenth Kabbalistic Sephirah, the Kingdom. It has been called a number of divinity—throne of God.

The Wheel of Fortune is a Trump which, at first glance, is the most simplistic of all the Golden Dawn Tarot cards yet that simplicity hides a very real and masterful system that includes many of the Golden Dawn's sub-systems. In the Levi version, from which many of the modern copies developed, we are told:

> *The Wheel of Ezekiel contains the solution of the problem of the quadrature of the circle and demonstrates the correspondences between worlds and figures, letters and emblems; it exhibits the Tetragrammaton of characters analogous to that of the elements and elemental forms. It is a glyph of perpetual motion. The triple ternary is shown: The central point of the first Unity; three circles are added, each with four attributions and the dodekad is just seen. The state of universal equilibrium is suggested by the counterpoised emblems and the pairs of symbols.*

Although from a slightly different viewpoint many of the above comments apply equally to this version of the Trump although some of the symbols apparently differ in their framework of application. The title 'Wheel of Fortune' is a misleading one for many think of the good luck syndrome attached to this card, possibly due to its planetary association. If you consider the old fairground concept of the Wheel of Fortune then you will be closer to the truth for good luck only falls for one, while many are disappointed if they lose. This shows, from an esoteric viewpoint, the karmic patterns of life, the law of Cause and Effect.

The Kabbalistic path associated to the 'Sepher Yetzirah' is: The twenty-first path is the Intelligence of Conciliation and is so called because it receives the Divine influence which flows into it from its benediction upon all and each existence. This path joins Chesed and Netzach and relates to the divine emanations which flow through from the Higher to the Lower Self. In many respects we have in this instance a perfect alignment of the subtle bodies of man so that there is no impediment and things have a chance to operate freely with various physical and mental benefits. From these man looks up to the Spiritual and worships it, so that the flow from the spiritual to man is received and returned back to its source. A cyclic concept of both giving and receiving.

The Hebrew letter associated here is Kaph, meaning hand, and relates to a semi-closed fist though it can be applied to any hollow object. This letter has a numerical value of 20 with a final value of 200. The word Kaph has a value of 100 and relates to other words such as KLKL 'nourish', showing the functions of the cupped hand and LAa 'to absorb' or 'swallow', which further extends the original meaning. Also when the word AaL 'exalted' is applied one has the experience of exaltation, which can be further applied to the meaning of the Trump itself as well as to the function of the hand. As a letter, Kaph was said to have come from Cheth which comes from Heh, with Gimel as the main force behind all these letters.

The Alchemical Stage that this Key represents is Sublimation. This takes place when matter is placed in a container (usually with a long neck and over heat). Vapour or essence is then extracted from the matter and remains in the top of the neck of the flask for a short time and then descends back down the tube into the Matter again at the bottom of the flask. Now the whole process is a cyclic action which is shown by the Wheel in the Key. Part of the essence is taken from the matter, is strengthened—which is shown by a fusion of the Elements in the form of the Sphinx, then returned to it, making the matter changed in its composition. The ape shown at the bottom of the wheel is the measurer and balancer of the Philosopher's Fire, which burns underneath an apparatus in which the substance is being sublimated. This is the key to the Wheel.

The Astrological association to this card is through the planet Jupiter. One of Jupiter's titles is 'the great benefic' which, when applied to this Trump, hints at its generosity. This application is general to life influences and not relating to any particular aspect. Its basic concepts relate to growth, expansion and exaltation, an aspect which further closely allies this association with the meaning of Kaph.

The Chakra associated here is the Sacral. The sacral associated physical glands are the Gonads. This also relates to the release of testosterone from the Leydig (Lyden) cells. It is very powerful in the release of sexual energy and sex instinct. There is also a water empathy here due to release of body fluids during orgasm and also the association to the genitourinary tract. This chakra is also the centre where karmic patterns of the past will come back into play during successive incarnations. This chakra helps ground the emotions as it is strongly attached to the Emotional Body. It is a point where the past and the present meet and this centre must accommodate both of these before any next level of awareness can be reached.

Another influence is through the Sephirah of Chesed and the cohesive concept of its nature, for under its Rabbinical title of 'the Lesser Countenance' or 'Microprosopus' it refers to the manifested universe as a whole. This further relates to the unification of both the active and passive parts of nature so that a type of cyclic action exists, that each part is different yet joined, in much the same action as the revolving wheel. We are told that in the fourth path, relating to the influence of Chesed, it 'emanates all the spiritual virtues with the most exalted essences'.

The Psychological Mode of Action that this card expresses is someone who is a constant striver, not the fanatic, but someone whose growth potential is consistent with these abilities. Much is attempted in a very balanced manner. In many ways it shows the sacrifice of the Self to the greater cause of the Path that one has vowed to take in life. The framework from which this individual may operate will alter, though the prime directive to succeed will not.

The Sphinx lies above the Wheel, but does not touch it. Its symbolism is extremely complex, depending on the level on which one wishes to view it, although in the Golden Dawn ritual of the thirty-second path we are told:

> *The Sphinx of Egypt spake and said I am the synthesis of the Elemental Forces. I am also the symbol of Man. I am life. I am Death. I am the Child of the Night of Time.*

The best way to understand its functions is to apply its application through the framework of the Four Worlds of the Kabbalists. Through the World of Atziluth, its highest function, the Sphinx shows the perfected being, a combination of all the best attributes. As such it is the supreme being of the Spirit that expresses itself through a given framework which it is recognizable to us. The Briatic influences show the accumulated experiences of the Soul through various karmic patterns lived by man. The Yetziratic emanations deal mainly with the Ruach of Man and the various patterns man must experience. The influence of Assiah on the Self, shows the development of the body and intellect where both work in harmony with each other to a very high level, which is continually developing. The Sphinx however, puts the checks and balances on the wheel so that all is worked out in the end for it is the Law of Cause and Effect.

The Sphinx is also a composite of not only the Elemental Forces but of the forces of the Macrocosm. In previous Keys relating to this card, the Kerubic forces were present in each corner. The Sphinx also is analogous to those ideals with four principle forces here, but they are merged in a uniform nature. Each part must support the other and overlap it. The ideal of each fixed point controlling a certain position is not so defined due to the multi-layered nature of the Beast. The face of Man relates to Aquarius and the New Age that is about to approach us, an age of learning and understanding. It is the Soul of nature personified. The Paws of the Lion show the zodiac sign Leo and Strength to carry out a sense of purpose and Will. The Body of the Bull shows the procreative properties while the Wings of the Eagle show the soaring of the spirit, a sense of renewal.

The Wheel, like the Sphinx, also has many meanings but only two have any real importance in this instance. The first is an application to the Macrocosm. Here the Wheel represents the cosmic cycle of both the physical Universe and the Spiritual one and shows a gradual unfolding of both. It is the central force which all things gravitate to and from and which all things emanate from, shown by the central hub of the Wheel. The second meaning that primarily concerns us is that of the spokes of the Wheel relating to the twelve astrological houses, or the twelve phases of human existence, which the Soul of man must work through in his various incarnations. The central hub relates to the Higher Self which co-ordinates and directs these impulses through varying lives.

Mathers stated when looking at the Wheel from a totally different perspective (downwards), the Adept will notice that it resembles the circular flower at the top of the Lotus Wand. The central staff is hidden but each section relates to the twelve Signs of the Zodiac and the forces of Light and Darkness that balance them. On the Hub of the Wheel of Fortune is written the words 'Ashtaroth' which is the dark side of the light of the Sun, discussed in the above paragraph. This shows that all who fall from the Wheel will come under the influence of this Qlippothic Force. The Central Hub of the Wheel can represent both Light and Darkness.

The Ape, which sits on the lower portion of the card, is the Cynocephalus which, apart from being a simple animal with desires of his species, is also the one who was stationed in the Hall of Judgement as depicted in the Egyptian Book of the Dead. His function was to preside over the scales and tell Thoth if the deceased's good actions had outweighed the bad ones. In many respects the Ashtaroth is from the Mathers' association to this key. We have decided not to include it. In in the actual drawing functions of the Sphinx and the Ape are similar, for the Ape is also man and the Sphinx is what man strives to be through his Karmic patterns of life, as shown by the Wheel.

The Egyptian myth is that of Atum or Temu which he is sometimes called and often known as 'Father of the Gods'. Atum was one of the very early Egyptian Gods who was later identified with the Sun God. He was a force that was clearly shown to exist before creation. In Greek mythology the god form of Zeus applies. To a certain extent he is Cronus, because Cronus was also considered to be responsible for creation itself. The Roman theme shows variations on Jupiter.

Divination

Good fortune, good health, luck, change in life pattern (whether for good or evil), a journey. The 'Mercy and Magnificence of Victory' and Jupiter acting through Jupiter directly on Venus— Lord of the Forces of Life.

This is the Wheel of Life and of Change. Which direction of change, good or bad, is often dependent on the surrounding cards in your spread. In some instances it is self realization and a breakthrough, but in a natural manner. Unexpected luck or bad luck can be shown, but this card often works in the positive. Wherever it falls in your divination, it will show change of some sort. The energy of change is with you, use the moment.

I welcome change and am ready to receive my destiny.

XI

JUSTICE

Key 11—Justice

Title	:	Daughter of the Lord of Truth, The Holder of the Balances
Number	:	Eleven
Astrological	:	Libra
Kabbalistic	:	Twenty-second Path—Faithful Intelligence
Tribe	:	Asshur
Hebrew Letter	:	Lamed
Alchemical	:	Cohobation
Mythology	:	Maat, Themis, Fates
Sound	:	F Sharp
Colour	:	Sap Green; Blue; Bottle Green; Pastel Turquoise; plus complementaries

Key 11 is a powerful number of Truth. Firstly, if you take 11 and break it up into 10 and 1, you will have in the 10 a divine spark (0) contained in the manifestation of Man (1). This number then, speaks of the Law of Mankind. It also represents violence and power, which is a sad history of mankind in the wielding of its many Laws. But it can also be revelation. Spiritual Truth (1) unites in the material plane (10), the Kingdom. However, 11 also rules sins, penitence and striving for liberty and knowledge.

One hidden number in the name Justice is 8 (Strength), using the Pythagorean system. Key 8 is the spiritual cosmic Law and Truth, which subtly guides Mankind in their earthly Law, Key 11. Using the English Kabbalah system, the other hidden number is Key 6, harmony and balance is sought by Man with divine blessing.

The Golden Dawn version of this card, for the most part imparts a traditional Western archetype of the figure of Justice with esoteric symbolism around it. In many ways, both directly and indirectly, this appears to have come from the Egyptian Book of the Dead—the Judgement of Ani before Osiris. This takes the concept of Justice beyond the Physical law and gives it the seal of Karmic evaluation as well. This shows that judgement and the law of cause and effect, better known by the name of karma, is all encompassing and all embracing. None escape its wrath, whether in this world or the next. As the last word, it is absolute.

The Hebrew Letter associated here is Lamed which means 'ox-goad' due to its symbolism of an outstretched arm, or, wing or an appendage that could suddenly whip out from a folded position. It has a numerical value of 30. This letter is of extreme importance when placed beside the letter Aleph for together as AL they represent the concept of power extended. An example of this is in the word ALOHIM which brings forward this concept almost to the point of infinity. The concept of A and L together signifies unknown limits or quantity which have come from the abstract to the concrete. It also expresses any form of conjunction that could help or propel a desired object. As a word Lamed has a value of 74, which further relates to such words as YSD 'to create the foundation of' and NKD meaning 'posterity'.

The Kabbalistic association to the 'Sepher Yetzirah" comes from the twenty-second Path and is called the 'Faithful Intelligence' because by it spiritual virtues are increased and all benefit from this type of influence. This relates to the concept of increased virtues for all of those who dwell in the light or who we would commonly call the Faithful and indicates that these clearly are the majority. The faithful are, of course, those individuals or groups who follow a Divine plan of the Light and adhere to its doctrines.

The Tribe of Israel associated with this card is Asher, for Jacob says, 'Out of Asher his beard shall be fat and he shall yield royal dainties'. Moses says, 'Let Asher be blessed with children, let him be acceptable to his brethren and let him dip his foot in oil. Thy shoes shall be iron and brass and as thy days, so shall thy strength be'. All of this coincides with the nature of Venus and Libra and the reference to the feet show the sign of Pisces which Venus is exalted in.

The Alchemical stage represented by the card Justice, is Cohobation. This is where a series of successive Distillations take place where the volatile substance is repeatedly poured back over the dried Matter and redistilled. This process loosens any fixed structure of the matter taking with it, during the Distillation, the soluble from the insoluble leaving the insoluble fixed. By this process many things become their opposite—sour becoming sweet, sharp becoming soft. The second stage within Cohobation is Imbibition. Mercury and sulphur are combined as a liquid and are joined very gradually to the body, the salts, where they are reabsorbed and retreat into the body. This washes the body with frequent lustrations until it is wholly coagulated within and unable to rise but remains fixed. When applied to this Key, the scales are the balance, while the figure between the pillars is transmuting the process between the two opposite poles. A further glance at the chequered floor shows this from yet another perspective, the positive and negative in juxtaposition with each other.

The Astrological connection to this card is through the Sign of Libra, the scales. This sign stresses balance and shows the path or middle way and as such appeals to many because it first appears to be all things to all people. The Arabic name for this constellation is called 'Al Zubena' meaning 'redemption' or 'purchase' while its Hebrew counterpart is Mozanaim meaning 'scales'.

The Psychological Mode of Expression is a harmonising or balancing, not only of one's conscious nature, but of the unconscious as well. Communication is also a very important part of Justice as well as a sacrificial quality which shows that the individual will sacrifice himself for the good of all. Extreme versatility is required to adapt to circumstances that require constant changing of conditions so that an even balance can be maintained, adjustment.

Justice is very much the balance between Emotion and Will as expressed through the energy of the Sephiroth of Tiphareth and Geburah. The concept here is especially allied with some of the pictorial aspects from the Egyptian Book of the Dead and with an added meaning of the earthly desires being held in check under the foot of the figure. The figure seated on the throne is the figure of Maat in the Judgement Hall of Two-fold Truth and behind her is the power of Osiris. Her function in this Hall was to test the scales of the dead with a feather against the heart and it was to her whom the petition of the dead was said. The throne on which she sits represents her power and authority and 'the unshakable Truth', for it is the centre of two extremes shown by the Pillars of Severity and Mercy. On the top of the Throne and placed either side of the figure, are two lotus flowers. These are analogous to the Sun and Moon and are two extremes shown by the twin Pillars. They represent purity and truth and the path that Justice must work within. The Scales also represent the Sun just quitting its point of balance—the Equinox.

The sword she holds is the sword of the Imperator which the Current of Nephthys acts through in the Neophyte ceremony and helps keep balance in the Hall. The tip of the Sword represents Geburah and the double-sided blade is the Path of Mem. The blade of the sword shows that it is a time of reflection and all who come into contact with it must reflect on their past nature. The tip of the sword shows the might of Geburah and will place the Severity of that Sephirah upon all those who have not reflected on their actions. While the sword shows the Power of Geburah, the set of scales are the symbol of the Path that one must take to uphold the law. One shows the power of Justice, while the other shows that Mercy can only be given once the consequences of one's actions have been considered. If the scales are heavy, then the power of the sword takes over; if they are light then the influence of Mercy will come through that Pillar and through the influences of Chesed.

The fox held firmly under the foot of Maat shows that Justice triumphs over the slyness and cunning of those with evil intent. It also shows that no matter how clever one is, the Law of Cause and Effect applies to all and eventually all will have to pay for their own actions on the earthly plane. The chequered floor is divided into forty-four parts. These stand for the twenty-two paths of Light and the twenty-two Paths of Darkness that are held in perfect balance for man to choose his path. Each Path has an Angelic Guardian and Qlippothic host and both influence us along the path of life. The Egyptian mythological figure associated is as mentioned above, Maat, the Goddess of Truth and Justice. The Greek Goddess linked to this card is Themis. She was a goddess who directed the Oracle at Delphi and was known for her accuracy in matters of divination. She also presided over vetting of the petitions men made to the Gods and only asked for what was just. In return, she made sure the Gods fulfilled their promises. The Roman association is that of the Fates (daughters of the night). These are the three sisters who determined the course of life by weaving the destinies of mankind.

Divination

Justice, balance and harmony; force used in matters of Law, legal matters to be seen to; a decision is being made and there may be a gap of time and space before it is acted out; timely action. The Severity of Beauty and Sovereignty and Mars acting through Libra upon Sol—Daughter of the Lord of Truth, Holder of the Balancers.

As a decision and judgement card, Justice will always show the balancing of ideas, forces, events, etc., in one's reading. Clearer focus appears to be applied, as quite often the querent will admit their awareness of a matter when this card turns up. Legal matters may be judged and the outcome depending on surrounding cards. In some cases this card represents the lawyer. In emotional matters this card does not show support of feelings. It will show one weighing up matters logically and a clear mental picture of what the situation truly is. It has appeared in readings representing the dancer, or dance institutions—social arts.

I acknowledge the truth within and accept responsibility of that truth.

XII

☽ HANGED MAN ♆

Key 12—Hanged Man

Title	:	The Spirit of the Mighty Waters
Number	:	Twelve
Astrological	:	Neptune
Element	:	Water
Kabbalistic	:	Twenty-third Path—Stable Intelligence
Hebrew Letter	:	Mem
Alchemical	:	Cohobation
Mythology	:	Heqet; Poseidon; Neptune
Sound	:	G Sharp
Colour	:	Prussian Blue; Olive Green; Greenish-Lemon; White flecked with Black; plus complementaries
Chakra	:	Brow (Ajna)

The number twelve is considered a Divine number of measurement, of involution and evolution, life cycles, a number of grace, time, knowledge, experience and perfection, but also of danger, changes and sadness. Material, emotional and spiritual suffering are depicted because Key 12 is one of growth through release of self. Self-sacrifice and suffering is experienced if this release is resisted. The reduction of 12 is 1 + 2 = 3 (Empress). The Empress holds the Orb of the World which mankind must strive for through Key 12 and the twelve experiences of life (the Zodiac) to attain. The Empress also wears a belt of twelve zodiac signs which symbolise the above. Pythagorean numerology analyses the name of the 'Hanged Man' to be Key 10 (Wheel of Fortune), which is also called the wheel of life and alludes to the cycles of life and fate within which Key 12 operates. Through these cycles humanity and all that is in our solar system, experience. The hidden number of 10 is 1 (Magician), which is the attainment of adeptship and can only happen once one has experienced and mastered all facets of mind, body and soul. Another analysis of the name 'Hanged Man' comes to 4 (Emperor), using the English Kabbalah, which shows a hidden purpose, which is to master the material plane.

The Golden Dawn version of the Hanged Man seems at first glance to resemble the traditional concept of this card but, in fact, this is merely on the surface. With most of the recent innovations of the last 150 years or so, we see in the traditional versions of this card, that the Hanged Man is suspended from a wooden frame, which some have related to the Tau Cross. Of this older version of the figure we are told:

> *It is the ancient symbol of Life: The union of the girdle of the Great Mother with the Tau Cross of Death;*
> *It is the emblem of that eternal life of the Spirit which the Divine ones pour forth upon Men, delivering him from the body of death.*

The Hebrew letter associated with this card is Mem and is a sign of passive action and a protective aspect of the creative power. When vocalised it means 'water'. This is always used in the plural since Mem Final is collective, as water, as in the condensation of moisture. When prefixed with the letter Shin the word SHAMAIM is formed and refers to the Heavens, ethereal water or atmosphere. When utilised as an article or prefix, Mem relates to 'as from' or 'out of, with' or 'among'. Hieroglyphically Mem indicates a rough water, sea, or waves, while Mem Final indicates calm water, silence and peace. As a word Mem has a value of 90 and is analogous to such words of similar value such as PY 'mouth of a well or entrance' and SL meaning 'raise or exalt'. If you study the outline of the cove in the card you will find that it is in the shape of Mem, which shows the framework from which these influences operate.

The Alchemical stage that this Key represents is Cohobation, a final step after Purification. Like the other two main stages on this level, Cohobation has a number of minor stages included in its terms of reference. Basically, it refers to successive distillations which have the effect of unifying Sulphur, Salt and Mercury and bringing them to the required vibrational rate. This is shown pictorially by the figure of the Hanged Man who is totally submerged in water, with a faint glow emanating from his head. The figure of the man represents the three essences of Mercury, Sulphur and Salt in the form of Spirit, Soul and Body respectively (its true associations). The figure in Key 12 is subjected to rising and falling tides, which provide the effect of Cohobation. On another level it represents the Salt which is the Body.

The association to the 'Sepher Yetzirah' comes in the twenty-third Path which is 'Stable Intelligence' and is called this because it has the virtue of consistency among all numerations. The key concept depicted in this explanation is one of stability through the consistent process of restriction and through the emanations of Geburah upon Hod. Geburah has restricted the growth factor of Hod and has made it channel its influence to a very severe degree, making the emanations or growth patterns fight all the harder to attain their desired goals. It is very much the old axiom of 'no pain, no gain' that is referred to here.

There are two astrological associations to this card: the first is the Element of Water. This element is best shown by the Apas Tattwa, which relates to the Water element and is symbolised by a silver crescent. By direction the crescent has a downward movement, showing contraction and relates to any form of liquid formation and to man's sense of taste. The beings linked to this world are the Elemental Undines who are ruled by their King Necksa. The second astrological association is to Neptune and shows that extreme pressure is placed on the psyche, where prophecy and other forms of psychic perception can result. Neptune is the planet that produces extremism and release on one hand and containment on the other. It is a case of the containment being necessary for the release to take place and when it does there are virtually no boundaries to it.

The Chakra that this Key refers to is the Brow centre with its physical root in the Pineal and Pituitary Glands. It works on the intention to create and expresses Imagination and Desire in their highest forms. This centre has two petals that are symbolically shown as the arms of the cross where a man is crucified. This in turn releases energy (Kundaline) from the spine to flow to the head centre, which is adequately shown in the archetype of the inverted figure.

The Psychological Mode of Expression shows a shattering of one's previous belief structure and opting for a new one. In many ways, it is the rebirth principle and for the Eastern system of beliefs it is allied with reaching a certain level of enlightenment. Jung found this type of mode of expression analogous to the alchemical state of the dissolution factor where the negative elements are expelled or purged out of the system—the end result being a total change in character. The Leopard skin worn by the figure in this card relates to animal nature in all humans. This nature is eventually shed through release of the spirit—shown by the glow around the figure's head.

One will also find a very strong link to the Sephirah of Kether here as well, for Neptune relates not only to this Path but also to the Sephiroth. Kether is, of course, the beginning of the Tree of Life and, as such, its influence is reflected here.

In Egyptian mythology we have Heqet, the frog-headed deity who presided over death and birth. Her function was to try and ease the transition from one state to another—such as birth and death. The Golden Dawn also used the Greek myth with this card for its interpretation showing Poseidon's triumph by overcoming the giant Polybutes, whom he hurled off a cliff into the ocean, for the inlet from which he hangs was carved by Poseidon. This is why the common title of this card used in both the Golden Dawn and Wake's Holy Order of the Golden Dawn was the 'Drowned Giant'.

The actual geometrical shape of the figure is of prime importance for it has two basic hidden configurations attributed to both the Outer and Inner Order. The first is that the crossed legs represent a cross and the shape of the elbows form a triangle. These show the cross above the inverted triangle with light radiating from it, which is symbolised by the Altar diagram in the 3 = 8 ritual, attributed to the element of Water, which says:

> *The Cross above the Triangle represents the power of the Spirit of Life rising above the Triangle of the waters and reflecting the Triune therein, as further marked by the lamps at the angles. Whilst the Cup of Water placed at the junction of the Cross and Triangle represent the Mother letter Mem.*

The Inner Order or second method of interpretation shows the influx of the formula of Divine White Brilliance—commonly called the LVX invocation. The figure when viewed from this perspective has the shape of the letters for the Legs crossed as the 'L', the forearms the 'V' and the crossed wrists the 'X'. This is the formula of Osiris sacrificed in YEHOSHUA. Within the invocations of this formula we invoke *Virgo, Isis Mighty Mother* which relates to the Womb and the letter Daleth further shown by the letter Mem in the card (as the surrounding cove) and showing the baptismal process. Then comes *Sol, Osiris, Slain and Risen* which is the resurrecting form of Osiris and is analogous to the insertion of the Hebrew letter Shin in the name YHVH, which is the hidden aspect of spirit. The phrase *Scorpio, Apophis, Destroyer*, in fact, is the destruction of the old Ego due to the transformative process, so there is no turning back.

The Hanged Man depicts a nightmare-type journey in which he has to confront not only his own feelings and emotions but a whole belief structure that surrounds him. It is an individual put under enormous pressure with the result being a shattering process of old ideals and values. Mathers' explanation of the Hanged Man is as follows:

> *'The twelveth Key of the Tarot, 'Hanged Man' but also more properly called the Drowned Giant and its position is horizontal rather than perpendicular. In this position, the lower side of the Key represents the Bed of the waters and the upper side the Keel of the Arc of Noah, floating above the Drowned figure. Or, in Egyptian Symbolism, the Baris or Sacred Barque of Isis; whilst the Figure is one of the Bound and Drowned followers of the Evil Forces; though yet again, in another sense, it may represent the Body of the Slain Osiris in the Pastos, sent down the Nile to the sea: Whilst above is the Keel of the Baris or Barque of Isis in which she travelled to seek him.*

Divination

Enforced sacrifice, punishment, loss, suffering but with the end process showing a stronger individual, self-analysis, the Severity of Splendour, execution of Judgement and Mars acting through Water upon Mercury—Spirit of the Mighty Waters.

Everyday life is not always emotionally traumatic, but when the Hanged Man appears in a reading, it strongly depicts specific issues that must be dealt with, whether they be emotional or not. If not dealt with, some form of suffering or sacrifice takes place. Very often this card shows that a person has merely been delving into their own inner being in an attempt to come up with the truth of a matter, or the truth of what path he or she should really be walking. In other cases it is a person wrestling with themselves—blind to the divine Will, searching for an answer. However, emotional upsets and trauma are prevalent, or even alcoholism and drug abuse. The 'Hanged Man' may appear as a warning of a dangerous situation. For example: in a reading the Hanged Man came up in a travel position with the 3 of disks accompanying. The middle-aged couple being read for were going on a holiday and were informed that they were headed where there was a lot of water, where they would travel over that water and, at times, would be in water, and they were warned of danger. They said that this was not possible as they were travelling over land only and only crossing a few rivers, although they might do a bit of swimming. Months later they returned and reported that they in fact did do the trip and were surrounded by water. The region they travelled to had severe floods and continuous downpouring of rain. They had indeed felt as if they were in danger the whole time while making their way through the deep floods.

I release myself to the Divine Will, which guides me safely through life.

Key 13—Death

Title	:	The Child of the Great Transformers, Lord of the Gates of Death.
Number	:	Thirteen
Astrological	:	Scorpio
Kabbalistic	:	Twenty-fourth Path—Imaginative Intelligence
Tribe	:	Dan
Hebrew Letter	:	Nun
Alchemical	:	Digestion/Ferment
Mythology	:	Apepi; Prometheus; Vertumnus
Sound	:	G Natural
Colour	:	Bluish Green; Sky Blue; Azure Blue; Aqua-Sapphire Blue; plus complementaries

The number thirteen is sacred and relates to transmutation and transformation. With transmutation, however, there can be death and destruction and so many connect this number with evil omens. The number thirteen, is the urge to end a cycle, to transform and change (evolve) into a new cycle. All debris and rubbish is swept out in this transformation. It is a number of Karma.

The numerical reduction of Key 13 is 1 + 3 = 4 (Emperor). Key 4 then is its counterpart and where Key 13 is more likely to disintegrate, or be unmanifested, Key 4 manifests. An analysis of the name 'Death' in Pythagorean numerology is 10, which in turn reduces to 1. Therefore, unless via Key 10, Key 13 cannot return to Key 1, the beginning, to rebirth into a new cycle. Another analysis, using the English Kabbalah, comes to 20 (Judgement), which shows that at the gates of death comes the Final Judgement.

This card is very much in the traditional mould and shows that death affects us all. The Golden Dawn version of this card, though, has some very subtle symbolism that shows not only the physical death but the liberation of the spirit after physical death and these be must considered. The Hebrew letter associated with this card is NUN which, hieroglyphically, represents a 'Fish' and also represents the image of produced or reflected existence, whether it be animal or vegetable. When joined with Beth it now becomes a sign of interior action for BN, or Ben, means 'a Son'. This is clearly realised when we consider that NUN Final is augmentative and emphasises the individual concept. NUN at the beginning of a word suggests passive action, or contemplation, while at the end of a word it is a converse or unfolding principle. Applied to this card we have the eternal and a new beginning, as shown by the Ben and illustrating a continuing line from the original seed that is totally changed yet still retaining a basic framework. NUN has a value of 50 and relates to other words of the same value such as BMCh 'to be high or elevated' or MTA 'reach unto', both of which relate strongly to the concept of Death.

Within the Portal ritual of the Golden Dawn we are told:

> The Twenty-fourth Path of the 'Sepher Yetzirah' to which the Tarot Key Death is referred, is the Imaginative Intelligence and it is so called because it giveth form to all sorts of similitudes which are created in like manner similar to its harmonious elegances. For the outward form always follows the Hidden Law, thus from Chaos is produced Harmony, just as a beautiful flower is produced from decaying matter.

Alchemically we are looking at the stage of Digestion. Within this process is also fermentation and corruption. This is where mild heat is applied over a long period of time, to the Matter, which gives up its vital essences. This process is also called Maceration. It is where the gross elements become much lighter as the essence is removed and to a certain extent Separation occurs. The Death card shows the corruption of the matter as a death process, which is essential before the life forces of the Matter are released as a state of birth. Transmutation then occurs.

The Astrological association of this card is Scorpio representing extremes of one's nature and a pool of emotional depth. It rules reproduction and sexuality. There is a certain destructive quality about this sign though it shows the power of the Spirit through new frameworks of operation through the concept of desire. The old Hebrew name for Scorpio was Akrab, meaning 'conflict' and the Arabic name is Al Akrab, meaning 'wounding the one who comes' while the Coptic title is Isidis, meaning 'oppression or attack'.

The Tribe of Israel here is Dan, for Jacob says: 'Dan shall judge his people as one of the Tribes of Israel. Dan shall be a serpent by the way, an adder on the path, that biteth the horse's heels, so that his rider shall fall backward. I have waited for thy salvation, O Lord'.

The Psychological Mode of Expression is transformation through an emotional content of sexual energy (the Freudian Libido). It shows an instinctive process overcoming us by taking ourselves into an extreme of our nature. This is transcendence of a person's present framework, as one then goes to the next level. When a person has actually gone to the limit he must now transform to something else or destroy himself. It is also sacrifice of the Self to the Greater Whole so that one can successfully transform.

Mathers says of this card in the Portal ritual:

> The thirteenth Key of the tarot represents the figure of a Skeleton, upon which some portions of flesh still remain. In a field he is reaping off with the Scythe of Death the fresh vegetation which springs

from corrupting bodies buried therein, fragments of which, such as hands, heads and feet appear above the soil. Bones are also strewn upon the surface. One of the heads wears a kingly crown; another is apparently that of a person of little note showing that Death is the equaliser of all conditions. The five extremities, the head, hands and feet, allude to the powers of the number five, the letter HE, the Pentagram, the concealed spirit of life and the Four Elements, the originator of all living form.

The Sign of Scorpio especially alludes to the stagnant and fetid water, that property of the moist nature which initiates Putrefication and decay. The eternal change from life into death through death into life, is symbolised by the grass which springs from and is nourished by putrefying and corrupting carcasses; the herbage, in its turn affords food to animals and man which when dead, nourisheth vegetable life and bring to growth and perfection the living herbage. This is further shown by the figure itself putrefying and decaying as it reaps the grass of the field. 'As for man, his days are as grass, as a flower of the field so he flourisheth'. The top of the scythe forms the Tau Cross of Life showing that what destroys also renews. The whole is a representation of the eternal transmutation of the life of nature, which reforms all things into fresh images and similitudes. This symbol represents the corrosive and destructive action of the infernal fire as opposed to the Celestial, the Dragon of the Waters, the Typhon of the Egyptians, the Slayer of Osiris which latter yet rises again in Horus. The Scorpion, Serpent of Evil, delineated before the figure of Death in the more ancient form of the Key, refers to the mixed and transforming, therefore deceptive, nature of this emblem. Behind him is the symbol of the Nameless One, representing the seed and its germ, not yet differentiated into Life, therefore incapable of definition. The Scorpion is the emblem of the ruthless destruction; the Snake is the mixed and deceptive nature, serving alike for good and evil; the Eagle is the Higher and the Divine Nature, yet to be found herein, the alchemical Eagle of Distillation, the Renewer of Life. As it is said: 'Thy youth shall be renewed like the Eagle's.' Great indeed and many are the mysteries of this terrible Key.

Apart from the above statement by Mathers there are a number of other aspects associated with this card. The drawing of the Solar Annular Eclipse at the top of the card relates to the Neshamah blocking out the expression of the Ruach. The Annular or Ringed Eclipses, as they are sometimes called, relate to a completion of a cycle on a Higher Plane which is analogous to forcing the Nephesch to release itself from its two senior counterparts which results in the termination of death of the physical body.

The whole concept can be likened to that of the many lives of man, who is completely renewing himself through the spirit and who experiences life both as a King and also as pauper, in his many incarnations leading to perfection. Further figures of mythology that relate to this card include the Egyptian Apepi—the Serpent. It was he who attacked Ra and was beaten each day. This God was a symbol of the darkest hour of night. The fight with Ra on the daily basis was to try and prevent the Sun god from spreading his light and warmth over the land and its inhabitants. Apepi was the opposite, signifying everything that Ra was not and the personification of evil. Prometheus was one of the Greek myths here associated. The legend states that an eagle would come to visit Prometheus and feed upon his liver by day, which would then in turn grow back at night. This was repeated daily. (He was eventually rescued by Hercules.) The Roman myth is Vertumnus, the changeling. He took on many different forms in order to seduce Pomona.

Divination

Time, age, transformation. Sometimes death and destruction are signified but rarely the latter unless queries specifically relate to health. It is a card of transformation and rebirth. A letting go or sweeping away the debris of the past. Other meanings include: change of attitude to one's friends and family; the Sovereignty and result of Victory; Sol acting through Scorpio upon Venus, or Osiris under the destroying power of Typhon afflicting Isis—The Child of the Great Transformers, Lord of the Gates of Death.

Certainly this is the most misconstrued card in the deck. Very rarely does it represent the death of a person and never does it represent evil or nasty happenings. The Death card is a symbolic death, which leads to an inner and sometimes outer transformation and birth of a new personality or situation. It is the natural working processes of nature. Nothing is sudden unless surrounding cards depict this. The Death card has often shown a relocation from one country to another, or a major lifestyle move within one's country. In many other matters it often is the end of a situation and the birth of another, such as a relationship, job, home, etc. For matters of health there may be an actual death, however, in a lot of cases the individual is going through a cleansing of his or her body, purging the dead cells and wastes. Wherever this card turns up, it is showing the end of a cycle where old moulds are broken and new formed. The birthing process, however, can take anything from a day to years and the operation of change is a gentle, natural one.

I allow myself to transform through the ever changing conditions of life, death and rebirth.

Key 14—Temperance

Title	:	Daughter to the Reconcilers, the Bringer Forth of Life
Number	:	Fourteen
Astrological	:	Sagittarius
Kabbalistic	:	Twenty-fifth Path—Intelligence of Probation
Tribe	:	Benjamin
Hebrew Letter	:	Samekh
Alchemical	:	Sublimation
Mythology	:	Chiron; Sati/Satet; Diana
Sound	:	C Sharp
Colour	:	Deep Blue with hidden Red; Pale Slate Grey; Pale Grey Blue; Mauve Grey; plus complementaries

Key 14 is a number of constant movement from unity to disunity and back again. In some states it is fusion and in others dissolution. Because of this, fourteen has been given both positive and negative meanings, such as: Ignorance and forgetfulness, trials and dangers from natural forces and energy, university, unity, alchemical marriage, nature, preparation and formulation.

The numerical deduction of 14 gives 1 + 4 = 5 (Hierophant). Key 5 is the four elements plus spirit, therefore hidden in Key 14 is the power of nature guided by spirit. The English Kabbalah system of numerical analysis of the name Temperance produces 10 (Wheel of Fortune) giving an underlying factor of change to Key 14. Another analysis reduces the name back to 14, hence a reproduction and reunion of itself. Creation is in the making in full force, through trial and blind force of all elements (4), but under the gentle direction of the Spirit (1).

The card Temperance is really quite unique among the Golden Dawn Tarot for in fact two cards were presented to the aspirant during ritual and showed the former version which to a large extent was taken from Levi and also the later attempt. The form of this card clearly was taken from Chapter 10 of Revelations, with a few modifications, which said:

> And he had in his hand a little book open and his right foot upon the sea and upon the Earth and lifted his hand to heaven.

These were what some in the Golden Dawn described as the Secret Keys of the tarot by aligning certain figures with Biblical phrases to try and get a clearer perception of their meaning. As a word, Temperance means moderation and self-restraint and Mathers said of the second form of this Key:

> This later form of Temperance is the usual figure of Temperance, symbolising in a more restricted Path form than the preceding, the peculiar properties of this Path.

The Hebrew letter associated with this Key is Samekh, which means 'prop' or 'support'. It also relates to the hissing sound of Zain linking to a Bow that has just released its arrow, for its image is that of something circular or spiral in movement. This of course relates directly to the astrological sigil of the Sign of Sagittarius. Samekh has a numerical value of 60 and relates to other words of the same value such as BNCh 'to build a house' and YKL 'power or ability'. The word Samekh has a value of 120 and relates to words such as NAa 'to move or agitate' and SS 'being active' along with TZL 'shade or shelter'.

The Portal Ritual says:

> The Twenty-fifth Path of the Sepher Yetzirah to which the Tarot Key of Temperance is referred, is called the Intelligence of Probation and it is so called because it is the primary temptation by which the Creator tries all righteous persons. That is, that in it, there is ever present the temptation to turn aside to the one hand or to the other.

The astrological influence is also discussed in this ritual:

> From the many coloured Bow, is loosed in Yesod, the Arrow of Sagittarius-Samekh, soaring upward to cleave open the Veil into the Sun in Tiphareth. Thus it is a fit symbol for hope and aspiration, for the Sign of Sagittarius, Jupiter, ruler of Kaph is Lord. Thus, by this straight and narrow way only, is advance between the dangers that have threatened you, possible … But Sagittarius the Archer is a bicorporate Sign—the Centaur, the Man and the Horse combined … For thus will thou cleave upward by the Path of Sagittarius, through the Sixth Sephirah into the Path of Teth, answering to Leo the Lion, the reconciling Path between Mercy and Severity, Chesed and Geburah, beneath whose centre hangs the glorious Sun of Tiphareth. Therefore by the straight and narrow Path of Sagittarius, let the Philosophus advance like the arrow from the centre of Qesheth, the Bow. And this Sign of Sagittarius lieth between the Sign of Scorpio—Death and Capricornicus—the Devil, so had Jesus to pass through the Wilderness, tempted by Satan.

The Tribe of Israel associated here is Benjamin, for Jacob says: 'Benjamin shall ravin as a wolf: In the morning he shall devour the prey and at night he shall divide the spoil'. Moses says: 'The beloved of the Lord shall dwell in safety by him: And the Lord shall cover him all the day long and he shall dwell, between his shoulders'.

The Mathers description of this Key is as follows:

> It represents an Angel with the Solar emblem of Tiphareth on her brow, the wings of the Aerial and Volatising nature, pouring together the fluidic Fire and the fiery Water, thus combining and harmonising and temperating those opposing elements. One foot rests on dry and volcanic land, in the background of which is a volcano whence issues an eruption. The other foot on the Water by whose border springs fresh vegetation, contrasting strongly with the arid and dry nature of the distant land. On her breast is a square, the emblem of rectitude. The whole figure is a representation of that straight and narrow way of which it is said 'few there be that find it', which alone leads to the higher and glorified life. For to pursue that steady and tranquil mean between two, opposing forces, it is indeed difficult and many are the temptations to turn aside either to the right or to the left, wherein remember, are but to be found the menacing symbols of Death and the Devil.

The Alchemical association to this card is Elevation. This is the process where the spiritual or ethereal essence is removed from the corporeal or gross, the volatile from the fixed (such as vapour), through the process of Fire or heat. The first version of this Key seems to relate more directly to this with the figure over the heated cauldron. The second version here is more subtle and as Mathers notes 'more restricted in meaning'. However the water jugs being poured, with the volcanic fire in the background, make it plain that the Elevation process is not a dry one, or humid (as in the first version of this key), but is more liquid in orientation and is more closely allied with (though not identical to) higher distillations.

The Psychological Mode of Expression shows, to a certain extent, an isolated individual, away from any pressures that might distract him from his task. He is an individual that has channelled all of his creative energies into a desired task and does so very successfully.

A myth associated with this Key is that of Chiron, the centaur, who was considered the perfect balance between animal and man and who, as a teacher, was an individual who tried to help man raise his level of awareness. Egyptian mythology, with this Trump, relates to Sati or Satet as she is known generally. Her name means to 'pour out' for she was a Goddess of fertility and often shown carrying bows and arrows as well as carrying water pots. Both of these myths are very heavily associated to this Key.

Divination

Combination of Forces, Realisation, Growth built of a fast-growing but firm foundation; Support while going through an adjustment period; Things happening very quickly. Beauty of a firm basis; taking a balanced path, manoeuvring, mergers, marriage. The Sovereignty of Fundamental Power. Sol acting through Sagittarius upon Luna—Daughter of the Reconcilers, the Bringer forth of Life.

This card has many colours and has played many roles in readings. It has represented activities in the creative arts, drama, films, education and travel. It has even represented commercial or domestic efforts in the culinary arts, design, dressmaking, etc. Under business matters a merger of people, companies or ideas can take place. On relationships it is a union or marriage. Temperance is likened to the mixing of ingredients until that perfect result is obtained. This shows a person or persons taking the right steps at the right times, manoeuvring him/herself to the right results. Unification and balancing are its key meanings. Often Temperance has played the role of medicine, the doctor or natural health practitioner. More often the latter.

I use my creative energy whenever I choose, I unite the forces of my life.

Key 15—The Devil

Title	:	Lord of the Gates of Matter, Child of the Forces of Time
Number	:	Fifteen
Astrological	:	Capricorn
Kabbalistic	:	Twenty-sixth Path—Renewing/renovating Intelligence
Tribe	:	Zebulon
Hebrew Letter	:	Ayin
Alchemical	:	Coagulation/Cibation
Mythology	:	Pan; Set; Mendes; Faunus
Sound	:	A Natural
Colour	:	Indigo Blue-green; Yellow; Pale Bluish Grey; Dark Greenish Brown; plus complementaries

This number, Key 15, was considered in days of old to be one of magic and evil. It is considered to be a fatal number of troubles, but also of marriage and eloquence, bondage, magnetism, gaiety, desire. The numerical reduction of 15 becomes 1 + 5 = 6 (Lovers) which is divine union. Whereas Key 6 is a spiritual marriage, Key 15 is a marriage of matter, the flesh, which brings commitment and limitation.

The Numerical analysis of the name 'Devil' reduces to 7 in the English Kabbalah system. The number seven is also a magical number and as a hidden number to fifteen is magic of the earth plane, magic in incarnation. The Pythagorean analysis brings forth 9. Again, 9 reproduces itself through the Keys of the Tarot. Here, blending into Key 15, it shows the law of Karma, the law of cause and effect, action and reaction.

The title of this card originates from the Latin word *Diablos* which means 'adversary'. The Golden Dawn version of this Key is very much in the traditional mode and is an exact opposite of the preceding Key of Temperance. Where Temperance tries to build, the Devil tries to make man live for the moment and have him captivated by his senses. In this way man is a slave to desire and cannot rise above his current station until he acknowledges that he has a higher spiritual path to contemplate, for the Devil brings out the obsessive nature of man and captivates him. Levi, links the Devil to Baphomet and says:

> He is the guardian of the key to the Temple. Baphomet is analogous to the dark God of Rabbi Simeon. He is the dark side of the Divine face. That is why during the initiation ceremonies, the member elect must kiss the hind face of Baphomet or to give him a more vulgar name, the Devil. Now in the symbolism of the two faces, the hind face of God is the Devil and the Devil is the hieroglyphic face of God.

The Hebrew letter associated is Ayin which means eye. It has a numerical value of 70. A look at the letter will show that at first glance it is nothing like an eye for which it is named. A closer inspection of it shows that the two YODS at the top of the two branches resemble the eyes. Inside us we have the ductless glands of modern physiology—the Pineal and the Pituitary and these, when exercised correctly, can actually play a role in the awakening of the third eye. Phonetically Ayin represents the opening of the glottis (in the throat) and makes a guttural sound transliterated as AA-OO-WH. This symbolises an interior hollow sound, or noise and connotes materialism or emptiness, sometimes falsity or perversity. It represents the physical aspect of Vau and when used as a consonant almost always has an evil implication. Ayin has a value of 130 and relates to SML 'image or idol of worship' which also relates to eyes and their visual stimulus. The Zohar says:

> To the letter Ayin, the initial word Avon (which means evil act), though it is claimed the origin of Anyana, the Holy One said: 'I shall not create the world by thee and forthwith Ayin departed'…

The twenty-sixth Path of the 'Sepher Yetzirah' to which the Tarot Key of the Devil is referred, is called the Path of Renovating Intelligence. By it, God the Holy One, reneweth all changing forms which are renewed by the Creation of the World. This is the growth of consciousness which, while transforming, still retains a basic essence or structure which man has to transcend.

The Holy Tribe of Israel, Zebulon, is associated here, for Jacob says: 'Zebulon shall dwell at the haven of the sea and he shall be for a haven of ships and his border shall be unto Sidon'. Moses says, 'Rejoice Zebulon in thy going out and Issachar in thy tents and they shall call the people unto the mountain, there they shall offer sacrifices of righteousness, for they shall suck of the abundance of the sea, of the treasure hid in the sands'.

Alchemically the Devil symbolises Cibation. Cibation is the concept of wetting or feeding dry matter. It is part of the integration process where it impregnated itself. Its own liquid has been dropped into its own dried matter and in this way feeding itself, eating its own flesh (sometimes called the Peacock's flesh). That which eats its own tail is called the Uroboros. The metamorphosis that takes place is associated to this Key in the sense that it is self-renewal, but still limited to a category where one part is life-sustaining for the other. Hence the limitation, shown by the two figures (brother and sister or twins) which are restricted by chains. Like the devil, this action shows the eating of their own Spirit.

The astrological sign of this key is that of Capricorn the Goat. This rules the hair and outer layers of the body including joints and bone structure in general. Capricorn can also introduce a strong tendency towards inhibition as this Key shows. The spiritual aspect shows separation from the source, so that a whole is not fully comprehended.

The psychological mode of expression that this card displays is that of the opportunist. An individual who will prey on others to fulfil his or her tasks no matter how big or small. This stems from the concept that his mind is so attuned to the physical senses that he is unaware of any spiritual influence, or of the concept of right and wrong. Winning is the only thing that counts for him. Ego inflation takes place to the point where concern for Self takes precedence over everything else. Sexuality here is also a very vital part of one's nature at this level but, instead of being constructive, it is destructive, self-indulgent and possessive, sometimes obsessive.

Mathers says of this Key in the Portal Ritual:

> *The fifteenth Key of the Tarot represents a goat-headed, satyr-like Demon whose legs are hairy—his feet claws, standing upon the Cubical Altar. He has heavy bat-like wings. In his left hand, which points downwards he holds a lighted torch and in his right, which is elevated, a horn of water. The left hand points downwards to show that it is the infernal and burning, not the celestial and life-giving flame which is kindled at his torch—just as when the Sun is in Capricorn, to which cold and earthy Sign this Key corresponds. Solar Light at its weakest and the natures of cold and moisture triumph over heat and dryness.*
>
> *The Cubical Altar represents the Universe—right and left of it, bound thereto by a cord attached to a circle which typifies the centre of the Earth, are two smaller demons, one male and one female. They hold a cord in their hands. The whole figure shows the gross generative powers of nature on the material plane and is analogous to the Pan of the Greeks and the Egyptian Goat of Mendes (the symbol of Chem).*
>
> *In certain ways this Key represents the brutal forces of nature, which to the unbelieving man only obscure and do not reflect the Luminous Countenance of God. It also alludes to the sexual powers of natural generation. Thus, therefore, the Key fitly counter-balances the symbol of Death on the other side of the Tree of Life. Of the smaller demons, one points downwards and the other upwards, answering to the positions of the hands of the central Figure.*
>
> *Beneath his feet are Pentagrams on which he tramples (whence comes their title of Wizard's Foot) and his head is covered with the evil and reversed Pentagram. As his hands bear the torch and the horn, the symbol of Fire and Water, so does his form unite the Earth in his hairy and bestial aspect and the Air in his bat-like wings. Thus he represents the gross and materialised Elemental Forces of Nature; and the whole would be an evil symbol, were it not for the Pentagram of Light above his head which regulates and guides his movements. He is the eternal renewer of all changing forms of Creation in Conformity with the Law of the All-Powerful One (Blessed be He) which controlling law is typified by the controlling force of the Pentagram of Light surmounting the whole. This Key an emblem of tremendous force; many and universal are its mysteries.*

Divination

Materiality; temptation; and obsession in general; deceit; mistrust; sexuality; power; cunning; devilment. Associated symbols are the Sovereignty and Beauty of the material (and therefore false Splendour). Sol acting through Capricorn on Mercury—Lord of the Gates of matter, Child of the forces of Time.

Although this card represents the pro-creative energy of life, it is also the limitations that manifested life must work within. Hence, the meanings of commitment, responsibility and restriction apply. In matters of employment, hard work where the individual has to stay in a profession with little hope of leaving it for the time concerned. In business and economics, success is within the limits of current conditions, but power and growth are depicted. In relationships we have sexual attraction, sexual activities, karmic ties, sexual harassment. Often the querent will be dealing with greed in others, or themselves and those of self-concern only. Here the querent will have to be warned to look out for themselves. The Devil card also talks of a person having to learn to take hold of their own power and master themselves and their surroundings.

I master myself, I master my life.

Key 16—Blasted Tower

Title	:	Lord of the Hosts of the Mighty
Number	:	Sixteen
Astrological	:	Mars
Kabbalistic	:	Twenty-seventh Path—Active or Exciting Intelligence
Hebrew Letter	:	Peh
Alchemical	:	Calcination
Mythology	:	Anher; Ares; Mars; Cyclops
Sound	:	C Natural
Colour	:	Poppy Red; Primary Red; Scarlet; Poppy Scarlet rayed Amber; plus complementaries
Chakra	:	Solar Plexus

Key 16 is a great force which follows a course of awakening of the inner, spiritual self through sudden happenings, which may have been shock, upsets, or clear flashes of insight. It is a number of atonement, weaknesses revealed, catastrophes and accidents. The numerical breakdown of 16 is 1 + 6 = 7 (Chariot). The power of the Divine (1) illuminates the mystical union of Spirit and Matter (6), causing an awakening of Man, thus his mind and body knows his true potential (his soul) and is now awakened from ignorance (7).

Numerical analyses of the name 'Tower', using the Pythagorian and Hebraic systems, and the English Kabbalah, all give 9 (Hermit), which is someone who has forsaken all and gone towards a spiritual path. Another view-point is how the Edomite Kings built false values and walls which are shattered by the reality of spiritual awakening. In contrast, Key 1 (Magician) brings about an awakening of the senses, or, perhaps, awareness, through study and learning.

The Blasted Tower of the Golden Dawn is very much in a traditional mould. In the preceding Key, the Devil showed two small figures chained to his world of materialism. In this card the story unfolds yet further, for these two figures are blasted away from the shackles that bind them, through the lightning anger of YHVH. The entire concept of this card and its predecessor is shown in the story of the Tower of Babel, where Nimrod persuaded the post diluvians from worshipping the Creator and to concentrate on life's pleasures. Instead of worshipping God in man's image they decided to return the complement by building a huge tower that would reach heaven itself. Confusion and misunderstanding struck however when they could not all speak the same language, which was said to be Divine retribution.

The Hebrew letter associated with this Key is Peh which means mouth and symbolises speech, hence its direct relationship to the Tower of Babel for speech was a very important step for people to communicate with each other. Without it there would be chaos as shown in this Key. The letter Peh has a value of 80 and relates to other words such as YSOD 'Foundation' and VAaD 'union' which share a strong link and show the method of the Tower's construction. Since the word Peh has a value of 85, other words such as MYLH meaning 'circumcision', also have a part to play in understanding the meaning of the Tower. Here we have something split open and this action is very much in accord with the pictorial imagery of the Key. The Zohar says of Peh:

> *I am the beginning and deliverance and thou wilt execute in the world … but thou also gives rise to evil and thy form resembles animals that walk with bowed heads, like wicked men who go about with bowed heads and extended hands.*

Peh also reinforces the letter Beth by virtue of its shape which gives Peh an outlet, from the concept of the pronunciation of speech as given in the Key, The Magician.

The Blasted Tower relates to the Solar Plexus Chakra (and the adrenal glands, spleen and stomach) which has been called by some esoteric philosophers as the 'great clearing house of energy below the diaphragm'. It is the chakra that controls the lower chakras for it is the most independent of the four lower centres. It is the point where all emotional desires build up and need release, dispersing latent energies so that the individual has clear expression without the lower desires getting in the way. As the Blasted Tower cleans away the unwanted people in the Tower, so does this chakra get rid of the Astral and Emotional dregs that have prevented it from performing its function correctly.

In the Philosophus Ritual we are told:

> *The twenty-seventh Path of the Sepher Yetzirah which answered to Peh is called Exciting Intelligence and it is so called because by it is created the Intellect of all created Beings under the Highest Heaven and the excitement or motion of them. It is therefore the Reflection of the Sphere of Mars and the Reciprocal Path connecting Netzach with Hod, Victory with Splendour. It is the lowermost of the three Reciprocal Paths.*

There is a strong influence also through the Sephiroth of Geburah which helps feed the energy of this Path and the Key. Here we have the overreaction of the martial side of nature shown by its title of 'Severity'. This is also helped by the Yetziratic title of this Sephirah, 'Radical Intelligence', all of which and more apply here to this Key.

Alchemically this key is the First Stage of the Calcination Process. This is where the Prima Materia or First matter is reduced in volume due to direct burning, which reduces the Prima to first black then changes to white ashes. It is a destructive purgation process in order to get rid of the excessive material or dross that is not needed. With reference to this Key we find the Lightning is the direct flame and the correct setting (for the flame) is shown as the ten-stage Tree. On the other side of the Tower the Qlippothic eleven-stage Tree shows that there are still more impurities to transmute. All figures leaving the Tower are the unwanted dross, impurities.

The Astrological association here is the planet Mars, which represents the aggressive and dynamic tendencies of man's nature. Mars governs the muscular tissue of the body and, to a certain extent, the nervous system and the excretory organs and the red corpuscles in the blood.

The psychological expression of this Key relates to the Will of Man's mind pushing the physical body to its limits and beyond, resulting in some sort of breakdown. It is the individual who, driven by power and conquest, destroys all those in his path in an effort to achieve his own ends. Like the card the Devil, the person here is after self-gratification with disastrous results; someone completely out of control.

The Blasted Tower tells the story of the expulsion of the Dukes or Kings of Edom who reigned the Earth when it was formless and void. The wars between these Kings shown in this card are symbolised by the lightning which is sent from a Light Bearer and which caused the unbalanced forces to ebb away. The 4 = 7 Ritual of The Golden Dawn goes into great detail on the subject of the wars with the Edomite Kings and this should be studied carefully with the meaning of the Key. In his notes to the translation of the 'Book of Concealed Mystery', Mathers says:

> The Kings of Ancient Time mean the same thing as the Edomite Kings; that is, they symbolise the worlds of unbalanced force, which according to the Zohar, preceded the formation of this Universe.

Within the Ritual of the twenty-seventh Path in the 4 = 7 Grade the following speech on this Key is read out to the Postulant:

> It represents a Tower struck by a Lightning Flash proceeding from a rayed circle and terminating in a triangle. It is the Tower of Babel struck by Fire from heaven. It is to be noted that the triangle at the end of the lightning Flash, issuing from the circle, forms exactly the astronomical symbol of Mars. It is the power of the triad rushing down to destroy the Column of Darkness. Three holes are rent in the walls, symbolising the establishment of the Triad therein and the Crown at the summit of the Tower is falling, as the Crowns of the Kings of Edom fell, who are also symbolised by the men falling headlong. On the right-hand side of the Tower is LIGHT and it is the representation of the Tree of LIFE by ten circles thus disposed. On the left-hand side is DARKNESS and eleven circles symbolising the QLIPPOTH.

In many respects Man and the Tower are analogous to each other and the Freedom of Will concerning which Path to choose is of paramount importance in this life. If that choice be a negative one, then Mankind will suffer the fate of the Kings of Edom. Within the four inner concentric circles of Mars, from where the energy of Light originates we have the Holy name of YHVH which eventually formulates into the twelve points. Each of these points represents one of the twelve Tribes of Israel which were sent to bring Order in Edom and expel their Kings. These are directed through the three final circles, which shows the framework of the Ain Soph Aur— the Limitless Light manifesting itself in Darkness causing light and balance. The Crown of Five points shows the energy of Geburah being unbalanced by a greater force.

The Egyptian god form of this Path is Anher (Anhert) and personifies the most warlike attributes of Ra of which he is a derivative. The Greek god form is Ares and the Cyclopes (Arges, Brontes and Steropes) who represent the various elements of destruction. They made the thunderbolts of Zeus and built fortresses for the Gods. Mars is the Roman god form.

Divination

Ambition, fighting, war, courage, destruction, bad health, accidents, disruptions in general, shock, shifting, the unexpected, victory over Splendour. Venus acting through Mars upon Mercury: Avenging Force—Lord of the Hosts of the Mighty.

Wherever this card is laid in a reading, it will show an area of life where a disruption or awakening takes place. This disruption can be serious or slight. Often it is serious and a shock to the querent. The Tower has represented shifting house and/or environment and changing job under sudden and sometimes unpleasant circumstances. Other times it is a realization of the truth of a situation, usually painful to the querent to accept. Here the debris and negative is thrown out, so that the good and positive can grow. Quite often a situation is out of the querent's hands to control. The Tower shows a purification process. The Tower depicts influences in people's lives that make them turn around and look at themselves. In personal matters, like relationships, this card will show an argument or break-up.

I accept my situation and release what holds me back from my full realization.

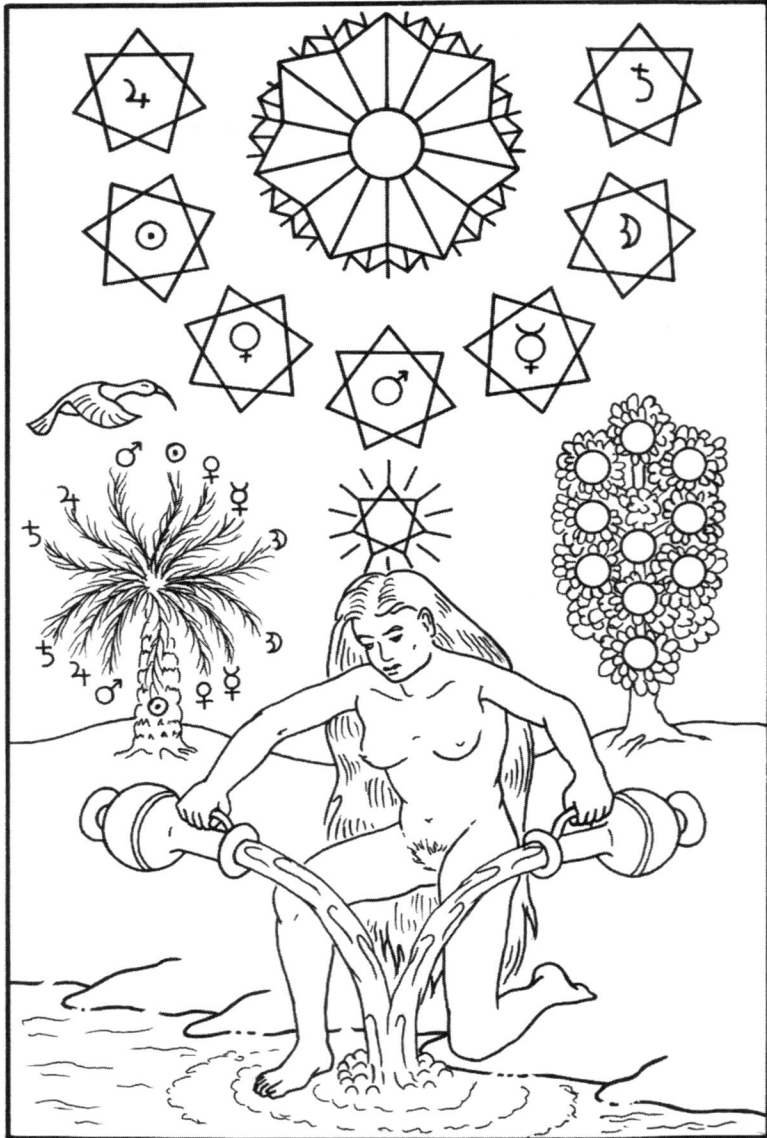

Key 17—The Star

Title	:	Daughter of the Firmament Dweller between the Waters
Number	:	Seventeen
Astrological	:	Aquarius
Kabbalistic	:	Twenty-eighth Path—Natural Intelligence
Tribe	:	Reuben
Hebrew Letter	:	Tzaddi
Alchemical	:	Congelation
Mythology	:	Hebe; Nut; Juno
Sound	:	A Sharp
Colour	:	True Purple; Dove Colour; Soft Lilac Grey; Buff flecked White; plus complementaries

Attributed to number seventeen are immortality, love and hope, the dreams and hopes of mankind, promised rewards and advancements, truthfulness and revelation. From the destruction and awakening states of Keys 15 and 16, Key 17 redeems and restores. The numerical reduction of 17 is 1 + 7 = 8 (Strength), which is hidden in 17 as a promise of eternity through perpetual motion of the forces of life. This motion of the life forces is shown through the Pythagorean numerical analysis of the name 'Star', giving 10 (Wheel of Fortune). The English Kabbalah analysis gives 13 (Death), the transformation of a soul through death and rebirth. Key 17 symbolizes the cyclic process which one must go through to gain access to the Tree of Knowledge (evolution), or the Tree of Life (involution).

At first glance the Golden Dawn concept of this Key is traditional, but when considering the ritual explanations of the Path of Tzaddi in the 4 = 7 grade of the Golden Dawn Order, other meanings of this card are brought to bear. The Star is something of a paradox, for though an

Air Sign, the whole concept of this card is in fact Water. The Three Goddesses involved with this Key are: Isis who governs the Rain and stimulates growth; Nephthys who governs the Dew and shows the effect of growth through the Darkness of Night; and Athor who Rules the Atmosphere of Earth. These Goddesses are representations of the Mother Supernal or AIMA ELOHIM which, in turn, can be simplified as one title of Mother Nature herself. Of this Mathers says:

> All things bow before the Three Supernals. The first Course is sacred but in the midst thereof another, the third aerial, which cherisheth Earth in Fire and the Fountain of Fountain of All Fountains; the matrix containing All. Thence springeth forth abundantly the generation of Multifarious Matter.

The Hebrew letter associated with this Key is Tzaddi, which represents all concepts of severance or solution and, as a hieroglyph, is represented by a Hook by which something may be caught or ended. In sound it falls into the same group as Zain and Samekh though it is harder and more abrupt. Placed at the beginning of words it indicates the movement which carries us on towards an end. Placed at the end as a final, it indicates the end accomplished. On a higher level it represents a refuge for man. The letter Tzaddi has a value of 90 which equates with other words of the same value, such as SL 'exalt', or PY 'mouth of a well or opening of a garment'. As a word its value is 104 and relates to QD 'divide' and DQ 'beat'. One of the original symbols for Tzaddai was a rod, the masculine principle which was later divided into two, symbolic of the feminine principle, which then unify together at a later stage.

Mathers says:

> The twenty-eighth path of the Sepher Yetzirah which answereth to the letter Tzaddi is called Natural Intelligence and is so called because through it is consummated and perfected the Nature of every existing being under the Orb of the Sun. It is therefore a reflection of the Airy Sign Aquarius, the Water-Bearer, unto which is attributed the Countenance of Man, the Adam of the restored World.

The Alchemical stage of the Star is the Congelation process. This is where an object is thickened or gelled and is likened to ice over water, for within it, it contains a fluid substance. When the surface is broken the essence flows out. This is analogous to this Key where the hard surface of the Star is shown above and the liquefaction of the matter is shown below.

The astrological Sign of Aquarius is associated with this Key and is the Fixed Sign of the Air Element. It relates to the lungs and the circulatory process. This Sign also shows achievement through spiritual growth of an impersonal nature. Aquarius, is of course, governed by Saturn (though Neptune has its exaltation here), but using the modern psychic approach to the meaning of this planet, which is that of a 'reconciler' according to psychics (Edgar Cayce and Arthur Ford), the main theme behind the Sign is then revealed, for in relation to Binah, which is associated with Saturn, we have 'Understanding'. Both of these concepts link into the symbology of Key 17.

The associated Hebrew Tribe is that of Reuben, for Jacob says: 'Reuben, thou art my first-born, my might and the beginning of my strength, the excellency of dignity and the excellency of power. Unstable as water, thou shalt not excel, because thy went up to thy father's bed and defiles thou it; he went up to my couch'. Moses: 'Let Reuben live and not die and let not his men be few'.

The psychological mode of expression represented by this Key is that of the perfectionist. This is an evolvement process which has reached a high point and now must veer off in a new direction for additional stimuli. It is very much a coming of age of concept where the child becomes an adult and must choose the Path which he or she has mapped out. There is no turning back, however, and this is the beginning of the cultivation of new experiences.

The Golden Dawn ritual of the 4 = 7 grade says of this Key:

> *The large Star in the centre of the Heavens has seven principal and fourteen secondary rays and this represents the Heptad multiplied by the Triad. This yields twenty-one—the number of the Divine Name EHEDEH which as you already know is attached to Kether. In the Egyptian sense, it is Sirius, the Dog-Star, the Star of Isis-Sothis. Around it are the Stars of the Seven Planets each with its sevenfold counter changed operation. The nude figure with the Star of the heptagram on her brow is the synthesis of Isis, of Nephthys and of Athor. She also represents the planet Venus through whose sphere the influence of Chesed descends. She is Aima, Tebunah, the Great Supernal Mother—Aima Elohim, pouring upon the Earth the waters of Creation, which unite and form a River at her feet, the River going forth from the Supernal Eden which ever floweth and faileth not. Note well that in this Key she is completely unveiled while in the twenty-first Key she is only partially so. The two Urns contain the influences from Chokmah and Binah. On the right springs the Tree of Life and on the left the Tree of Knowledge of Good and Evil whereon the Bird of Hermes alights and therefore does this Key represent the restored World, after the Formless and the Void and the Darkness: The New Adam, the Countenance of the Man which falls in the Sign of Aquarius. And therefore doth the astronomical symbol of this sign represent, as it were, Waves of water; the ripples of that River going forth out of Eden. But, therefore also, it is justly attributed to Air and not to water because it is the Firmament dividing and containing the Waters.*

Within the New Zealand Order, the Star has many additional considerations apart from the quotation above. The Seven Stars are analogous to the Seven Branched Candle Stick diagram that is shown in the 1 = 10 ritual. They are also related to the Seven Seals of Revelations and to the Seven Psychic centres of Man (Chakras) for these must be awoken in harmony before man can transcend to newer horizons.

The Tree of Knowledge of Good and Evil as shown on the left of the Key gives the structure that man must work through and eventually transcend with either positive or negative results. The Tree has seven upper and seven lower branches which relate to the Seven Heavens and the Seven Hells of the Kabbalists. The Bennu Bird above the Tree is the release of the Spirit after it has travelled the many paths of the Tree. On the right side of the Card we have the Tree of Life which is the Eternal Structure of the Spirit.

The Star directly above the head of the figure has seven points and alludes to the Sephirah of Netzach or 'Victory'—the seat of Venus, who governs it. This is the Star of Sirius and the seat of perfection and harmony, which will be released into a new form of consciousness.

The Egyptian god form associated here is Nut, the Sky Goddess, who was the heavens and night embodying the stars above the earth and was the daughter of Ra. The Greek Goddess

Hebe is also associated and is the wife of Heracles and daughter of Zeus and Hera. She lost the office of goddess of youth and the cup bearer of the gods when she presented a posture that was indecent, when pouring nectar to the gods during a festival. Her other duties were domestic, but she also had a healing power and was able to restore to men and gods their vigour. Juno has also been associated with this card.

Divination

Hope, faith, unexpected help, dreaminess—deception, if negatively aspected by its position; The Victory of Fundamental Strength; gradual crystallisation of one's efforts. Venus acting through Aquarius upon Luna—Daughter of the Firmament, Dweller between the Waters.

Ideas and inspiration, vision and self-awareness, are represented by this card. Very often the Star turns up in a reading representing situations that have been resolved, realised and put into a positive direction. There is a sense of serenity and beauty in matters depicted by this card. It shows a need to be alone for personal development, rather than in a relationship. A larger and more humanitarian view comes to awareness which can sometimes leave a person with a feeling of awe. Events will unfold in their own time according to the plan of the universe, therefore the querent must be instructed in patience. Your hopes and dreams will crystallize in their own time.

I open my mind to a greater awareness that is beyond my individual existence—yet I know I am a part of the whole.

XVIII

MOON

Key 18—The Moon

Title	:	Ruler of Flux and Reflux, Child of the Sons of the Mighty
Number	:	Eighteen
Astrological	:	Pisces
Kabbalistic	:	Twenty-ninth Path—Corporeal Intelligence
Tribe	:	Simeon
Hebrew Letter	:	Qoph
Alchemical	:	Conjunction/Impregnate
Mythology	:	Upuau; Odysseus; Venus and Cupid
Sound	:	B Natural
Colour	:	Deep Crimson; Warm Golden Brown; Oxide Red; English Red; plus complementaries

Key 18 is a number of the elements and is reflected light. Its counterpart, 1 + 8 = 9 (Hermit) sets out with his Lantern to follow the path of the Sage, but at Key 18 he enters the twilight and walks through the path of temptation, trickery and deception. On this path, if he follows the light, though reflected, he emerges knowing his own strengths and weaknesses. In fact, the light must be reflected, for the full blast and sight of the 'Light' would blind him. The strength he draws from and finds is shown through the hidden number of the name 'Moon' which is Keys 1 (Magician) and 8 (Strength).

This Key applies to vivid imagination, dreams and the subconscious, which is a realm the adept must know how to 'walk'. It is also a number of body care and one's inner healing forces. The English Kabbalah analysis of the name 'Moon' comes to twenty-one (Universe), showing the end of the path is close by and such awareness guides the adept through the darkness,

151

(involution). On an evolutionary path, twenty-one is the power with which the postulant comes and walks with.

The Golden Dawn version of this Key is very much in the traditional approach but seen through the framework as given in the 4 = 7 Ritual. In the 4 = 7 grade ritual of the Golden Dawn, a general overview of the Key is given, with Osiris as the pool, representing the resurrected past producing Horus as the Crayfish, with Isis as the stream of life flowing into the pool.

The associated Hebrew letter is Qoph which has a value of 100. Hieroglyphically it resembles an ear and also the back of the head. Symbolically it becomes an implement, or instrument, by which man may accomplish an act or defend himself, marking force and restraint. It is significant of repression and decision. It is the harder and more guttural sound of Kaph. Abstractly, a regular succession can be traced of descent and development which has Heh analogous to Universal Life, pure being and Cheth the Life of Nature, manifest existence, with Kaph as Assimilated Life hiding natural form and Qoph as Material Existence giving the means of form which is the very nature of this Key.

The Kabbalistic association of the 'Sepher Yetzirah' says that the twenty-ninth Path is called Corporeal Intelligence because it forms the very body which is so formed beneath the whole Order of various plans of existence and their amplification. It is therefore a reflection of the Watery Sign of Pisces on the twenty-ninth path connecting the Material Universe, as depicted in Malkuth, with the Pillar of Mercy and the side of Chesed, through the Sephirah of Netzach. Through Netzach to Malkuth the Waters of Chesed flow.

There are actually two Hebrew Tribes of Israel linked to this Key, which are Simeon and Levi, for Jacob says: 'Simeon and Levi are brethren; instruments of cruelty are in their habitations. O my Soul, come not thou into their secret, unto their assembly, mine honour, be not thou united; for in their anger they slew a man and in their self-will they dug down a wall. Cursed be their anger, for it was fierce; and their wrath, for it was cruel: I will divide them in Jacob and scatter them in Israel'. When applying the above to this Key, we see the splitting apart of the two as illustrated by the two Watchtowers on either side of the stream from which the two emerge.

The alchemical stage referred to here is the Conjunction/Impregnation. This is a bringing together of the separated parts of the experiment into one homogenous commodity. It is the final step in which all the component parts of Matter which have been separated, are strengthened and placed back together, so that it is stronger than when the experiment first started. The Green Lion becomes White, so that White may become Red. In this Key the Moon represents fertility and impregnation which is shown by the Crayfish emerging from the pool, the point of conception. This is a very dangerous state, for one slight error will ruin the experiment. The Red Crayfish travels on the Path towards the White Luna influence.

The astrological association is the Sign of Pisces in which Venus is exalted and is governed by Jupiter. Applied to the Tarot we have an empathy with the Empress (Venus) who has just given birth in Pisces (shown by the crayfish in the pond, an archetypal symbol of life in the womb) in this Key and is governed by the Wheel of Fortune showing the beginning of a cycle of change. The Sign of Pisces is a hieroglyphic symbol of two fishes bound with rope and is a symbol of bondage and captivity, relating strongly to the Biblical quotation in the preceding paragraph. In human physiology this Sign covers the lymphatic system and body fluids.

The psychological mode of expression are various forms of escapism and a possibility of the danger of drug abuse. It shows other individuals asserting their will and influence on people who are very susceptible to any form of influence. On a more positive note, however, transcendence into a spiritual nature and universal oneness will be a prime focus. Insight into the needs and pain of others together with an ability to heal on a psychic/emotional level. The Mathers version of this Key is as follows:

> *The eighteenth Key of the tarot … represents the Moon with four Hebrew Yods like drops of dew falling, two dogs, two Towers, a winding Path leading to the Horizon and, in the foreground, Water with a Crayfish crawling through it to the land.*
>
> *The Moon is in its increase on the side of Mercy, Gedulah and from it proceeds sixteen principal and sixteen secondary rays, which make thirty-two, the number of the Paths of Yetzirah. She is the Moon at the feet of the Woman in Revelations, ruling equally over the cold and moist natures and passive elements of Earth and Water. The Four Hebrew Yods refer to the Four letters of the Holy Name reconstituting the destroyed world from the Waters. It is to be noted that the symbol of the Sign is formed from two Lunar crescents of Gedulah and Geburah bound together. It thus shows the Lunar nature of the Sign.*
>
> *The Dogs are the Jackals of the Egyptian Anubis guarding the gates of the East and West, shown by the Two Towers between which lies the Path of all heavenly bodies, ever rising in the East and setting in the West. The Crayfish is a Sign of Cancer and was anciently the Scarabeus or Khephera, the emblem of the Sun below the Horizon as he ever is when the Moon is increasing above. Also, when the Sun is in the Sign of Pisces the Moon will be well in her increase in Cancer as shown by the Crayfish emblem.*

Additional to the Mathers' explanation is that the four Yods represent the Eternal River of Eden, which has four heads and finds correlation in the four triplicities of the Zodiac. The Watch-Towers symbolise the Forces of Darkness and show the borders of Hades on either side of the narrow stream of life. Their function is to give alarm, if man, symbolised by the Crayfish and as a wandering Soul, enters their Kingdom, for they are warring factions and will compete for his capture. The Jackals below them are their followers who will attempt to drag the Crayfish and devour it if it gets too close to them. The River or Stream of Life separates the two 'borders' for none can stand the Lux, Light of Life in the Kingdom of Darkness. The Four Yods fall into the stream which nurtures the Pool of Stagnation so that it in fact becomes a Pool of Life at the appropriate monthly astrological time. Here Man has a distinct choice to make as he climbs up the stream of Life concerning what direction to take and ultimately this Key relates to a matter of choices.

The Egyptian myth of Upuaut means the 'opener of the way'. Upuaut was a wolf-headed god and Lord of the Underworld and Necropolis and known as a warrior god of power. This was before the development of Osiris and was later merged in meaning with Osiris. Upuaut was depicted on the Boat of Ra and also a guardian of Osiris. He acted as a guide to Ra and a scout to the gods. The Greek myth is the voyage of Odysseus where he travelled to Aeaea. This was where he resisted going to the call of the Sirens by lashing himself to the mast of his ship. Another myth is that of Hero and Leander, two lovers divided by a large body of water. From her tower, Leander shined a light to guide Hero as he swam over, but one night the light went out and Hero drowned. She followed him into the water where they united in death. The Roman myth is that of Venus and Cupid when they sat of the bank of the Euraphrates river. Typhon approached scaring them into the water, where two fishes saved them. Another myth associated with this card is that of Matsya, the fish avatar. This is an Indian myth and another story in itself, still connected to water and fish.

Divination

Forced to take a decision; to see a project or situation through; blindness to dangers; exhaustion, hidden enemies, dissatisfaction; victory over the Material. Venus acting through Pisces upon the Cosmic Elements, the deceptive effect of the apparent power of the Material forces—Ruler of Flux and Reflux, Child of the Sons of the Mighty.

In relationship matters this card represents heavy emotional issues, mistrust, fear deceit. Often a person is leaving a situation or relationship. In home/environmental matters a shift or new situation is sought as an escape from unhappy times or circumstances—again emotional issues are prevalent. The Moon warns a person not to stray from their goals and to keep a clear mind as illusion and temptation will fall in their way. To some, they feel as if they are walking through a dark tunnel, but can see the light, now, at the end of it. It is subconscious and hidden issues which must be dealt with. In health matters good nutrition is important. It can show menstrual/hormonal problems in women and fluid retention. Midnight drawing forth to Dawn, bringing on new levels of future awareness. It represents a time of ordeal—life's tests—and warns one to maintain a true and correct way or conduct. If one can lift above base emotional instincts to a more spiritual energy and higher reasoning the card promises a difficult path but great rewards. A card of dreams, mystery and imagination.

Although I may not see my way clearly, I remain true to myself and my life's path—I trust my instinct.

Key 19—The Sun

Title	:	Lord of the Fire of the World
Number	:	Nineteen
Astrological	:	Sun
Kabbalistic	:	Thirtieth Path—Collective Intelligence
Hebrew Letter	:	Resh
Alchemical	:	Tincture/Lapidication
Mythology	:	Aten; Helios; Apollo
Sound	:	D Natural
Colour	:	Clear Orange; Golden Sunflower Yellow; Deep Melon Yellow; Amber Yellow rayed Red; plus complementaries
Channel	:	Pingala

A powerful number is Key 19 and the numerical reduction of this key is: 1 (Magician) + 9 (Hermit) = 10 (Wheel). The change takes place for the Magus as he brings himself to completion. He went forth to accomplish a mission (1), thus grasping it, he enters the path of wisdom (9) and after trial and ordeal he finally enters into manifestation united with the Divine (19), grasping his good fortune. Key 19 is a number of success, esteem, honour, marriage, happiness, leadership, love, agriculture, tests of courage, obstacles overcome, drive and ambition. The Numerical analysis of the name 'Sun' is 9 (English Kabbalah) and 6 (Pythagorean). Wisdom, harmony and beauty. Through 9 we see a cycle completing and through 6 we see the final marriage—union.

This Golden Dawn Key is very much in the traditional mould. The Sun is, of course, the very core of our Universe and is the very essence that gives Life to our World. Since the Golden Dawn is a solar-orientated Order the Sun has a very special place in it.

The Hebrew letter Resh is the letter par excellence and represents movement. Hiero-glyphically it is the head of Man for Resh directs the movement of the body and initiates any form of movement, especially any which helps sustain life; hence, the title of RASHITH HA GDLGALIM which 'talks' of the vortex, or the beginning of movement from the primal centre, that is, renewed by any form of movement. Resh has a value of 200 and relates to other words of similar value such as YTzQ 'pour out', QLAa 'casting a net'. The value of Resh as a word is 510 which relates to YRSh 'gain by succession' and NThS 'destroy' or 'spoil' showing both the positive and negative aspects of the Sun.

The Kabbalistic Sephirah of the Sun is Tiphareth, which means Beauty and is in the cen-tral position of the Tree of Life and has a direct influence on the other Sephiroth around it. In many ways Key 19 is similar to the meaning of Tiphareth, for it is the passive framework of Tiphareth coupled with a positive expression of the thirtieth Path which one must travel on the way to reach Tiphareth. In many ways this represents the Astrological concept of the Sun as the giver of Life to all, that which rules our lives and regulates the seasons and is the centre of our solar system.

The alchemical stage that this Key represents is the Elixir Lapis Philosophicus and/or Lapidi-fication, which is the Lapis Aureus (the Golden Stone). This is the end result of the experiment and where the finished product can be increased in quantity. Here the twins stand outside of the boundaries of their garden while the energy of the Sun above increases their vitality.

The Thirtieth Path of the Sepher Yetzirah on which this Key is placed, is called 'Collecting Intelligence', because from it Man measures the concept of time and judgement from the influ-ence of the Sun, the planets and their relationship to the Stars. It is the Path connecting Yesod to Hod, linking both Foundation and Splendour.

Astrologically the star which is the sun, as a meaning on its own, is the Soul, vitality and life-force. Only through the zodiac does it take on a personality. Therefore its meaning is coloured depending on what zodiac sign it shines through. This is very relevant when relating the Sun to the Key 19. The influence of Key 19 will depend very much on the personality of the quer-ent or person working with the card and it will typify our Soul nature, or essence of ourselves. Therefore the psychological mode of expression of this card is multifaceted by encompassing all potential expression and depending on the zodiac sign of the individual.

The Sun rules the Heart which is the pulse of our life and centre of our circulation of blood, which affects all parts of our body. Here again you see the holistic effect the Sun will have over the macrocosm and microcosm.

Like the High Priestess, the Sun has no chakra associated, but represents the Pingala, a channel that goes up the right-hand side of the Sushumna channel in the spine. Its effect is to counterbalance Kundaline energy and give it strength to rise and go through the various chakras. When energy is needed by the chakras the Pingala will perform this function and counterbalance with the Ida, which will help cool the energy if things get out of hand. Both these channels form a type of magnetic polarity which together helps the Kundaline to rise and perform its function correctly. The following description of this card is taken from the Golden Dawn's Practicus Ritual:

The Nineteenth Key of the Tarot … The Sun has twelve principle rays which represent the Twelve signs of the Zodiac. They are alternately waved and salient as symbolising the alternation of the masculine and feminine natures. These again are subdivided into thirty-six Decanates or sets of ten degrees in the Zodiac and these again into seventy-two, typifying the seventy-two quinances or sets of five and the seventy-two-fold Name Schemphamphoresh. Thus the Sun embraces the whole of creation in its rays. The seven Hebrew Yods on each side, falling through the air, refer to the Solar influence descending. The Wall is the circle of the Zodiac and the stones are its various degrees and divisions. The two children standing respectively on Water and Earth represent the generating influence of both, brought into action by the rays of the Sun. They are the two inferior or Passive Elements, as the Sun and the Air above them are the superior and Active Elements of Fire and Air. Furthermore, these two children resemble the Sign of Gemini which unites the Earthy Sign of Taurus with the Watery Sign of Cancer and this Sign was, by the Greeks and Romans, referred to Apollo or the Sun.

Also on the far left of the card beside the male, are three sunflowers which show the unified process of higher forms of the Kabbalistic Soul as it journeys through the sojourns of the Zodiac in each life, for these are the mysteries of the Supernal. The man and woman are joined for these are the forms one takes in the varying incarnations on Earth and they are permanently entwined. In this key they stand outside the Zodiac Wall and have transcended beyond their physical limitation. This card shows us the blueprint not only of the old Garden of Eden but also of the new one which man will eventually assume in future years as he sets foot on new worlds. It is a cyclic enfolding pattern that the thirty-six Decanates are divisions made of a 360 degree circle. The Decanates are ten degrees each, three of them allotted to each zodiac sign, so that each sign is thirty degrees. The 360 degree circle can also be divided every five degrees, which gives seventy-two divisions called decads or quinances. There are seventy-two bricks in the wall around the hill in this card as well, representing the seventy-two quinances (seventy-two angles of the Schemphamphoresh) continuous in its development.

Aten is the Egyptian god form here associated. Aten was a god of the Sun and Spirit and had a relationship as Aten-Ra, acting as the physical vehicle of Ra. The Roman god form is Apollo who was considered the elemental form of the Sun. The Greek god form is Helios, who drove over the sky in a golden chariot to find a golden cup of Hephaestus, found on the island of Hesperides. He would travel all night to return the contents of the cup to his family (who became many—humanity), only to repeat his journey over again every day and night.

Divination

Liberation; rejuvenation; going to areas where one has never been before; new ideas, fertility, riches of the Soul; collective experience; holiday; vitality; love; affection; friendships; achievement. The Splendour of the Material World. Mercury acting through the Sun upon the Moon—Lord of the Fire of the World.

Joy and richness of life with personal wellbeing—vitality and good health. Happiness in friendships or partnerships. Creativity, love and fullness of life where goals are fulfilled; spiritual fulfilment; birth of clarity and consciousness. Often the Sun represents a country or area with a sunny climate, e.g., Australia.

I open myself to fulfilment and experience the richness life offers in every moment.

JUDGMENT

Key 20—Judgement

Title	:	The Spirit of the Primal Fire
Number	:	Twenty
Astrological	:	Pluto
Element	:	Fire
Kabbalistic	:	Thirty-first Path—Perpetual Intelligence
Hebrew Letter	:	Shin
Alchemical	:	Purification
Mythology	:	Mau; Hades; Pluto
Sound	:	C Natural
Colour	:	Orange Red; Vermilion; Red; Paprika Red flecked Green; plus complementaries
Chakra	:	Spleen

Through Key 20 is a final awakening. Standing at the many crossroads of life, decisions are made and unmade, destiny is dictated, or changed. This is a 'make or break' point and already the beginning of the manifestation of matter and entry into the Kingdom. The counterpart to this Key is 2 + 0 = 2 (High Priestess) which involves the sacred portals through which one passes. The hidden essence is 'zero', the Fool. In all respects, twenty is life and the impulse is good, but this depends entirely on one's previous actions. From an involutionary perspective, it is passing through the sacred womb into life. From an evolutionary perspective it is a return to the sacred womb.

This Key also has the numbers nine (English Kabbalah) and ten (Pythagorean) associated as hidden numbers. As said before, nine and ten are completions of cycles and changes into new cycles. Key 20 is analogous to this as well, however, its state of cycle is more significant in change as one stands before the threshold (Universe card) deciding on which direction to walk and viewing what was, is and will be. This, in turn, involves the consequences of one's actions, past, present and future being, or to be, experienced.

In the Golden Dawn version of this Key there is a great deal of hidden symbolism. The Hebrew letter Shin, thus associated, is said to represent the teeth, due to a hissing sound made in pronunciation of this letter. It completes the symbolism of Zain and Samekh and is, in a sense, bound to them for Zain is like an arrow and Samekh the bow string, so Shin symbolises the bow itself.

In the Golden Dawn rituals, we are told that the three Paths on the Tree of Life (Qoph, Shin Tau) form the word QUESHETH, the Bow, which is the material sign of receptivity between God and Man. Shin is a symbol of movement and duration. Used as a prefix it can communicate a double power of movement as well as conjunction. It may be pronounced either SS or a Sh and it usually has a point above it to indicate which sound is to be used. Geometrically it represents the semi-arc of a circle, whereas Resh is a directly forward movement of a radius and Samekh a spiral. The Divine Name SHADDAI represents the overarching Heavens protracting the fecundity and abundance of Nature or providence.

The astrological association of this Key was once accepted as the Element of Fire, but since the discovery of Pluto, most modern-day Golden Dawn Temples tend to use the planetary association here. Pluto rules Scorpio and is exalted in Leo showing the link to the Keys of Death with Strength, the two concepts of Death and Regeneration, for Pluto denotes the aspect of Resurrection, which the Key adequately shows. Pluto rules the unconscious and shows radical changes within it.

The chakra that this Key refers to is the Spleen centre. Its function is to absorb prana (energy) from the atmosphere then distribute it through the physical body's energy centres for continual rejuvenation. The energy is then sent to other chakras, channels, nerves and the blood supply. It is the centre of rejuvenation and controls the rate of flow of the new incoming energy into the physical and etheric bodies. This chakra works strongly with the Astral Body and helps with work such as dream control and some Astral journeys.

The Thirty-First Path of the 'Sepher Yetzirah' associated with this Key is called 'Perpetual Intelligence' because it regulates the motion between the Sun and Moon in their correct order. It is, therefore, a reflection of the Sphere or influence of Fire and the Path connecting the Material Universe, as depicted in Malkuth, with the Pillar of severity and the side of Geburah, through the Sephirah of Hod.

The psychological mode of expression analogous to this Key can only be described as a type of rebirth or repolarisation of one's goals and attitudes. There is a very prominent spiritual direction in this rebirth which shows an individual coming into attunement with his actions, past and present, thus trying to adjust to a new set of values.

Alchemically this card, Judgement, is the stage of Purification, which in itself comprises a variety of smaller alchemical stages. It refers to separating the solids or faeces from the liquid so that regeneration can occur. This is shown very adequately in this key by the division of Land and water—Liquid and solid, with a regenerating figure emerging from a coffin. Purification is continuous where Separation leaves off and takes the three components of Sulphur, Salt and

Mercury, purifying them to a very high degree. On another level, it is the individual component of Sulphur, the Soul. Mathers' description of this card as given in the 3 = 8 ritual says:

> *The Twentieth Key of the Tarot … to the uninitiated eye it apparently represents the Last Judgement with an Angel blowing a trumpet and the Dead rising from their tombs, but its meaning is far more occult and recondite than this, for it is a glyph of the Powers of Fire. The Angel encircled by a rainbow, whence leap coruscations of Fire and crowned with the Sun, represents Michael, the Great Archangel and the Ruler of Solar Fire. The Serpents which leap in the rainbow are symbols of the Fiery Seraphim. The Trumpet represents the influence of the Spirit descending from BINAH, while the Banner with the Cross refers to the Four Rivers of Paradise and the Letters of the Holy Name.*
>
> *He is also Axieros, the first of the Samothracian Kabiri as well as Zeus and Osiris. The left-hand figure below, rising from the Earth is Samael, Ruler of Volcanic Fire. He is also Axiokersos, the Second Kabir, Pluto and Typhon. The right-hand figure below is Anael, the Ruler of Astral Light. She is also Axiokersa, the third Kabir, Ceres and Persephone, Isis and Nephthys. She is, therefore, represented in duplicate form and rising from the waters. Around both these figures dart flashes of Lightning.*

The Three principal figures form the Fire Triangle and further represents Fire operating in the other Three Elements of Earth, Air and Water.

> *The central lower figure with his back turned and his arms in the Sign of the 2 = 9 Grade Sign is Arael, the Ruler of latent heat. He is rising from the Earth as if to receive the properties of the other three. He is also Kasmillos the Candidate in the Samothracian Mysteries and the Horus of Egypt. He rises from the rock-hewn cubical Tomb and he also alludes to the Candidates who traverse the path of Fire. The three lower figures represent the Hebrew letter Shin, to which Fire is especially referred, the seven Hebrew Yods allude to the Sephiroth operating in each of the Planets and to the Schemphamphoresh.*

The Triangle in the Key also represents three main aspects of Fire. The Apex represents the Fire of the Intellect (AUR), while the left basal angle of the Triangle denotes Volcanic Fires of eruptions deep within the Earth (AUD). The remaining Right basal angle shows the Astral Fire. This is not the Sulphur of the raw element sulphur that is found in the earth and is mined. This is the Sulphuric essence, the Fire of all things existing. This is the Soul (AUB). These three concepts are shown in the Ritual of the 3 = 8 grade as Latent Heat, Active Heat and Passive Heat.

The twentieth Key of the Tarot should be studied very carefully, for it strongly equates with the Ritual of the 5 = 6 Grade. The rainbow of Seven circles relates to the number of the Kabbalistic Sephirah of Netzach, which is also the planet association of the Wall of the door from which the Vault can be entered. The Serpents flashing around it are the serpent of Wisdom in both a higher and lower form. The Angel Michael comes from the Sephirah of Hod, to which the path of Shin leads, showing its Splendour. Each of the three groupings of figures has a Yod from the Letter Shin within them, giving the power of Shin. The right figures are in water which shows their passive state and also the Pillar of Mercy. The Left Figure on land shows Fire erupting around him and is the Pillar of Severity, both extremes finding that there is no resurrection, while the

Middle way shows the grade sign of Air. The Seven Yods are the seven Seals of the Apocalypse and only those who know the way will be saved.

The Egyptian myth associated with this card is the legend of Mau the Cat Goddess who was a variation of Ra. She had a fight with Neb-er-tcher which was another version of the myths of how day and night are created. Mau, always victorious, brought forth the rays of Dawn. The Roman god form is Pluto—son of Saturn and Ops—and is the counterpart to the Greek Hades. Both were Lords of the Underworld, Winter and Darkness, Hell. They sat in judgement and whisked away the Goddess of Summer for six months of each year.

Divination

Final decision; sentence; determination of a matter; repolarising; self-awareness; crossroads reached; decisions to be made; confrontation; realisation; the hidden revealed. The Splendour of the material world; Mercury acting through Pluto upon Fire—Spirit of the Primal Fire.

Key 20 is a card of decisions and crossroads, where a choice must be made. There is no turning back. Whichever decision that is made paves one's future destiny. Key 20 has come up in situations mainly requiring an awareness of one's own actions. In health matters it reveals birth and the opening up of and drawing out of problems. It is the 'great revealer'. What is revealed now, is what one has brought upon oneself, whether it be conscious or unconscious. Judgement also quite often represents situations brought upon one where there is no choice but to make a choice and make a change, as circumstances are beyond one's control. Self-analysis and self-reproach.

I am not afraid to step forward—I am not afraid to look at myself and accept my destiny and accept that I make my own destiny.

Key 21—The Universe

Title	:	The Great One of the Night of Time
Number	:	Twenty-one
Astrological	:	Saturn
Kabbalistic	:	Thirty-second Path—Administrative Intelligence
Hebrew Letter	:	Tau
Alchemical	:	Coagulation
Mythology	:	Mut; Gaea; Saturn
Sound	:	A Natural
Colour	:	Darkest Indigo Blue; Soft Black; Blue Black; Black rayed Blue; plus complementaries
Chakra	:	Base

Key 21 is a number of honour, truth, success and advancement. A number of the Universe—the crown of the Magi which is only gained after his many tests, trials and ordeals leading ultimately to victory. Therefore, we have the threshold of a new world. This is the end and the beginning. Reducing 21 brings 2 + 1 = 3: the formula of life. 1 = masculine, plus 2 = feminine, equals 3, reproduction of life. Key 3, the Empress, in this state is mother nature.

Numerical analysis of the name 'Universe' (using the Pythagorean system) gives 13 (Death) which is transformation from one phase into another and is exactly what this card the Universe, means. Another hidden number (using the English Kabbalah) is five (Hierophant), which is the four elements and spirit within Key 21. This is shown by the four Kerubs, one in each corner of the card and the female figure in the centre.

The Golden Dawn version of this Key is a radical departure from most previous descriptions. The Name of this Key was changed from the 'World' to the 'Universe' to incorporate the full impact of the Macrocosm and the Microcosm.

The Hebrew letter associated with the 'Universe' is Tau, the last letter of the Hebrew alphabet, which has a value of 400. As a glyph Tau stands in the ancient form of a cross which has been ascribed to Thoth. Some have considered it an elaboration of Resh. It is an extremely sympathetic sign and when joined with the first letter of the Hebrew alphabet, Aleph, forms the prefix of ATh meaning 'essence' which is analogous to the Divine Spark of a person or thing that gives life. It is said that Moses quite often used this prefix in his account of Creation, to indicate that he was not describing a material or individual, but essentially a process that is developed from a higher plane, preliminary to any physical manifestation. Other words of the same value of Tau are ShAal 'a hollow concave form', ShQ pushing forward and QSh 'gather together'. The meaning of all these words combined shows varying aspects of this card. The alchemical stage that this Key represents is Coagulation. This occurs when all parts of the experiment are reunited and are brought back together as a solid or thicker substance when the liquid has evaporated. Applied to this Key we find that the formation of the figure is the substance in question, with the four Kerubics as the fixed aspect of the experiment. This can then be applied to the final stage of the Great Work bringing the resulting form into a solid, completed and exalted substance if done by heat, or a liquid if by cold. It is the Philosopher's Stone, or Elixir of Life.

The astrological association is a double one, for it relates not only to the Element of Earth but to the planet Saturn. This planet does not have a very good meaning in mundane astrology because everything connected with this planet's influence takes time and nothing is easy or done through a limited framework of operation. Saturn was referred to as the Lord of Karma and sometimes as Cronos. Due to the works of Psychics, such as Edgar Cayce and Arthur Ford, a further understanding of this planet is that of the 'reconciler', showing that patterns of reconciliation have to be worked out through Saturn's influences (which makes a lot of sense since Saturn is exalted in Libra). In short it makes us know ourselves so that we can evolve spiritually. Since Saturn is also related to Binah we have the influence of 'Sanctifying Intelligence' emanating through its feminine disposition and association with the 'Great Mother' which shows the receptive quality of its nature through absorption of all energies.

The Chakra associated here is the base Chakra where the Kundaline energy is stored. It is the supporter of all the other Chakras. The Four Kerubs around the edge of this Key are analogous to the four outermost petals of the Lotus, which is the Eastern description of this chakra. The naked lady is the representative of raw Kundaline energy, as also shown by the snake. The wands she holds represents the Ida and Pingala, the two channels of balance on either side of the spine that help stabilise the influence of this energy when it begins to rise. It is the reconciler that integrates all the all phases of the personality and subtle bodies. It is the first chakra of Initiation of the Personality.

The Yetziratic Title of this Key is 'Administrative Intelligence', because it is directly associated with the operation of the Seven Planets and their various paths through the heavens. Because of this therefore we attribute to it the Seven Abodes of Assiah, the Material World, shown by the Apocalypse of the Seven Churches. This in turn relates to the Universe of the Four Elements, the Qlippothic and the Astral Plane. Apart from being a reflection of the Sphere of

Saturn it is the link between the Kabbalistic Worlds of Yetzirah and Assiah, the Formative and Material Worlds. It also shows the above framework passing through the Astral Plane, Elemental Kingdoms and the Qlippothic. It is the rendering of the Veil of the Tabernacle on which the Four Kerubim and Palm Trees are depicted and the passing through the Gate of Eden.

The psychological mode of expression relates to an individual trapped in a situation that he has to learn to live with. The potential he has is way beyond the limit or structure he has to work with in life and he must learn to accept things as they are and see the other person's viewpoint. In many respects it is very much a calming down or 'back–to–reality' situation for an individual who may have a very inflated ego. A great deal of mental discipline is required so that things can be accepted as they are.

The Kerubs in each corner of the card relate to the lower earthy nature of man, the desires. The Calf relates to the Base Chakra, the Man to the Sacral Chakra, the Lion to the Solar Plexus Chakra and the Eagle to the heart Chakra. These four animals are also representative of the Ego which encompasses the Physical Body, the Etheric body, the Astral/Emotional Body, the Lower Mental Body. These are the four sheaths that fall away after death leaving the Higher Mental, Casual and Spirit as the immortal aspect of man that survives ensuing reincarnation. Mathers' description of this card says:

> The twenty-first Key of the Tarot … Within the oval formed of the seventy-two circles, is a female form, nude save for a scarf that floats around her. She is crowned with the Lunar Crescent of Isis and holds in her hands, two wands. Her legs form a cross. She is the Bride of the Apocalypse, the Kabbalistic Queen of the Canticles, the Egyptian Isis of Nature now shown partially unveiled, the great feminine Kerubic Angel Sandalphon on the left hand of the Mercy Seat of the Ark.
>
> The Wands are the directing forces of the Positive and Negative currents. The Seven pointed Heptagram or Star, alludes to the Seven Palaces of Assiah: The crossed legs are a symbol of the four letters of the Name. The surmounting crescent receives the influences of Geburah and Gedulah. She is the synthesis of the thirty-second Path, uniting Malkuth to Yesod. The oval of seventy-two smaller circles refers to the Schemphamphoresh, or Sseventy-twofold name of the Deity. The twelve larger circles form the Zodiac. At the angles are the Four Kerubim which are the vivified powers of the Letters of the Name of YOD HEH VAU HEH operating in the Elements.

Where this Key ends, the Fool starts, as this card is the ending of a karmic cycle. These two Keys are the Alpha et Omega. The Universal Spirit thus manifested in material terms.

The figure of the woman shows the Animus Mundi or World Soul. It also represents the Macroposopus, the Greater Face that organises our Karmic existence that it is in tune with everyone else. This is further emphasized by the twelve Zodiac signs around her, all of which the Soul must travel through to experience Life to its fullest capacity, both good and bad. It is this cycle that the Soul yearns release from and must complete. The two wands which the figure holds are the dual polarity that she must constantly separate. One wand symbolises the convoluted forces and the other the involuted forces. Both these forces work on a spiral that is never ending, for these are the energies that govern and give life to the chakras. If they spin too erratically then disease can occur and if one chakra is out of balance, whether it be a higher chakra or a lower, another must compensate.

The Egyptian goddess associated here is Mut, who represents the 'great Mother'. She was known under many names and depicted with a vulture crown. Mut was the wife of Amen-Ra and formed from Nu as a personification of the 'great Mother'. Her title was 'Lady of the two lands'. The Greek association is the legend of Gaea, also known as the Earth. She was a fertility goddess and goddess of healing. The Roman myth involved here is Saturn who was seen in two roles: the releasing of restrictions and giver of freedom, and the devourer of children.

Divination

The end of a matter; synthesis; success; change; attainment of a long sort-after goal. The Foundation of the Cosmic Elements and of the Material World; stepping out into a new threshold. Luna acting through Saturn upon the Elements—The Great One of the Night of Time.

The Universe card generally depicts the World as we know it and often shows overseas travel, or one shifting overseas. An end of a cycle takes place followed by a new beginning. You are what you have made of yourself, and you will be what you are still to make yourself. The future is pure potential. In most cases, however, the completion is through success, but this will depend on surrounding cards. In most issues there is liberation, finished karma, freedom. One with the universe. It crystallizes the querent's question into an actuality as the circumstances will be absolute and irrevocable in the momentum in which they flow.

I fear nothing and trust that the Universe provides.

COURT CARDS AND THE ZODIAC

The Court Cards

The Court Cards of the Golden Dawn and those later used by the Stella Matutina, were the cards that underwent the most changes and alterations in tarot design. The above diagram applies the Court Cards to the Zodiac belt which is the twelve astrological Signs. These show a number of overlaps occurring and at this point there is bound to be some confusion as to why they do not fit neatly into one zodiac sign each (Princesses excluded). Taking the Knights as examples: All the Knights gain their strengths from the four Mutable signs, which are of Gemini, Virgo, Sagittarius and Pisces. These deal mainly with imminent things, which are, of course, the actions of the Knights. The initial impetus of the Knights is not in the Mutable Signs, however, but the last decanates of the preceding fixed Signs. This is where the influence of the Mutable Signs begins to come in and that of the Fixed Signs weakens. The strongest influence of each Sign is in its centre, the second decanate and anything before it is growing and anything after it is said to be weakening in its zodiac influence, or changing from one state to another. The same principle then applies to the King and Queen of each suit, as you will see in the above diagram.

We have given in the following descriptions more emphasis on the personality profiles of the Court Cards. More often than not, they relate to a certain type of personality. They can also, however, represent the forces of the elements, as well as the actions of a person. Over the last few years we have had a chance to experiment with literally thousands of Tarot readings with the Golden Dawn Cards and find that the meanings of the elemental forces should not be ignored. For example, sometimes instead of meeting a woman with light brown hair who will influence a person in some way, the querent might be going through an influence of what that woman represents. A good example of this is the Princess of Swords which we have found, on a personal level, does not always represent a separate individual, but rather the querent who is subject to working in the background and not being appreciated enough. This is shown in the card by the smoke that tends to obscure things around her, to use but one example.

The psychological approach to the Court Cards also does not rest in an individual psychological description of each card. Each category can become representative of the varying stages of the human Psyche itself. The Knights are masculine figures on horseback and can also be equated with the Animus, the masculine kernel of a feminine shell. The Queens relate to the Anima, the feminine centre with a masculine shell. Both of these are reflective of the deep emotional states that emit from the archetypal imagery of the Collective Unconscious. These are of course states that are deep within the Psyche and far removed from the Rational Mind. The Rational or Conscious Mind is in fact represented by the King (Prince) and is intrinsically a state, framework or storehouse, with its only action being the expansion and contraction of its borders as information is gathered and processed. It is regal in nature, like an office of state, such as Kingship, but with all Kings they are only as good as their subjects—the contents of the mind itself. The Princesses are allied to the Freudian concept of the Unconscious, where instincts are formulated.

When we first consulted our old Tarot notes for the basis of the Court Card section of this book, we found we had to do more work on the actions of each of the three decanates for the Knights, Queens and Kings. Later, when we compared these with Mathers' explanations, we found they matched perfectly together with their elemental actions. We mention this because an enormous amount of thought went into the construction and meanings of these cards by the Golden Dawn.

We have also included a mythology section for each of the Court Cards. For those of you who are familiar with the Golden Dawn system, you will notice that the Egyptian associations are also utilised in Enochian Chess.

In going along with what he considered the traditional approach, Regardie decided in both his publications (which he changed from the original manuscripts) to call the figures on horseback Kings and those in the chariots Princes. In this regard his influence is very evident in the Wang pack, while the descriptions in the original Golden Dawn papers often contradict each other in this respect. The Court Card descriptions throughout this book have been rewritten with this in mind. I have been assured by Jack Taylor that in the Golden Dawn proper, it was Knight, Queen, King and Princess and so I have followed suit. It would be fair comment however that not all in the Golden Dawn went along with this association.

If the subtleties of the Court Cards are studied, then the dual titles of the King/Knight and King/Prince becomes apparent when they are applied by association to the Four Elemental Kingdoms. As Aleister Crowley has said before in his Book of Thoth, the Court Cards are the one area that have a great deal of overlap and one must take this point very seriously. We have found a good example of this in the physical description of the figures, which in fact relate more to the various elemental families that they belong to than to an actual person. Possibly the best method is to ignore the descriptions and concentrate on the actions and character makeup of the Court Card figures. In our own experience it has been found to be very important not to confuse the physical characteristics and the personality.

The Wands are associated with the Salamanders. These are Fire Elementals, as they are sometimes called and are beings that in fact go way beyond the Material World of Assiah and can, in one form or another reach the Kingdom of Atziluth (though they are limited to being Angelic subjects). They are also called the Lords of Fire or Flame. They work primarily through friction and at the direction of their angelic hosts. In the higher planes they are the Divine Sparks that grow in each level until we have the material view of them as Fire. Their main function is to 'start the train in motion' of manifestation, in one form or another.

The Cups are linked to the Undines. These are Water Elementals. Madame Blavatsky made the following comment: 'Elementals have not form and in trying to describe what they are, it is better to say that they are 'Centres of Force' having instinctive desires, but no consciousness, as we understand it. Hence their acts may be good, bad or indifferent'.

The Undines work mainly through the Emotions and manifest in the Material World as cloud formations, streams and water in general.

The Swords are related to the Spirits of the AIR and are called Sylphs. These Air Elementals are considered the closest to Man in empathy as they have three senses—Hearing, Touching and Sight. Their intelligence is close to that of man as well and far above the other Elemental Kingdoms but generally they lack individuality and work more on a collective basis.

The Disks are in empathy with the Spirits of the Earth that we call Gnomes. These Spirits have an enormous amount of different species, depending on the geographical location which takes distance as well as height into location (Mountain areas as opposed to plains). When people move from place to place they attract different types of Gnomes who tend to alter the individuals' awareness to a certain degree through the geopathic density of magnetism given out by different areas (such as Ley lines and other places where certain actions of High Magic can be performed).

Included in this section are the I Ching association with the Court Cards. Though popularised by Crowley in his Book of Thoth, a number of early Golden Dawn Adepts also used this association, which brings yet another added dimension to explaining the actions of the Court Cards from the Chinese point of view.

The alchemical association with the Court Cards is a dual one. The first is that of the Elements proper and the second is that which can be applied to the four colouring steps of alchemy. The Disks are applied to the Blackening process, the level of the Calcination process where the colour of the Prima Materia turns black due to applied heat. The Blackening process, however, need not be totally Calcination as at certain levels the separation process will also bring about these colours. The Swords are applied to the Whitening process. This is the purification occurring when the Spirit is released then reunited with the Prima Materia so that 'a Phoenix' or resurrection quality is then apparent. This happens usually through the multicolours of the experiment, the Peacock's tail, which eventually leads one back to a pure state.

The Cups represent the Yellow state. Though this state is not referred to much among alchemists, today it can be easily seen during the Calcination process when the Prima Materia takes on a Yellow tinge, especially in Herbal Calcination. The Wands represent the final state of the Reddening process which is also part of Unification where a final Conjunction is formed.

On studying the Westcott drawings of the Court Cards we are of the opinion that they were the original sketches, or prototypes which were changed at a later date when the descriptions were draughted up. In some cases the drawings and the descriptions differ, but for the most part, these are minor, with the exception of the directions the figures faced. We have made the appropriate footnotes where the changes occurred.

The directional facing of the Court Cards has always been something of a mystery as the original Westcott prototypes followed the trend of the French designs. The improved versions we have seen, both from Mathers and Felkin, also, in our view omit a few vital points. In our opinion the Court Cards would be best if they faced the same direction as the YHVH letters on the Enochian Tablets. Each Court Card is analogous with a quadrant in the four tablets, each tablet having four quadrants. From the viewing perspective, this would have the Knights facing right, the Queens facing left, the Kings facing left and the Princesses facing right.

After studying this carefully, this is the pattern that we personally have opted for, as it is also painted on the outside Walls of the Vault of the Adepti and places the direction focus of these cards in some sort of logical sequence. The general rule of thumb is that in the later versions of the Court Cards the figures would always be looking at the symbol of the element which they held, even if it was a slight turn of the head.

When a number of Court Cards are turned up in a Divinatory reading it is well to know how they react to each other and the best method with which to approach this is to try to understand them from the principles of the Four Elements, following the Golden Dawn paper (adapted from the works of Agrippa) explanation:

Therefore, there are Four Elements, the original grounds of all corporeal things, viz: Earth, Air, Fire and Water, of which elements all inferior bodies are compounded, not by way of being heaped up together, but by Transmutation and union; and when they are destroyed, they are resolved into elements. But there are none of the sensible elements that are pure. They are more or less mixed and apt to be changed, the one into the other, even as earth being moistened and dissolved becomes water, but the same being made thick and hard becomes earth again and being evaporated through heat as it passes into Air and that being kindled into Fire; and this being extinguished into Air again; but being cooled after burning becomes water again, or else stone or sulphur and this is clearly demonstrated by lightning.

Now every one of these Elements has two specific qualities: The former whereof it retains as proper to itself; in the other as a mean, it agrees with that which comes directly after it. For Fire is hot and dry; Water is cold and moist; Air is hot and moist; and so on in this manner, the Elements, according to two contrary qualities are opposite one to the Other, as Fire to Water and Earth to Air.

Likewise the Elements are contrary one to the other on another account. Two are heavy, as Earth and Water; and the others are light, as Fire and Air. Therefore the stoics called the former 'passives', but the latter 'actives'. And Plato distinguishes them after another manner and assigns to each of them three qualities, viz: To the Fire—brightness, thinness and motion. To the Earth, darkness thickness and quietness. And according to these qualities the Elements of Fire and Earth are contrary. Now the other Elements borrow their qualities from these, so that Air receives two qualities from Fire, thinness and motion and from the Earth one, darkness. In like manner Water receives two qualities from the Earth, darkness and thickness; and from Fire one, motion. But Fire is as twice as thin as Air, thrice more moveable and four times lighter. The Air is twice more bright, thrice more thin and four times more moveable than Water. Therefore as Fire is to Air, so is Air to Water and Water to Earth. And again as Earth is to the Water, so is Water to Air and Air to Fire. And this is the root and foundation of all bodies, natures and wonderful works …

Now each of these Elements has a threefold consideration, so that the number of four may make up the number of twelve; and by passing the number of seven into ten, there may be progress to the Supreme Unity upon which all virtue and wonderful things do depend.

On the first Order are the pure Elements, which are neither compounded, changed nor mixed, but are incorruptible and not of which but through which the virtues of all natural things are brought forth to act. No man is fully able to declare their Virtues, because they can do all things upon all things. He who remains ignorant of these, shall never be able to bring to pass any wonderful matter.

On the Second Order are Elements that are compounded, changeable and impure, yet such as may, by art, be reduced to their pure simplicity, whose virtue, when they are thus reduced, doth above all things, perfect all occult and common operations of Nature; and these are the foundations of the whole of natural Magic.

Of the Third Order are those elements which originally and of themselves are not elements, but are twice compounded, various and changeable unto another. These are the infallible medium and are called the Middle nature, or Soul of the Middle nature; very few there are that understand the deep mysteries thereof. In them is, by means of certain numbers, degrees and orders, the perfection of every effect in what thing so ever, whether natural, celestial, or super-celestial. They are full of wonders and mysteries and are operative in Magic, natural or divine. For, from these, through them, proceeds the binding, loosing and transmutation of all things—the knowledge and foretelling of things to come, also the expelling of evil and the gaining of Good Spirits. Let no one, therefore, without these sorts of Elements and the true knowledge thereof, be confident that he can work anything in the occult science of Magic and Nature.'

The Elemental attribution explained in the above paper can be shown by the following association to the Court Cards:

Knight of Wands	Fiery part of Fire
Queen of Wands	Watery part of Fire
Prince of Wands	Airy part of Fire
Princess of Wands	Earthy part of Fire
Knight of Cups	Fiery part of Water
Queen of Cups	Watery part of Water
Prince of Cups	Airy part of Water
Princess of Cups	Earthy part of Water
Knight of Swords	Fiery part of Air
Queen of Swords	Watery part of Air
Prince of Swords	Airy part of Air
Princess of Swords	Earthy part of Air
Knight of Disks	Fiery part of Earth
Queen of Disks	Watery part of Earth
Prince of Disks	Airy part of Earth
Princess of Disks	Earthy part of Earth

These above attributions also apply to the Tattwas. Therefore we can assume that each Court Card is applied to a Tattwa. The difference here is that there are twenty-five Tattwas. Sixteen of these are applied to the Court Cards, four to each element in spirit (ether) which are applied to the Aces and the other five relate to the spirit essence, the Akasha itself and its subdivisions. However, the later five are not applied to the cards. Tattwas are atomic and are five modifications of the 'Breath' (Prana), which have distinct vibrating motion. They are the power of the elements and varying movements of the elements. They are a mode of motion and the central impulse which keeps matter in a certain vibratory state. Every form and motion is a manifestation of a Tattwa or a combination of such currents, as shown below.

Akasha Tattwa (Ether/Spirit) = sonoriferous ether, sound.

Vayu Tattwa (Air) = locomotion, touch, tangiferous ether which impulse fills space with auditory vibrations, but falls back on itself along with its path, hence a blue circle filled of space is chosen for its symbol.

Tejas Tattwa (Fire) = colour, perception and light, expansion. Luminiferous ether and its vibrations take place at right angles to direction of wave, hence a red triangular form is its symbol.

Apas Tattwa (Water) = contraction and smoothness, taste. Gustiferous ether, which breaks the Apas circle and vibrates in a downward direction causing contraction, hence a silver half-moon on its back is its symbol.

Prithivi Tattwa (Earth) = odoriferous ether, smell, cohesive resistance. It is quadrangular in shape and moves in the middle rather than at any angles, but on the line of the wave in the same plane as the quadrangle. Hence the yellow square is its symbol.

The application to the cards are then:

Tejas of Akasha	=	Ace of Wands
Apas of Akasha	=	Ace of Cups
Vayu of Akasha	=	Ace of Swords
Prithivi of Akasha	=	Ace of Disks
Tejas	=	Knight of Wands
Apas of Tejas	=	Queen of Wands
Vayu of Tejas	=	King of Wands
Prithivi of Tejas	=	Princess of Wands
Tejas of Apas	=	Knight of Cups
Apas	=	Queen of Cups
Vayu of Apas	=	King of Cups
Prithivi of Apas	=	Princess of Cups
Tejas of Vayu	=	Knight of Swords
Apas of Vayu	=	Queen of Swords
Vayu	=	King of Swords
Prithivi of Vayu	=	Princess of Swords
Tejas of Prithivi	=	Knight of Disks
Apas of Prithivi	=	Queen of Disks
Vayu of Prithivi	=	King of Disks
Prithivi	=	Princess of Disks

We have also applied by association to the Court Cards the figures of Geomancy. Geomancy is a method of divination where the judgement is rendered by lot or destiny. The figures are made up of odd and even numbers of points. Hence each figure is four rows of one or two dots each. To each of the sixteen geomantic figures astrological and elemental associations are given. There is an overlap with the geomantic associations when applying them to the elements and to the signs of the zodiac. Through this we were able to apply the sixteen geomantic figures to the sixteen Court Cards.

Note

The authors take no responsibility for the artistic license taken by the artist in his drawings of the anatomical forms in the Court Cards.

To further understand the construction and method of divination of Geomancy, read *Terrestrial Astrology: Divination by Geomancy* by Stephen Skinner, Routledge and Kegan Paul, and *The Oracle of Geomancy* by Stephen Skinner, Prism Press.

KNIGHT of WANDS

Knight of Wands

The Lord of the Flame and Lightning;
The King of the Spirits of Fire

Element   : Fiery part of Fire
Symbols   : Black Horse, Waving Flames, Club, Scarlet Cloak, Wings
Emblem/crest   : Winged black horse's head
Scale   : Circle within a circle divided by a cross
Command   : King of the Salamanders
Myths   : Ra, Conlai
Kabbalah   : Yod of Yod, Abba-Chokmah
I Ching   : Fifty-first Hexagram
Zodiac Rule   : Twenty degrees Scorpio to twenty degrees Sagittarius
Tattwa   : Tejas
Geomantic   : Aquisito
Colour   : Red-gold hair; hazel eyes; Red and Green; Black crest and horse

The symbols and divinative meaning and nature of the Knight of Wands: he wears wings on his crown and body which show the swiftness of his nature and his essence having a soul and spiritual origination. The emblem of the winged horse's head which he wears on the head, heart and feet, represent an instinctive nature and that his mind, emotions and body are ready to act in accordance with them. He wears a scale upon his helmet and his club, which shows the division of a circle within a circle, divided by a cross. This is the Divine seed or cosmic egg giving birth through the framework of the four elements.

He is the King of the Salamanders (whom some referred to as Djinn), who move rapidly over short distances in such Elemental forms such as Lightning. It is the function of the King of the Salamanders to start movement patterns, enough for the next in line to take over. As such, like lightning, his movements are violent, sudden and swift. As an initiator of action he expects quick results from any order he gives and does not tolerate fools gladly. His influence on matter and form is a vast one but only as an initial impetus, which will not repeat itself if matters do not get going on the first burst of energy.

The Egyptian myth of Ra is associated here and is a visible symbol of the Sun, which as seen from the earth moves quickly across the sky until nightfall. In many respects this is the action of the Knight of Wands, bright, fiery and fast-moving. Ra, in the early dynastic periods, was also considered Father of the Gods and, as such, is the vital essence of the Yod of Yod formula, the first manifestation or impulse of the heavens. The Celtic myth linked to this card is that of Conlai, son of the hero Cuchulainn. He went to Ulster where he defeated Conlai in battle and was eventually challenged to fight by his father, who did not recognise him until it was too late.

The Chinese I Ching Hexagram 51 is linked to this Court Card. It relates to Thunder and Shock. Both Upper and Lower Trigrams relate to the eldest Son who has a great deal of energy and strength and is able to initiate people that surround him into action. Chen itself is success in fields of communication, such as television, radio, movies, theatre, advertising, etc. The energy factor of the young man is, however, limited and indicates an initial burst of action only, something not often to be repeated. The I Ching cautions against first associations, whether business or relationships, but does give its approval for second-time around ventures in both these areas.

The Sigils of the Scale, which appear only on the Court Cards of the Golden Dawn pack, are in fact based on heraldic symbols that appeared on the early cards. Many of these symbols were from important families who had decks printed. Some of these symbols were later modified by the Golden Dawn for their own esoteric purposes. The later version has this Knight and his horse going in the opposite direction.

The influence of the last decan of Scorpio shows the development of a strong intuitive and psychic faculty which allows him to penetrate the veil of mystery. His emotional sensitivity can change rapidly, due to Mars' rulership of Scorpio. The first twenty degrees of Sagittarius depict the expansive growth of the Knight's energies, which are enhanced by Jupiter which is the planetary rulership of Sagittarius. The second decanate is of Jupiter and shows that he initiates many religious, cultural and militaristic operations. If negatively aspected, the Knight will become a racial, cultural and religious bigot with his only loyalty being to power.

This card represents the Fiery part of Fire, which is fire in its pure essence and the birth or manifestation of this element and as such he is a very active individual who spends little time resting. He will try to get others to follow in his footsteps as he is an initiator of things to come, the herald of a new era. By nature he is an impulsive person who lives on his wits and reacts unconsciously to friend or foe alike. If an insult or injustice is done to him, he will strike out blindly in retaliation. His attitude, from a negative perspective, shows he is capable of being a bigot and brutal. Right or wrong he believes totally in what he is doing until proved wrong, though his impulsiveness has a lack of staying power. He is also the Yod of Yod, the very beginning of the masculine impetus, showing a very pliable but powerful force that can and will eventually grow as he adapts to new experiences. Speed is his key essence in both defence and attack.

The Tattvic current of Tejas is associated to the Knight of Wands, but it must not be confused with the manifested element of Fire. It is the movement behind the element of fire and operates as perception, light and expansion. Its symbol is a red upward-pointing triangle.

The Geomantic Figure is Aquisito—'generally good for profit or gain'. This indicates success through travel and shows many of the fortunate benefits of Jupiter. This is achieved however by direct result, inquiry and by an aggressive business sense. Other meanings associated here are grasping, possessing, receiving, force. All of these meanings relate directly to the nature of the Knight of Wands.

Divination

The Knight has too much energy or force in most matters. A shortened force, with no staying power. This can lead to destruction or creation. For example, instigating new enterprises, projects, etc., or sudden endings, dangerous situations. This Knight is a catalyst to circumstances wherever it turns up in a reading. As an archetype he is an innovator, but tends to act too hastily, or burns himself out from too much effort and energy, therefore overly active and restless. Problems can occur when dealing with others due to self-centredness and unrestrained desire to act directly. Abrupt and aggressive, given to exaggeration, very passionate, over-confident and self-indulgent. As a Mars force his actions allude to a Mars affect such as combativeness, executiveness, that which concerns energy and sex, physical activities, accidents, quarrels, courage or daring. On a positive level, this force and energy can cause a breakthrough to success for an individual.

QUEEN of WANDS

Queen of Wands

Queen of the Thrones of Flame

Element	:	Watery part of Fire
Symbols	:	Leopard, steady flames, wand with heavy head
Emblem/crest	:	Winged Leopard head
Scale	:	Pyramid of Fire
Command	:	Queen of the Salamanders
Myths	:	Sati-Ashtoreth; Scathach
Kabbalah	:	Heh of Yod, Amia-Binah
I Ching	:	Seventeenth Hexagram
Zodiac Rule	:	Twenty degrees Pisces to twenty degrees Aries
Tattwa	:	Apas of Tejas
Geomantic	:	Puer
Colour	:	Red-Gold hair; blue eyes; Blue, Red and their complementaries Orange and Green

The symbols and divinative meaning and nature of the Queen of Wands: she wears an emblem of the winged leopard's head which shows the swift ferocity which she is capable of, but also this power is contained as shown by the couchant leopard at her feet. The head of the wand, which she holds, resembles a type of Yod while the sigil of the scale which is repeated on the Wand, throne, belt, knee armour and neck broach is the pyramid of Fire, as viewed from different angles and is a symbol of the Tejas Tattwa. On her crown and on the uprights of her throne, the pyramid of Fire is repeated with the upturned Water pyramid beneath it, to modify its temperament. The combination of these two pyramids is depicted as the symbol of the scale.

As a Queen of the Salamanders, her function is to modify and direct the commands given to her by the knight and to temper them if need be. As 'Queen of the Thrones of Flame' her function is to help spread the load or burden of the Knight and direct his command or energy into areas that he may not anticipate when the Order is issued. This force is materialised by the rainbow that often appears after the fierceness of storms. Like a rainbow the division of the Knight's command are prismatic, in empathy and go to every corner of his reign though it is but a reflection of his original command.

The Egyptian myth of Sati-Ashtoreth is associated here with the Queen of Wands. This is, in fact, a merging of two female God-forms. The first is Sati (from the root 'sat' meaning to throw or eject, which is connected to both speed and Water) and associated with the fertile waters of the Nile and fertility. Sati was also a Goddess of the hunt. The second is Ashtoreth, often drawn with the head of a lioness, which is shown on the crown of the Queen of Wands. She was a Goddess of War. The combination of the two names indicates a very powerful warlike figure who is not to be trifled with. In Celtic mythology she is identified with Scathach, one of the important martial arts teachers of Cuchulainn. It was she who gave Cuchulainn the spear (which she holds in the card) 'Gale-Bolg' which was feared in battle.

The Chinese Hexagram for this card is Sui/Following which is the seventeenth Hexagram of the I Ching. The Lower Hexagram is Chen while the Upper is Tui which relates to the beauty of Autumn. Combining the two trigrams into the Hexagram we have the Tui (Lake), over Chen (Fire), the Watery part of Fire. The combination of two trigrams also shows that Thunder grows weaker in the advent of Autumn, beauty. Although it augurs success, this will be short-lived. It cautions that darkness is fast approaching and it is a time for rest, for Chen indicates motion and Tui indicates pleasure. The combination of the two can be an exhaustive state, for Tui relates to pleasures and excitement taken to the extreme.

The Queen of Wands rules the last decanate of Pisces. These ten degrees concentrate a great deal on the subconscious, which is a hidden aspect of her nature. The influence of Jupiter, which rules over Pisces in this Sign, is also fused with Neptune, Pluto and Mars, showing her very occult nature and concern with spiritual growth. She rules the first and second decanates of Aries as well. The first decanate portrays her impulsiveness, while the second decanate of Aries brings her authority and generosity to rule, which can come and go very suddenly but, while it lasts, is very strong.

The Queen of Wands represents the Watery part of Fire. In this instance, Fire has been tempered by its Watery aspect which is emotional enthusiasm. This produces a personality which is quick-tempered, but is triggered by her intuitive insight into a clear perception of the truth. She also tends to go all out in displaying her emotions and, for those in her favour, there is very little she would not do, though this could be short-lived. Badly aspected, she will display all the negative Fiery temperaments of revenge and temper tantrums. As the Heh of Yod, she is the transmutation of the masculine into the feminine, which results in the aggressive aspect of the Yod force as a primary driving impetus, tapered through an emotional feminine framework giving more resilience and adaptability than the Knight.

The Tattvic current applied here is Apas of Tejas, which is the moving energy of water expanded by fire, very much like boiling water and steam. Its vibration is a silver crescent on its back within a red triangle. Therefore Tejas is drawn down to release the contraction of Apas.

The Geomantic figure is Puer which is Latin for 'Boy' and means someone who is beardless, rash and inconsiderate. This figure is basically neutral, although in most meanings Puer comes across as destructive and evil, except in matters of War and Love. However, generally the over-all energy is perhaps too much energy with a need for an outlet. Some may have thought this figure applies to the Knight, however, in keeping in line with the Golden Dawn system of associations it is essentially the Queen, as her main astrological affinity is Aries and Aries rules Puer.

Divination

Persistent energy, calm authority, kindness, generosity and a capacity for friendship and love, but at her own initiation. There is much pride, charm and social ease with popularity. Adversely positioned, she shows impatience, brooding, gullibility and one who harbours revenge. She has a sharp tongue and cruel wit and may tend to intoxication during periods of melancholy. Adjustment, adaptation, successful achievement, balance and harmony lie within one's power. There may be initial obstacles but success after disorder. General impulsiveness to situations without pre-thought, if you allow matters to influence you on a subconscious level.

KING of WANDS

King of Wands

Prince of the Chariot of Fire

Element	:	Airy part of Fire
Symbols	:	Waved and salient flames, fire wand of Zelator Adept, Lion and Chariot
Emblem/crest	:	Winged Lion's head
Scale	:	Hexagram with a circled cross at centre
Command	:	Prince of the Salamanders
Myths	:	Toum; Cuchulainn
Kabbalah	:	Vau of Yod
I Ching	:	Forty-second Hexagram
Zodiac Rule	:	Twenty degrees Cancer to twenty degrees Leo
Tattwa	:	Vayu of Tejas
Geomantic	:	Fortuna Major
Colour	:	Golden hair; Blue-Grey eyes; Yellow, Red and complementaries Violet and Green

The King of Wands, like the Knight, is winged, showing his link with a spiritual source and a swift masculine approach. The winged lion's head emblem displayed on his breast, knees and above his crown symbolises his strength, power and leadership, for zero degrees Leo is the beginning of the Golden Dawn zodiac, as shown by the Lion pulling the chariot. His Wand is double-ended and has a conical top, which is the Fire Wand of the Zelator Adeptus Minor with Yods painted on it. At the other end of the wand is the emblem and sigil of the scale. This is a Hexagram with a circled cross at the centre. The Hexagram brings through the influence of the Zaur Anpin (and the six Sephiroth of Yesod to Chesed) that the King, as the Vau force, has as

189

his seat of power. The cross with the circle in its centre symbolises the Fiery heart of the four divisions that the King must control.

As a King, he carries out the duties of his Mother the Queen and now that the Queen has issued more widely-based instructions the Prince must travel widely to bring them about. As 'Prince of the Chariot of Flames' he represents the rays of the Sun in motion bringing light to wherever he travels. He is a more steady force of energy than his father the Knight and a force that is more long-lasting.

Toum is the Egyptian God associated with this card. One of Toum's titles (as Tern) was 'Father of the Gods who maketh Life'. He was also the 'closer of the day' (as Atum) and was said to have later taken over the position of Ra (through force). As the Airy part of Fire we have Vau, the Son, manifesting and eclipsing the Yod force of the Knight. His being seated in the chariot reminds us of the Egyptian Sun boat which crossed the heavens each day. The Celtic myth linked with this card is that of Cuchulainn, the great Irish hero who won many battles and was possibly the most feared and loved of the Irish heroes. His most famous incident is when he single-handedly defended Ulster during the war of the Tainn.

The forty-second Hexagram of the I Ching linked to this card is 'Yi' which means Increase. The Lower Trigram is Chen, Thunder and Trees and the Upper Trigram is Sun, Wind and Air over Fire. It can be looked on as shrubs and flowers. Combined, these two trigrams become T, which is a lush, vegetated area of flowers, shrubs and trees in bloom, suggesting Spring, a time of growth.

The King of Wands rules the last ten degrees of Cancer. His high spiritual and cultural inclinations are enforced by a high psychic perception though the influence of both Jupiter and Neptune, who co-rule this Sign. He also rules the first and second decanates of Leo. The first decanate of Leo relates to his authority and magnetic personality coupled within a spiritual framework, through the power of the Sun which rules Leo. The King can be, if ill-dignified, accused of having an over-inflated Ego. The second decanate of Leo is also influenced by both Jupiter and Neptune, to a certain extent, showing the King to have the ability to control the masses through public opinion and the media.

The King of Wands represents the Airy part of Fire, which is energy and Will, the intellectual and spiritual aspect of the Fire element. In many respects this is the governing point of Fire for, from here, one is at the very heart of its nature. The King has aggression and a temperament to advance in almost any condition but also has the intellectual prowess to rationalise his strengths and weaknesses. He is steady, commanding, just and feared, he moves fast but never without thinking his actions out first. If the card is ill-dignified he will be cruel and vengeful but worse than the Knight of Wands for the King plans his strategy and does so mercilessly, leaving no stone unturned. As the Vau of Yod, the King is the third or rationalised neutral impetus showing a rapid expansion of the Yod force through the power and energy of applied thought.

The Tattvic current is Vayu of Tejas, which is the moving energy of air given light and expansion by fire. This vibration forms a circle within a triangle.

The geomantic figure is Fortuna Major which rules fortuitous things, assistance, safety on entering and greater fortune in general. It tells of protection and help given from within, possessions and daylight hours and like the tattvic current alludes to light and life—the sun.

Divination

This is an individual who is eager for action and who has strength and drive to carry through his effort. When this card is placed in a fighting situation it reads as aggressive, being supported by strength and energy. A definite direction is being applied, as this is not a scattered force. The situation can be volatile however, so it must be directed by Will. Expanding horizons will be seen and plans carefully applied. This card warns of the tendency of not being able to settle on anything in a situation that may require a decision. Positively aspected however, this card shows strength and decisiveness, independent thought and reason. Negatively aspected you will see a force that cannot be stopped, which will influence everything around ignoring all resistance. Business matters move in a forward motion with little holding him back. Travel takes place only with a purpose and not for recreation.

PRINCESS OF WANDS

Princess of Wands

Princess of the Shining Flame; the Rose of the Palace of Fire

Element	:	Earthy part of Fire
Symbols	:	Tiger, leaping flames, gold altar, long club largest at bottom
Emblem/crest	:	Tiger's head
Scale	:	Ram's head with spirals of energy emitting
Command	:	Princess of the Salamanders
Myths	:	Anouke, Dornall
Kabbalah	:	Heh final of Yod
I Ching	:	Twenty-seventh Hexagram
Zodiac Rule	:	Rules from North Pole to forty-five degrees Leo Latitude and from zero degrees of Cancer to thirty degrees of Virgo
Tattwa	:	Prithivi of Tejas
Geomantic	:	Cauda Draconis
Colour	:	Red-Gold hair; Blue eyes; Green, Red and colours from Malkuth of the Queen Scale

The Princess of Wands stands with her hand on an altar. The altar is the seat of her power showing an ever-present spiritual framework from which she works. The Tiger's head above her crown and on her belt and knees, is the symbol of her dual nature of both creator and destroyer. On her crown and club is the Sigil of her scale, the hieroglyphic symbol of a ram's head with spirals of energy emitting therefrom, but it is reversed revealing the feminine polarity with masculine traits. The Fiery club she holds is also reversed for the same reason. The ram's heads circling the altar are masculine, procreative energy and power which she emits. Her practical, earthbound energy puts energy into form.

193

The Princess of the Salamanders works directly under her brother, the King, in carrying out the Orders of her father the Knight. Her functions on the Material Plane are a direct application of both heat and Fire in the physical sense. She is a force that produces intensity in the Fire of the Salamanders. Her title is 'Rose of the Palace of Fire' and her actions are likened to the 'unfolding Rose' which starts as a small bud that gradually blossoms into full bloom. It is she who controls the volume or capacity of the fire element.

Anouke (Anuket/Anquet/Anukis) is the mythical figure associated here and her name means 'clasper'—she who clasps the riverbank of the Nile. Her function was to help give life to the Nile and, to a certain extent, this Goddess of the cataracts was associated with the aggressive Goddess of War. As the Earthy part of Fire we find that she is a black Goddess. In Celtic mythology she is Dornall (Big fist) daughter of Domhnall who helped train Cuchulainn. She was in love with him but when he rejected her advances she sought out vengeance on him by splitting him up from his two companions Laoghaire and Conlai.

The twenty-seventh Hexagram of I Ching linked to this card is 'I' meaning Nourishment. The Lower Trigram is Chen, Thunder, trees, etc., while the Upper Trigram is Ken which means Mountain and relates to non-movement. Thunder at the foot of the Mountain suggests rain, mist and nourishment for vegetation by way of rain which nurtures the soil. The combination of movement of the lower and stillness in the upper Trigrams duplicates the mastication of the human jaw in eating and in speech. This Hexagram advises caution and moderation in both speech along with eating and drinking and working in harmony in those areas.

The Princess of Wands represents the Earthy part of Fire or the material aspect of Fire (concrete action). This combination is very powerful in the sense that it shows not only strength and energy but the physical, initiating result of any situation. The Princess has received the power of her Mother and Father and she is a trained woman warrior who commands vast numbers. The Earthy part of this card implies that she is in touch with reality but sees things very simply. Her greatest forte is that she is in harmony with her surroundings, yet still manages to operate with speed. She is, however, held in check by her materialistic outlook. In anger or love she is quick to act, which shows a marked desire for power due to her upbringing. As the Heh Final of Yod, the Princess is the last bastion of an old era and is prepared to fight to the finish before she unites with the King to start yet another dynasty.

The Tattvic current in motion is Prithivi in Tejas—earth consumed by fire, like burning wood. The vibration gives a square within a triangle—a single plane releases into a trine.

The Geomantic figure is Cauda Draconis, which is the lower threshold and a going out. This is the dragon's tail of the constellation Cauda Draconis. It is the lower kingdom which in divination is good for terminations of any kind, but harbours disaster for other matters. As the Princess of Wands is the most manifested state of fire, it is a threshold out to the next element and acts as the lower kingdom of the fire element.

Divination

The Princess is a very powerful personality, fully able to back up her needs and commands. She is strong-willed and forceful, but generally able to control her emotions, although ready to fight if challenged. If the ultimate goal will benefit her she will conform to conditions around her. She can create and destroy depending on her position at the time. Negatively aspected she tends to be wanton and a bit loose with her virtues. She makes her own mind up on matters and if told what to do, will go in the reverse direction and can also show a situation where sudden concrete action is taken after a period of stillness. This action is sometimes impulsive and sometimes calculated, depending on the surrounding environment, but any action taken will be strongly felt.

KNIGHT of CUPS

Knight of Cups

Lord of the Waves and the Waters; The King of the Hosts of the Sea

Element	:	Fiery part of Water
Symbols	:	White Horse, Crab issuing from Cup, Sea, Wings
Emblem/crest	:	Peacock with open wings
Scale	:	Tortoise shell
Command	:	King of the Undines
Myths	:	Sebek, Bran
Kabbalah	:	Yod of Heh
I Ching	:	Fifty-eighth Hexagram
Zodiac rule	:	Twenty degrees Aquarius to twenty degrees Pisces
Tattwa	:	Tejas of Apas
Geomantic	:	Laetitia
Colour	:	Fair hair; Blue eyes; White horse and crest; Blue, Red and complementaries Orange and Green

The Knight of Cups has a winged crown and body identifying his link with his soul. His emblem is a peacock, the bird of storms, rains, resurrection and immortality. The sigil of the scale on his crown, broach, cup and belt, signifies a tortoise shell which relates to the Waters of Creation and is very similar in meaning to that of the crab issuing from the cup that he holds.

The Undine associated with the Knight of Cups is King Necksa. His power is strong in swift movements of water, such as waves coming into a beach, sudden changes of tides, waterfalls, water gushing from springs, rain, fast-moving streams and rivers, for all these are the actions of the King of the Undines. As King, it is his function to initiate any movement of water in any sudden or direct manner until the Queen can take over from his action. His movements are usually spasmodic, however, when left to their natural patterns (without any interference from man). He helps govern emotions by inspiring people to act, whether positively or negatively.

In Egyptian Mythology Sebek (Suchos) the crocodile God was said to have aided Set when he killed Osiris. He was a God who wanted sacrifices to appease him. In his early years he was allowed to wander the fields and eat whoever he pleased, so sacrifices were eventually incorporated to appease his predatory nature. He was a very unpredictable God at the best of times. In Celtic mythology Bran (Son of Febal) is linked here. Bran was enchanted by a beautiful woman while walking near his fortress and after she left he then made a voyage to find her. His voyage and adventures duplicated to a certain extent those of Jason and the Argonauts.

The I Ching association is from the fifty-fourth Hexagram, Kuei Mei, 'The Marrying Maiden'. The bottom trigrams is Tui-Lake, the beautiful youngest daughter. The top trigram is Chen-Thunder representing the eldest Son. This is a combination of youthful inexperience that tends to rush into things too quickly. This Hexagram relates to a union of sorts, such as marriage or a partnership, but this merger will be short-lived. The further combination of the two trigrams is rain in the form of thunder (Chen) which overflows the lake (Tui), showing quick rise and fall of water—a shallow individual with little staying power.

The influence of the last decanate of Aquarius gives ambition in group activities at their initial inception, especially in any area where exploration of the mind or social conscience is utilised. This Knight, like all the others, is a vanguard of these types of organisations. The first decanate of Pisces relates to a Jupiter influence of growth and expansion, but this is limited to the realm of the mind where there can be development of one's clairvoyant faculties through emotional drama. This is due to the Knight being so impressionable by nature. The second decanate of Pisces represents occult activity at its deepest point, due to influences of the three outer planets, which will also bring out a deep emotional intensity in a person's nature.

The Knight of Cups represents the Fiery part of Water, which relates to the active or fast flowing energies of this elemental combination. As an individual, the Knight is emotionally volatile, but in a superficial manner. Negatively he is not to be relied on for any long-term commitment as he is too easily influenced by his emotions and is inclined to go wherever he is pulled. The Watery impetus stimulated by Fire brings turmoil and continuous movement, never settling down to anything. He is the Yod of Heh and as such has a limitation to his aggressiveness as Heh calms Yod. Since Fire and Water are in reality antagonists, they both stimulate each other into restless movement. The Fiery essence can be smothered so that the Watery part is stimulated into movement, shown by the ground swell in the card. At his best, his nature makes him artistic in perception and ever-enthusiastic, honourable, kind and loving, passionate and romantic. But if ill-dignified, he will be an utter disaster in relationships and an eternal dreamer.

The Tattvic current is Tejas of Apas, which is Fire generating Water and being encompassed by Water: for example, electrically generated by the movement of water. The vibration is a red triangle within a silver crescent on its back.

The Geomantic figure is Laetitia, a figure of freely expressed joy, health, laughter. Laetitia is described as a bearded figure but pleasing in appearance with beauty and grace.

Divination

Good fortune, apart from what has been discussed above. Careful discrimination; knowledge transferred; however, if negatively positioned a limitation and communication breakdown. Desires can become greater than one's ability, or be contained too much below the surface. The position of this Knight will show what is being hidden in a person's thoughts, or where a situation or a person is impressionable and may react too strongly to external impetus rather than to their own drive. The archetype is one of emotional feelings without true control and responds more to desire. Positively aspected this Knight indicates the illumination of thoughts and ideas; an understanding of cause and effect; strength and outer protection; a person who can shield you from difficulty; a Mars force working in an undercurrent, e.g., behind the scenes.

QUEEN of CUPS

Queen of Cups

Queen of the Thrones of Waters

Element	:	Watery part of Water
Symbols	:	Crayfish issuing from river
Emblem/crest	:	Ibis
Scale	:	Reflection of Water in movement
Command	:	Queen of the Undines
Myths	:	Thouerist, Boann
Kabbalah	:	Heh of Heh
I Ching	:	Fifty-eighth Hexagram
Zodiac Rule	:	Rules from twenty degrees Gemini to twenty degrees Cancer
Tattwa	:	Apas
Geomantic	:	Populus
Colour	:	Gold Brown hair; Blue eyes; Blue and Orange

The Queen of Cups has an Ibis on her crown and the emblem of an Ibis on her breast and knee guards. This relates to the Soul in flight, as shown by its open wings and deep attunement within the self, working through one's higher aspirations. The Sigil of the scale on her crown, belt buckle and cup, is a reflection of Water in movement. The Crayfish emerging from the cup shows new beginnings which surround her. The lotuses on the Water in front of the throne are, in fact, passing her in the current and are the illusory nature of what she sees.

In Egyptian mythology Thouerist (Taurt, Taueret, Apet, Opet) is the Goddess of Childbirth and symbolised maternity and nursing infants. She is a combination of crocodile, hippopotamus, human breasts and lion's feet. She was both protector and avenger (if the need arose) at the same time. In Celtic mythology Boann is linked to this card. Boann was a Water Goddess and wife of Nechtan. She did not fully appreciate the subtleties of her husband's magic and brought sorrow to herself for not listening to him when he forbade her to approach the magic well. She quickly went into hiding when the well chased her.

As Queen of the Undines she represents quieter water habitations than her husband and commands the still pool, calm rivers and streams. Like the Queen of Wands before her she must take the Knight's aggressiveness and transpose it into something she can deal with. It is her function to look and study clearly the orders given by the Knight and translate them into some form of logical sequence so that they can be understood.

The I Ching association to this card is the fifty-eighth hexagram, Tui/Joyousness. Both Upper and Lower Trigrams are called Tui. This Trigram is associated to a Lake and anything happy or joyous in nature. The archetypal association is to the youngest daughter, and the body part that Tui represents is the mouth, which shows success in public speaking and the ability to transmit one's message to people. In the business sense Tui relates to Gold and old artefacts. In romance Tui is a complicated situation where two women compete for the same man.

The Queen of Cups rules astrologically twenty degrees Gemini to twenty degrees Cancer. The last decanate in Gemini relates to intuitive insight due to its Uranian ruler and the exaltation of Mercury is a rare but incredible combination which can bring flashes of insight and awareness. The first decanate of Cancer is ruled by the Moon which implies moodiness and unpredictability. The second decanate of Cancer is ruled by both Mars and Pluto implying a stubborn defensive quality especially where relationships are concerned.

The Queen of Cups is the Watery part of Water symbolising emotions at their greatest depth and, if well-dignified in a reading, reveals a very great attunement with one's Higher Self. The Queen can allude to an excellent companion on any trips due to her good nature, but will not help much if relied heavily upon as she is often in a dream state. If ill dignified, her emotions swamp reality as her imagination takes over and becomes a reflection of other people's projections, thus showing little substance of her own. She is the Heh of Heh, the feminine aspect of a feminine framework. The Yod has been taken to the point where it must now separate and form its own polarity, stirring deep emotional intensity for it cannot manifest as yet on a material level.

The Tattvic current is Apas. This is the gustiferous ether which breaks the Vayu circle and vibrates a downward direction causing contraction, thus the symbol is a silver crescent on its back. The motion of Apas is smoothness and contraction, a holding together—attraction and subject to gravity.

The Geomantic figure is Populus. This figure holds the concept of groups of people, the family or gathering, community or city. It is neither good or bad, but neutral and subject to the whim of the crowd.

Divination

Further divinative meanings are: beauty and purity with infinite subtlety; a highly imaginative person who is artistic, very intuitive, receptive and transmitive of surrounding influences; success and benefits in day to day affairs; talk and social enjoyment. If adversely positioned she is a dreamer who is reflective of outside influences or other people's thoughts, so much so, that none can see through her to the truth. Sometimes pervasiveness and distortion of facts. Very moody, however, psychic ability and sometimes prophetic. If adversely affected by other cards you must check your actions to avoid danger, be careful and patient, and beware of trickery and deceit. There may be difficulty in growth or movement. A waiting period is shown but if this Queen is weakly positioned it may show a lack of incentive to get moving and change matters.

KING OF CUPS

King of Cups

Prince of the Chariot of Waters

Element	:	Airy part of Water
Symbols	:	Scorpion, Eagle-serpent issuing from lake
Emblem/crest	:	Eagle
Scale	:	Four Scorpion tails in the form of a swastika
Command	:	Prince of the Undines
Myths	:	Hapimon, Nechtan
Kabbalah	:	Vau of Heh
I Ching	:	Sixty-first Hexagram
Zodiac Rule	:	Rules from twenty degrees Libra to twenty degrees Scorpio
Tattwa	:	Vayu of Apas
Geomantic	:	Rubeus
Colour	:	Brown hair; Grey or Brown eyes; Yellow, Blue and complementaries violet and Orange

The King of Cups has an eagle drawing his chariot and has a crest above his crown, on his breast and knee guards. This shows his airy nature; swift and continuous though still above the water beneath him. The serpent issuing out from the cup relates to secretiveness and evil intentions, but is balanced with the lotus as a symbol of purity. The Scorpion on the rim of the wheel of the chariot shows the influence of the zodiac sign and the destructive influence in which he moves. The Sigil of the Scale is of four Scorpion's tails in the form of a swastika, which relate to a negative influence that will one day sting him if he drops his guard. The four dots separating each tail from the one beside it are the checks and balances he has set for himself. Like all masculine figures in the Tarot Court Cards, he is winged.

The Egyptian mythological figure associated here is that of Hapimon (Hapi) who had the figure of a man and the breasts of a woman. He was a Cataract God where he poured water to both heaven and earth from his urns. When the Nile was low it was to Hapi that his devotees prayed to increase the Nile's water level, necessary for prosperity. The Celtic link here is to the Water God Nechtan, husband of Boann, whose function was to guard the sacred Well 'Segais', the source of all knowledge. In many respects he was allied to the Arthurian myth of Sir Gwain, for Nechtan was one of four who were cup bearers to the Well.

The Prince is associated to the Undines of the oceans and their overall effect on the rest of humanity. The Oceans are of a constant state of flux, constantly replenishing themselves with sea life which in turn helps produce the air in our atmosphere. The Prince has taken the message of the Queen and is taking it to the four corners of the earth so that every Undine in his realm fully understands the tasks the Queen has required of him. There is little permanence here in the ebb and flow of the oceans, mainly unseen by human eyes, for this is in accordance with the actions of the Prince.

The I Ching association is to the sixty-first Hexagram, Chung Fu/Inner Truthfulness. The Lower Trigram is Tui, meaning the happy youngest daughter while the Upper Trigram is Sun, the eldest daughter—wood and penetration. Wood over Water tends to show boats travelling over the ocean and there is no disharmony between them. The whole Hexagram relates to people respecting and helping each other and travelling or movement. For romance the two trigrams relate to two people who are happy together and trust each other.

The last decanate of Libra is ruled by Mercury and influences communication in its many forms, but tends towards superficiality in areas of the emotions. The first ten degrees of Scorpio is ruled by Mars and Pluto and as such, relates to a strong sexual appetite, resourcefulness and secretiveness. The second decanate of Scorpio is ruled by Jupiter and Neptune and strongly influences the intuitive and emotional side of one's nature leaning to channelling or mediumship.

The King of Cups represents the Airy part of Water, an individual who can be subtle, violent, crafty and artistic. The Air nature is the power of the intellect rationalising, while the deep-seated emotions of the water element which govern the knight are never seen. He has a fierce drive but a calm demeanour. The King gives a very superficial and false impression of himself. He has secret designs and there is a strong tendency for evil influences if he falls in with the wrong people. As the Vau of Heh, he shows the point of breaking away from old values and substituting new ones. His intellectual framework will be spurred on by very deep and powerful emotions and this will be his realisation for all his pent-up energy.

The Tattvic current is Vayu of Apas—air being contained by water. Would the fish be able to survive in water without the water being oxygenated? Therefore it alludes to the oxygen/hydrogen content of water. Its vibration is symbolized by a blue circle in the centre of a silver crescent which lies on its back.

The Geomantic figure is Rubeus which was considered one of bad temper, passion, a head of red hair, and sexual violence. Rubeus's power can be turned to good if positioned well. However, the nature of one with Rubeus energy is extremism.

Divination

Further divinative meanings are: superficiality when coming into a situation; something which cannot be trusted; something is being kept secret; hidden depths have not yet been reached or penetrated; continual voyaging, unrest, travel; this is a transitional state in all matters where the surface is just being skimmed; from harmony and balance to penetration and transformation. As an individual you will be dealing with someone who has control over emotion and who can act objectively. However, such controlled emotions are not resolved and dam up causing an overflow at times. One who can apply himself to a task and with plenty of drive, but he uses any means to obtain the desired result without consideration for others. Action is a means to release emotions. Positively aspected he is objective and willing to look for causes of problems and then get rid of them.

PRINCESS OF CUPS

Princess of Cups

Princess of the Waters; the Lotus of the Palace of Floods

Element	:	Earthy part of Water
Symbols	:	Dolphin, Lotus, sea with spray, Turtle from cup
Emblem/crest	:	Swan
Scale	:	Lotus
Command	:	Princess of the Undines
Myths	:	Shooeu-tha-ist (Hathor); Aine
Kabbalah	:	Heh final of Heh
I Ching	:	Forty-first Hexagram
Zodiac Rule	:	Rules North Pole forty-five degrees Lat from zero degrees Libra to thirty degrees Sagittarius
Tattwa	:	Prithivi of Apas
Geomantic	:	Via
Colour	:	Brown hair; Blue Brown eyes; Green, Blue complementaries Red, Orange; and colours from Malkuth in the Queen Scale

The foaming spray at her feet relates to her elemental structure while the dolphin is her guide to the underworld and represents the womb, giving her warmth and comfort. The crest of the swan is worn above her crown, on her belt and knee guards. It stands for the transmutation process that she is undergoing. The turtle emerging from the cup is a life force emerging, or new beginnings. The Sigil of her scale on her crown is a lotus, something she also holds. The lotus represents the aspirations of the Soul's deepest yearnings.

As Princess of the Undines her power is through the muddy waters that nurture the soil near the riverbanks and gives fertility and life to those that live near her domain. Out of all the Cups she is the closest to humanity for she directly feeds humanity through the natural process of the rivers, through the waters and silt washed up on the land during the floods. Like her elemental nature she at times works deeply beneath the surface of consciousness. Those around her are mainly unaware of her actions for she will obscure their vision. Any change she makes will be harmonious and beneficial.

In Egyptian mythology the association is with Shooeu-tha-ist (Hathor) a nature goddess who was also described as the Star Sothis. In the form of a Cow she gave new life to the Dead when they entered the Underworld. To a certain extent she was a healer and teacher of the Dead. She was also the patroness of Love. In Celtic mythology she is linked to Aine, the Goddess of Love, who was constantly conspiring with mortals over affairs of the heart. She was raped by Ailill, but she killed him afterwards through magic. She is worshipped on Midsummer's Eve and also guards against sickness and infertility.

The I Ching association is the forty-first Hexagram of Sun/Decrease. The Lower Trigram is Tui—Lake and the Upper Trigram is Ken—Mountain. It shows the mountain being eroded by the lake below it so that the mountain eventually falls into it and as a result of this shows decrease or loss. In a business situation the profits are gradually eroded away. As a form of action to take in business, Sun suggests reducing costs and overheads as restraint in this area is called for. In affairs of the heart we have a good situation. The Youngest Son (Ken) is quite stubborn but is eventually influenced by the happy Youngest daughter, who sets about changing him for the better (through her speech).

The Princess of Cups is the Earthy part of Water. The Earthy part of her nature is the one which gives her foundation, strength and energy to accomplish whatever goals she sets out to achieve, motivated by her emotions, together with a very strong strength of purpose. The watery part, is the initial impetus from which she works. She is a person who finishes everything she sets out to do and, as such can be heavily relied upon for comfort and support. Her emotional framework has a deep response within her to the tasks she undertakes and she is firmly and emotionally behind everything she sets out to do. She is a romantic by nature and is a very genuine and caring person who will fight for her beliefs. She is very much a Joan of Arc type character. If ill-aspected she can be selfish and indolent. She is the Heh Final of Heh, the formation or crystallisation of a matter that is undergoing a gestation period where she can work her energy to the full within the framework of her emotions through which she operates.

The Tattvic current is Prithivi of Apas which is earth smoothed and broken down by water. Its vibration is a yellow square within a silver crescent on its back.

The Geomantic symbol is Via which means a direct way, street or path, highway, a way through, which is good for journeys taken by direct routes. It is a neutral figure which is reflective like the moon, of the nature of the surrounding influences.

Divination

The individual represented here is soft but determined in nature, although rather dreamy. However her tremendous strength of purpose can turn dreams into reality. Most of her actions are emotionally charged, so emotional involvement is rarely avoided. Her beliefs and convictions are strong, though she usually acts in harmony with the times. There is no forgiveness for those who cross her and she can set up quite a campaign against her enemies. She likes to share her experiences and her expression is to create.

In the divinative side of dreams she shows ideas are being crystallized. People are being nourished and educated and the battle of life is being won. Turmoil and chaos may be around, but it will not directly influence one. If positively aspected nothing will sway the querent from a task. If this card is situated in a position where she is not influencing any situation it shows too much time can be spent on entertainment and self-indulgence.

KNIGHT of SWORDS

Knight of Swords

Lord of the Winds and Breezes; King of the Spirits of Ain

Element	:	Fiery part of Air
Symbols	:	Winged brown horse, driving clouds, drawn sword
Emblem/crest	:	Winged hexagram
Scale	:	Arrowhead
Command	:	King of the Sylphs
Myths	:	Seb; Cairbre
Kabbalah	:	Yod of Vau
I Ching	:	Thirty-second Hexagram
Zodiac Rule	:	Rules twenty degrees Taurus to twenty degrees Gemini
Tattwa	:	Tejas of Vayu
Geomantic	:	Albums
Colour	:	Dark brown hair; dark eyes; Red, Yellow and complementaries violet and orange, brown horse

The Knight of Swords holds a sword which is the penetrating aspect of his nature, where he is ready to inflict punishment or uphold a law. As with all the other Knights his body and crown are winged to show their swift nature and link with their soul or spiritual nature. He wears the crest of the winged Hexagram on his crown, breast and knee guards. This is power of the Ruach pushing him forward. The Sigil of his scale is, in fact, an arrowhead showing his violent and swift, penetrating nature. On the arrowhead is a small circle which represents the Vayu Tattwa. The dark stratus clouds beneath him are the potential growth of things to come under the Knight's influence.

The King of the Sylphs is called Paralda and like the other Kings before him, he expects quick obedience to his orders. His direct force of governance are the Winds which blow over every quarter of the earth. He charges the atmosphere with either positive or negative ions and as such can alter the disposition of all those who come into contact with his winds of power. He also governs the mind and thinking process and will either stimulate or hinder those he comes into contact with (depending on the circumstance).

The Egyptian myth associated here is that of Seb (Geb/Keb) who, on being parted from his sister/wife Nut, lamented both day and night. He was originally a God of mischief but was eventually taught a lesson by the other Gods, settling down to become an excellent administrator. In Celtic Mythology he is linked to the baird Cairbre. When he was insulted by King Bres, in retaliation for the way he was treated, Cairbre then made up a bairdic tale which in turn insulted King Bres so badly that he had to retire from his reign of Kingship.

The I Ching Hexagram is the thirty-second, Heng/Duration. The Lower Trigram is Sun and relates to Wind (and the Eldest Daughter) and shows the penetration and gentle approach. The Upper Trigram is Chen meaning Thunder and is the more powerful of the two main Trigrams. Thunder and Wind are very compatable forces when combined. In affairs of the heart we see the submissive woman giving support to the strong man, which in Chinese society shows something in step with their culture and so promises duration. In business it rules success and duration through help and advice from either a stronger partner or another.

The last decan of Taurus is ruled by Saturn with Mars in exaltation which is ambition and organisation carefully tempered with aggression. The first decanate of Gemini is ruled by Mercury relating to travel and communication. The Third decanate of Gemini is ruled by Venus with Saturn exalted, a combination that shows strong emotional attachments that are not long-lasting.

The Knight of Swords is the Fiery part of Air. Swift in his actions and the vanguard of Air, his fiery nature shows the force of Will applied to an intellectual level and as such, he is clever, active, subtle, fierce, delicate, courageous and skilful with an inclination to domineer. He is, however, a force that is an initial impetus only, hence energy is not long-lasting. If ill dignified he can be deceitful, tyrannical and crafty. As the Yod of Vau, this is a masculine aspect of a neutral force. After a great deal of rationalisation has been done a build-up of energy will be released simultaneously and rush forward with tremendous attacking speed.

The Tattvic current is Tejas of Vayu, a locomotive energy. Air is set into motion by fire, hence rushing, moving and storms. The vibration is symbolised by a red upward-pointing triangle within a blue circle.

The Geomantic figure is Albus which is good for profit and starting undertakings. The term Albus means 'white head' and alludes to fairness, wisdom and clear thought. Albus, through its zodiac attributions rules the nervous system, communication and ideas.

Divination

This is an archetype who gives orders and directives, a quick mind, fleetness of purpose. As a thinker and planner he can be the architect of many things, however to actually get anything done reinforcements must be brought in. He can be a teacher, a good listener and give an objective opinion about things. He can brood too much which brings storminess in nature and can bring harshness to a situation. He represents travel and movement. If he is left to sit too long in one place problems begin to show. There must be short, swift bursts of energy in a matter to keep the impetus up, otherwise a situation, or person will crumble. Distinction is made as to what is good and in sympathy with the question and what must be judged and swiftly dealt with. The Air Knight represents communication being made and future events shaped or planned. Wherever he is matters of swiftness are depicted. He is a Jupiter force showing new vistas and opportunities, speculation and travel. If well-positioned, cheerfulness and good hopes; if negatively positioned the Air Knight shows risks taken, waste of energy or material goods.

QUEEN OF SWORDS

Queen of Swords

Queen of the Throne of Air

Element	:	Watery part of Air
Symbols	:	Head of man severed, Cumulous Clouds, drawn sword
Emblem/crest	:	Winged child's head
Scale	:	Circle within a circle
Command	:	Queen of the Sylphs
Myths	:	Pekht; Erain
Kabbalah	:	Heh of Vau
I Ching	:	Twenty-eighth Hexagram
Zodiac Rule	:	Rules twenty degrees Virgo to twenty degrees Libra
Tattwa	:	Apas of Vayu
Geomantic	:	Puella
Colour	:	Grey hair; light brown eyes; Blue, Yellow complementaries Orange and Violet

The Queen of Swords holds a sword that is a symbol of her office and authority. The bearded head held in her left hand implies strength, the power she has over life and death. The beard on the head represents wisdom, therefore, she has both strength and wisdom firmly within her grasp and control. Her emblem is a winged child's head, the Cherub of Air who guides and influences her, bringing ideas into actions. The Sigil of her scale, on her crown, broach, sword and belt buckle, is a circle within a circle which is the symbol of the Holy Palace of Water which she rules over.

As Queen of the Sylphs she is personified through the actions of humidity in Air. This affects humanity on much the same lines as the geopathic stress felt from the magnetic fields of the earth. Humidity can also affect the emotions depending on its density which, in turn, is very much like an aerial magnetic field. Humidity can either lighten moods or dampen them and this is where the Queen of the Sylphs is at her best, in shifting the balances of the atmosphere.

The Egyptian mythological figure given to the Queen of Swords is that of Pekht (Pasht) who was one of the cat goddesses. She was a Goddess of Music and Dance and protector of men from sickness and evil spirits. In Celtic mythology the Queen of Swords symbolises Erain, wife of Ogma. In one myth that is appropriate she is pursued by the Love God Midair. When he found her he blasted her with a wind that lasted for seven years.

The I Ching association of this card is Hexagram 28, Tau Kuo/Great Excess. The Lower Trigram is Sun—Trees, shrubs, foliage and the Upper Trigram is Tui—Water or Lake. When combined they show Water over the Trees which suggests a flood. Since Tui also relates to something broken, the flood is caused because some container was not strong enough to support the weight of the water. The Hexagram suggests a great beam which is unable to sustain its own weight due to lack of support or strength. In affairs of the heart an older and younger partner have no happiness between them. For business situations this is a time to withdraw and the present situation cannot go on for it suggests a state of collapse about to occur and advises any action is better that non-action.

The last ten degrees of Virgo are ruled by Venus and with the Moon exalted therein, which shows a liking for the aesthetic in personal possessions and a keen intuitive insight into the emotions of others. The first decanate of Libra is ruled by Venus with Saturn exalted showing socially inclined individuals who are capable of strong relationships and sharing love and affection. The second decanate of Libra is ruled by Uranus with Mercury exalted. This leads to unusual or occult-orientated groups and friendships and spiritual development within these boundaries.

The Watery part of Air shows the emotions motivating the intellect. In nature we have the accumulation of rain clouds analogous to an elemental influence of potential nourishment to all things. As an individual she is intensely perceptive and a keen observer of things, whose actions are subtle and quick. She makes a good confidante and consultant for those around her with her soundly based objective opinions. She often gets caught up in superficial things but always sees them through to the finish. A graceful individual, she is fond of dancing and enjoyment. If ill dignified, she can be cruel, sly, deceitful and unreliable though still with a good exterior. As the Heh of Vau, the Queen shows receptivity and anticipation towards the birth of Vau.

The Tattvic current is Apas of Vayu. Here water is set in motion by air bringing rain and mists. Its vibration is symbolised by a silver crescent on its back within a blue circle.

The Geomantic figure is Puella that stands for 'a girl' and one with a pretty face. Although this figure implies pleasantness, it is generally not fortunate as surface beauty and harmony hides much turmoil within. On matters relating to women Puella is good, also for relationships that must be met on equal terms.

Divination

This is an archetype with the power of transmission and indicates an intelligent and complex person who pays attention to detail and accuracy. She is a keen observer, graceful and skilled at balancing situations, therefore versatile. Adversely positioned, she is cruel, sly, a foil of half-truths and quiet slander and her superficial beauty and attractiveness aid in deceit.

In her movements she shows how a person can take hold of matters and turn them to one's advantage. There is always a struggle but there is plenty of ability for great undertakings if one wills it. Sometimes ambitions are greater than abilities. The untrustworthy must be avoided so work to improve a situation and ones will attract success, then one's potential can be fulfilled. This card shows breakthroughs and situations being dealt with before they become too dangerous. Badly aspected, she may show someone laying the law down to others concerning a situation and dealing with them in an arrogant manner.

KING OF SWORDS

King of Swords

Prince of the Chariot of Swords

Element	:	Airy part of Air
Symbols	:	Arch-Fairies winged. Dark clouds Nimbi, Drawn Swords
Emblem/crest	:	Winged Angel's head
Scale	:	Winged Pentagram in a circle
Command	:	Prince of the Sylphs
Myths	:	Shu; Ogma
Kabbalah	:	Vau of Vau
I Ching	:	Fifty-seventh Hexagram
Zodiac Rule	:	Rules twenty degrees Capricorn to twenty degrees Aquarius
Tattwa	:	Vayu
Geomantic	:	Tristitia
Colour	:	Dark hair; dark eyes; Yellow and Violet

The King of Swords wears an emblem which is a winged child's head with a Pentagram above it on the King's crown and breast. This relates to the intellect at its quickest, governed by the unseen power of the Kerub of Air. The sword and sickle he holds shows he rules with the former and slays with the latter. The sigil of his scale is a winged pentagram in a circle showing the concept of Spirit, of which he is and something that is not tangible. The Pentagrams on the heads of the Arch Fays who draw the Chariot also stand for Spirit, for they are the same substance as the King and are being directed by the intellect of the driver.

The Prince of the Sylphs portrays himself in his elemental attributions in cloud formations. At the direction of the Queen he will gather up the water in the air (atmosphere) and transports it to other areas as clouds, sending it where it will be the most effective. Clouds indicate nourishment but also a certain lack of direction for the clouds dissipate if not directed by the wind. There is a scattering of energies here as the Prince tries to do everything at once and he needs to call on many of his Elemental helpers.

The Egyptian myth associated here is that involving Shu (meaning to 'raise' or 'hold up'). Shu is the God who supports the Sky and was the one who separated Seb from Nut and held Nut aloft from her brother/husband. He succeeded Ra but eventually fought his children and won. Upon another revolt he then became tired of governing and fled to the sky where he remained. In Celtic mythology the King of Swords is the myth of Ogma, God of literature and War. He claimed the sword (this was called Orna) of Tetra (which he holds in the card) after he defeated Indec (son of the Goddess Orna). He also doubled in being associated to the Greek Charon—who conveyed the sons to the Underworld after their death during battle.

The I Ching link to this card is the fifty-seventh Hexagram of Sun/Penetration (Wind). Both the Upper and Lower Trigrams are Sun—Wind, Gentle, Wood, Penetration. These both show the attitude of flexibility allied with docility and penetration. Sun indicates a place of a garden or wood in windy weather. The combination of the two bring a scattering process of the seeds so that they are allowed to germinate elsewhere. The entire concept is that one will be successful elsewhere, like the transplanted seeds. In business it is particularly auspicious for any condition involving travelling. The growth period will show minor delays before success comes. In affairs of the heart it advises that one should look elsewhere, for any success in the present situation will be short-lived.

The last decanate of Capricorn is ruled by Mercury and relates to professional prestige and a bureaucracy: an individual caught up in the non-personalised field of statistics. The first decanate of Aquarius is ruled by Saturn and Uranus with Mercury exalted. This combination produces the person who is always seeking new horizons; though impartial, he also relies on his intuition to guide him. The second decanate of Aquarius is ruled by Mercury and influences an individual in the area of the intellect and communication skills, especially in group areas with a strong tendency to travel.

The Airy part of Air is the intellectual thinker and planner who is full of ideas, thoughts and designs but also careful and sometimes overcautious, although firm in friendship to those he trusts. Because of his Airy nature he is continually changing his mind and cannot make a decision or stick to it, for he is the abstract thinker who has, to a certain extent, retired from the reality of a situation and could be accused of 'living in ivory towers'. If ill dignified he can be harsh and malicious, plotting, obstinate and indecisive. This card also shows someone at the crossroads of life with multiple choices available to them but who is unable to make a firm decision on what route he will take. As the Vau of Vau he is a neutral force that dares not move unless moved by others.

The Tattvic current is Vayu. Vayu is the tangiferous ether. Its impulse fills space with auditory vibrations but falls back on itself along its path, hence a blue circle of filled blue space is chosen for its symbol. Its vibrations are spherical and locomotive.

The Geomantic figure is Tristitia and means sadness, melancholy, grief, condemnation and bad in all things. Matters must be fortified and retrenched. The exception is where indulgence—debauch—is implied. These vibrations don't necessarily fully apply to the King of Swords, however, but can be the case if the card is ill dignified.

Divination

The Prince/King of Swords shows areas of no restriction and goes where his whim takes him. Energy may be wasted and answers may become elusive. It can show one's mind racing too fast. As an individual the Prince/King is the thinker and planner who handles matters skilfully. Vast plans are brought into action, however, this person can be very abstract and is in danger of loosing sight of the goal. Negatively placed the reality of a situation can be disassociated from, especially when dealing with people's emotions. Usually this person will be travelling or handling matters alone. Energies can be scattered in too many directions—matters happen too fast and confusion can set in. Too many people are having their say which confuses matters even further. There is indecision and one ends up not getting anywhere but running in circles. Positively aspected caution is applied together with a willingness to try on all accounts. Old values are broken for new concepts to follow.

PRINCESS OF SWORDS

Princess of Swords

Princess of the Rushing Winds; Lotus of the Palace of Air

Element	:	Earthy part of Air
Symbols	:	Silver Altar, smoke, Cirrus clouds, Sword
Emblem/crest	:	Medusa with serpents as hair
Scale	:	Two links of a chain
Command	:	Princess of the Sylphs
Myths	:	Tharpeshest; Tuireann
Kabbalah	:	Heh final of Vau
I Ching	:	Eighteenth Hexagram
Zodiac Rule	:	Rules from North Pole to forty-five degrees Latitude and from zero degrees of Capricorn to thirty degrees of Pisces
Tattwa	:	Prithivi of Vayu
Geomantic	:	Fortuna Minor
Colour	:	Light Brown hair; Blue eyes; Green, Yellow, complementaries Violet and Red; colours of Malkuth from the Queen Scale

The Princess of Swords wears above her crown and on her belt and knee guards, the symbol of the Medusa with serpents as hair. This signifies the crystallisation of a matter, as all those who gazed upon the face of Medusa turned to stone. The smoke from her altar is yet another aspect of her heavy, but Airy nature, while the sword she holds is to rule. The Sigil of her scale is two links of a chain. Since the chain is analogous to Air, the two links show its binding qualities, for as the Princess is bound to rule with the Sword she is also bound to the altar to uphold the spirit so that the material and spiritual are interwoven and firmly linked together.

As Princess of the Sylphs she rules the Rushing Winds and the creation of the vesica, which is the portion in common between two overlapping circles. Her function is not to be confused with that of the King who initiates the start of the winds while the Princess must keep them going and give them some sort of direction. It is her function to integrate the winds with the rest of the functions of the Sylphs. She gives strength to the winds for better or worse. At best she will produce a mild wind and at worst she will be the instigator of tornados and the like.

The Egyptian myth associated with her is that of Tharpeshest (Tefhut), the Goddess of dew and rain. Tharpeshest helps Shu support the Sky each morning and waits for the Sun to break free from the mountains. She is the air god, Shu, sister/wife. In Celtic mythology Tuireann, daughter of Etain and Ogma, is linked here. Tuireann was bewitched by a Druidess who was in love with her husband Ullan and who changed Tuireann into a bitch. In order to turn his wife back into a human being, Ullan agreed to go away with the Druidess, who then restored Tuireann back into her original shape.

The I Ching association is the eighteenth Hexagram, Ku/Stopping Decay. The Lower Trigram is Sun—Wind, Gentle, Wood, Penetration. The Upper Trigram is Ken—Mountain, Stillness. The Combination of the Two Trigrams is a strong one on top of a weak one which shows a lack of growth due to the product being spoiled. In this case it could represent too much earth over the scattered seed so that growth is either impossible or a long time in coming. The nuclear Trigrams (Chen and Tui), however, give more information on this and point to improvement (of one's position) that will bring growth. The Lower Trigram shows the crossing of wooden boats over the lake (with the help of Wind). For business there is shown to be an impossible situation which needs movement or reorganisation. In romance an older man loves a younger woman but she is eventually stifled with the relationship and it comes to naught.

The Princess of Swords is the Earthy part of Air. She is an individual who has a firm grasp of the practical limitations of her intellect but applies herself in such a way that she has a better control over her abilities than that of any of her predecessors. She has wisdom, strength, acuteness, subtleness in material things, grace and dexterity; logic towards a definite conclusion is her aim. As the Heh part of Vau she is the final part of the neutral essence of Air and, as such, is dull and heavy in physical movement, but still a very quick thinker. If ill dignified she is frivolous and cunning.

The Tattvic current is Prithivi of Vayu, symbolized by a yellow square within a blue circle. Earth is set into motion by air (sand, dust, movement of trees).

The Geomantic figure is Fortuna Minor, 'lesser fortune': a safeguard in going anywhere; external help and protection. The Sun at night.

Divination

This is an individual with a practical grasp of a situation and who needs to express herself through an abstract, quasi-intellectual manner. However, material matters sometimes do not move as fast as the mind's conception of plans, therefore, she can get very frustrated when everything moves slowly. Patience needs to be learned.

Her framework relates to matters social and communal integration. Ideas are materialised. People are benefited rather than the individual. Goals must be worked for. In tense situations she may be the bearer of exciting news. Negatively aspected she can snatch Victory away just to get her own selfish ends. Negatively aspected she shows no compassion for others and only intellectualises situations, e.g., if she has not experienced it she will not understand it.

KNIGHT of DISKS

Knight of Disks

Lord of the Winds and Fertile Land; King of the Spirits of Earth

Element	:	Fiery part of Earth
Symbols	:	Light brown horse, ripe corn land, Sceptre with Hexagram as Z.A.M.
Emblem/crest	:	Winged Stag
Scale	:	Hexagram within a circle
Command	:	King of the Gnomes
Myths	:	Horas; Dagda
Kabbalah	:	Yod of Heh final
I Ching	:	Sixty-second Hexagram
Zodiac Rule	:	Rules twenty degrees Leo to twenty degrees Virgo
Tattwa	:	Tejas of Prithivi
Geomantic	:	Conjunctio
Colour	:	Hair dark, eyes dark; red, green and colours of Malkuth in the Queen Scale

The Knight of Disks, like all the other Knights, is winged in body and helmet. Above his crown, on his breast and knee guards, is the emblem of a winged stag which relates to the natural growth factor, which is his nature, and to his aspirations, through the framework of the Tree of Life. The sigil of his scale is a hexagram within a circle. It is engraved on his crown, belt and in the disk which he holds. The emblem relates to the seven-stage system of nature. Beneath his feet are cultivated corn fields. They signify potential growth that is awakened in mankind.

The Elemental King of the Gnomes is Gob and his Elemental realm is in the form of Mountains. His strength is in the size of his Kingdom and of the various elemental members of his Kingdom. Gob is not only associated with slow but sure actions, he is also linked as King to Volcanic activity, if one gets on the wrong side of him. He is also responsible for earthquakes. In Egyptian mythology

Horus is associated here. He is Son of Osiris and Isis. He defeated Set in a final showdown when the Evil God threatened the Kingdom with perpetual Night. It is said that night and day represent the battle between Horus and Set, the forces of Light and Darkness. In 1. Spiritus; 2. Flesh of Christ; 3. Flesh of Adam; 4. Archaeus; 5. Evestrum; 6. Hiastri; 7. Limbus (Corpus).

In Celtic mythology we have Dagda (the 'Good God') who was also called the God of Tire and 'Great Knowledge'. He was often shown riding his horse 'Acein' and carrying his gigantic magical club. The Dadga was also called leader of the Gods. His cauldron of food was so vast that no man who ate from it ever went away hungry.

The I Ching association is to the sixty-second Hexagram, Hsiao Kuo/Slight Excess. The Lower Trigram is Ken—Mountain stillness, Youngest Son, while the Upper Trigram is Chen—Thunder, Eldest Son and movement. The Upper Trigram appears stronger than the lower resulting in excessive movement. The Symbol shows Thunder above a Mountain typical of the bully. Similarly it indicates one who goes to excess and cannot gain any real advantage from it for the Judgement says Undertaking in small things, not great things. Also this hexagram warns of someone striking from behind.

The last decanate of Leo is ruled by both Mars and Pluto with the Sun exalted and relates to resilience, physically and morally and an ability to overcome any obstacle. The first decanate of Virgo is ruled by Mercury and shows people concerned with the practical side of life, especially hygiene, tending to leave no stone unturned in their observations. It shows a keen intellect, someone who is mentally alert. The second decanate of Virgo is ruled by Saturn and has Mars exalted. This signifies a person who is reserved and prefers the traditional and practical approach but is very skilful and hard-working at what he does.

The Fiery part of Earth describes a strong and dull but patient person. This perhaps disguises his underlying volatile nature. In many respects the Knight could be described as resembling a dormant volcano that may be ready to erupt if pushed in the wrong direction. If ill dignified he is avaricious, grasping, jealous and not very courageous. As the Yod of Heh Final, he is a masculine force which has to be expressed through a feminine framework, for he implants the seed of his efforts into the environment, making things he touches grow. This relates strongly to an instinctive side of his nature that guides him through both beneficial and harsh times by motivating him to prepare for the future. Though he is the initiator he will also see things through to the finish and can be relied upon if everything is made clear to him as to what his tasks are.

The Tattvic current is Tejas of Prithivi, the vibration of which is symbolised by a red upward-pointing triangle within a yellow square. This is fire controlled by earth; heat and energy/life within matter; activity.

The Geomantic figure is Conjunctio which heralds a coming together and joining. It is neutral however, and is good with good and evil with evil. Conjunctio is cold and analytical, resourceful and precise.

Divination

Nourishment and abundance, fertility and wealth are depicted here. If positively positioned the Earth Knight shows growth, regeneration and prosperity, but this is only while there is purpose and direction to the Knight's moves or position, otherwise a situation may be considered sterile, static or inert. He shows where there is potential and hope. The archetype is one who wants more of everything, a 'well-to-do' person, or one who has attained a lot through hard work. Sometimes extravagant, exaggerative and over-confident, but very practical. A warm character who can be very giving under the right circumstances. The Earth Knight's effect on influencing his surroundings is not as quick as the other knights, but it is still a catalyst and things do happen as he is a prime mover of things to come. His effect is longer-lasting with a powerful momentum. The Earth Knight is a Jupiter force of a beneficial material nature.

QUEEN OF DISKS

Queen of Disks

Queen of the Thrones of Earth

Element	:	Watery part of Earth
Symbols	:	Barren land, face light one side only, Sceptre with orb of gold
Emblem/crest	:	Winged Goat's head
Scale	:	Cube
Command	:	Queen of the Gnomes
Myths	:	Isis; Brigid
Kabbalah	:	Heh of Heh final
I Ching	:	Thirty-first Hexagram
Zodiac Rule	:	Rules twenty degrees Sagittarius tc twenty degrees Capricorn
Tattwa	:	Apas of Prithivi
Geomantic	:	Career
Colour	:	Dark hair, dark eyes; blue, green and complementaries red and orange; splashes of colours from Malkuth cf the Queen scale

The Queen of Disks wears her emblem of a winged goat's head above her crown, on her breast and knee guards. This relates to fertility and procreation, as does the goat beside her which is the influence of Capricorn in her nature. The sigil of her scale is a cube which she has on her throne, crown and sceptre. This cube represents the Salt of the Earth which is the stabilisation of things becoming and yet to become.

As Queen of the Gnomes she is present where there is any form of vegetation. It is here that muddy waters sustain and give life to the arid areas of lesser growth. She is the patroness of agriculture and is present in any such concept as a dam, or stream, where water is used as a Life Force to nurture the Earth.

In Egyptian mythology this position is taken by the Goddess Isis, wife of Osiris and mother of Horus. She was the one who searched for the scattered body parts of Osiris (after his battle with Set) and restored him to life. She was the Mother figure of the Egyptian Gods and was initially known as a Fertility and Agricultural Goddess. Gradually her fame increased and she presided over women's affairs. In Celtic mythology the Goddess Brigid (one of the triune Goddesses) was the daughter of Dadga. In one form she presided over healing and the making of weapons and farm implements (part of her duties as a Smith) and became the Goddess of fertility and poetry.

The I Ching association is the thirty-first Hexagram of Hsien/Attraction-Stimulation. The Lower Trigram is Ken—Mountain, Stillness, Strength of a Young Man. The Upper Trigram is Tui—a Lake, Marsh, Young Woman. The Weak is above the Strong and as such, forms an attraction. In Romance this is a good Hexagram and the Judgement says: 'To many a girl is good fortune'. Also prosperous for any business ventures, it shows a time of expansion. The indications are that the weak partner should know their limitations and try not to lead the stronger.

The last decanate of Sagittarius is ruled by the Sun with Pluto exalted. This relates to the eternal optimist who is in a powerful position in religious or cultural organisations and one who has a great deal of staying power. The first decanate of Capricorn is ruled by Saturn with Mars exalted and shows a person who has worked hard to get in a prominent position in life and shows swift decisiveness in her actions. The second decanate of Capricorn is ruled by Mercury with the Moon exalted. This relates to a workaholic or over-achiever who tends to be very materialistic in her outlook.

The Watery part of Earth shows that her emotional nature is the framework on which her material outlook expresses itself. As such, she is kind and generous to others, intelligent, moody and reliable. Because she has to express herself practically and materially she will help through that medium though her emotive responses will guide her. One of her motivations is fertility, both spiritual and material. If ill dignified she will be undecided, foolish and very changeable with her emotions constantly placing her in a state of flux where she feels she can attain nothing or finish anything she begins, with a strong inclination to both alcohol and drug abuse. As the Heh of Heh Final, the Queen brings a feminine aspect of new structure and this produces a type of receptivity that inclines towards both union and cooperation with others.

The Tattvic current is Apas of Prithivi symbolised by a silver crescent on its back within a yellow square. This is water restricted by earth and earth nourished by water; an underground well, pool, stream or lake, moisture within the earth.

The Geomantic figure is Carcer which is considered an evil figure of prison, restriction, capture, delay.

Divination

This archetype has quiet qualities, a 'down-to-earth' person, compassionate and a lover of luxury, collector of possessions. She can give great affection and is very forgiving, hard-working and sensible. She is usually domesticated and not intellectually inclined. Adversely positioned there can be debauch, spendthriftness, general extravagance, narrowness in sight and abuse of alcohol or drugs. She could be too materialistic, dull and/or foolish.

The Earth Queen governs areas or situations where there is attraction, stimulation, co-operation and merging of separate parts, relationships between people and gatherings. She shows that there is enough success in a matter to continue and all is being nourished for growth. Adversely influenced by other cards it is not a good time for movement. Wait for a more appropriate time for change.

KING OF DISKS

King of Disks

Prince of the Chariot of Earth

Element	:	Airy part of Earth
Symbols	:	Flowery land, Bull; Sceptre with orb and cross. Orb held downwards
Emblem/crest	:	Winged Bull's head
Scale	:	Hexagram within a square
Command	:	Prince of the Gnomes
Myths	:	Aroueris; Daire
Kabbalah	:	Vau of Heh final
I Ching	:	Fifty-third Hexagram
Zodiac Rule	:	Rules twenty degrees Aries to twenty degrees Taurus
Tattwa	:	Vayu of Prithivi
Geomantic	:	Amissio
Colour	:	Dark brown hair, dark eyes; Yellow, green, complementaries violet, red; splashes of colour from Malkuth from the Queen scale

The King of Disks wears a winged bull's head emblem above his crown, on his breast and knee guards. This emblem represents quick application of strength, power and determination and it is also linked to his Taurean nature. The sigil of his scale is a hexagram within a square. This differs from that of the Knight because the King is more stable, hence the square Prithivi Tattwa of Earth shows solidarity. The Wand he holds has a cross, a symbol of spirit descending into matter through Earth into the Septenary which binds him to matter. The orb he holds is reversed showing that he has not utilised its power correctly. The flowers beneath him are life and growth.

As Prince of the Gnomes he acts through the gaseous nature of Earth that is entrapped below the Earth's surface. He is responsible for helping humanity through this type of fuel and frequently he will also work with other elementals as well, especially the Knight of Disks and King of the Salamanders. He often considers himself a guardian of the earth's hidden treasures and will prevent humans from finding them by protecting them with his gaseous nature, especially in tunnels and mines.

The Egyptian association here is to Aroueris. This is in fact Horus the Elder (Heru-ur) who was the Son of both Ra and Hathor and was 'Great God and Lord of heaven … among all the Gods, whose power hath vanquished the foes of his father Ra'. In Celtic mythology Daire (Son of Fachtna) is linked to this card. He was the owner of Donn, the brown Bull of Cuailgne (shown pulling the chariot) which Medb (a triune Goddess) who collected bulls, wanted him to sell to her, but he refused. Medb then enlisted Ailill to help her steal it from Daire and in doing so started the war of the Tain. In another myth Daire became high King of all Ireland when he caught the golden fawn. On his helmet is the symbol of the white, winged bull which further attests to his sovereignty.

The I Ching association is through the fifty-third Hexagram, Chien/Gradual development. The Lower Trigram is Ken—Mountain, Stillness, Youngest Son while the Upper Trigram is Sun—Eldest Daughter, Wind, Gentle Wood, Penetration, Slow Growth. Combined, these two Trigrams imply trees growing on a mountain. The two Nuclear Trigrams, however, are yet another structure of the Hexagram. The Upper, Li, relates to a flying bird that leaves the Water, represented by Kan, the Lower Nuclear Trigram, which gradually wings its way to the Primary trigrams by flying towards the Trees on the Mountain top. Everything moves at a steady pace and is good for any type of union, whether romance or any business venture.

The last decanate of Aries is ruled by both Jupiter and Neptune which relates to ambition through cultural and religious organisations and to a very socially orientated person who likes being in a position of authority. The first decanate of Taurus is ruled by Venus with the Moon exalted. This combination shows a monument builder, but also an over-inflated ego—self-importance. The second decanate of Taurus is ruled by Mercury and depicts wealth and security that is accumulated through a careful and analytical plan.

The Airy part of Earth is the intangible aspect of Earth. Its nature is that of the theorist who has risked all on a plan towards a material goal. However, he is a steady and reliable individual who will apply himself practically towards an increase in wealth through grand schemes. If ill dignified, he is material in his outlook and also stupid but eruptive if aroused. He is not like the Knight in this regard for the Knight is spontaneous. The King would think and plan before he acted and it would be done coldly, without any feeling of remorse. He is the Vau of Heh Final and as such shows new growth and independence of thought.

The Tattvic current is Vayu of Prithivi and its vibration is symbolised by a blue circle within a yellow triangle. Air is redirected and permeated by earth, as occurs, for example, when there is air within soil.

The Geomantic figure is Amissio. This is bad for any effort for personal gain, but good for leaving or giving up something. This is contrary to the astrological meanings and would perhaps be the negative potential only.

Divination

Wherever this card is placed positively in a reading one will see prosperity and growth; matters operate slow but sure; seasonal changes, fertility and matters of development; everything must be timed if one wishes success; matters materialise and all efforts and theory take root as the final formula is put into place. Therefore the material result of all one's efforts are beginning to show. As an individual it is someone who actively seeks comforts. However, he will take everything in his stride, one day at a time. Both intellectual and physical effort is applied to anything that is desired. He is generous and loving. Situations of gain, movement, shifting from one place to another and taking all your possessions. In the business world everything is obtained through progression. Negatively, he is greedy and too materialistic, making an excuse for everything.

PRINCESS of DISKS

Princess of Disks

Princess of the Echoing Hills; Rose of the Palace of Earth

Element	:	Earthy part of Earth
Symbols	:	Grass, Flowers, grove of trees, Sceptre with disk, pentacle as well
Emblem/crest	:	Winged Ram's head
Scale	:	Cube divided into five levels
Command	:	Princess of the Gnomes
Myths	:	Nephthys; Macha
Kabbalah	:	Heh final of Heh final
I Ching	:	Fifty-second Hexagram
Zodiac Rule	:	Rules North Pole to forty-five degrees Latitude and from zero degrees Aries to thirty degrees Gemini
Tattwa	:	Prithivi of Prithivi
Geomantic	:	Caput Draconis
Colour	:	Rich brown hair, dark eyes; Green, complementary red; colours of Malkuth from the Queen scale

The Princess of Earth wears a winged ram's head emblem above her crown, on her belt and knee guards. The ram's head is the influence of the zodiac sign Aries. She carries a wand with the sigil of her scale. This is the same cube as that of the Queen of Disks only this time it is sub-divided into another four levels, which relate to entering a new era in material matters. The disk she holds is like that of the Ace and shows the influence of matter through the twelve astrological houses—all phases of life. She is Persephone which is shown by the vegetation and growth on the right side of the card and barrenness on the other.

The Princess of the Gnomes expresses herself through minerals and rock formations of the earth, especially hilly areas, hence her title. It is her task to show humanity where and what to find in order for it to develop further. She will also hide certain minerals from us if she thinks humanity is not ready for them. She will often reveal her nature through mines and excavation work and occasionally she will work directly on the earth's surface.

The I Ching association is through the fifty-second Hexagram, Ken/Stillness. The Two Trigrams of Ken over Ken show a still situation on the outside. There is no apparent movement here though the Nuclear Trigrams are Chen—Thunder over Kan—Water which can be a potentially dangerous situation, as all of one's concentration is on the inner workings and not the external. It is good for prayer or meditation and planning.

In Egyptian mythology the Goddess associated here is Nephthys, the faithful shadow Goddess and sister to Isis and Osiris. It was she who saved the life of the younger Horus when he was stung by the Scorpion. It was she who helped Isis gather the limbs of Osiris. She was known as a Goddess who gave protection to those who asked for it. The Celtic Goddess to this card is Macha, a Fertility Goddess and another triune Goddess. She was said to make weaponry and use magic against her enemies and help those who ask win battles. She was a deity who forced the sons of her enemies to build the fortifications of her capital fortress.

As the Earthy part of Earth there is no other choice for her but to transform herself otherwise she will become dormant, a rock. The Princess is kind, generous, diligent, benevolent, careful, courageous and preserving. Quite often during divination with this card it will relate to a location change, either at work or in the home. If ill dignified she is wasteful and prodigal. As a woman she is the last of the line and must join another for procreation so that her line will live on in a new era. The Tattvic current is Prithivi, the odoriferous ether of cohesive resistance. Its vibration is quadrangular in shape and moves in the middle rather than at any angles, but on the line of the wave in the same place as the quadrangle. Hence the yellow square is its symbol. Prithivi is solid matter, earth, rock.

The Geomantic figure is Cauda Draconis which is known as a good figure. An entrance, going in, coming to, generally good news in matters of gain, but mainly neutral and influenced by whatever surrounds.

Divination

A receptive, fertile situation is depicted here, where the Princess divines matters of finality which now must open up and be receptive to a new cycle. To those of fixed expression and pursuits it must be a time of contemplation as a revision of goals must take place, where the old is discarded. New ventures are begun; new ground entered on, for example, a new home or job. Concerning growth, the potential is to be great, but it depends entirely on the individual. Good luck is depicted, however it can be the reverse if adversely aspected. Often the Princess of Disks depicts pregnancy.

The Minor Arcana

One of the origins of the symbols in the four suits of the Pip Cards (Minor Arcana) seems to have its roots in the Four Grail hallows, popularised by Geoffrey de Monmouth around the middle of the twelfth century. The Cups related to the Holy Grail from which Christ drank at the last supper. The Sword was that of King David. The Lance was that of Longinus, which pierced the side of Christ as he was nailed to the Cross. The Plate (Platter) was the one used to consecrate the bread at the Last Supper. There is a strong link or at least a parallel one, between the Four Talismans of Ireland (see under The Fool) and the symbols of the Minor Arcana. Mathers, however, makes it clear that the Golden Dawn Symbols, the Wand, Cup, Sword and Disk, are directly related to the Four Elemental weapons that the Zelator Adeptus Minor must make and consecrate:

These are the Tarot symbols of the letters of the Divine Name YHVH and of the Elements and have a certain bond and sympathy between them. So that even if only one is to be used (the elemental weapons) the others should be also present, even as each of the Four Elemental Tablets is divided itself into Four Lesser Angles representing the other three elements bound together therewith in the same Tablet. Therefore also let the Z.A.M. remember that when he works with these forces he is as it were dealing with the Forces of the Letters of the Divine Name. … The Wand … is for all workings of the nature of Fire and under the presidency of Yod and of the 'Wand of the Tarot'. … The Cup … is to be used in all workings of the nature of Water and under the presidency of the letter Heh and the 'Cup of the Tarot'. … The Air dagger is to be used in all works of an Airy Nature and under the presidency of the 'Sword of the Tarot'. Let there be no confusion between the Magical Sword and the Air Dagger. The Magical Sword is under Geburah and is for Strength and defence. The Air dagger is for Air, for Vau of YHVH and is to be used with the other three implements. They belong to different planes and any substitution of one for the other is harmful. … The Pentacle … is used in all works of the nature of Earth and is under the presidency of Heh final and the 'Pentacle of the Tarot'.

Each suit of the Minor Arcana also equates with one of the Four Worlds of the Kabbalah and with each suit there is the appropriate Kabbalistic symbolism. By applying this methodology the Minor Arcana then become living symbols of the Sephiroth of the Kabbalah and can be studied as such. As an example, the Wands represent action on the Spiritual plane, the Cups the instinctive reaction, the Swords the counterbalancing and checking of dynamic power so that it can be brought under control, the Disks the nature of the material manifesting through the Sephirotic framework. Also in like manner, the Soul is applied to the Wands; Vision or Spiritual Experience to the Cups; Vices and Virtues to the Swords; and Symbols to the Disks. Each card in the Minor Arcana also relates to the symbols of the Kabbalah in the Four Worlds.

The Minor Arcana cards represent a more personal or 'tuned in' meaning than that of the Major Arcana. Their key meanings come from both astrological and Kabbalistic origins, with the drawing (design) on the card being the framework or modifier of both these influences. Quite often in the past people tend to simply use the astrological meaning of the Minor Arcana without even considering what the drawings on each card meant in real terms. Within the Golden Dawn and later in the New Zealand Order, the Adept had to do his or her own commentary on what each card meant, based on the descriptions in the Order papers. This led to a very intuitive individual development, albeit based on the Golden Dawn correspondences.

There are two main astrological associations of the Minor Arcana. The first one is from the concept of a Planet in an Element and this influence is from the Kabbalistic Sephirah with which the individual cards are associated. The astrological action of the Sephiroth is the point or direction which the background influence of the card comes from, while the Planet in a Sign is more in line with the direct meaning of the card itself. Sometimes the astrological meanings will relate directly to the cards and other times they will not. In these instances then, the drawings or symbols of what the cards represent take on paramount meaning in the card itself.

It is important that the meanings of the symbols drawn on the cards are understood clearly for they are the doorways through which these forces are interpreted. Otherwise we may as well have white cards with astrological symbols on them and nothing else.

On a personal note we have found over the years that symbols or drawings on the cards eventually open up certain latent layers of the psyche and help tap into deeper levels when doing readings. We have heard it said that the Minor Arcana are not important enough to meditate on. When we first began Golden Dawn training, Jack Taylor insisted that we lock ourselves away for hours on end with the cards and write down our impressions of them through meditation. It was only after then that we completely appreciated the full extent of the Golden Dawn symbolism. We suggest the same to others. Once this has been achieved one can build up a rather fuller picture of the abstract symbolism given on each of these cards. Taylor first instructed us to meditate on the black and white deck and, after this was done and we were familiar with the colour scales, we then painted them. This added further deeper insight into their meanings. The whole process can take months, or even years, but is the fundamental basis to understanding and, most important of all, of linking yourself up to these cards and the energies they emit.

Like the Major Arcana and the Royal Arcana, we have included in each card alchemical associations. It is important however, to note that the formula of alchemy does not necessarily run consecutively through the cards from Aces to tens and so on. On a general level, however, the alchemic applications to the four suits would go like this:

Wands are the motivating forces in alchemy and are the actions and energy within the alchemic workings.

Cups are the liquids, menstrums and containers/vessels. The perfection of the liquid stone is described by the cups.

Swords are the gasses and vapours during the transitory stages of the experiments. Disks are the raw material, faeces, salts, powders and solidifying processes through to the solid stone.

Watching and understanding the alchemic processes through the cards reveals a fascinating and exciting world of creation. This is the essence and perfection of life. Words cannot describe it. Like the Court Cards, the following explanations of the Minor Arcana are merely an introduction to them and we suggest that readers start their own research into this area. When searching for divinatory meanings, study the text of the whole card first and then record each impression in a notebook. Consistent meditation will bring a great many meanings for each card. The section on 'brief meanings of the cards' covers divinatory explanations of the Minor Arcana and will give you a kick start in this direction. Ultimately, it is up to you through meditation and the experience of using the cards, to build up your concepts of what these cards mean. The object here is to try and make this deck personal and that can only be done through experiencing the cards at many different levels.

Ace of Wands

Title	:	Root of the Powers of Fire
Element	:	Fire
Force	:	Yod
Alchemic	:	The three principles of the Invisible Fire—The Furnace
Kabbalistic World	:	Atziluth
Sephirah	:	Kether
Holy Name	:	AHIH
Soul	:	Yechidah—Divine Consciousness
Planet of Sephirah	:	Neptune
Archangel	:	Michael
Astrological	:	Fiery part of Neptune
Myth	:	Labours of Hercules
Colours	:	Wand and Yods red; background green; clouds and hands white

An angelic hand emerging from clouds grasps a flaming wand which separates into three forks. Each fork ends in flames, the right and left-hand forks in three flames and the centre in four flames. This yields ten which is the number of the Sephiroth on the Tree of Life. The entire concept here is one of potentiality, the seed of an idea or impulse, force, vigour and strength which can be used for good or evil depending on the dignity of the card. Surrounding these flames leap twenty-two Yods alluding to the Paths on the Tree of Life in the King Scale (Atziluth): three to the right for the three Mother letters of the Hebrew alphabet, Aleph, Mem and Shin. Seven Yods leap above the centre representing the seven Double letters of the Hebrew alphabet and thus the paths associated. The rest of the leaping Yods are twelve in number representing the Single letters.

The Sigils of the Scales on the three branches are taken from the Court Cards. The left-hand branch has the sigil of the Knight of Wands. The three-sided pyramid plus its base on this branch, equates to four sides which multiplied by twelve produces the months of the year, cycles of life. On the middle branch, the sigil is of the King of Wands, which is the Hexagram within a circle, symbolizing the seven planets contained in the four elements. The right-hand branch has the sigil of the Queen of Wands, a circle divided by four which shows the four elements. The Fourth sigil of the Scale is in fact hidden by the hand grasping the Wand.

The Wand itself is in fact the club of Hercules which he used during his Twelve Labours. The Yods on the right and left Branches stand for the following twelve labours:

1. Killing of the Nemean Lion.
2. Killing of the Hydra.
3. Capturing the boar of Erymanthus.
4. Capturing the Arcadian Stag.
5. Driving away and destroying the birds of lake Stymphalus.
6. Retrieving the girdle of Hippolyta.
7. Cleaning the Augean stables.
8. Capturing the Minoan Bull.
9. Capturing the mares of Diomedes.
10. Bringing the oxen of Geryon.
11. Plucking the apples of Hesperides.
12. Bringing Cerberus up from the underworld.

In addition, the remaining ten Yods relate to the ten commandments of YHVH given to Moses. It is the law by which man will be governed.

On the shape of the Wand, Mathers says:

> *The symbol of the Triad represented by the three lopped branches; it is the symbol of the Almighty Strength within the Cube of the Universe.*

This adheres to the blueprint of Creation given in the Book 'Sepher Yetzirah' which can be expanded into the Cube of the Universe.

The Ace of Wands, on the Kabbalistic Tree of Life, is placed in Kether and shows the influence of Yod of Kether, in Atziluth, which is raw energy just manifesting in a new state of awareness. Its influence is very pliable, as an initial impetus to establishing oneself into a given framework. In many ways the Ace represents the Creative Will and impulse behind the planning and directing stage of formation, which has yet to be fully realised but signifying everything is about to begin.

The Holy Name manifesting for Kether in Atziluth is AHIH meaning 'I am, I was and I shall be'. This is very much the formula for self-manifestation and as such is extremely far removed from the conscious state of 'knowing'. It is the impetus of an idea in an unmanifested form in a totally alien framework. AHIH is the Divine spark of the establishment of the state of existence itself, ready to take new and as yet unmoulded energy into a new era of development so that it has a chance to grow in its new environment. Kether is of course the Sephirah of the Crown when placed on the figure of Adam Kadmon, the Heavenly Man or Man of the Macrocosm.

When YHVH first appeared to Moses, 'the angel of YHVH appeared to him in a flame of Fire out of the midst of a bush: and he looked and, behold, the bush burned with Fire and was not consumed' (Exodus 3: 2-4). When asked by Moses the name of the God who spoke to Him the voice replied, through the Flaming Bush, 'I am that I am' (AHIH).'.

The Ace of Wands is also associated to the Yechidah, the most primal point of the Kabbalistic Soul, of which Mathers tells us:

Thus Yechidah is called Divine Consciousness—Conscire means 'to know with' and 'to be in touch with' and only your Kether can do this as regards the Divine and your Kether is then Divine Consciousness.

The Kabbalists sometimes call this HUA or Holy Guardian Angel. Through the three branches in the Ace of Wands we can see the Soul of Man coming into manifestation on three levels: an Individual Task to perform, Group Karma and Individual Karma. All of these three principles must be harmoniously merged to produce a cohesive effect as the individual grows, in the lower Trees.

The Archangel is Michael who biblically ranks greater than all angels and is 'chief of the order of virtues, chief of archangels, prince of the presence'.

Kether's Planetary association is Neptune, a planet so broad in scope that it is difficult to judge it except in terms of pure insight and thought. In this instance it is Neptune in the Fire Element. This can be equated with the Three Branches of the Ace, for Neptune in the Fire Element has three principles of growth. The first shows important development in mystical religious concepts, the second is the creativity of performance and idealism and the third is formations of the higher ideals expressed through a religious framework.

The alchemic concept of the Ace of Wands is that of the three principles of the Invisible Fire. For this explanation we quote from the 'Golden Chain of Homer'. The Universal Spirit in its three powers is described:

Thus God created first this invisible fire and endowed it with an unerring Instinct and a Capacity to manifest itself in 3 Principles. [The right-hand branch:] In its Original most Universal state it is perfectly invisible, immaterial, cold and occupies no space, in this tranquil state it is of no use to us, yet in this unmoved state it is omnipresent. [The right-hand branch:] In its second state it is manifested by motion or agitation into light. In this state it was separated out of the Chaos, when God said, 'Let there be Light.' Yet it is still cold. When gently moved or agitated, it manifests warmth and Heat, as in the case in all Frictions and in Fermentation of moist things. [The central branch:] When collected in a sufficient quantity, and violently agitated it is manifested into burning fire. This continues burning as long as it is agitated, and has a fit subject to act upon; when that fails, it returns to its first state of tranquil Universality.

Another alchemic concept of the Ace of Wands is Raw Power.

Divination

Divine purpose; aspirations, the first inspiration, or gestation of some matter whether it be an impulse, idea, or life form (conception); pure force and spontaneity with no controlling principle. In material matters little control or manifestation on a practical level; the beginning of matters showing great potential; integrity; action; favourable for commencing new projects; however, usually referring to undecided plans. In matters of life and death the Ace of Wands will refer to the new beginning of either, although it is more likely to refer to life. Illnesses associated are cancer, fevers, sudden onsets of acute conditions, viruses. The life force and one's actual vitality. Intense motion; procreation; spontaneous combustion; kindling of relationships; truth being the better part of valour; purists; morality; making haste. The Ace of Wands can be good with good and bad with bad, therefore the reverse interpretation to the above can be emphasised if this card is negatively aspected in a reading.

Two of Wands

Title	:	The Lord of the Dominion
Element	:	Fire
Force	:	Yod
Alchemic	:	First Stage Calcination—Blackening
Kabbalistic World	:	Atziluth
Sephirah	:	Chokmah
Holy Name	:	YAH
Soul	:	Chiah—Living Creatures
Planet of Sephirah	:	Zodiac/Uranus
Angels	:	Uhauel, Deneyael
Astrological	:	Mars in Aries zero–ten degrees
Colours	:	Wands Poppy Red; background Blood Red; clouds Bluish White; complementary colours used for shading, shaping, flames and zodiac symbols; White hand

The Two wands are held in a single grip portraying harmony in direction for the hand grips easily, no other support is needed. This also relates to self-containment, independence and justice, where one has a firm grip on the situation in hand. Where the Ace showed the first impetus, the two of Wands is the joining or conception.

An X shape is formed by the wands, where the concentration of energy is in the centre of the X, a point where the powers of opposites, above and below, meet at the centre and are as yet undivided. The 'Emerald Tablet' of Hermes (Trismegistos) tells us of the similarity between that which is above to that which is below. The X also symbolizes St Andrew's Cross, which also speaks of the union of the upper and lower worlds and a force unified. In the two of Wands this is the last stage before the final monadic force of the Ace of Wands and in manifestation it is the division that the Ace of Wands must make towards creation.

The X is also the alchemical symbol of the union of the elements in the beginning. An early alchemical text, the 'Anthroposophia Theomagica' explains this when quoting from Esdras:

> *'Upon the second day thou madest the spirit of the firmament' for it is 'the bond of all Nature' and in the outward geometrical composure it answers to 'the middle substance', for it is spread through all things, hinders vacuity and keeps all the parts of Nature in a firm, invincible union.*

The two of Wands is also the Blackening which is the first stage of calcination when intense heat is applied.

The two of Wands is associated with the Kabbalistic Sephirah of Chokmah. The portion of the Kabbalistic Soul is the Chiah ('living creatures'). Mathers indicated that the Chiah is the first real beginning of man. By this he meant that the real self is in Kether and the Yechidah and the framework of expression is in the Chiah. To a certain extent the Chiah is still undeveloped and is partly a blind force hence its equation with living creatures.

As Chokmah of Atziluth, the Two of Wands has the God Name YAH (a variation of YHVH). The Gematric considerations show that IH (pronounced YAH) has a value of fifteen which relates to 'He who impels force' and as such is directly linked with the Two of Wands and its title of 'Dominion'. This dual concept of Fire brings forward the concept of Polarisation, hence the Two Wands and two letters of the Holy Name IH, which brings about balance and support, hinting at hidden impregnation as the two opposites unite into a homogeneous unit.

The two angels ruling this card are Uhauel and Daneyal. Uhauel's title is 'Great and Lofty'. Uhauel aids in the expression of ideas and their ultimate success once acted upon, while the title of Deneyal, is 'Merciful Judge'. The nature of these two angels suggest that we have a favourable framework to help and guide one through initial growth, with the latter angel helping to balance the energies of the former.

Uranus is the influence from the Sephiroth. Uranus in a Fire Element symbolizes a quantum leap to freedom and social reform, a shattering of restrictive or oppressive structures. Individual freedom is an important necessity in this instance. This vital need for freedom of expression also goes into the sexual area of expression and will differ from the morality of the day. Leadership in the arts and sciences is also indicated as one will have a need to express creative urges through an existing framework. Strong desires to enter into fields of religion, science and politics and a certain amount of eccentricity will be apparent in the approach to such areas.

Mars in Aries represents willed energy translated into direct action. An outlet is needed and when an existing framework is utilised, those working within that framework will give their support, due to the popularity Mars in Aries endures. There is a certain impulsiveness here that must be curtailed somewhat or a tremendous energy will burn itself out. Mars in Aries people need to constantly prove their power and tend to respond very quickly to anything going on. Adversely there is little control over these people, as they pave their way towards being masters of their own destiny. Physical disciplines help in this area.

Divination

Chokmah of Yod is a planning and thinking stage which now puts theoretical concepts into forceful action, under the guidance of some authoritarian framework. This is a positive card, although, with such raw energy negative circumstances can arise. Assertion of individuality and a need to be noticed; fight for values; rashness although intentions may be good; careless with money, although aggressive in obtaining money and possessions; impatience with others; best interacting when playing sport or working with another; sharp verbal approach; restlessness; rages; ever active; difficulty in resting; competitive sport; fastidious pride in work; bored quickly, needing new challenges all the time. Uniting forces; dominating another; joint resources and activities. If ill-dignified then 'overkill' is present, something that has got out of control and does not know when to stop, thus introducing ferocity, tenacity, angry outbursts and revenge; spoiling for a fight; domestic battles; not good for relationships.

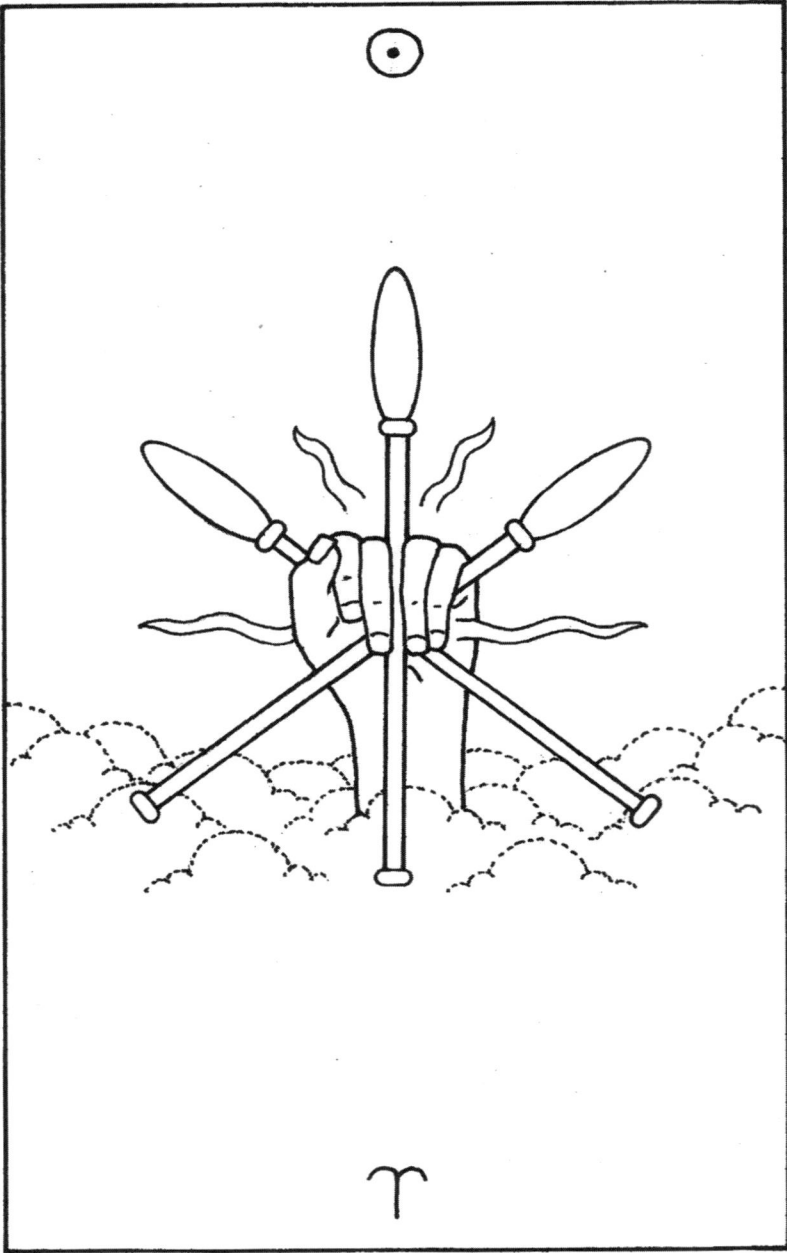

Three of Wands

Title	:	Lord of Established Strength
Element	:	Fire
Force	:	Yod
Alchemic	:	Second Stage Calcination—Whitening Symbols: three Wands forming sextile held by one hand issuing from clouds, flames from a hand
Kabbalistic World	:	Atziluth
Sephirah	:	Binah
Holy Name	:	YHVH ELOHIM
Soul	:	Neshamah—Breath
Planet of Sephirah	:	Saturn
Angels	:	Hechaseiah, Amamiah
Astrological	:	Sun in Aries ten–twenty degrees
Colours	:	Clear Orange Wands; Blood Red background; Translucent Crimson clouds; White hand; complementaries as zodiac symbols, flames and shading

A single hand issues from the clouds grasping firmly three wands crossed in the centre where flames issue at the point of junction. A third wand is now shown upright in the centre of the X of the two of Wands, emphasising further strength, but the maximum one hand can hold. The three Wands symbolize a reflection of the Holy Trinity in the Ace of Wands. The sextile formed by the wands is a symbol from the Greek alchemical tradition. The energies of a sextile are universal, spiritual and work on an internal level, tapping into deeper dimensions, hence its use as a six-pointed star. Where the two of Wands was the formation of the elements, the three of wands is the formation of the planets, with the Sun as the central force. Hence this card's planetary association is the Sun. Here, in its trinity, there is the union of spirit, soul and body (mercury, sulphur and salt). This is also the second stage of calcinations, bringing in the whitening. The heat is still intense but more controlled. Where we saw the monad in the Ace, the duality in the two of Wands, the three of Wands is the birth of the third principle, as discussed below. The sextile symbol also alludes to prayer and is the sixty degree aspect in astrology.

This card is very much like its predecessor except that a central wand has now been introduced to give additional strength and also help stabilise the situation. This results in Established Strength, for the additional wand has taken away the volatile aspect of the former card. Here success has been achieved after a struggle and material success and power through independence will be achieved.

The Holy name of Binah of Atziluth is YHVH ELOHIM. There is more than one interpretation of the meaning of this Name; such as 'Lord my God' and 'It is, it was and it shall be'. When this is expressed through the framework of Binah it would be advisable to study the name of Binah as well, for it breaks down into two names: BN (Ben–Son) and IH (Yah) which is a combination of both Binah and Chokmah. The receptive feminine nature of Binah is important here for in the Three of Wands we see that impregnation has given birth to a third principle, which is depicted by the Third wand, as the Son. In essence, the Father, Mother and Son triad are associated. This however can only be accomplished by the feminine principle giving in to its own nature.

In this respect the Kabbalistic Soul this card is related to is the Neshamah (breath). This state of the Soul is part of an impregnation and unification process. It is from here that the Neshamah will formulate a new Ruach with each incarnation and at the end of each life the vitality extended into each Ruach will be withdrawn, along with all the memories and experiences of each life. The Neshamah has the function to merge higher aspects of the Soul with each new personality.

Therefore its function is to search for prospective parents where Soul is breathed into the existing foetus in the womb. It tries to establish a family for souls as they enter the World. As it performs this function it must work through the angels of Karma which give the Neshamah certain instruction about any physical restrictions, Karmic debts, group Karma, etc. All of this information is merged with the messages from the Chiah on what the main function of the individual on earth will be. All of these greatly restrict the Neshamah's options for a suitable body to infiltrate. In many respects this is closely applied to the function of the Three of Wands.

The first angel who rules over this card is Hechaseiah, who is titled 'Secret and Impenetrable'. The inference is in something hidden and unrevealed. The second angel Amamiah's title 'Covered in Darkness' also relates to hidden motives. Both these titles are operations being kept in secret by a powerful group or organisation that leaves nothing to chance. What these angels conceal, in fact, is the actual Path to Binah which must come from Daath, across the Abyss, so that the Qlippothic elements cannot climb the Tree into the realm of the Supernal.

The planetary influence of Binah is Saturn in a Fire Element. An initial need to discipline and to acquire material possessions, leading to hard work, detail, accuracy and perfectionism and in every aspect Saturn in this element represents the workaholic and overachiever. This whole concept is fuelled by strong ambitions in such fields as business, science or politics. There is no rest for Saturn in the Fire Element and there is a constant need to transcend one's boundaries and self-efficiency and independence.

The Sun in Aries symbolizes vitality and advances being made on a number of different levels indicating general wellbeing, assertiveness, the leader of a field and explorer of new schemes yet a certain sensitiveness. It is life force in an outgoing form. Those under the influence of Sun in Aries catch the attention of others. They appear to shine and be very popular. Their energy is warm and they have a sense of identity, needing to create a name for them where there is recognition. A negative expression is egocentricity, over-zealousness, excessive pride, authoritarianism and self-admiration.

Divination

As Binah of Yod, Understanding is at the very beginning of things or initial comprehension. Perseverance is very strong here as well but it is limited to its framework of operation. Here is the beginning of organisation being formed in a frontier state of being; acquiring money, possessions; self-worth being important; organization of others; gathering friends; good luck; gentle momentum; travel for pleasure; meeting challenges with strength; co-operation between fellow workers; participation. In relation to health, speedy recovery, positive thinking, an increase in vitality and life force. Relationships get built on, friendships grow, tolerance and persistence. Dedication to path; the ability to succeed and develop an identity. Artistic expression and the richness of living enhanced through recreational activities. Established independence and strength. If ill-dignified, this shows conceit, self-assumption, insolence and arrogance; imperfections physically, emotionally or psychologically are amplified; and all of the above reversed in nature.

The meaning we have given here differs from that given in the original manuscripts and is extremely positive in outlook compared to the negative comment given on Chokmah of Yod in 'Book T', which is more in line with Saturn and not Binah. The new meaning we have given is also more in line with the general meaning of the card itself.

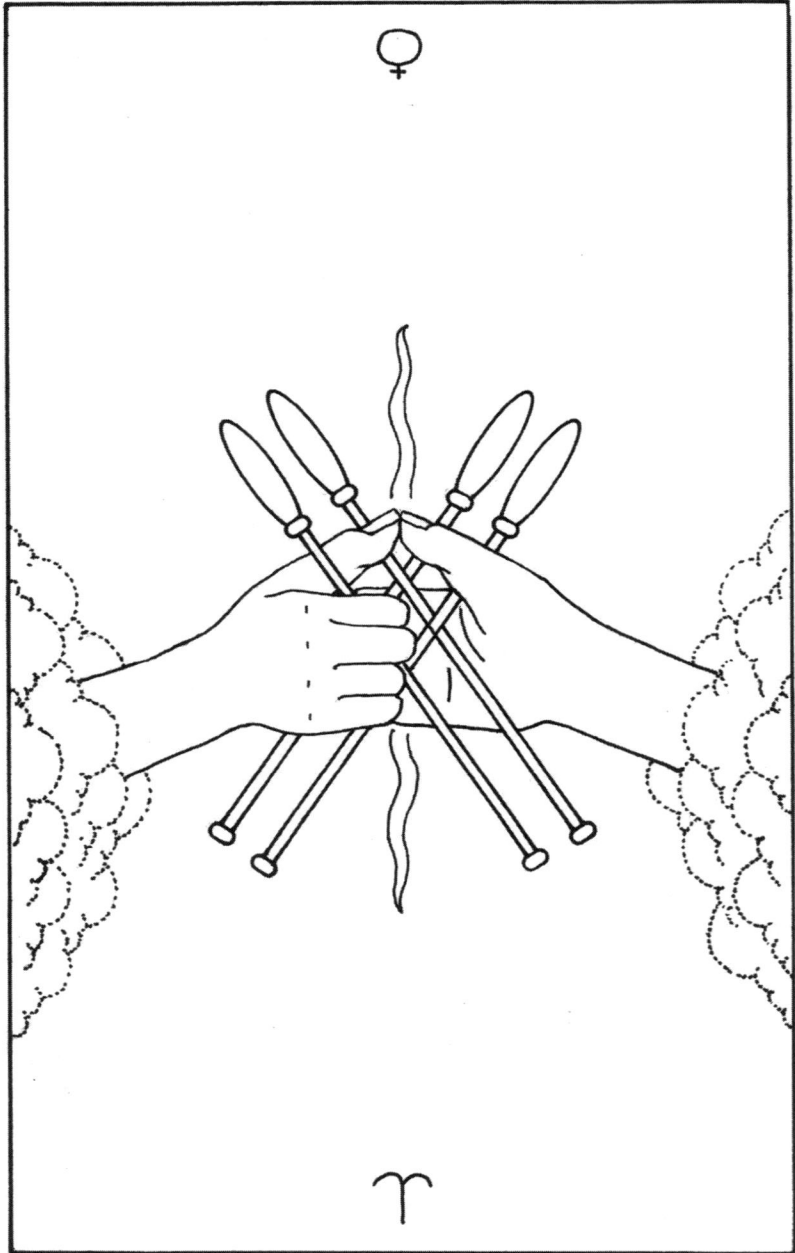

Four of Wands

Title	:	Lord of Perfected Work
Element	:	Fire
Force	:	Yod
Alchemic	:	Third Stage Calcination—Reddening
Kabbalistic World	:	Atziluth
Sephirah	:	Chesed
Holy Name	:	AL
Soul	:	Ruach—mental body
Planet of Sephirah	:	Jupiter
Angels	:	Nanael, Nithael
Astrological	:	Venus in Aries twenty–thirty degrees
Colours	:	Emerald Green wands; Blood Red background; Deep Violet clouds; White hands; complementaries for shading, flames and zodiac symbols

This card is the first of the Wands that introduces two hands holding the Wands instead of one. Two hands are needed to hold the Four Wands, giving additional help in balancing a situation. The duality here of the two hands, with two sets of Wands shows perfection and harmony through merging. The clouds have risen to each side of the card where the hands each issue, revealing an exalted state.

A double cross is formed by the positioning of the wands, with each end of the wands pointing to the four points of the earth, the four elements in their primordial form. Like the two of Wands, the four of Wands shows the unified force of the upper and lower worlds, however, a further form of perfection occurs with the double cross, hence the title Lord of Perfected Works.

This is an alchemical symbol of Ashes (Cinders) and alludes to the concept of the Phoenix which rises out of the ashes. This can happen two ways: Spirit being born into nature, or birth of the Higher Self. With birth, there is some form of death and transformation and purification. As this is a purified state, we now have the final stage of calcinations where there is a reddening. The reddening is the most pure state that is brought about by intense, but controlled heat.

Chesed of Atziluth has the God name of AL which means simply 'God' or 'Might'. AL is important for its energy is twofold. It needs our love and adoration to exist and in return we expect certain favours from AL. The God in AL is not to be confused with YHVH for in Chesed, AL becomes the God in Microcosm (or Microprosopus), separated by the Abyss and the shadow Sephirah Daath which divides Chesed from Binah, the next higher Sephiroth. AL in Chesed is an expendable God for its truer nature is above it. The tempering framework of AL's nature by Chesed restricts it by forcing it to give way, or give Mercy.

The Kabbalistic Soul, of which Chesed is but a part, is called the Ruach. To New Age groups this would be referred to as the Mental Body where all the thought processes are stored and refined. It is here that the impetus that comes across from the Abyss is adapted to suit specific components of the psyche. The faculty of Memory has been associated to Chesed by modern occultists.

The first angel of this card is Nanael, who is titled 'Caster down of the Proud'. His function is to inspire growth (but not at the expense of others) and when Ego inflation and self-importance arrive his function is to bring people back to reality and see things in real terms. The second angel is Nithael, who is titled 'Celestial King'. This is a highly evolved figure in authority that has never lost touch with his spiritual awareness. All of these functions this angel will try and impart to others. These two angels provide a modification of power, authority and haughtiness, by making people more spirituality aware of themselves and their actions in dealing with others.

The Sephirotic associations are Jupiter in a Fire Element. There is a strong indication for a leadership role to improve social, educational and mystical areas. An element of reform also creeps into this concept and the desire to convert others to a special type of metaphysical or religious belief. Due to a huge energy influx, Ego inflation is something which often occurs here and will have to be controlled, or rashness and impulsiveness take over. Total confidence and a strong support base, however, gives a high degree of prestige, and fulfilment in matters of romance, unless negatively aspected.

Venus in Aries symbolizes creative activity, enthusiasm in social gatherings, beauty and grace with keen insight, love and affection which is difficult to restrain once accepted. There is a tendency to rush into things of a romantic nature (such as marriage). Anything to do with finance is favourable but there is also a tendency to rush out and spend it just as quickly as it is received. Love of the arts and appreciation for all things beautiful. Meeting life with open arms; a feeling of self-worth; seduction; attractiveness; optimism.

Divination

Chesed of Yod relates to a neutralised force being satisfied with what it has, a settlement or completion of an action. A person has completed a goal and finds that the existing framework is now not enough. In employment it indicates that someone may be finishing a project, or may leave a job (of their own volition) to look for something better. It is a time of change and to tidy up loose ends so that what is good can be got on with. One must also, however, realize one's limits and work within the boundaries of the present. Possessions are of importance in all forms; pleasure-seeking activities; social engagements; family focus towards gathering loved ones around one; readiness for new states of development; restlessness. In matters of sport, preparation and premeditation; careful timing. Relationships promise to be fruitful; one reaches out to those around; contracts and improving partnerships; loyalty. Fortunate in finance, efforts will be rewarded. In spiritual matters a sense of unity and awareness is felt; idealism and dreams. In other situations, retirement; the arts; complete use of resources; friendship; whole of healing. Negatively aspected this card will portray the reverse to the above; an unfinished situation, instability, something being rushed through before it is checked properly with a good chance of it being unsafe or unsound.

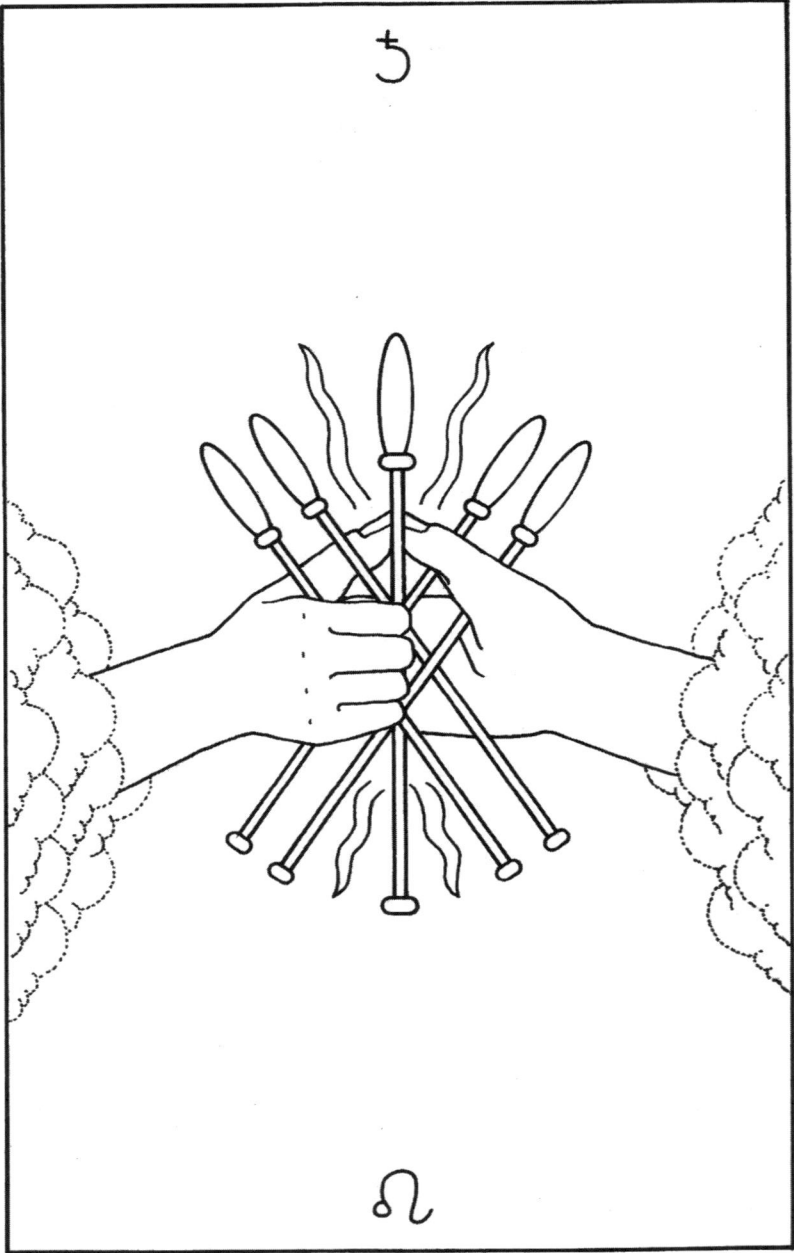

Five of Wands

Title	:	Lord of Strife
Element	:	Fire
Force	:	Yod
Alchemic	:	First Stage Putrefaction; corrosion
Kabbalistic World	:	Atziluth
Sephirah	:	Geburah
Holy Name	:	Elohim Gibor
Soul	:	Ruach-Will
Planet of Sephirah	:	Mars
Angels	:	Vahuaih, Yelauel
Astrological	:	Saturn in Leo zero–ten degrees
Colours	:	Wands Darkest Indigo Blue; background Sun Yellow; clouds, Deep Orange; White hands; flames and zodiac symbols and shading in complementaries

The Five of Wands shows the perfection that the previous card attained is now unbalanced by the central wand which has no foundation or support from either hand and, as such, brings confusion and interrupts communication between the two hands, thus acting more as a wedge than a support. This leads to violence and strife and two impossible choices; one is damned if one does and damned if one does not. However, this force is necessary for disruption of old states which become too harmonious to grow. Therefore the fifth wand forces growth and change, a challenge is presented.

The clouds have grown larger, almost taking up the complete sides of the card, implying a storm brewing. The wands form the symbol of the Laborum. This was Constantine's emblem and it was believed that it drew the protection of Christ to those who wore this symbol. It was also the emblem of the Chaldean sky god and worn for good luck and an emblem associated to the Alpha et Omega occult order and inscribed on tombs.

The alchemic emphasis of the unbalanced cross, by virtue of the fifth wand through the middle of the four, is corrosion and alludes to the first stage of putrefaction—dying. The central wand creates a passage for spirit to be drawn into matter where there is imperfection. With the power of the fifth principle, there can be violent energy, although, this energy can be turned into a powerful creative force. The Golden Tripod says:

> All flesh that is derived from the earth, must be decomposed and again reduced to earth; then the earthy salt produces a new generation by celestial resuscitation.

Geburah of Atziluth has the Holy name Elohim Gibor ('God's war' or 'battles'). One Golden Dawn member has this to say on the subject:

> Elohim Gibor, carries the force on manly, strong hero-gods. It refers to an evolved man who has attained to somewhat advanced Christliness; but which is of too masculine nature. He is necessarily destined to a training which will develop his Chesed nature; which when accomplished, entitles him to another name which has a correspondence, but which is never mentioned in connection with this topic.

This is the trial or initiation through awakening of the senses, to which, to some extent, we are slaves. The energies of Chesed have shown us love and now we must fight for what is correct, even if it means a vital loss in the process.

The part of the Ruach that this card relates to is the Will or desire to succeed at all costs. This is vitally important for the Will is a part of the vital force of the Higher Self that has flowed through Kether. It is something that we cannot escape from and must follow through. When the Will is expressed through the framework of Geburah a very powerful emotive force is then unleashed and is almost unstoppable until completed. Will is tempered also by Desire and man and woman will constantly try for some sort of balance. A Psychological approach to Will relates to the impulse to act (mainly on one's own) in various stages of development.

The first angel of this card is Vahuaih, who has the title of 'God the Exalter'. Vahuaih gives spiritual support to any cause that exalts the name of God. The second angel Yelauel is titled 'My Strength'—support and strength and hints at both of these being martial and spiritual at the same time. Both fortify the concept of strength through God's name or some sort of Holy cause that must be pursued to the finish.

Through relationship with Geburah, Mars in a Fire element is expressed here. This is Mars in its own element and symbolizes too much applied force for any framework to accommodate it. As such, it causes much disruption for it is Mars almost out of control. The reason for this is that any passions expressed will come on suddenly and be extremely hard to limit as there is very little self-restraint. There is a strong tendency to achieve power and fame at the expense of others. All of this relates to gaining experience through hardship.

Saturn in Leo brings restructure, for a situation has reached a point where it cannot go on as it is and shows a constant struggle for control and power. There is however a strong support base here in any new form of development. As a result of this there may be gifts or legacies to help with the struggle. Saturn in this Sign also shows problems with any situation involving romance. Hesitation brings delays and there is difficulty in being sure of oneself and expressing personal creativity. A lack of love is emphasised and these types of people can become workaholics.

Divination

Geburah of Yod relates to fighting and aggression, boldness, lust and desire. This is the card of indecision. A person is faced with two strong choices and only one will suffice. The only respite one can claim is to stall while contingency plans are made. Arguments in relationships; self-blocking and rigidity; over work and energy loss. Domination and pressure from a person or work situation; disruption in environment; many demands from self and expectations of peers. Demands to face up to new conditions and not resist them; restructuring; struggle and need to improve skills, health and surroundings; too much discipline brings rebellion; break-ups in families or other relationships; obstacles and conflicts in most matters; security threatened; excessiveness. High blood pressure and loss of vitality. Difficult competition. Ultimately however, one can win out through perseverance.

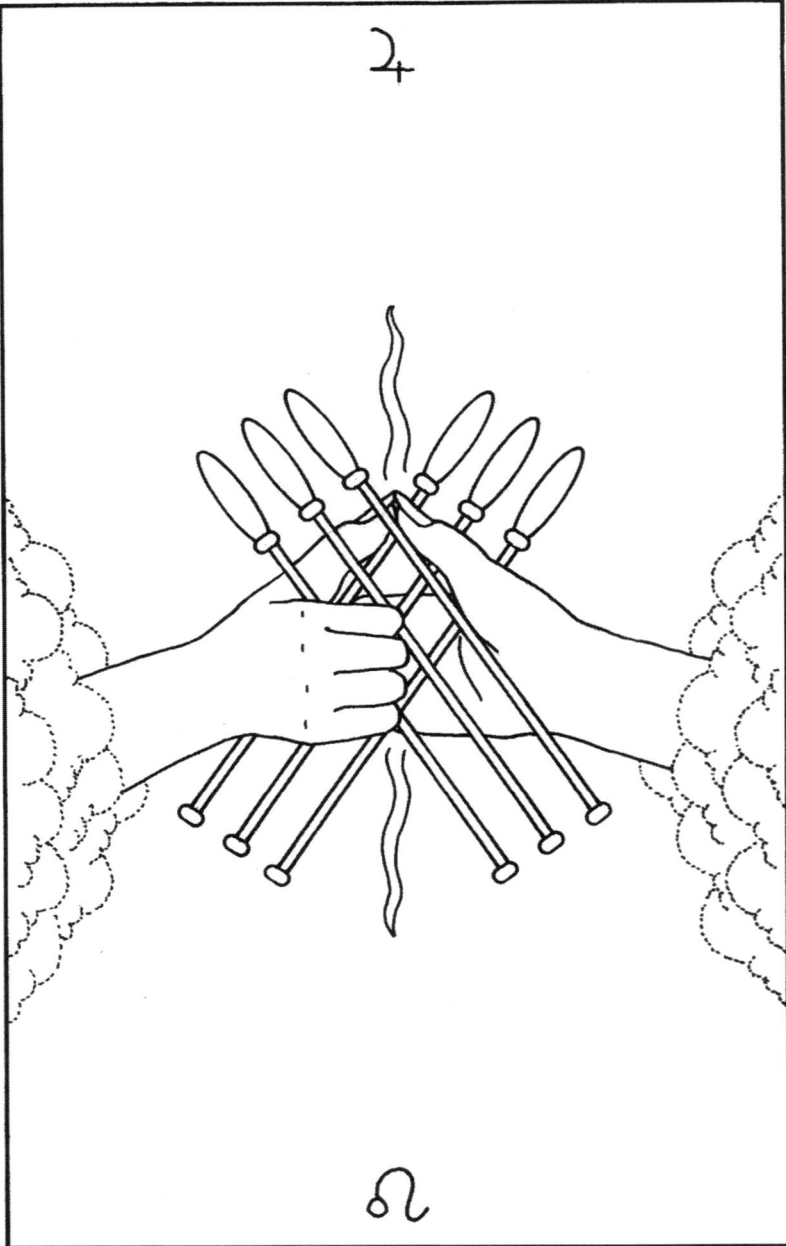

Six of Wands

Title	:	Lord of Victory
Element	:	Fire
Force	:	Yod
Alchemic	:	Second Stage Putrefaction—Gestation
Kabbalistic World	:	Atziluth
Sephirah	:	Tiphareth
Holy Name	:	Eloah ve Daath (Gods Knowledge)
Soul	:	Ruach
Planet of Sephirah	:	Sun
Angels	:	Saitiel, Nghelamiah
Astrological	:	Jupiter in Leo, 10–20 degrees
Colours	:	Wands Violet; background Sun Yellow; complementary colours for shading, flames and zodiac symbols; Rose Pinkish white for clouds; White hands

The two hands each hold the maximum they can hold individually, crossing at the centre creating consolidating power, alluding to victory through unification. Tiphareth lies in the centre of the crossed wands and this is also shown by the four diamond patterns formed, that when acting in the fire element allude to a mystic centre and luminous being. The Six of Wands levels off from the disharmony of the Five of wands, bringing equilibrium, hence its name Lord of Victory, although more appropriately Victory over Strife.

The alchemic emphasis here is an exaltation after resurrection, which also alludes to gestation within the second stage, putrefaction. From the 'Works of Thomas Vaughan' it says:

> *Of a truth God Himself discovered this thing to the first man, to confirm his hopes of those three supernatural mysteries—the Incarnation, Regeneration and Resurrection. ... Let me tell you then that the period and perfection of magic is no way physical...*

The wands form Twelve points, alluding to the zodiac in all its colours, with the Sun as Tiphareth in the centre. This joining of the celestial energies holds within the triad, as the wands point in threes to the four corners of the universe. The Alchemical text 'Open Entrance' is worth relating to as well as describing a more practical aspect of what this card represents:

> *Black Saturn is succeeded by Jupiter, who exhibits diverse colours. For after Putrefaction and conception, which has taken place at the bottom of the vessel, there is once more a change of colours and a circulating sublimation. This Reign or Regimen, lasts only three weeks. During this period you will see conceivable colours concerning which no definite account can be given*

The God name of Tiphareth of Atziluth is 'Eloah ve Daath' ('God's Knowledge' or 'Because of Knowledge') this is not only revealed but realised knowledge and is the point of re-birth ('for the truth will set ye free') for Tiphareth is on the Middle Pillar and a point of central focus of the Tree of Life. It is in Tiphareth that both Osiris and Christ were sacrificed but both of them emerged with a new nature after resurrection. The Tiphareth are the Gods of Illumination for it is this that changes what we are forever. Here we have a brief glimpse of what is beyond the physical.

Tiphareth is a vital central point of the Ruach. It relates to the concept of Imagination but in reality it is the area where the archetypal imagery is formulated. Jung states the following concerning the archetypal image:

> *A process of nature with a symbolic image, which apprehends the nature process just as the eye catches the light. And in the same way as the eye bears witness to the peculiar and independent activity of living matter, the primordial image expresses the unique and unconditional creative power of the spirit.*

All of the archetypal imagery works on different levels, some of the imagery is from day-to-day association and most of it comes from Geburah through the concept of Will.

The first angel who governs this card is called Saitiel and is titled 'Refuge, a Fortress'. This refers to an inner sanctuary where one can rest unmolested while the brain and body heals. This angel will aid in these comforts. The second angel, Nghelamiah, is titled 'Concealed, Saving'. It is similar in meaning to the previous angel except this one's main concern is with the spirit, while the former is more with the material. Combining these concepts one reaches safety and saves one's strength for both body and soul.

The Sephirotic association of the Sun in a Fire Element is one of a strong energising influence in getting things started in a new framework or idealism. Quite often this framework is expanded and adapted to suit the ideal of a situation in a fully individualised situation in which all the practicalities are explored. These are acted upon so that the ideas are taken and acted on in the highest level of the existing framework available. There is a resistance until a new framework is created and until the ideas are fulfilled.

Jupiter in Leo symbolizes one who functions to excess in all things, with panache. Self-expression is creative, spacious and self-aggrandising, although anything that is done, is done well. Play hard, love passionately and lead others down the garden path. This person has to be noticed, is very dramatic and makes a good actor; everything is expressed to the fullest. This sort of person has the capacity to expand on even the smallest of ideas, as capacity for vision is unlimited. They like to challenge life at every step. All of this is not necessarily negative, however. Such a person would naturally have the magnetism, or public image to lead very worthy causes, as Jupiter in Leo people are very humanitarian.

Divination

Tiphareth of Yod is the beginning of success. The initial impetus of the Yod's function is now exposed through its heart or centre. This card is a very fortunate one and relates to an individual going up against competition and winning. It is also taking the proverbial 'Long shot', going against all odds and succeeding where others around fail. Reaching an important goal or destination; victory after strife; success through energy and industry. Travel is indicated, sports for recreation, deep commitment to convictions and plans. In relationships there may be difficulty in staying faithful, although intentions are good. Freedom at all costs. A partner must be able to have interests outside the partnership. In matters of material possessions, there is generosity, fruitfulness, windfalls, inheritances, arrival of good news, fulfilment of one's hopes, diplomacy and success after hard work. If ill-dignified, plans can become too large for one person to handle, over-production and overdoing things; success but at too heavy a cost to be called victory; insolence and too much pride.

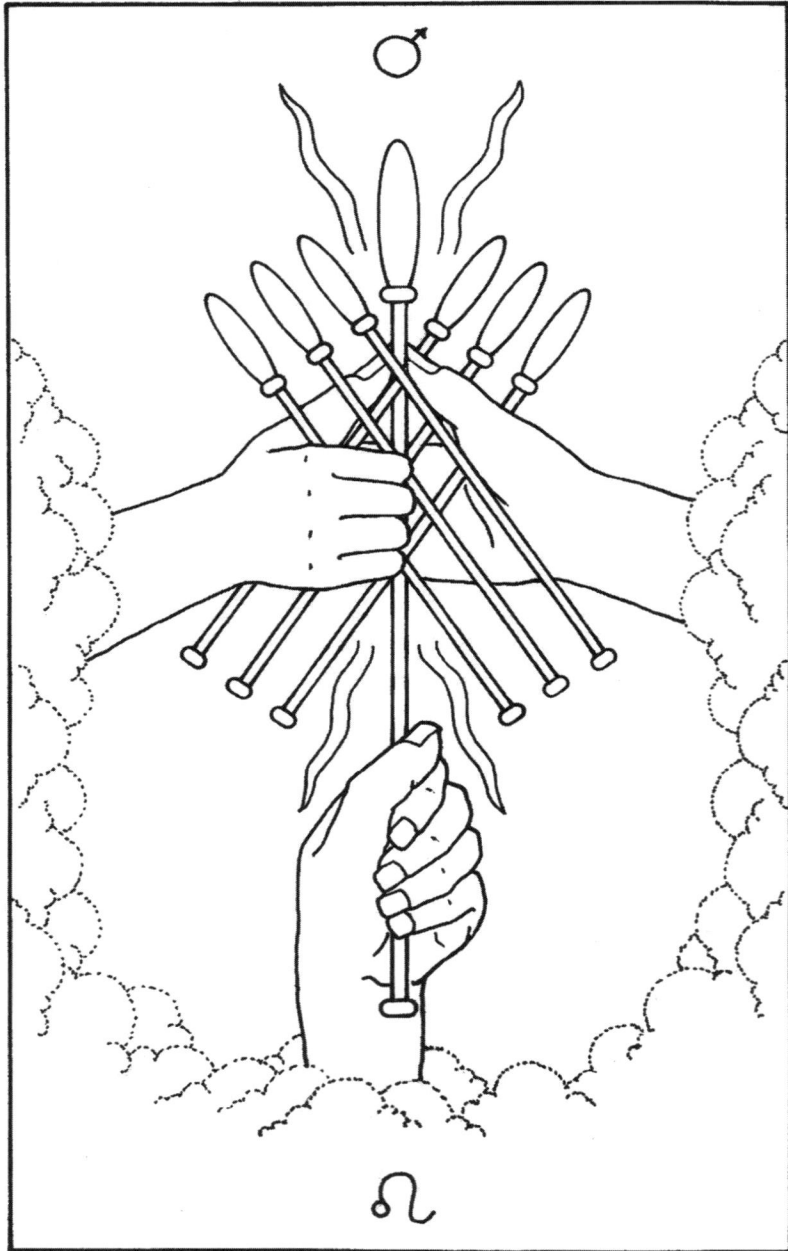

Seven of Wands

Title	:	Lord of Valour
Element	:	Fire
Force	:	Yod
Alchemic	:	Third Stage Putrefaction—Rebirth.
Kabbalistic World	:	Atziluth
Sephirah	:	Netzach
Holy Name	:	YHVH Tzabaoth
Soul	:	Ruach—desire
Planet of Sephirah	:	Venus
Angels	:	Mahashiah, Lahahel
Astrological	:	Mars in Leo, twenty–thirty degrees
Colours	:	Wands Poppy Red; background Sun Yellow; Clouds Amber Yellow; White hands; shading, zodiac symbols and flames are in complementaries

The Seven of Wands shows that the harmony of the previous card is now being further strengthened by a huge central Wand held by a third hand from below. This additional support does, however, throw a disruption of sorts into things, while it gains its new equilibrium. During this period an additional struggle begins while things are quickly sorted out as the two lots of three Wands come to grips with the third powerful force. The Alchemical association of this card is the Third stage, putrefaction, which is likened to a rebirth. Again quoting from the Golden Tripod:

At the end of the world, the world shall be judged by Fire and all those things that God has made of nothing shall by Fire be reduced to ashes and from the ashes the Phoenix is to produce her young. For in the ashes slumbers a true and tartaric substance, which, being dissolved, will enable us to open the strongest bolt of the royal chamber. After the conflagration, there shall be formed a new heaven and a new earth and the new man will be nobler in his glorified state than he was before ...

The clouds now have joined at the bottom of the card obscuring the wands from what is below while this 'new heaven and earth' is being formed.

The God-name of Netzach of Atziluth is YHVH Tzabaoth (meaning 'Lord of Armies'), which has carried over from Gnosticism, and tells that Tzaboath was one of the seven archons who created the Universe. It is the affirmation of the battle and supremacy of this force and hence its title of Victory. Issiah 6: l–3 tells us that the whole earth is for the glory of YHVH Tzaboath. From this we can deduce that a Victory here is a Victory over the flesh and a triumph of the Spirit.

The part of the Ruach that is linked with Netzach is our Desire nature. This is also the cleansing and purification process in which man must do battle and win over his earthy nature. On a wider scale this Sephiroth when applied directly to the soul nature, deals with the instruction of the Soul (this is applicable both during life and after death), and the beginning of the teaching and learning process. The Soul is forced to question his nature and his mortality for the flesh cannot enter the kingdom of God. The first angel governing this card is Mahashiah, who is titled 'Seeking safety from trouble', which indicates refuge from trouble. The second angel is Lahahel who is titled 'Praiseworthy, Declaring', showing one who is free from blame for any actions taken whereas the former angel is not so sure of himself and his tasks. Both relate to safety from struggle and effort.

The Sephirotic planetary association is Venus in a Fire Element which characterises difficulty in restraining one's affections, but bodes well on matters of finance; a strong attraction of people who will gravitate to the energies in this sign; amusements and pleasure of sorts; an appreciation for the arts and travelling; a lack of staying power in projects; a certain amount of opposition, yet the courage to continue on is also indicated, though this is temporary.

Mars in Leo is a very powerful combination, characterising a competitive spirit in life, love, work and creativity; daring, an adventurer, impulsive, a large amount of strength and courage. It also shows the patronage of people in powerful positions and being treated as one of them. There is much enthusiasm here plus the stamina to initiate almost any project. Extravagance is usually expressed in most activities; strong individualism and independence. In areas of work one would run roughshod over co-workers and always in a hurry. With love a 'Mars in Leo person' will rush into relationships, be very passionate and when it is not reciprocated suffer a very hurt pride. There is danger of taking hurt and aggression out on others.

Divination

Netzach of Yod shows the taste of victory, something just reached but without the chance to enjoy it yet. Here we have the problem solver. A person who is inundated with problems and handles them with relative ease, even under the most adverse difficulty. Possible victory, depending in the energy exercised, courage and valour. The additional wand brings direction in one's intent, therefore progress. However, one can drive too hard for what is wanted only feeling battle weary at the end of the road. Hard-working and often winning; many pressures and obstacles along the way. Energy problems are indicated and much effort in motivating others to co-operate. In financial matters there is a strain and one may suffer from impulsive spending. Relationships have to be worked at and could be too argumentive to cope with; usually there are many against one; family needs are pressing along with the demands of friends and work colleagues. When getting this card remember 'survival of the fittest'. Difficulties can be overcome however if one is persistent. Responsibility, intense concentration. If ill-dignified one has opposition, quarrelling, difference and pretension.

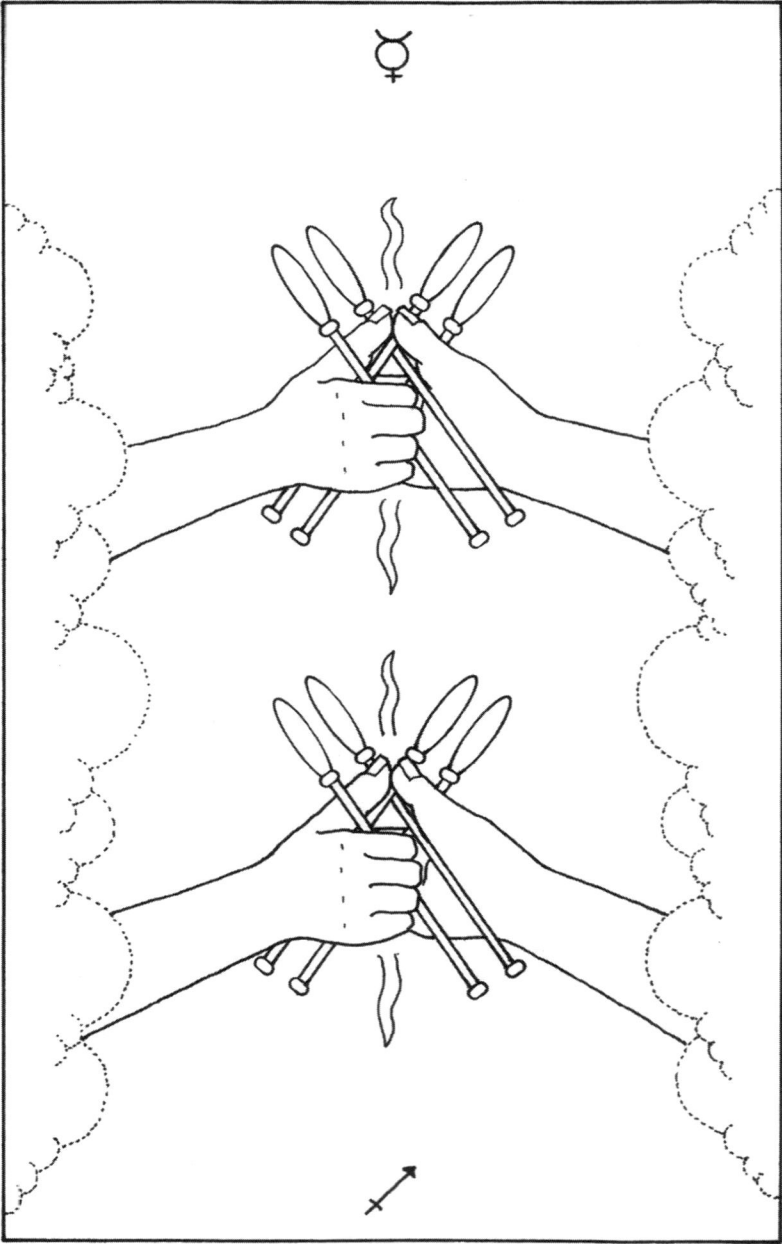

Eight of Wands

Title	:	The Lord of Swiftness
Element	:	Fire
Force	:	Yod
Alchemic	:	First Stage Fermentation—Introducing of substance
Kabbalistic World	:	Atziluth
Sephirah	:	Hod
Holy Name	:	Elohim Tzabaoth
Soul	:	Ruach—reason
Planet of Sephirah	:	Mercury
Angels	:	Nethhiah, Heeiah
Astrological	:	Mercury in Sagittarius, zero–ten degrees
Colours	:	Wands Primrose Yellow; background Deep Blue Hidden with Red; Clouds Translucent Deep Violet Purple; White hands; shading, zodiac symbols and flames complementaries

The Eight of Wands shows four Wands in two sets of hands. Although each set shows perfection in its own right, there is no real connecting force to unite them, resembling a dynamo which produces magnetic and electrical energy from whence the card derives its name of Swiftness.

The Alchemical theme of this card is part of the Fermentation process. The clouds have now separated from the bottom again and span the whole sides of the card. This shows that the obscurity of the previous card is cleared now and a separation is forming depicted by the two sets of hands and wands. Energy is formed in this fermentation process and with the interaction between above and below an electrical or magnetic charge builds. Hence an invisible substance is introduced and transmits through matter. Communication and energy is passed between the two sets of wands, where the energies rise and fall with the transmission of energy and light. To quote from the Emerald Tablet again:

> *It rises from earth to heaven and comes down again from heaven to earth and thus acquires the power of the realities above and the realities below. In this way you will acquire the glory of the whole world and all darkness will leave you.*

The God-name of Hod of Atziluth is Elohim Tzabaoth ('Lord of Hosts'). Tzabaoth in the previous card was associated to 'Armies' by the Golden Dawn and in this card the word is interpreted as 'Hosts'. Elohim is from the Pillar of Severity and YHVH from the Pillar of Mercy. The distinction between the two is more than Masculine versus Feminine; it is Hermaphrodital. Hod is on the pillar of Severity, headed by the 'Great Mother' in Binah and as such cannot be anything else but a strong feminine nature. The Name 'Tzabaoth' is a very powerful one and had to be split into two divisions. Netzach took the Martial sense and Hod took the resulting framework which was greatly increased from Tiphareth. The concept of 'Splendour' is a result of the expansionist policies of Netzach. Tiphareth was 'Beauty' and this was coveted by Netzach who conquered it then left its beauty intact. The 'Beauty' now is reverted to the name 'Splendour' displaying pomp and circumstance and being only an outward reflection of its former self. This is the exploitation of Beauty and to a certain extent natural growth from a state of innocence, a concept of survival necessary to obtain results.

Part of the Ruach that is related here is the faculty of Reason. Jung says of this:

> *Reason, always seeking to avoid what is an unbearable antinomy, takes its stand exclusively on one side or the other and convulsively seeks to hold fast to the values it has once chosen. It will continue to do this so long as human reason passes for an 'immutable substance', thereby precluding any symbolical view of it. But reason is only relative and eventually checks itself in its own antinomies. It too is only a means to an end, a symbolical expression for a transitional stage in the path of development.*

The first angel governing this card is Nethhiah, who is titled the 'Enlarger'. This relates to an expansionist concept due to a need of self-protection. The second angel is Heeiah, who is titled 'Hearer in Secret'. The two concepts show growth in communications, but in secret.

The Sephirotic Planetary association to the Eight of Wands is Mercury in a Fire Element, which produces quick communications on a variety of different levels (especially on subjects of Philosophy, Religion or Science). Short journeys are also indicated and finance is indicated in short-term business projects.

Mercury in Sagittarius is a combination of speed and efficiency, especially through any form of communication. There is an inclination towards any form of metaphysical study especially through fields such as writing. This also shows things happening fast, but at a late or intermediate stage in a project. There is good support among one's peers and possibly a co-authorship in a metaphysical subject may eventuate. This person can stand back from any issue and look from a broader perception understanding is believed only through intellectual figuring. Beliefs can be fanatical unless many perspectives are studied. The law and 'word' can be taken too literally.

Divination

Hod of Yod is rapid expansion of surrounding energy. Love of freedom and open spaces are also shown. Electricity, radio/phone communications, transmission, depending on the dignity, enthusiasm, quick mind, logic, self-awareness. Most issues are dealt with swiftly. Under material matters this card quite often represents the ideas/inspiration stage before the planning stage. Frequent travel and many activities in one's private life, with much communication, social involvement, sport and recreation. In areas of employment it may be temporary. If looking for employment, one will be employed soon, but not necessarily where expected. Often wishful thinking. Popularity and many friends. If you have a partner all is going well. If you are single, no one on the horizon yet. Everyone else is rushing around too much to notice each other, although lots of interaction socially. In matters of health, the etheric electrical body (nadis) may need treatment; try acupuncture. If ill-dignified, this card shows violence, insolence, repression, eloquence yet untrustworthiness, theft and robbery and the use of the media. This force has been applied too suddenly, with a very rapid rush but too quickly passed and expended.

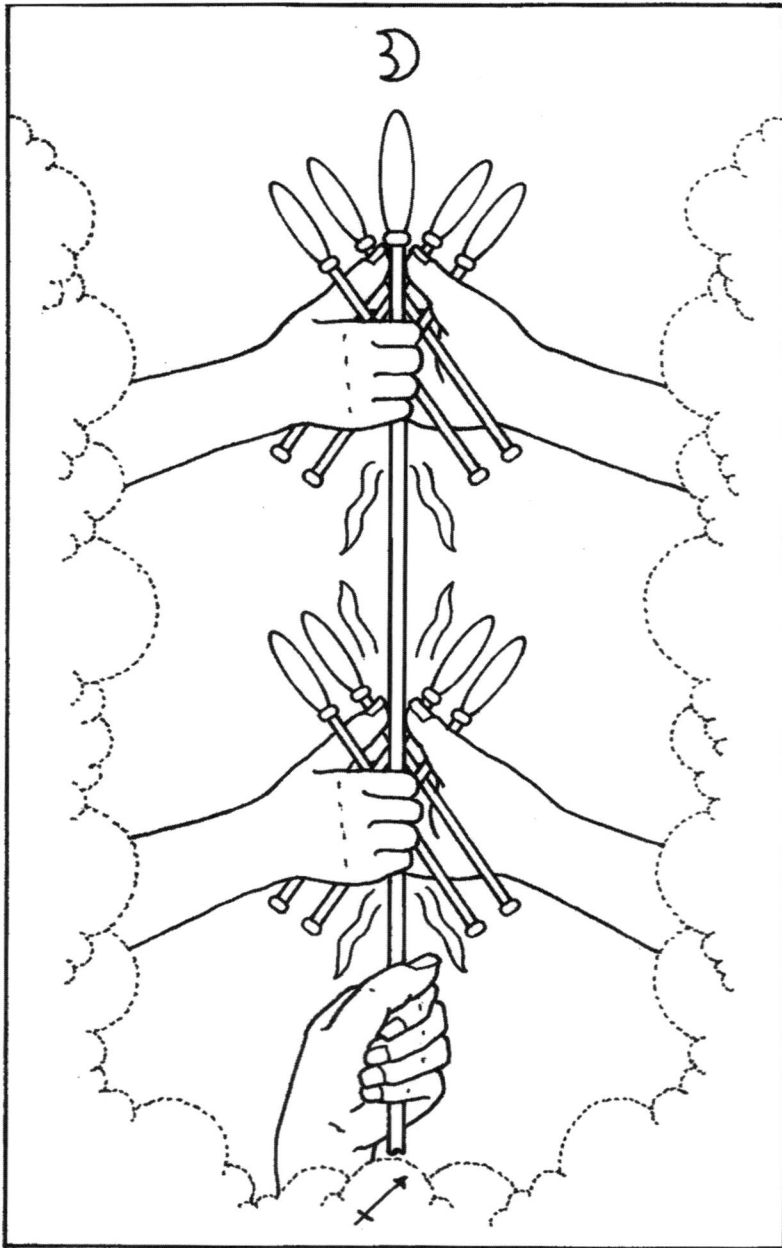

Nine of Wands

Title	:	Lord of Great Strength
Element	:	Fire
Force	:	Yod
Alchemic	:	Second stage Fermentation—Fermenting
Kabbalistic World	:	Atziluth
Sephirah	:	Yesod
Holy Name	:	Shaddai El Chai
Vision	:	Nephesch
Planet of Sephirah	:	Moon
Angels	:	Irthel, Sehaiah
Astrological	:	Moon in Sagittarius, ten–twenty degrees
Colours	:	Wands Pale Silvery Blue; background Deep Blue Hidden with Red; Clouds Dark Indigo Blue; White hands; shading, zodiac symbols and flames complementaries

A fifth hand issues from the bottom clouds which have again joined from the sides. This hand holds an additional large shaft bridging the gap between the two sets of four wands each held by two hands. These upper hands do not struggle to grasp the central wand and they give not only support but additional strength.

Alchemically we have the second stage of fermentation, where a cooking heat produces gases which again obscure the fermentation which transforms the matter below where sulphur and mercury are developed, through the influence of the powers above. The Sun and Moon work in equal balance strengthening and reinforcing the alchemic process.

The God-Name for Yesod of Atziluth is Shaddai El Chai ('Mighty Living One'). By Association to the genitals on the body of man in the Microcosm its higher association in Atziluth is fertilisation, procreation and generation. All of these lead towards a growing embryo, no matter what level it is on. The Atziluthic emanations are of things on a vast and grand scale and do not deal with the Microcosm. The entire concept is the creation and formation of a new era, or generation that works in with grand karmic plans for major groups and countries.

The Kabbalistic part of the Soul dealt with here is the Nephesch. When allied to the psychological, it is the Unconscious, where Automotive reflexes are housed. Jung considers the Unconscious as an area which has unlimited Wisdom and which is closed to us in our waking state. This is because the Unconscious in the Microcosm of the Collective Unconscious is the Macrocosm. It is from this line that man has the ability to adapt and grow through the ages. There is a strong instinctive urge here to release or contact the Kundaline energy stored within us, so that the normal internal blocks to our waking state are removed and we can then advance into the state of Super consciousness.

The first angel governing this card is Irthel, who is titled the 'Deliverer', which relates to a promise being made and kept. The second is Sehaiah, who is titled 'Taker away of Evils'. Both these titles refer to banishing negative activity through some form of help, hence this card's title, 'The Lord of Great Strength'.

The Sephirotic planetary association is the Moon in a Fire element, implying impulsiveness and volatility with a definite aggressive and martial attitude. Some form of authoritative position and a certain degree of publicity is indicated together with a certain degree of secrecy, a good degree of psychic perception and a love of the arts and an active love of exercise.

The Moon in Sagittarius characterises mental stimulation through speech and communications; a spellbinding orator and teacher who can use his or her gifts intuitively; an ability to see the outcome of situations; receptivity to religion, mysticism and the occult and a large part of that energy will come through that particular framework; faith; adaptation. There is a certain amount of restlessness here and a fondness for travel and life in foreign countries. The Moon in this position is powerful but not for any long duration. Embarking on new adventures; publishing and writing.

Divination

Yesod of Yod relates to strength and power in the initial stages. Pressure is bought to bear on a person and as a result of this the individual concerned summons up enough strength to push away the obstacle or person who is applying the pressure. A strong steady force that cannot be shaken; scientific analysis; more than one occupation attracts; personal power; resources gained; investment in oneself; unopposed; broadened spectrum; aggressiveness in communication; inspiring. In matters of love, fertility; sharing activities; balance in romantic relationships; lasting partnerships. In work and career matters, gaining ground; physical and mental energy absorbed into work; getting on well with co-workers; reaching ambitions and goals; the negative dispelled before it can do harm. Old ties and issues will be shed; a time of getting out with others and outdoor activities; perseverance to win over life's difficulties; water sports; many friends. If ill-dignified one still has success but with strife. Victory before apprehension and fear are also indicated. Procrastination after success can allow matters to slip back. Over-enthusiasm and vision, so that one may feel let down by the reality of the matter.

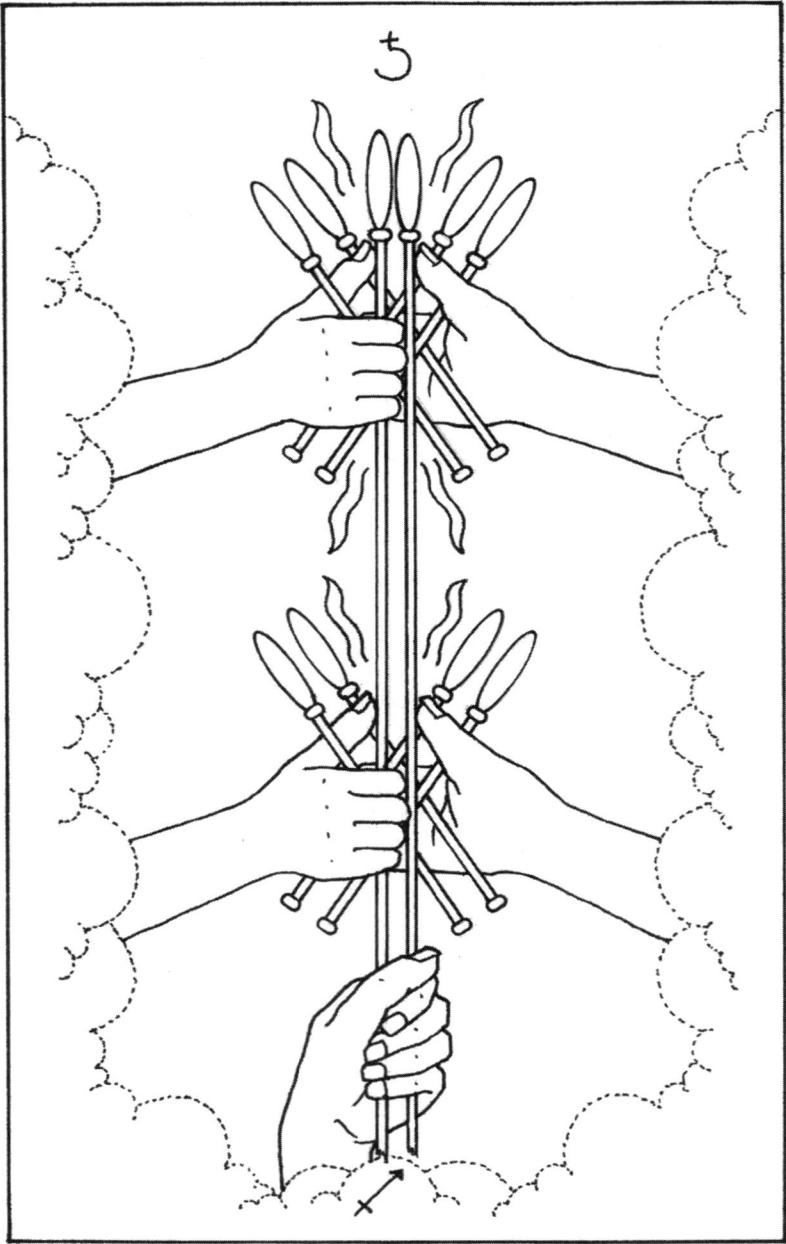

Ten of Wands

Title	:	The Lord of Oppression
Element	:	Fire
Force	:	Yod
Alchemic	:	Third stage Fermentation—Heat
Kabbalistic World	:	Atziluth
Sephirah	:	Malkuth
Holy Name	:	Adoni ha-Aretz
Soul	:	Nephesch
Planet of Sephirah	:	Saturn
Angels	:	Rayayel, Evamel
Astrological	:	Saturn in Sagittarius, twenty–thirty degrees
Colours	:	Wands Darkest Indigo; Background Deep Blue with Hidden Red; Clouds Vivid Yellow; White hands; complementaries for shading, flames and zodiac symbols

The Ten of Wands is very similar to the previous card with an additional Wand to reinforce its centre. This additional wand, however, brings in too much strength and force, over-extending the energies available. The hands from each side of the card are prevented from clasping the central wands due to the bulk, making the entire situation ready to break. This pressure is also likened to too much force from above rushing to below through the central wands, causing a great deal of movement and impetus to a new cycle that this card precedes. To those not ready to move into a new state, however, the influence would feel like oppression. Hence, the name Lord of Oppression. Alchemically we have the third stage of fermentation which is an intense build-up of heat. If at this stage the vessel's lid was opened you would have an explosion of energy emitted. The pressure in the vessel is extremely intense with all matter within oppressed so much that it is forced to give up its last virtues to the transformation. Hermes, the Father of all Philosophers, discloses in his 'Book of the Seven Treatises' that fermentation whitens the confection, hinders combustion and altogether retards the flux of the tincture, consoles bodies and amplifies unions. He explains that this is the key to the end of the work.

The God-Name of Malkuth of Atziluth is Adoni ha-Aretz ('My Lord' or 'Master of Earth'). There is some confusion here as to the meaning of the 'earth' being the element, or the planet, or the earthy plane. We must consider though that we are dealing with the world of Atziluth and, as such this does not directly refer to the planet (for that is Assiah), but more in line with 'earth the element' at the Atziluthic level, for this is the first tangible element of the creation process. It is nourishment of matter, through a spiritual process, so that it can grow and develop. This nourishment works directly through the Incorporeal Elements to the Corporeal Elements so that any growth must be in a controlled framework.

The Kabbalistic Soul related to Malkuth is still the Nephesch, but is the lower form which we have called the Lower Nephesch. The best explanation of this I think is to ally the Lower Nephesch with the Etheric Body which is a combination of both matter and energy.

The first angel of this card is Rayayel, who is titled 'Expectation' and the second is Evamel who is titled 'Patience'. The two concepts relate to waiting patiently for things to turn in a more positive direction.

Saturn in Sagittarius relates to restructuring one's beliefs, especially in the religious field, where strong support and many friends are made. This is only done however, through a great deal of personal effort. There is some financial gain but a delay in receiving it. One-time Golden Dawn member A.E. Waite associated a man carrying a heavy burden with this card and in some ways this is quite correct, but patience must be utilised as well for success. Saturn in Sagittarius characterises those who are serious, methodical, conservative and apprehensive. Any form of authority is seen as oppressive and judgemental; scepticism and cynicism.

Divination

Malkuth of Yod shows restriction in getting things done due to the influence of matter and difficulty in movement. Apart from the above: strength too strong to be controlled that it ends up controlling the one who originally sought help; it is a force that is cruel and overbearing but applied to selfish and material ends; it is ill-will, levity, malice, slander, obstinacy; a waste, self-sacrifice without a good result, incredible opposing forces, blindness to an easier way, violence, exhaustion. Something must be dealt with and not brushed aside. An individual would appear too pushy, violent or oppressive to others. Relationships can get very violent; anger, rage and psycho-trauma. Children become uncontrollable. On a positive side, however, the Ten of Wands can represent power which is created through an individual or situation that can be turned to greater things. Great drive, willpower and force to achieve what has to be done. In matters of health: physical exhaustion, spinal injuries. Financially, conditions can weigh one down. Fear in taking a further step; frustration; burden of authority and duties; great anger building up within. The task here is to break from tunnel vision or a locked-in direction and look at different approaches to one's problems; enlarge your vision and understanding and learn to use the tremendous energies which are available around you and within you.

Ace of Cups

Title	:	Root of the Powers of Water
Element	:	Water
Force	:	Heh
Alchemic	:	Great Mother—the menstrum—Azoth
Kabbalistic World	:	Briah
Sephirah	:	Kether
Holy Name	:	Metatron—Prince of Countenances
Vision	:	Union with God
Planet of Sephirah	:	Neptune
Archangel	:	Gabriel
Myth	:	Holy Grail
Colours	:	Blue Cup and letter Heh; Orange background, lotus pods and Lotuses; white clouds and hand and fountain water; the sea is white with reflections of blue from the cup and letter Heh

This card is under the influence of Kether of Heh, the feminine energy that has just established polarity in an attempt to renew itself through the actions of the fountain in the card. The Ace of Cups is like the Fountain of Life in its actions, with the Four Rivers (representing the Spirit of Azoth) gushing from it. Mathers says:

The Ace of Cups is of Egyptian origin, which can be more easily seen in the Spanish Tarot. The figure, like an M placed over the Cup is all that remains of the Egyptian twin Serpents which originally deco-rated the cup below it. The M in this instance is not inverted (which is the old method of association) but placed above the Cup and it represents the Waters of Creation in the first chapter of Genesis. The old inverted M symbol shows the impurity of the quintessence has been contaminated by matter, but placed above the Cup it is a symbol of power which receives and modifies.

The entire card shows the Creation myth from the perspective of the first six days of Genesis. The letter Heh above the Cup symbolises the Great Supernal Mother from which all things come and to which all things return. The actual shape of the Cup can be likened to the Tree of Life and also the symbols of the Tattva of Apas, representing Water, shown by the lunar crescent of the Cup itself. The Vayu Tattva, representing Air, joins the cup to its foundation, the triangle, which represents the Tejas Tattva of Fire. This entire concept is one of transmutation. There are three Lotuses and four lotus pods representing Spirit descending into matter.

This card is associated with the myth of the Holy Grail. The aim of those seeking the grail is spiritual attainment and earthly perfection. The Grail symbolises divine life, love, wisdom and understanding. The path to the Grail is the journey of the soul in its trials and ordeals, which are depicted in the many myths which tell of such journeys. One well-known legend is that of King Arthur. The Grail is like a universal magnet drawing mankind to its ultimate goal. It is also the fountain of life, as spoken of above.

Kether of Briah is exemplified by the name of the Archangel Metatron (said to be from the Latin 'metator'—a guide or measurer), called 'Prince of Countenance'. In Hebraic literature this archangel has many functions. He has been associated with Sandalphon, in Malkuth and also as the man Enoch, made by God into the spirit Metatron. When he was allowed to enter heaven he was given thirty-six wings and became God's right hand, eclipsing all other archangels. He was the angel of deliverance and also the angel of Death and the teacher of the souls of children in Paradise.

The Spiritual Experience or Vision of Kether is the Union with God. To a certain extent this is self-explanatory though in this union with our Creator it is still within our own framework of existence and as such it will be coloured by our own interpretation. It is a point where there are few boundaries and where there are boundaries, they do not matter because it shows complete control over the flesh and matter. In many respects this association is identical to what happened to Enoch/Metatron, Elijah, Christ and a few others. It is the bodily ascension of man or woman into Heaven itself.

The Sephirotic planetary association is Neptune in a Water Element. Neptune in this element has been described as the 'World of the Astral Voyager' for its focus and power. There are strong emotional feelings and attachments and a love of sensations, a willingness to share with others in need.

Alchemically, the Ace of Cups is the Lapis Exilis, the Azoth, as Thomas Vaughan describes from his 'Coelum Terrae':

In the first preparation the Chaos is blood red [Ace of Wands], because the Central sulphur is stirred up and discovered by the Philosophical Fire. In the Second it is exceedingly white and transparent like the heavens. It is … of a celestial transcendent brightness, for there is nothing upon earth like it. This fine substance is the child of the elements and it is most pure sweet virgin, for nothing yet hath been generated out of her. But if at any time she breeds it is by the fire of Nature, for that is her husband. She is no animal, no vegetable, no mineral, neither is she extracted out of them all, for she is the mother of them. [Shown by the letter Heh] … She yields to nothing but love for her end is generation and that was never yet performed by violence.

Vaughan goes on to talk about how she gives out the Virgin's Milk, which is the blood from her heart and thus presents the secret crystal. He describes her appearance as:

In the shape or figure she resembles a stone and yet is no stone, for they call her the White Gum and Water of the Sea, Water of Life, Most Pure and Blessed Water; … [This refers to the waters of the fountain in the card flowing from the cup into the sea]. … They call her also their twofold Mercury and Azoth, begotten by the influences of two globes, celestial and terrestrial. Moreover, they affirm her to be of that nature that no fire can destroy her …

In numerology the three lotuses and four lotus pods come to the number seven which is considered the lowliest of numbers. The gematrical value of seven is DG which is 'to multiply'. The lotuses are lowering, signifying immortality and spirituality. The seed pods allude to creation which will eventually burst new seeds which are the essence of new life.

The element of this card is Water, and its title, 'Root of the Powers of Water'. The water element is the sustainer of life and is considered feminine, passive and has Luna associated. The Psychological nature of those under the influence of the water element is one which brings deep emotion whether for love or hate. They operate mainly through instinct and intuition, as water rules the unconscious mind. These people are often psychic, dreamers, clairvoyants. Water people flow in their natures and are very adaptable.

Divination

The Cup represents productiveness, fertility, beauty, pleasure and happiness, a complete change in one's emotional state; creativity pouring forth from Kether (the Divine), love, joy. Negatively aspected it can show a complete break or change from one's chosen direction. The beginning of new emotional interests, celebration, joy, wonderful news. Deep yearnings of the soul; letting go of emotional waste; gaining consciousness; receiving light and understanding. From a personal perspective the Ace of Cups depicts pure happiness; trusting one's feelings; enjoyment of life; and shows the opportunity to lift off karma. In material matters this card is not very influential. It is more the hopes and wishes of such things rather than the reality of achieving them. In travel it refers to overseas travel and in some cases, depending on the surrounding cards, perpetual travel. In communication there is good interaction, love and joy. In matters of learning it can be effortless as understanding comes naturally. Environmental matters show peace and meditation and retreat. Spiritually an unconscious yearning and need to touch one's spiritual self. Work and employment issues bring good news and times of happiness with fellow workers. In partnerships or marriage there is union and love.

Two of Cups

Title	:	Lord of Love
Element	:	Water
Force	:	Heh
Alchemic	:	First Stage Conjunction—union of opposites
Kabbalistic World	:	Briah
Sephirah	:	Chokmah
Holy Name	:	Raziel
Vision	:	Vision of God
Planet of Sephirah	:	Uranus/Zodiac
Angels	:	Aiael; Chabeioh
Astrological	:	Venus in Cancer, zero–ten degrees
Colours	:	Background Heliotrope; Front Dolphin facing left is Silver and water cascading from it also; Dolphin facing right is Gold as is also the water cascading from it; Cups Light Sky Blue; water from lotus soft Bluish Grey, but sea below a mixture of Soft Bluish Grey, Silver and Gold; Lotuses, plant and astrological symbols and shading complementary colours to the cups and background. White Hand

The Two of Cups represents Chokmah of Heh, the Wisdom of the Great Mother, Aima. The energy of the previous card has now been polarised even further, as shown by the two dolphins of gold and silver that taint the pure white brilliance of the water into silver and gold streams, as it cascades off the dolphins. The dolphins are Argent and Or, representing the positive forces of the Sun and the negative forces of the Moon in juxtaposition, which is harmony and pleasure of the masculine and feminine united. The dolphins, together with the stem of the lotus plant form an emblem ascribed to Ceres who symbolized the sea and love. The dolphins represent the power of water and the soul's journey to truth and wisdom and act here as the axis mundi of the Supernal.

The two lotuses are the upper and lower forces (worlds) united by the stem of growth through which the sap of life rises from the waters below and transmutes at the top through the lotus pouring forth the Waters of Life. They are also a symbol of the Divine Source, spirituality, immortality.

Alchemically, we have here the first stage of conjunction which is the union of opposites. This is depicted by the different natures of the Gold and Silver waters. The Gold water becomes the male sulphur in the chalice and the Silver water becomes the female quicksilver in the chalice. They then pour into the sea which is the virgin's milk, or otherwise known as the Blood of the Grail. There they unite where the Mercurial water forms towards the philosophic gold.

Chokmah of Briah is the archangel Raziel, sometimes called Ratziel ('Secret of God' or 'angel of mysteries') and author of the book of secrets 'wherein all celestial and earthy knowledge is stored'. We are told in a targum (or rabbinical explanation) of Ecclesiastes 10:20 that Raziel stood each day on Mount Horeb and proclaimed the secrets of men to all mankind. His function is to give knowledge to mankind in the hope that it would gradually be understood as Wisdom and eventually be called upon for all men and women to live by.

The Spiritual Experience or Vision of Chokmah is the Vision of God, face-to-face. This experience is initially in accordance with our belief structure but as we become more aware of the experience it transcends beliefs and limitations set by man. It is the recognition of consciousness in its purest form with no distortion. Jung said of this concept:

> The 'seeing of reality' clearly refers to the Mind as the Supreme reality. In the West, however, the unconscious is considered to be a fantastic reality. The 'Seeing of the Mind' implies self liberation. This means psychologically, that the more weight we attach to the unconscious process the more we detach ourselves from the world of desires and of separated opposites and the nearer we draw to the state of unconsciousness with all its qualities of oneness, indefiniteness and timelessness ...

The Sephirotic association is Uranus in a Water Element. This is an instance of extreme sensitivity that must be channelled effectively. If the channel is too concentrated then problems occur as too much power and energy are flowing in one narrow direction. There needs to be a spreading out or sharing of the load, or framework from which Uranus in a water Element operates. When this is done the pressure is then released and the energy expenditure on the mental and physical capabilities is more easily handled.

The first angel governing this card is Aiael, who is titled 'Delights of the Sons of Men'. This is a strong indication of sampling the pleasures of life through strong sexual pleasures. The second Angel Chabeioh, 'Most Liberal Giver' is not much different except that he does not confine his bounties to the flesh alone, but for the spirit as well and helps the former angel in this respect by stabilising its influence in a more general concept. Both of these meanings however do show pleasure and love.

Venus in Cancer shows deep affection and emotions through a domestic framework of love and understanding. There are, however, some obstacles to be overcome, possibly due to outside interference on any harmonious situation by one or more parties. In some instances there is a difficulty of living in the real world as this planet in this sign show the emotions leading the mind: the 'dreamer'. There is a strong desire for peace and harmony and completion through uniting with a partner. There is a sense of enchantment, beauty and love. There is a deep need to establish a conservative approach with a strong set of values and standards by which one operates.

Divination

Chokmah of Heh relates to marriage, home, pleasure and family. Grace and an outgoing response, beauty and a happy outlook on life; domesticity; freedom from anxiety about material security; love and affection; celebration; support of friends and family gatherings; fraternal love and support; harmony and balance; attunement to one's inner nature and discovering the self on different levels. In matters of education there are interests in writing, poetry, love and intellectual pursuits. Anxiety is displayed when one meets the disapproval of others. Sincerity in all matters personal, integrity in all matters professional. Good health; pleasant surroundings. Regarding marriage and romance, usually this card portrays friendship linking up on a higher spiritual level, but at times is will portray marriage and a honeymoon. If turned up for questions on separation and divorce, these issues will be settled quietly, but sometimes imply a uniting of the couple on a different level. There may be financial gain through a partnership or estate. Negatively influenced emotions can be very intense and can be misdirected towards those who will misuse you.

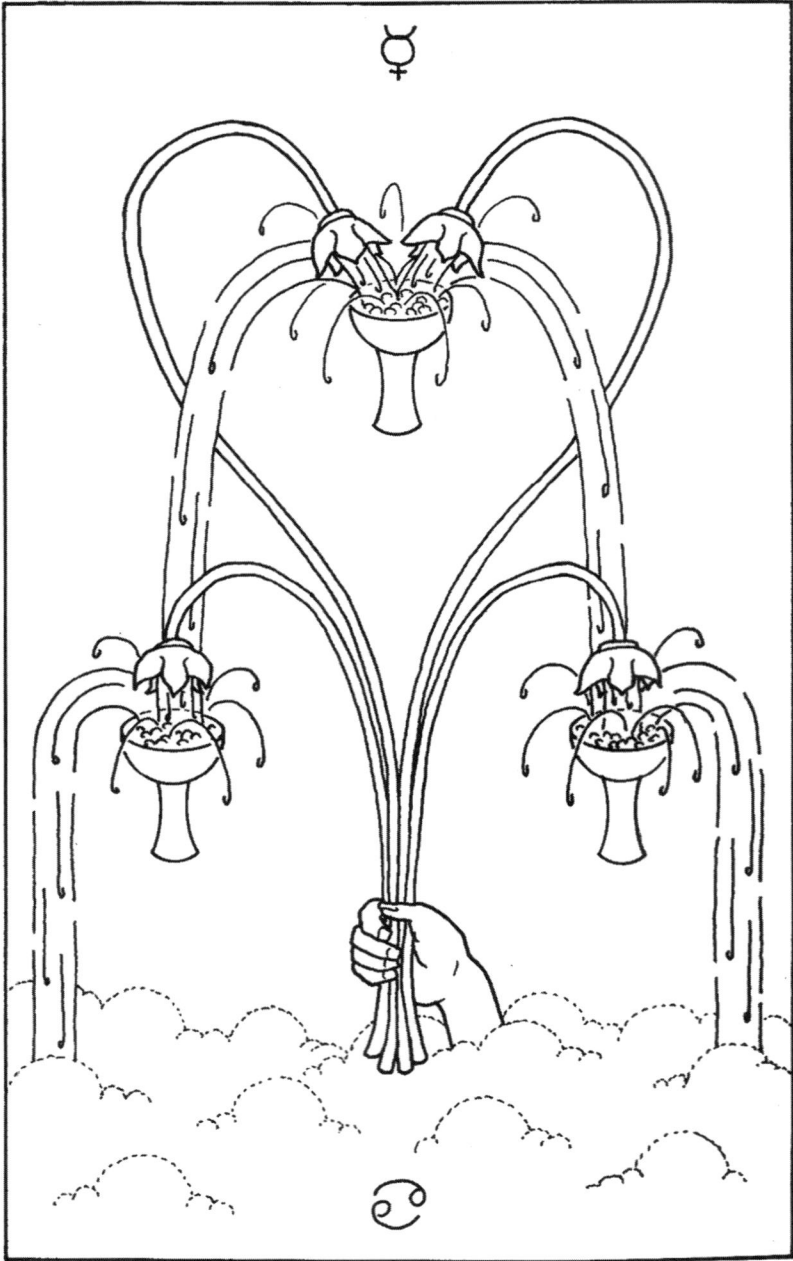

Three of Cups

Title	:	Lord of Abundance
Element	:	Water
Force	:	Heh
Alchemic	:	Second Stage Conjunction—impregnation
Kabbalistic World	:	Briah
Sephirah	:	Binah
Holy Name	:	Tzaphkiel
Vision	:	Vision of Sorrow
Planet of Sephirah	:	Saturn
Angels	:	Raphael; Yebamaiah
Astrological	:	Mercury in Cancer, ten–twenty degrees
Colours	:	Soft lavender Cups; Heliotrope background; Shading, astrological symbols, Lotuses and Plant complementary colours to the cups and background; Water White with shadings of translucent blackish Red from Binah. Hand White

In the previous card one is introduced to dualism in polarity but in this card we have the third and neutral concept being shown through the third cup. It is part of the other two extremes but meets it on middle ground bringing out the best of the positive and negative shown by the triangular formation of the Cups, for the triangle is analogous to Binah.

From the mud concealed within the sea (waters) below, nourishment is drawn up through the lotus plant to pour forth from the flowers. This quintessence pours forth into the other two cups where it overflows, cascading back to the sea where it is mixed again to recommence its cycle in the next card. This depicts a continuous nourishment and regeneration, where the elixirs are joined and mixed, only to produce a third elixir. The stems of the plant form the shape of a heart, which is the prime regulator of life.

Alchemically this is the impregnation and second stage conjunction, which can be better described as conjugium, which is copulation and the union of the man and wife in flesh; on another level, union of Soul and Spirit. This has also been described in three other ways: union of the spirit and earth; union of the ferment and the stone; union of the medicine and of the subject. Theophrastus states, however, that as the red man approaches the white woman by means of the water, the conjunction then is the copulation of congealed spirit with the dissolved body. The man then renders her fruitful.

In numerology we will also see within this card the twelve zodiac energies through the calculation of the three cups and four lotuses. Here Creative Will can operate.

Binah of Briah is the archangel Tzaphkiel 'Contemplation of God' and this indicates that this angel is forever watching us and nothing escapes his scrutiny. In many respects he is allied with the keeper of the records and in charge of issuing out karmic debits and credits. He is also related to the framework in which we operate and his function is to make us work through until we have completed our many tasks on the physical plane. Tzaphkiel's influence is through a bonding factor with others and he will help greatly in any group activities, especially through mystical or religious groups.

The Spiritual Experience or Vision of Binah is the Vision of Sorrow. Before the Fall, the point where souls were entrapped in matter, we were pure spirit. Now, we are trapped in the world of the senses and must go through seemingly endless incarnations before we get back to a state of Redemption and this process is where the Sorrow is recognised. Each life will be filled with certain trials and tribulations and the Higher Self must experience all these throughout the soul's journey back up Jacob's ladder. It is the growth we need to experience before reaching the point where no more incarnations will be needed.

The Sephirotic Planetary association is Saturn in a Water element. This is really not a good position for Saturn because of the constant changes and obstacles with the possibility of some of those changes being violent and sudden. Because Saturn is a planet of changes the aspect of it in a Water element shows it to be almost in a constant state of flux. In some situations this is good and for others it is negative, depending whether one wants stability or change. The constant change, though, does take the pressure off, especially if one is moving.

The first angel governing this card is Rahael, who is titled 'Beholding All' and the second is Yebamaiah, who is titled 'Producing All by his Word'. Both of these concepts relate to additional growth through which All is revealed.

Mercury in Cancer influences potentiality, genius and intuition and brings all these concepts out in the individual at the same time. It shows an easy-going attitude to life but with 'one's head in the clouds', so to speak. It also indicates that some of the inspirations and gifts are too scattered to have a chance to develop correctly. A firm system or structure is needed to help guide these types of energies into a practical basis. Restlessness leaves little need to settle in one place.

Divination

The Three of Cups relates to Binah of Heh or the Understanding of Heh, plenty, hospitality, eating, drinking, celebrating. This card relates to abundance, success, pleasure, sensuality, good luck emotionally, bounty and harvest. There is a great inclination to socialize and impress the concept 'my home is your home'. Reunions; group activities; good education; social conditioning; job satisfaction and self-expression; acquiring specialized skills and knowledge; good memory. In relationships this alludes mainly to friendships and happiness. On a one-to-one basis there may be conflicting emotions as there is a third party always involved. Pregnancy, sexual union, continuance of a relationship. Versatility in handling money and business; fortunes are attracted; overseas travel; generally abundance in all matters. Health problems could be nervous indigestion. If ill-dignified one has superficiality in all of the above; over emotionality which exhausts one and damages health; over-indulgence. Circumstance may fall short of one's expectations; goals not completely reached; underestimation.

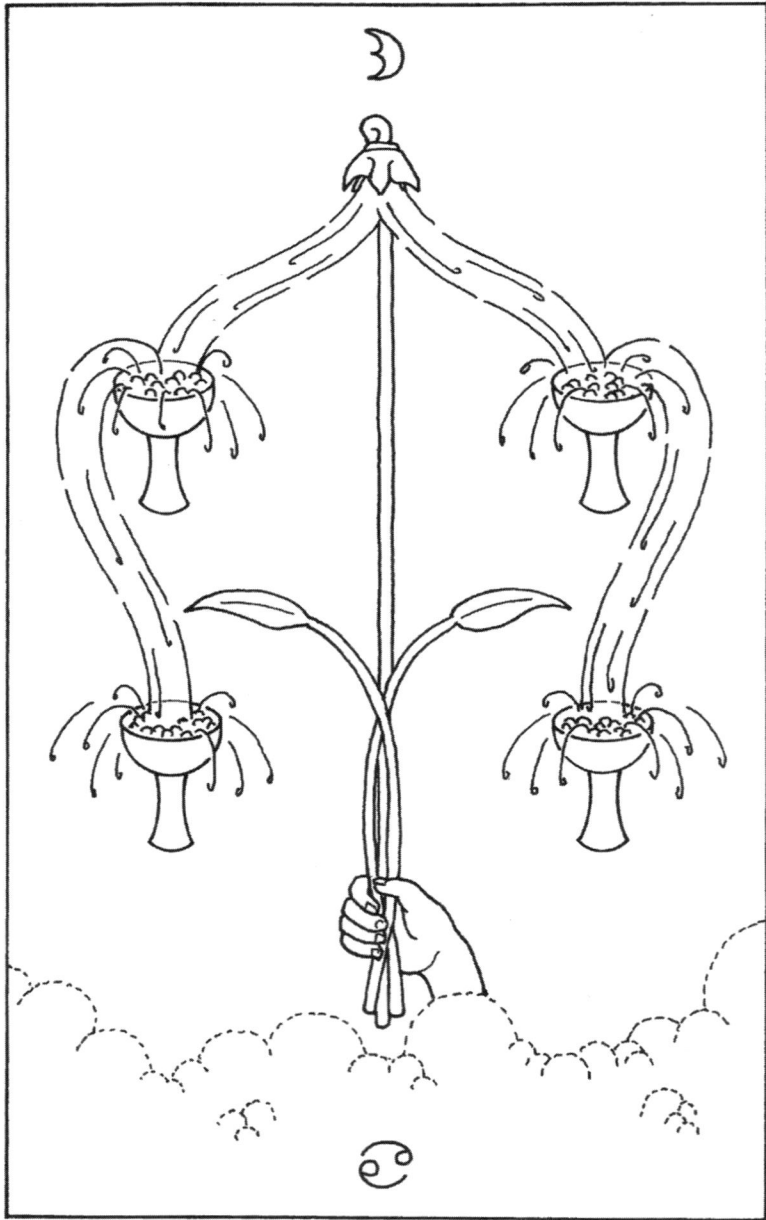

Four of Cups

Title	:	Lord of Blended Pleasure
Element	:	Water
Force	:	Heh
Alchemic	:	Third Stage Conjunction—blending
Kabbalistic World	:	Briah
Sephirah	:	Chesed
Holy Name	:	Tzadkiel
Vision	:	Vision of Love
Planet of Sephirah	:	Jupiter
Angels	:	Heyaiel; Mavamiah
Astrological	:	Moon in Cancer, twenty–thirty degrees
Colours	:	Silvery White Cups; Heliotrope background; complementary colours shading, astrological symbols; lotus plant and lotus; Translucent Vivid Blue Clouds; White Hand

The Four of Cups has each Cup placed so that a square is formed. The square is analogous with Chesed and the first step in the world of formation in Briah, being perfection and balance, seen also in the lotus plant which forms a cross of the four elements.

Alchemically the waters are now covered by a mist of cloud implying a distilling and purifying process in operation. These waters are blended below in a conjunction only to be again distilled over from the lotus where they are separated again into the separate cups ready for the next stage. Such repeated circulation over the last three stages of conjunction further purified and exalted the elixir. 'Lord of Blended Pleasure' seems very appropriate when looking at the card from the above alchemic perspective. The blending also speaks of Yin and Yang energies blending together for a brief time, germinating a further stage of development.

Chesed of Briah is conveyed by the Archangel Tzadkiel or Zakiel 'Righteous of God' or 'God's Justice'. This Archangel is associated with mercy, memory and benevolence and was also a standard-bearer for Michael when he did battle with the forces of darkness. He is the angel of the Law or pattern that we must follow through our karmic destiny and one of his functions is to keep our karmic debts in line by maintaining that the wheel of cause and effect is kept turning evenly. He is the angel of purification and, as such, is a hard task master, for the tasks that he sets us are designed to purify both the body and mind and lead the soul away from its attachment to the material.

The Vision, or Spiritual experience, of Chesed is a 'Vision of Love'. The Love referred to here is of a universal kind and has a deep reverence for all living creatures. For humans it is love in the fraternal sense and shows a deep emotive response that flows through from the Soul and makes us reach out and help when and where we can. It is harmony with one's surroundings at its best. In Psalms 25: 10: 'All the Paths of Tetragrammaton are Chesed and Ameth, Mercy and Truth'.

The first angel governing this card is Heyaiel, who is titled 'Lord of the Universe'. Heyaiel has a strong link here with control or dominion over the wild beasts. The second angel is Mevamiah who is titled 'End of the Universe'. Both these titles refer to the final decanates of the Zodiac of the Golden Dawn.

The Sephirotic association is Jupiter in a Water Element, which places strength on the emotional side of things with a fine interest in the arts and travel to many distant places, though there are problems due to travel. A love of the secret mysteries is indicated. There is a great abundance of enthusiasm about any undertaking, but although there is a certain expansive quality here it bodes ill for staying power.

The Moon in Cancer is the power of love being moved by the emotions through desire; excellent social intercourse with a fondness for the finer things in life. The moon in this sign shows a great deal of adaptability, especially when dealing through an established framework or group enterprise, which will be a large influence whether it be job or social. There is a need for integration into group activities here. There is a strong need for security and belonging, harmony in family matters. These individuals are highly attuned and sensitive to undercurrents in energy fields.

Divination

Chesed of Heh relates to receiving pleasure and giving it in return. This shows happiness, swiftness, hunting for pleasure and pursuit; celebration; religious and spiritual values; cultural activities; family and environmental growth and healing; loyalty; domesticity; good luck; ease and harmony in motion; family or other obligations; stability; content; plenty; confidence; recuperation. In employment one is content to stay where it is comfortable, although there may be no growth. In business all is made safe and secure, gatherings to celebrate contracts; public dealings. In financial matters one secures funds. In relationships it refers more to friendly, comfortable, family feelings, rather than romance. If ill-dignified we have a searching for pleasure and happiness for all the wrong reasons and it implies selfish interest at the expense of others; self-indulgence; complacency; laziness. Life may be too comfortable for one to be motivated to a challenge.

Five of Cups

Title	:	Lord of Loss in Pleasure
Element	:	Water
Force	:	Heh
Alchemic	:	First Stage Sublimation—make body spiritual
Kabbalistic World	:	Briah
Sephirah	:	Geburah
Holy Name	:	Khamael
Vision	:	Vision of Power
Planet of Sephirah	:	Mars
Angels	:	Livoih; Pheheliah
Astrological	:	Mars in Scorpio, zero–ten degrees
Colours	:	Cups Primary Red; Background Sky Blue; astrological symbols, shading, lotuses and plant complementary colours to the cups and background; Clouds Translucent Vivid Red. White Hand

The Five of Cups shows no Azoth issuing out of the Lotus stems and relates to the fact that the additional Cup has, in fact, exhausted its supply of nourishment, due to its central position, which is shown by the falling lotus flowers. The peculiar outline of the Cups in fact, is that of a Cup itself, the Cup of the Zelator Adeptus Minor, the inference here being that the cup is empty. The symbol of the North depicted by the position of the cups (the apexes of two triangles meeting in the centre), represents darkness, the barren and cold. However, energy is concentrated to the central point with this symbol sustaining life.

Alchemically this is the first stage of sublimation, which is essentially the first step to make the Body spiritual. To do this, however, the solution (Mercury, Sulphur and Salt) has to be placed into a Philosophic Egg and sealed so that nothing may evaporate. This Egg is placed into heat where the contents become resolved from above. Paracelsus says:

> Stand it in Athanor until, without any addition, it begins of itself to be resolved from above, so that it looks like an island in the midst of that sea, gradually decreasing every day and at last being changed into the resemblance of blackening. This black substance is the bird which flies by night without wings, which is the first dew from heaven, with its constant influence, its ascent and descent … (Sublimation).

This results in a feeling of losing contact with the spirit, generating awareness. Geburah of Briah is the Archangel Khamael or Camael ('He who sees God') and relates to the concept of 'Divine Justice'. Khamael was an angel of battles and appeared to Jesus, to give him strength, in the garden of Gethsemane and is the angel who wrestled with Jacob. He is an angel that gives us a martial framework to achieve the most good and helps channel our destructive tendencies in this area into constructive ability. Because of this angel, we become exposed to these destructive tendencies to give us additional experience in how to cope with them. Khamael is also said to be a tester of the darker side of our nature.

The Vision or Spiritual experience here is a 'Vision of Power' which relates directly to the strength aspect of the Sephirah. New energies, knowledge and contacts, places an individual in a position to control or influence others to a large degree. This comes both on the mundane and esoteric plane and it will take a strong individual not to abuse that power. The Golden Dawn related this directly with the grade of Adeptus Major where the power of the magus is starting to manifest and grow to a strong degree as he or she contacts the forces on the subtle planes that will both help, hinder and guide the individual for the rest of his or her life.

The first angel governing this card is Livoih, who is titled 'Hastening to Hear'. This angel listens to all those who petition him. The second angel is Pheheliah and is titled 'Help from Above'. Both these angels manifest a concept of crying out for help.

The Sephirotic association, Mars in a Water Element, produces an antagonistic situation. The energetic and martial side of Mars is held back by the watery structure and restricts its movements in all directions causing a great deal of confusion and a lack of direction. This can be an explosive combination where the emotions try to take control and lash out in any direction.

Mars in Scorpio characterises a certain amount of the self-destructive principle where the strong Mars type personality is trapped in a negative emotional framework. It relates to extremism of both sensationalism and negative emotions, such as jealousy. The sex instinct is likely to give trouble here as well as it goes out of control. There is a certain amount of self-destructiveness through brooding and the harbouring of old grudges. There is also, however, a tendency for sacrifice; identity with power and self-empowerment; meeting challenges more important than attaining the challenge. On a higher vibration level the Mars in Scorpio individual can give as much as they receive.

Divination

As the Geburah of Heh, we have a Severity of the feminine concept which shows one's emotions being shut down due to disappointments and loss in emotional situations. Loss of Pleasure;

individuals who are pressured into trying to enjoy themselves in an unsuitable situation. In friendships, relationships and job prospects it shows that they are unsuitable for the querent to push ahead into. There is also a tendency for the querent to be pushed into this unsuitable framework by others and he or she will have to stand up to these people and refuse to be bullied. Empty emotional response; termination of pleasure; disappointment, sorrow; anxieties, troubles from unexpected quarters, deceit, treachery and ill-will. Hopelessness, deteriorating principles; depression; loss. Giving up something that has lost its nourishment for one. Loss of prosperity; bad karma; malpractice; superficiality.

Six of Cups

Title	:	Lord of Pleasure
Element	:	Water
Force	:	Heh
Alchemic	:	Second Stage Sublimation—Spirit be corporeal and fixed to be substantial
Kabbalistic World	:	Briah
Sephirah	:	Tiphareth
Holy Name	:	Raphael
Vision	:	Vision of Harmony
Planet of Sephirah	:	Sun
Angels	:	Nelkhal; Yeisel
Astrological	:	Sun in Scorpio, ten–twenty degrees
Colours	:	Cups Golden Sunflower Yellow; Background Sky Blue; Lotuses and Lotus plant, shading, astrological symbols complementary colours to cups and background; White Hand; and Clouds Pastel Yellow

The Six of Cups shows that the lotuses of the previous card are being regenerated, due to its Solar influence resulting in an extra cup being formed. In order to balance the Cups on the stems, the central Cup has moved to be in juxtaposition with the other additional Cups. Water is now flowing and is filling the Cups but not to overflowing as its full strength is being contained by the framework of Scorpio. There is no strain or effort as the forces harmonize and regeneration begins.

The six lotuses and leaves of the Lotus plant are likened to the gift of purity that was presented to the Virgin by the Angel Gabriel. The six cups allude to the nurturing of the Soul into Form through the hexad.

Alchemically it is the Second Stage Sublimation—*Spirit be corporeal and fixed to be substantial*. One aspect of this is when the Alchemist takes the curcubite from the place of darkness and places it in the Sun for the contents to digest from the solar rays. This is where the waters are transmuted opening up new life. Paracelsus wrote that sublimation is a very important step in the transmutation of many natural objects. Within this process is exaltation, elevation and fixation, which is, in totality, not too different from distillation. In sublimation the lower is separated from the higher and releases the spirit into the atmosphere.

The Holy Name of Tiphareth of Briah is the Archangel Raphael ('God who has healed') who is the patriarch of journeys and a teacher of sciences. In the Book of Tobit, Raphael acts as companion and guide to Tobias (Tobit's son). As healer we find that this comes through his function as one of the 'Watchers', who is one of the four angels set up to oversee all diseases and wounds of men. The Zohar tells us 'Raphael is charged to heal the earth and through him … the earth furnishes an abode of man, whom he heals of his maladies'. His general function is to guide and teach those who seek knowledge when the veil of Paroketh is removed.

The Vision or Experience of Tiphareth is through the mysteries of the Crucifixion and a vision of the harmony of things. Both these two concepts actually work in tandem with each other for the mystery of the Crucifixion is a symbol of Self-sacrifice. It is a way of entry to this Sephirah and none other will be accepted for it also requires the death of the Ego. In every aspect this is the way shown to the entrance of YHVH's Kingdom and can only come about after death and the suffering one goes through during various incarnations. Then and only then, will the harmony of things be addressed and peace comes as a new realisation dawns.

The first angel governing this card is Nelkhal, who is titled 'Thou alone'. This relates to the concept of understanding the tasks allotted to us in this incarnation and being prepared to carry them out. The second angel is Yeisel, who is titled 'Thy right hand'. Here help has arrived in our new environment. The two concepts show growth and development starting in a new context.

The Sephirotic association is the Sun in a Water element which increases the devotional characteristics and a deep awareness of the emotional nature of mankind. This can be defined as love for our higher nature and wishing to adhere to the directions it gives us. Devotion is of course a necessary asset when one goes through the process of initiation and as such, this Sephirah of Tiphareth, influenced by the Sun, breaks away the veil of mysteries so that part of that Higher nature we aspire to is revealed.

The Sun in Scorpio is transformation through regeneration and is extremely durable as it is driven by the Will and the Emotive responses. It shows a person who will work to the letter of the Law and will not step outside of the framework he or she has imposed on the self. There is a great deal of secretiveness and intuitive insight as one is able to tap into the power coming down from the Higher Self. There is a great deal of independence shown by the Sun in this Sign and a strong urge to better oneself, almost at all costs. There are strong sexual desires that arise and sometimes there is a possessiveness and jealousy that is restricting. Overall though the card shows that people can go to great heights in their relative fields.

Divination

Tiphareth of Heh relates to the beginning of happiness and enjoyment. Socially this is a time of upheaval, but in the best possible way. There is a great deal of socialising and also romance indicated here. This card relates to any form of social activity that is pleasurable by nature. A steady increase, gain and pleasure, but in their commencement only. Physical wellbeing; self-protection; forming alliances; profit; gifts; accomplishments; balance and harmony. Happiness in matters of work and relationships; rewards of past efforts; problems solved; love and compatibility; a change of fortune is forthcoming; sexuality temporarily satisfied. Diplomacy, mending bridges, temporary sacrifices for future success. If ill-dignified it brings defective knowledge, contention, strife, arising from unwarranted self-assertion and vanity. Superficial feelings in relationship; impressionability; emotional dependency. The pitfall is being too casual.

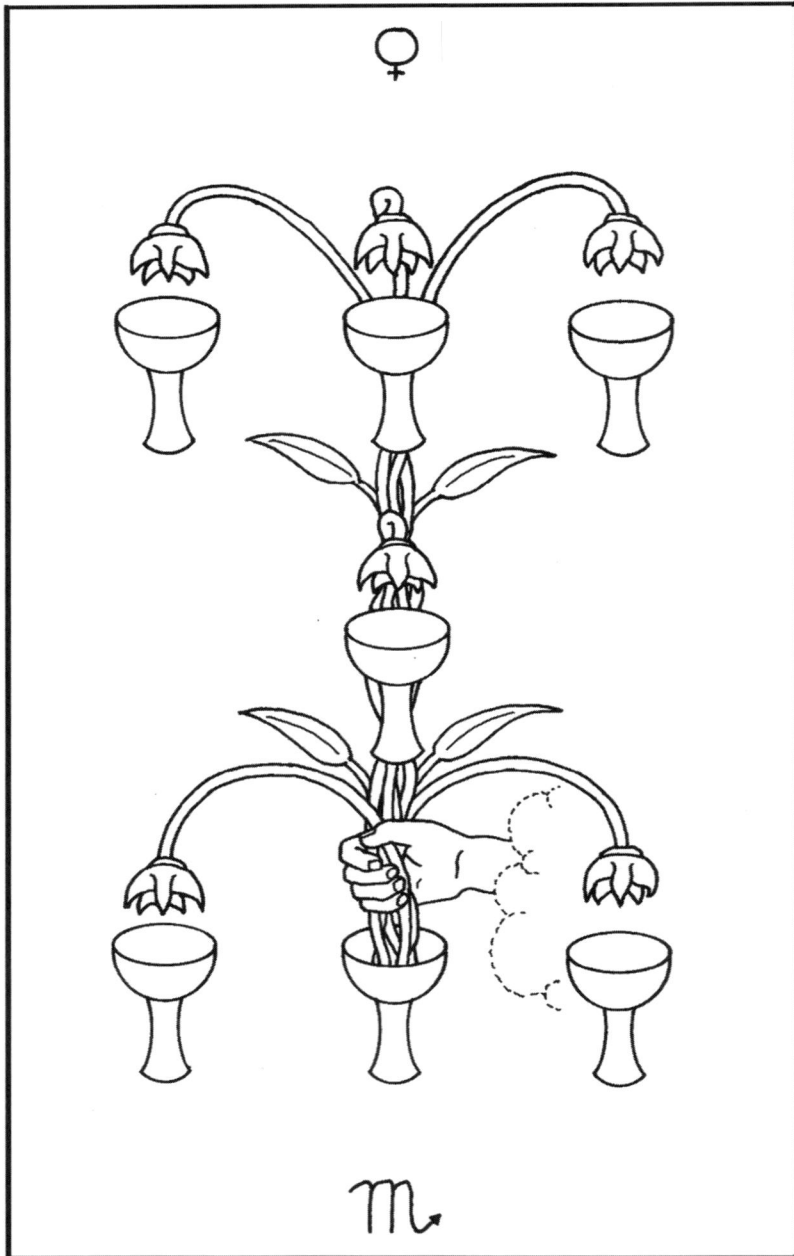

Seven of Cups

Title	:	Lord of Illusionary Success
Element	:	Water
Force	:	Heh
Alchemic	:	Third Stage Sublimation—be cleansed and fatness diminished
Kabbalistic World	:	Briah
Sephirah	:	Netzach
Holy Name	:	Naniel
Vision	:	Vision of Beauty
Planet of Sephirah	:	Venus
Angels	:	Malahel; Hahaviah
Astrological	:	Venus in Scorpio, twenty–thirty degrees
Colours	:	Cups Light Sky Blue; Background Sky Blue; Lotus flowers and plant, astrological symbols and shading the complementary colours to the cups and background; Cloud translucent Deep Green; White Hand

In the Seven of Cups, the additional Cup has drained the Azoth so that none flows from the Lotuses. The pattern has been rearranged so that though things are in equal balance, the central lower Cup has taken the nourishment resulting in no new growth of the Lotus pods. The hand issues from Netzach, the seventh sephiroth. The separation of the cloud from the waters to where it now shows, is a separation of the spirit from its source. This is also seen by the separation between the upper and lower row of cups by the central cup.

Alchemically the Seven of Cups is Third Stage Sublimation—'be cleansed and fatness diminished'. Sublimation purifies the Matter through dissolution and the reduction of the Matter into its constituents. In this way the 'fatness' can be diminished, the gross purified while separated from the subtle. It has been suggested that the cups in this card do not hold water, but a subtle powder. This can allude to many things, some being the crystallized salts or the crystallization of matter. With the separation of the spirit from matter, the appearance of matter brings forth superficiality, however, there is a potent force behind the symbology of this card, through its number, seven. Although there is corrosion within, there is clarity without which may hold the concept of illusion.

Netzach of Briah is the archangel Haniel ('Glory and Grace of God'). This angel's chief function is to take the devotional emanations from Atziluth and transmute them into something more tangible and this is done through the Religious Orders and the New Age Mystery schools, regardless of structure. Haniel is concerned with form and structure and will only work this type of format. His directions are instructional ones and he tries to keep basic common denominators in this type of area so that the various schools of learning do not stray from the correct Path of Initiation.

The Vision or Spiritual Experience of Netzach is the Vision of Beauty. This is the glimpse of Tiphareth (through the method of ascent) where we can glimpse Tiphareth but cannot as yet arrive there through the veil of mysteries. The veil has but only parted slightly for us as we have now attained a type of limited perfection and are ready to advance further into the mysteries. By way of ascent, we now look behind us and see the beauty and harmony as we now go into the World of the senses—the world of Illusion, hence the meaning for this card.

The first angel governing this card is Malahel, who is titled 'Turning aay from Evil'. This is the area of temptation. The second angel is Hahaviah, who is titled 'Goodness in Himself'. The two concepts relate to resisting temptation and remaining steadfast to one's ideals.

Venus in a Water Element is a time of obstacles where people are hindered, especially in emotional and material matters. The dreamer now comes into reality as all the facts are presented and the ideal clung to is lost. The framework is not suitable for success as the desire is greater than the abilities. Timing is also another reason why the energy and determination of Venus cannot survive in a wholly emotional situation as nothing concrete will develop.

Venus in Scorpio alludes to occult activity guided by intuition. The old saying of 'beauty being only skin deep' applies here very well as Scorpio destroys any chance of Venus bringing its full influence to bear, resulting in no or little permanence. It shows emotions being directed sexually and selfishly for there is a lack of reason due to the intense makeup of Venus in this Sign which results in an all or nothing situation. There is a strong attraction for the occult or mystical. In relationships or partnerships there is trouble indicated and the whole scenario is one to back away from.

Divination

Netzach of Heh shows the Victory of femininity but this is short-lived as it has no support and is an illusion. This is a time to take a low-key approach and not deviate from one's original plan. If any options come up to take on additional responsibility or get involved in a new venture then it would be unsuccessful. There is also a lack of healthcare indicated with signs of exhaustion. With women this can show difficulties with the health of their reproductive organs, such as endometriosis. This relates to deception in love and friendship and apparent victory, unfulfilled promises, lying, drunkenness, vanity, lust, jealousy, corruption. Often shows one who lacks acceptance in seeing the truth in a situation. Lack of reasoning. Sexual fantasies, and distortion in knowing how to deal with the opposite sex. Heavy emotional issues leaving one's subtle bodies heavily congested. Negativity. In matters of work and career there may be sexual involvement with workmates that lead to discomfort, misrepresentation of a project or promise. In matters spiritual the querent may have lost sight of the higher within and without and sees everything from a negative and sceptical viewpoint. A great lack of satisfaction in all matters; friends and acquaintances leaving an empty feeling in one.

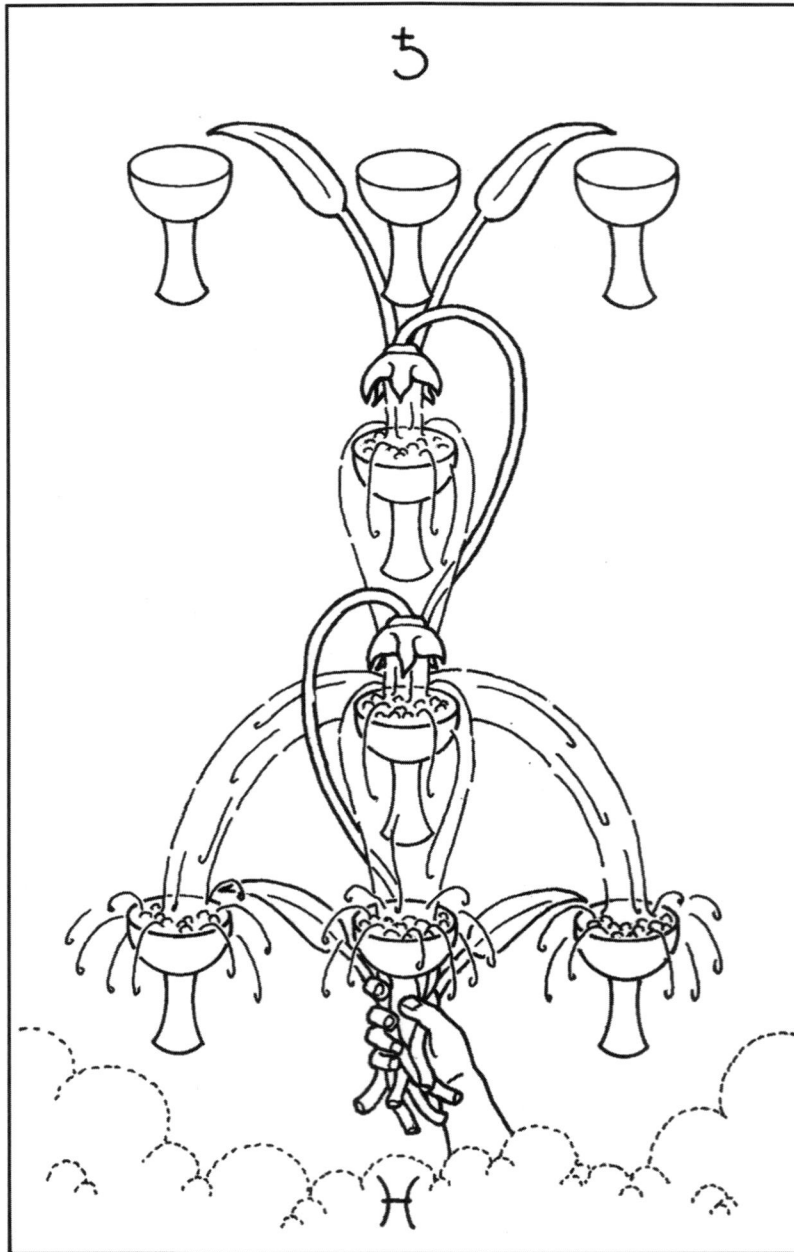

Eight of Cups

Title	:	Lord of Abandoned Success
Element	:	Water
Force	:	Heh
Alchemic	:	First Stage Projection—Transmutation
Kabbalistic World	:	Briah
Sephirah	:	Hod
Holy Name	:	Michael
Vision	:	Vision of Splendour
Planet of Sephirah	:	Mercury
Angels	:	Vavaliah; Ilnaiah
Astrological	:	Saturn in Pisces, zero–ten degrees
Colours	:	Soft Black Cups; Warm Golden Brown Background; complementaries of these as lotuses, lotus plant, shading, astrological symbols; Water, Clouds translucent Tawny Orange; White Hand

The Eight of Cups shows that there are only two lotuses to fill all eight cups and the two central cups are the only ones which get the Azoth, as there is not enough sap for the lotuses to reach above the upper cups to fill them. The whole scheme resembles success at a midway point and this success is not completely fulfilled. The two streams of Azoth resemble the Sigil of Saturn, one normal and the other in the mirror image.

Alchemically this card is the first Stage of Projection—Transmutation. Additionally, the symbol formed by the positions of the cups in this card is an 'I', which in alchemy symbolises Antimony Vitrum. This is a glass vessel of an antimony base and within this the first stage of

317

projection and the transmutation of the elixir takes place. A Projecting Medicine must be used however and this is where the Azoth, as the Tincture from the sea below, pours forth up through the Lotus plant and into the cups. This form of projection is, however, by violent interpenetration, through which, at the moment of ingression, the matter is transformed.

Hod of Briah is the Archangel Michael ('Who is like God') and his secret name is said to be Sabbathiel. Michael is the highest of the Archangels and his presence in Hod shows us that he is working to a Divine Plan through intellectual stimulation. One of his functions is to educate groups towards certain goals and open up doors of communication. He is also called the 'Protector of Kingdoms' and was the guide to Elijah.

The power of Hod is the Vision of Splendour. The Vision or Spiritual Experience of Hod is said to equate with that of Ezekiel 1: 4. It is also the unfolding vision of the Water Sephirah (by way of ascent) when the emotional content is intellectualised into a clear plan or framework. The entire plan or concept shows the Glory of Hod in its Splendour.

The first angel governing this card is Vavaliah, who is titled 'King and Ruler' and the second is Ilnaiah, who is titled 'Abiding Forever'. These concepts combine to show firmness in setting up rules and regulations.

The Planetary Sephirotic association is Mercury in a Water Element. The Water Element here shows gain, especially through any type of property. There is also a tendency to travel—mainly by water; investigation of occult subjects; harmony is an important factor, possibly through the arts and especially through music and it will be an outlet to bring about higher levels of awareness.

Saturn in Pisces characterises misfortune through illness and criticism. This is not a good combination and relates to unpopularity, hostility and public reprimand. It can effect the mind by producing neuroses through an overactive imagination. This is brought to the surface when the past cannot be forgotten or forgiven and this rises to self-pity. In most cases this can be rectified (on a personal level) through psychodrama and analyses. People so afflicted are afraid of what lurks beneath the surface of their own consciousness and tend to repress their drives and appetites. The unconscious is divorced from the conscious in order to feel safe. Fear, self-doubt, lack of confidence; fear of intimacy. If these people can take the whole realm of their unconscious seriously and investigate it, they, above all others, will be amply rewarded.

Divination

Hod of Heh shows superficial success, decline of interest, abandoned success. This situation shows an excellent beginning but a cancellation of plans at the last moment causing havoc. It bodes ill for any romantic or business ventures, both of which show initial success only. It is a stimulation of the mental faculties to a reasonably high degree by channelling our emotions into a framework we are comfortable with. Temporary success is indicated where things are thrown aside as soon as gained. The success is not lasting, even in the matter in hand and there is indolence in success. We find misery and ripening without cause and instability. There is wisdom in remaining within set boundaries of one's influence and strength. This card is not always a time of despair during abandonment. Often it arises during situations where there is a timely abandonment. Often also the querent is relunctant to admit how deeply a situation has affected them. Projects will not be finished; undertakings lose their interest. Low self-esteem; self-destruction and depression; a journey needed to self-awareness. Partings between people, or from places; parting of lovers; loss of love, or love for all the wrong reasons. Stagnating working conditions; chronic health problems. Often when this card turns up in matters of employment it shows that the person's current situation does not fulfil their needs.

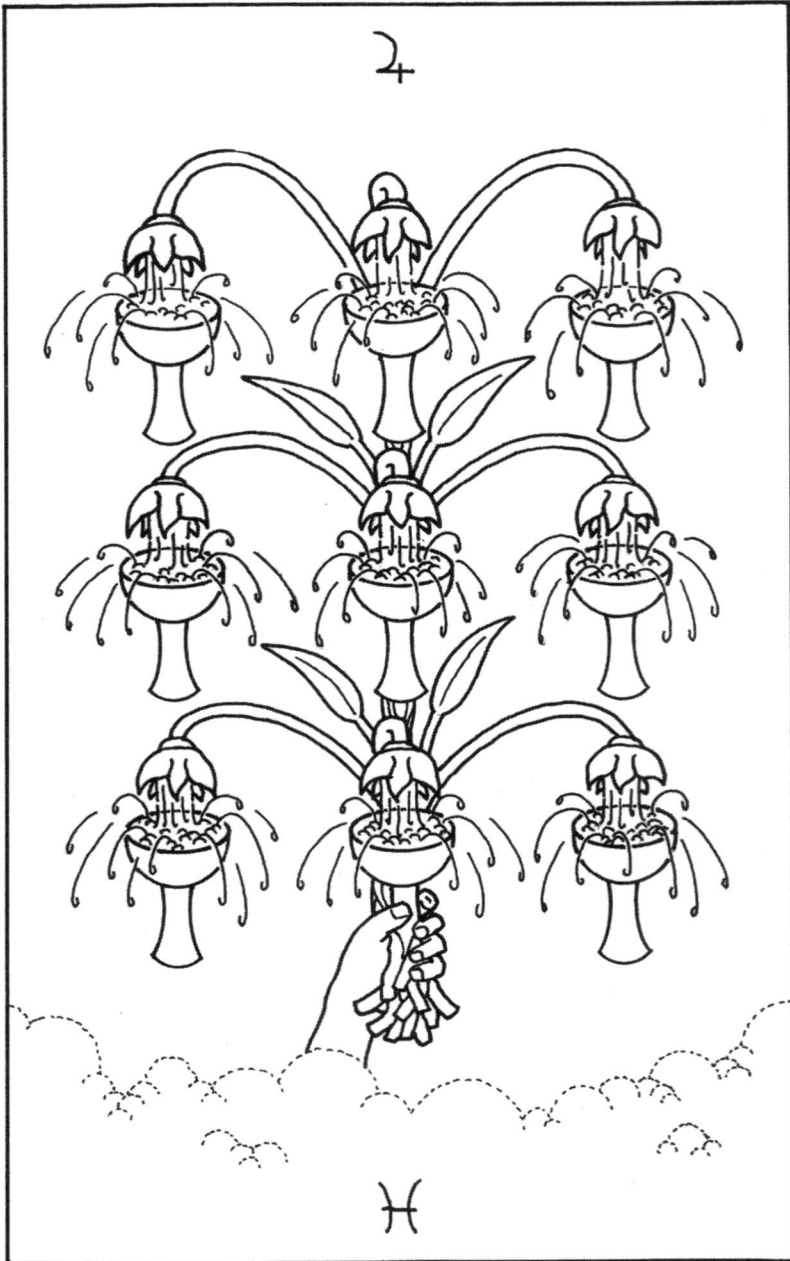

Nine of Cups

Title	:	Lord of Material Happiness
Element	:	Water
Force	:	Heh
Alchemic	:	Second Stage Projection
Kabbalistic World	:	Briah
Sephirah	:	Yesod
Holy Name	:	Gabriel
Vision	:	Vision of the Machinery of the Universe
Planet of Sephirah	:	Moon
Angels	:	Saelaiah; Naghazaiel
Astrological	:	Jupiter in Pisces, ten–twenty degrees
Colours	:	Princess Blue Cups; Warm Golden Brown Background; complementary colours to the cups and background for Lotuses and plant, shading and astrological symbols; translucent Dark Petunia for the water, clouds and White Hand

The Nine of Cups shows that every cup has a lotus flower above it pouring out Azoth into each cup until it starts to overflow. This alludes to the expansive qualities of Jupiter. The symbol portrayed by the cup and hand positions is the alchemic symbol of Jupiter (one middle vertical column and three horizontal lines with a central hand below). This formation also forms a square above a cross, which is a symbol of Sal Alkali, which is known as the Salt of Wisdom 'which causeth the Spirit to enter properly into bodies and permeate them'. Hermes Trismegistus said 'the vine of the wise is drawn forth in three'. Projection is a violent action and now that a violent penetration has taken place from the previous card, this card depicts now the moment of transformation. The elixir pouring forth is now composed of three virtues: philosophically sublimated Mercury (white or red ferment), metallic water and sulphur.

The Holy name of Yesod of Briah is the Archangel Gabriel ('Power of his Mightiness' or 'Strong one of God'). This is the angel that appeared to the Virgin Mary at the Annunciation and because of this is directly associated with Divine Creation. His power is to create or be the herald of a new era, not only in religious thought, but also in political thought, new states of awareness, or through music, and, as such, is the Archangel of a new generation. Gabriel works on vast international levels and is the instinct of the creative genius of men and women in all fields of endeavour (when for good).

The Vision or Spiritual Experience of Yesod is a Vision of the Machinery of the Universe. The actual title of this comes from an old woodcut where we see the dreamer fully awake in his dream and in front of him is a vision of the machinery that makes the universe. In many respects this imagery is quite correct for it shows the process of dream control. This is where we direct our dreams to go to certain areas to explore through the Astral Body. It is possibly the first vision of the higher planes man has, through the medium of dreaming. This is how man travels naturally through time and space to another dimension or reality.

The first angel governing this card is Saelaiah, who is titled 'Mover of All things' and the second is Naghazaiel, who is titled 'Revealer'. Both allude to revelation through growth.

The Sephirotic Planetary association is the Moon in a Watery Element. This shows a very sympathetic response to people and the possibility of living for those people and not for oneself. There are strong mystical and occult currents around and an individual is inclined to be at their mercy because of the extreme sensitivity of his or her nature.

Jupiter in Pisces brings forth the spiritual aspect in life along with deep sincerity. This is also associated with people who are inclined to self-sacrifice due to their passionate and generous nature. There is a deep spiritual yearning to be at peace spiritually and there will be an attraction to New Age Orders—as a follower and not as a leader—which could open such people up for manipulation by others if they are not careful, due to a 'live and let live attitude'. In Pisces, Jupiter rules the inner world or other worlds, where one searches for the meaning of life within rather than without. There is a strong sense of need for the truth in all matters. Meditation, prayer, retreat, music, the arts, healing.

Divination

Yesod of Heh is complete success, pleasure and happiness fulfilled. This card shows that the material aspect has gone far better than anticipated and that it brings about joy for celebration. This refers to complete and perfect realisation of pleasure and happiness. Manifestation; materialisation; abundance but not excessive; harmony; balance; equilibrium; regeneration; generosity; satisfaction. Ideas are spontaneous and inspired; friendships are good and many; love issues flow well. Good fortune in business and finance. Family matters are congenial, but perhaps a tendency towards being taken for granted. Travel over water (overseas); water sports and interests; music, arts; hospitals and healing; natural healing; alternative therapies. Gatherings; weddings. If ill-dignified it brings self-praise, vanity, conceit, overtalking and self-denial. One then becomes high-minded and not easily satisfied with small, limited ideas. One could be running round looking for answers and joy in all directions rather than looking within.

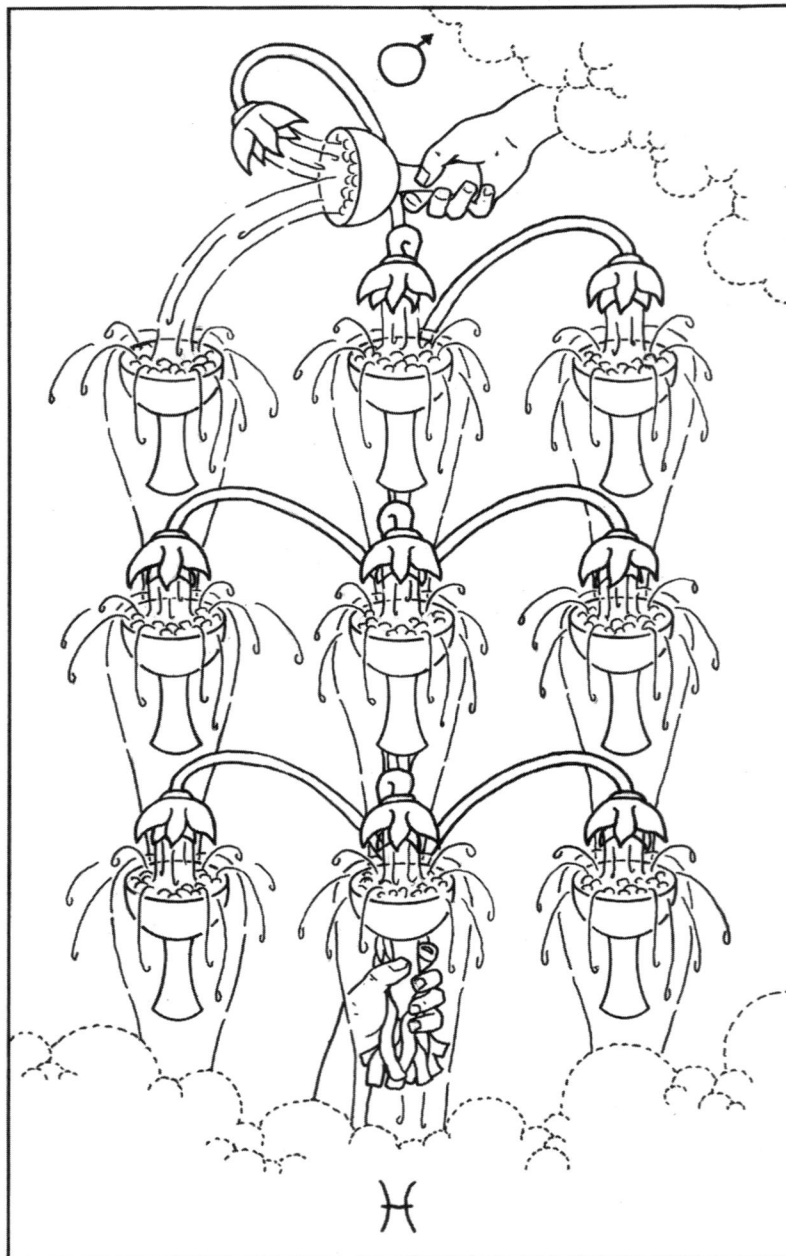

Ten of Cups

Title	:	Lord of Perfected Success
Element	:	Water
Force	:	Heh
Alchemic	:	Third Stage Projection—refined gold/the elixir
Kabbalistic World	:	Briah
Sephirah	:	Malkuth
Holy Name	:	Sandalphon
Vision	:	Vision of Holy Guardian Angel
Planet of Sephirah	:	Four elements
Angels	:	Aslaiah; Mihel
Astrological	:	Mars in Pisces, twenty–thirty degrees
Colours	:	Primary Red Cups; Warm Golden Brown Background; complementary colours of cups and background for shading, astrological symbols, lotuses and plant; Water and clouds coloured translucently in the tertiaries, colours of Malkuth in Briah; White Hand

The cups flow over as the water cascades from the lotuses, a symbol of plenty, abundance from the Azoth. There is perpetual motion of the elixir as it travels from the sea through the lotus plant, into the cups and then pouring back to the sea. This is the vitality of Mars acting in Pisces and is the end result of this particular stage where the elixir is strengthened and perfect in every way. Two angelic hands at the top and bottom of the card show the forces of 'Above and Below' working in harmony.

The alchemic symbols are the sigil of Mars and the mystic eye of eternity which represents enlightenment and the solar door to the celestial. Alchemically we have here the third stage of projection bringing forth the Aqua Philosophical, which has the power to distil itself into manifestation through the Art of Life. By some it is another name, for this can be the Aqua Permanens which is the Celestial Water where Sol and Luna are dissolved and united. Other names used for it are the Dragon's Tail and Flying Bird and the Mercury of the Philosophers, indicating that it has a sharp and clear Mercurial power and property.

The Holy Name of Malkuth of Briah is the Archangel Sandalphon ('Co-Brother'). He is the twin of Metatron and one of his functions is to sort through all the prayers and present them to the higher echelons where they are designed to go. He is an angel of presentation, especially in matters of prayer and birth, for it is his function to help decide the sex of the child in the expectant mother. In general terms he helps in the overall design of civilization and helps to streamline each generation.

The Vision or Spiritual Experience of Malkuth is the Vision of the Holy Guardian Angel. This title is a little confusing as to what happens in Tiphareth but in fact it refers to men and women being aware of their own spirituality. In Malkuth there are, in fact, four levels equating with the four elements and these have to be worked through in the process of initiation (there is an overlap here with the elements as applied to the Sephiroth). The whole concept is one of balancing polarity; the lower mechanism of the flesh in balance with the higher aspirations of spirit.

The first angel governing this card is Aslaiah, who is titled 'Judging' and the second is Mihel, who is titled 'Sending Forth as a Father'. Both relate to the concept of the strength of a man being reached through observation of the laws.

The Mars in Pisces character quietens down the active energies of Mars so that its thrusting and expansive energies are in tune with a more inner, Piscean framework. Pisces has modified the energies of Mars by the process of forethought. A strong depth of emotional feelings and emotive responses develop from this and they have to be channelled accordingly to be effective. It must be considered that it is Mars that must adapt to the framework of Pisces and not the other way around. A close study of this situation will reveal a very enthusiastic nature where strength and courage work hand-in-hand with each other. From the negative perspective of Mars in Pisces you have someone who is almost manic and very inconsistent in behaviour. Now you see him, now you don't! The natural aggression of Mars may be disguised as pure stubbornness and passive resistance, although underneath, this person will boil for a long time. This person may also complain about all that is wrong but not get up and do anything about it and usually baits someone else into expressing action or anger for them.

Divination

Malkuth of Heh concerns matters definitely arranged as wished and complete good fortune. This relates to permanent and lasting success, happiness due to divine inspiration. Stimulated ambition, but a need to do everything in harmony with life. Music and the arts; heightened creativity; fullness of experience; culmination of desires; enlightenment. Overseas travel for pleasure is often depicted; joyous occasions and celebrations. In family matters there should be ease of relationships and happiness. In love matters, love can be very expansive and felt very deeply. Marriage may be rushed into. This card can represent many children, but it usually depicts love working on a higher, more universal level. In recreational matters one may win a prize.

The unusual and unexpected. Trust in business and good working environmental relationships; overall support from others. Many social activities and a great deal of satisfaction in working to help others. Healing and health matters come to the fore. Healing oneself. Spiritualism and mysticism; solitude and rejuvenation of energy; perpetuity; honour; love and friendship. Recontact with those from the past; flooding of past memories, usually good ones. Selfless service; deep and hidden resources available; the unconscious flooding into the conscious.

If ill-dignified then dissipation, debauchery, excessiveness, wantonness, wastefulness results; a tendency to reject responsibility in favour of harmony.

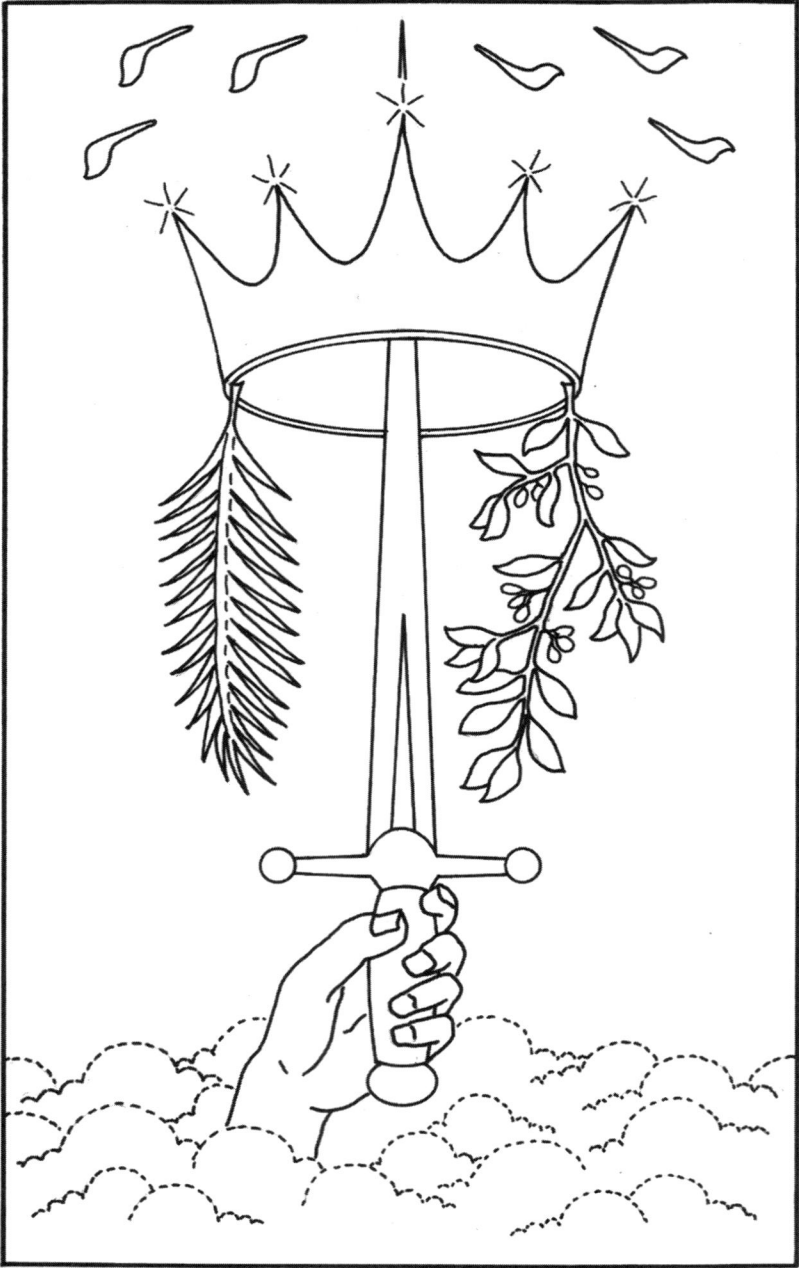

Ace of Swords

Title	:	The Root of the Powers of Fire
Element	:	Air
Force	:	Vau
Alchemic	:	Xanthosis
Kabbalistic World	:	Yetzirah
Sephirah	:	Kether
Angelic Choir	:	Chayoth Ha-Quadesh
Vice/Virtue	:	Virtue to complete task of the Great Work; Vice is the failure of the latter
Planet of Sephira	:	Neptune
Archangel	:	Raphael
Myth	:	Excalibur/Albion
Colours	:	Sword and Yods Vivid Yellow Gold; Background Mauve; Crown, Hand and Clouds White; Palm and Olive branches Green; Stars issuing from Crown Vivid Yellow Gold

This is Kether of Vau, the first process of the development of the Airy Element. The Sword, held upright in the centre of the card is a blind force which could invoke or evoke good or evil. Since Air and Spirit are linked to each other the sword upholds one's spiritual nature through the Ruach and, as such, is classified as invoked force (power). The six Vau around the Crown relate to the Six days of Creation and also to Tiphareth where the Ruach has its throne. The palm leaf and olive branch hanging from the Crown are divine truth and suffering (Chesed and Geburah). These are also symbolic of the twin Pillars of Mercy and Severity for the Sword in between them also is the Central Pillar of the Tree.

The Sword is symbolic of Invoked Force over Nature. In this card the sword is raised in an upward position towards the spiritual essences of Light which we all aspire to. If reversed it would show drawing on the energies of the Qlippoth and is an evil symbol. Hence the potential for great good and great evil, depending on the actions of the wielder. This is the ability to attain the heights of power and eventually transcend oneself, but only through help, be it Light or Dark. The Sword represents the higher mind and vehicle for the Will and it issues from Tiphareth surging up to pierce the crown in Kether, seeking unification.

Kether of Yetzirah works through the Order of Angels called the Chayoth ha-Qadesh (Holy Living Creatures) who take incorporeal elements and transmute them through the four radical processes needed to reduce them to a common structure or form. This occurs in order that these elements can prepare for entry into the next level. Another title or name which is applicable here is Rashish ha-Gilgolim ('Whirling forces'). The actions of the World of Formation in this Sephirah are to form the cell structure in nature for all living creatures and prepare the blue prints for life on earth. The actions work with the angels of Karma on this issue as well.

The Virtue of Kether of Yetzirah is to complete the task of the Great Work. This is a rather broad statement that is a 'double-edged sword'. The first aspect concerns the spirituality that we were born to aspire to, through various tasks and frameworks. The second relates directly to the secret tradition and what is called the 'Great Work' by the alchemists and which is the attainment of a certain Hermetic goal. Technically speaking Kether has no Vices, however, what could be considered as a Vice is the failure to complete the work mentioned above.

The Sephirotic planetary association of the Ace of Swords is Neptune in an Air Element. This is a sympathetic association. The vastness of Neptune's power is limited to an intellectual blueprint and promotes sympathy with others of like mind. It is establishment of a framework over a previous uncharted area or frontier state that Neptune produced.

The Ace of Swords also has been associated with the myth of Albion and Excalibur—the sword of power, mystery and magic. In this legend of King Arthur, the Lady of the Lake brought forth the sword from the waters and mists. In this card the clouds from which the Angelic hand issues could allude to these mists and the waters beneath the clouds, the Azoth, brought forth from the suit of Cups. Here then, we see the birth of Air from Water, as the Lady of the Lake gives up the Sword from the Waters, just as vapour rises and becomes air.

In Alchemy the element of Air permeates all stages of alchemical workings. The Ace of Swords alludes here to the Stage of Xanthosis—the yellowing, and also to the stage that is most visible of the Air element, the White Eagle, represented in this card by the Crown. The *Praxis Spagyrica Philosophica* says:

> The White Eagle is nothing else but the slowly rising Mercury/Sulphur (vapour), at the top of the digestion flask, from the calyx of gold (the sword)…

In many alchemical texts Air is termed as Wind, which referred to Life and Soul. In the Ace of Swords, the Sword representing the Air element, life and the Soul, penetrates through the centre of the crown. This alludes to the exaltation of the Soul and is also referred to as the 'Flying Eagle' which is stated to be Philosophical Mercury. Mercury, of course, is not 'Soul', but 'Spirit'.

This could cause confusion to those studying alchemy, as 'Eagle' represents 'the Water'. But when it is flying it becomes vapour and immersed in Air. Paracelsus explains this further:

> *Now, as to the philosophy of the three prime elements, it must be seen how these flourish in the element of air. Mercury, Sulphur and Salt, are as prepared as the element of air that they constitute the air and make up that element. Originally the sky is nothing but white Sulphur coagulated with the Spirit of Salt and clarified by Mercury. Moreover the air is breath, from which all draw their life. This is truly air itself and puts forth the air which nourishes the four elements and at the same time sustains the life of man....*

The Air element in astrology is described as a need for freedom of Will and Spirit; communication and need for a meeting of minds; curious, restlessness, explorative, the intellect, relationships, mental attitudes, knowledge, learning, all facets concerning the thought processes and the mind.

Divination

Additional to the above: a whirling force showing strength through trouble, the affirmation of Justice and upholding Divine Authority; additional responsibilities being given to persons and it is up to them how they perform. Power of the Will, Word and Intellect. The 'idea' in its manifesting form; relocation of work, home, country, or direct action taken, driven by one's will. Energy and invoked power which could be used for good or evil, depending on the intentions of the wielder. Justice, retribution, higher intellect, triumph and conquest. Often the Ace of Swords shows travel; direct communication methods; selfhood; awakening and pure clarity; reasoning and clear thinking.

Practical magic or some form of application of someone's Will. Domination of Will, unbreakable bonds. Plans and actualization of such. A relationship brought forth through one person's will or the Divine Will; legacies. Negatively this card would show the misuse of one's Will and Power, arguments, division between people; operations and sickness. Misuse of the power of the Word; over-ambitiousness; over-competitiveness; the manipulator.

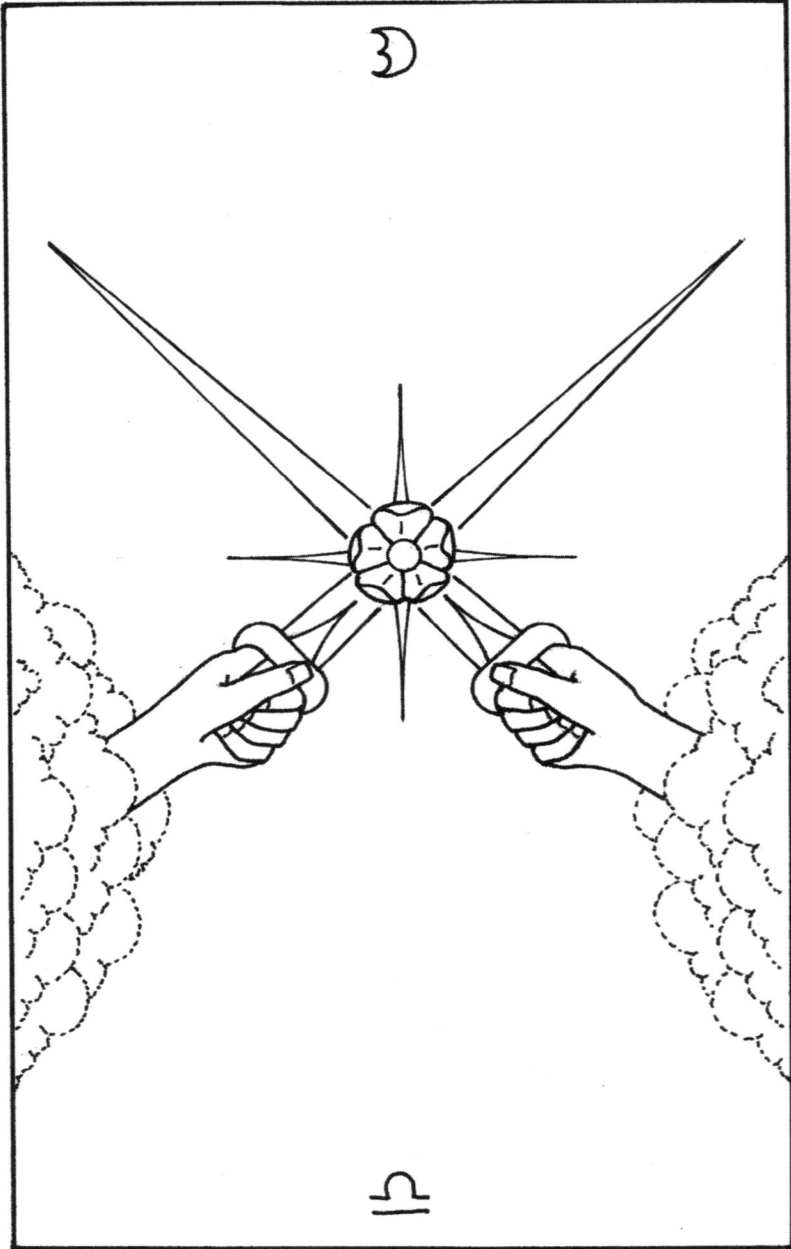

Two of Swords

Title	:	Lord of Peace Restored
Element	:	Air
Force	:	Vau
Alchemic	:	First Stage Cibation
Kabbalistic World	:	Yetzirah
Sephirah	:	Chokmah
Angelic Choir	:	Auphanim
Vice/Virtue	:	Virtue is devotion; Vice is obsession
Planet of Sephirah	:	Uranus
Angels	:	Iezalel; Mevahael
Astrological	:	Moon in Libra, zero–ten degrees
Colours	:	Swords very cold pale Blue; Background Bottle Green; Rose and Hands White; Rays and Clouds Bluish Grey; Shading, Astrological and sword symbols complementary colours to the Swords and Background

At the crossed point of the two swords the five-petalled rose sits binding them in harmony. Each sword is held by an angelic hand issuing from the central sides of the card, bringing balance and harmony. The white rose is spirit binding the swords (mind) into focus, concentration and meditation on the central point. This implies that one must centre oneself to know the essence of oneself. The centre is a point where the opposing forces of the universe unite.

Alchemically, the clouds have now risen from the mists over the waters and now depict the Flying Eagle. The two swords and rose form a cross with a circle in the middle. (This symbolizes Tutia, which is Tutty that cleaves at the top of the oven in its pure state.) It was also an ancient symbol for Pluto, salt and a stage of the Green Lion (crystallised verdigris).

The Two of Swords is the first stage of Cibation which is a stage between elevation and congelation—reuniting. Cibation is where a wetness is applied to a dry powder which produces growth and warmth. This relates to Spring. In many instances the seed which lays dormant during the Winter is now revived into a complete new cycle. So in fact it is a regrowth or reunion with water issuing from the clouds acting as a catalyst.

Chokmah of Yetzirah works through the Choir of angels, the Auphanim ('wheels' or 'many-eyed ones'). In applying these angels to the 'Wisdom' of Chokmah, we will find that they work not through the intellect but through the process of feeling or being in empathy with. They bring forth insights into the total picture or what is and how to act. They were said to have aided Solomon over the dispute of two mothers over a child. Being 'many-eyed' the Auphanim are able to see things at all levels that are invisible to us mortals. From their all-seeing capacity they will impart to us what they consider best for us under the existing circumstances. We will not be given the complete picture as they see it, but we will get a methodology of dealing with a problem, which goes way beyond any direct intellectual capacity.

The Virtue applied here is Devotion. This actually comes through the Briatic Vision of 'meeting God face to face' where an archetypal imagery of God can be contemplated. This contact is usually done through direct contact with one's own Causal Body. By the removal of all barriers between the Subtle Bodies a strong emotive tie that holds them together is revealed and the devotion to one's higher self is then felt as it gives out love and we give it devotion in return. The Vice here is Obsession. This usually happens when the inclinations of devotion are somehow interfered with. The impetus for devotion is present but the reason is now lost and it becomes mechanical and obsessive, completely devoid of love.

The first angel governing this card is Iezalel, who is titled 'Rejoicing over all Things' and the second is Mevahael, who is titled 'Guardian and Preserver'. Both concepts link to something being saved.

The Sephirotic Planetary association is Uranus in an Air Element. Overall this a good position for Uranus to be in and will establish an empathy with those around. Travel is also indicated, with favourable result. In any form of study or learning, Uranus is in its best configuration.

The Moon in Libra is superficiality, without cultural asceticism, being sacrificed through a very high emotional context. The superficiality is avoidance of reality. Harmony and peace are the main goals here and to a certain extent this is expressed in the title of the card itself. There is a great deal of adaptability here, especially when confronted with a superior strength, for example from a partner. Old stances and habits will change overnight if the majority wish it. On a higher level the Moon seeks union in Libra, just as the lower self seeks union with the higher self. On a negative level there is much changeability of emotions and mind with the Moon in Libra.

Divination

Chokmah of Vau—wisdom in thought. In relationship matters, as Peace Restored it shows a reunification after suffering and estrangement; tolerance where there was once intolerance; meeting people you have not seen for some time who are tied in with your past. A return to the old, reunions and a stabilization process where matters were volatile but now coming back to normal. In other matters, a stress-free situation; meditation; retreat to be alone to rethink matters; selfhood. In material matters, financial and business affairs are kept secret; life's affairs are regulated; business matters handled with skill and calm; however, matters tend to remain as they are. Intellectual pursuits; peace restored in disputes. If ill-dignified this card is a repetition of negative things in the past happening again and hurting someone without knowing it. However its main vibration is one of contemplation, peace of mind, meditation. This is very much the combination of pleasure after pain, recuperation after surgery or an illness.

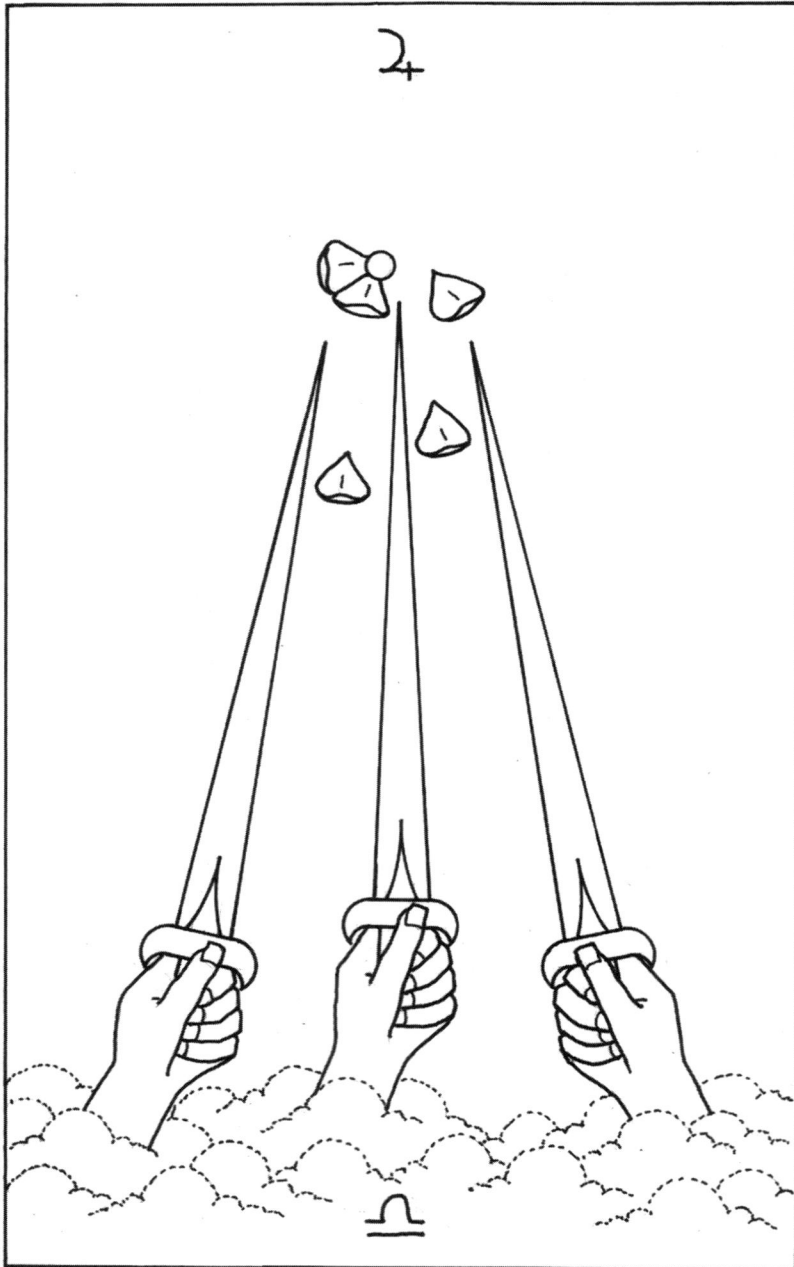

Three of Swords

Title	:	Lord of Sorrow
Element	:	Air
Force	:	Vau
Alchemic	:	Second Stage Cibation—Soul's return
Kabbalistic World	:	Yetzirah
Sephirah	:	Binah
Angelic Choir	:	Aralim
Vice/Virtue	:	Virtue is Silence; Vice is Avarice
Planet of Sephirah	:	Saturn
Angels	:	Harayel; Hoqmiah
Astrological	:	Saturn in Libra, ten–twenty degrees
Colours	:	Swords Blue Black; Background Bottle Green; Shading, Astrological and other symbols complementary colours to the words and background; Clouds translucent Crimson, with black edge and rays; Rose petals and Hands White

In the Three of Swords the rose of the previous card is being shattered as another Sword is introduced which shows reckless action losing the gentle penetration of the previous. The third Sword resembles the actions of a wedge thrust between the other two, tearing apart the five-petalled rose. The outside swords are the faces of creation and restoration, with the central sword the face of destruction/disruption.

As the second stage of Cibation, the Soul's return, the White Eagle descends back to the growing mists over the waters. This is depicted by the falling rose petals and increased clouds in the card. The Eagle now becomes a wingless bird and is now known as the 'Crow's Head'. The crow's head is known as the Nigredo. The anonymous author of the *Novum Lumen Chemicum* writes:

> *O our heaven! O our water and our Mercurius! O dead head or dregs of our sea! … And these are the epithets of the bird of Hermes, which never rests.*

and from the *Rosarium Philosophorum*:

> *And know that the head of the art is the raven, who flies without wings in the blackness of the night and the brightness of the day.*

This has been referred to as a restless, unsleeping spirit of aerial and volatile stone, that is the heaven and the scum of the sea. This darkening phase is one of death and resurrection.

The Three of Swords also symbolises the *Aqua Permanens* which is the morning dew. This is considered the tears of the moon that flooded the land mourning the death of night. Here you now see that the Three of Swords sheds its tears as the rose sheds its petals.

The Angelic beings of Binah of Yetzirah are the Angelic Choir called the Aralim ('Valiant ones' or 'Order of Thrones'). The throne is, of course, the foundation of a kingdom and Binah is this, because it is the first Sephirah of the Supernal (by way of ascent). When the Tree of Knowledge of Good and Evil broke at Daath, Binah was the Sephirah that stood guardian against the Qlippothic elements as they tried to rise through Daath, but were repelled. Its function and duty is to guard the upper realms against all of those who are unworthy and try to aspire to the heights of the Supernal.

The Virtue of Binah is Silence. We are told 'The seed of Wisdom is sown in Silence and grown in darkness and obscurity'. This relates to the initial formulation of Silence in Chokmah until it reaches its fullness in the darkness of Binah. This means forgetting everything we have learnt and just accepting the fact of being, for it is here that magical virtues come as the Postulant emerges into a different realm, compared to what he or she has been used to.

The Vice of Binah is Avarice where one enters a new realm and covets everything in sight, displaying a lack of restraint and direction. If Silence, under its Zen principle, were maintained, then the right knowing and thought would come and the confusion would not exist.

Saturn in an Air element brings construction and order to the thinking processes, but lacks humour and tends to weigh those of an airy nature down to moroseness. However, it brings powerfully concentrated thinking processes for those in professions which rely on the intellect and memory.

The first angel governing this card is Harayel, who is titled 'Aid' and the second is Hoqmiah, who is titled 'Raise up, Praying day and Night'. These two concepts show someone calling out for help.

Saturn in Libra relates to conflict but this is modified due to Libra's influence. An internal struggle that goes to extremes and introduces panic. Though Saturn is exalted in Libra and is fortunate, one must be extremely careful in seeing things in an abstract concept with no understanding of the real nature of the situation. It is a 'knife edge' situation with Saturn under control but still on the edge of a situation that could get out of hand if the balance is tipped in either direction. It is a situation of perpetual give and take, so that the balance is not tipped either way. This character has a fear of losing individuality which causes an estrangement in relationships. Companionship is needed, yet once attained, is torn apart. The lesson here is to meet all relationships with an inner sense of freedom.

Divination

Binah of Vau shows unhappiness, sorrow and tears. This is separation, quarrelling, mischief-making, betrayal of one party by another and interference where it is not wanted, deliberate callousness to hurt others by the actions of a third party, secrecy and perversion if taken to an extreme are also indicated. Dogmatism, ignorance, unhappiness, disappointment, disruption to any situation, sadness of parting, death and loss. Financial loss, delays, promises unfulfilled, lies, changes of direction which cause worry and difficulty. Interference in relationships by a person or a thing such as business, often through no fault of the individuals concerned. Estrangement and loneliness.

On a positive point old problems are swept aside. One's parting from people or a situation may be a happy event of choice. Isolation caused for personal growth. Time for change and reassessment in all matters this card connects to in your reading.

Four of Swords

Title	:	Lord of Rest from Strife
Element	:	Air
Force	:	Vau
Alchemic	:	Third Stage Cibation—the resuscitation
Kabbalistic World	:	Yetzirah
Sephirah	:	Chesed
Angelic Choir	:	Chasmalim
Vice/Virtue	:	Virtue is Obedience; Vice is Disobedience
Planet of Sephirah	:	Jupiter
Angels	:	Laviah; Keliel
Astrological	:	Jupiter in Libra, twenty–thirty degrees
Colours	:	Swords Blue Violet; Background Bottle Green; Shading, Astrological and other symbols complementaries to above; Rays, clouds Lapis Lazuli; Hands White

In the Four of Swords the central Rose is not pierced but rather enclosed and held by the four Swords. The Rose, as the central point, is intact but the swords still threaten it. The crossed Swords actually lock themselves together nullifying their own action. The Rose, as such, represents a haven from the strife of the Swords. The symbol formed by the swords and rose is the double cross, which implies, due to the presence of the rose, resurrection from the Cinders.

The alchemical association is the third stage of Cibation, which is a resuscitation, or resurrection as mentioned above. Although the clouds have lifted to the sides of the card, they still meet at the bottom. In the 'Treatise on the Great Art' Dom Antoine-Joseph Pernety says:

At all times bodies exhale a subtle vapour, this is manifested more clearly in summer. The warm air sublimates the waters into vapours and attracts them to itself. When, after a rain, the rays of the sun beam upon the earth, one sees it smoke and exhale itself in vapour. These vapours hover in the air in the form of fogs, when they do not rise far above the surface of the earth: But when they mount to the middle region, one sees them float, here and there, in the form of clouds …

The Crow's Head now rises, represented here by the White Eagle which flies up into the clouds, separating from the Green Lion.

The Angelic beings of Chesed of Yetzirah are the angelic choir called the Chasmalim ('Domi-nations'). Their function is 'to dominate'; procure liberty; vanquish enemies; give the authority of Princes over all kinds of persons—even Ecclesiastics. This choir is the one that gives us a breathing space to grow in strength before we come up against the negative aspects of the other Sephiroth, especially where karmic patterns are concerned. They also bring together people for common causes, especially where group soul growth is experienced, and control things more on a day-to-day basis.

The Virtue related here is Obedience. This is a wide-ranging term, but it is Obedience to the powers and emanations that come from Chesed and are the framework for our existence. At a certain point in time we must obey our higher nature, so that our soul attunes itself to us where we learn certain lessons that will help purify the spirit. The Vice is Disobedience and this is the oppo-site of the above. Here the needs of the flesh and desires have triumphed over that of the spirit and the individual indulges in self-gratification and neglects his or her true course or destiny.

The Sephirotic planetary association is Jupiter in an Air Element. This is a restless situation where there is constant movement and a lack of attachment to anyone, or thing, and a distinct lack of focus for any long period. There are certain leadership capabilities, but a lack of staying power to utilise the fullest potential.

The first angel governing this card is Laviah, who is titled 'Wonderful' and the second is Keliel, who is titled 'Worthy to be Invoked for Self'. The combined meaning of these two show optimism and resilience.

Jupiter in Libra shows the expansive qualities of Jupiter being equalised by Libra. This pro-duces the concept of the optimist as Law, order and discipline are merged with the expansive qualities Jupiter brings. In relationships, those with Jupiter in Libra are hard to pin down to a commitment and usually can't be trusted as they want to experience all aspects of many rela-tionships. On another level one may expect too much from a partner or society. This may seem quite different from the basic meaning of this card, however, meeting a person of this nature halfway is about the best you are going to get. Also calling on inner truth is essential in this character and those dealing with him or her. Libra, when accustomed to its higher vibration, balances the exaggerated qualities of Jupiter.

Divination

Chesed of Vau is convalescence, recovery from sickness, change for the better. This card shows a time of quietness is now enforced and people tend to block out negativity towards them. A trip is indicated and possibly a holiday; Optimism and Freedom. It is a time to get away from the worries of the world and relax. This shows rest from sorrow, strife and problems in general. A period of rest and recuperation, recovery from sickness, a holiday away from things. Refining, channelling, confirming, drawing a balance. Truth outer and inner is needed for insight and inner peace. In relationships people must realize they can't extract any more out, only draw a truce or compromise. A partner may not be trusted. Business affairs must be kept as they are, impulsiveness must be controlled. A person may be talented in many areas, but expert at none. This card is favourable for study, exploration and social activities. A time of rebalancing and thought; fairness in results and actions. Rest after a struggle; recognition of achievements; opposition falls away; counsellors; an impasse; a waiting period.

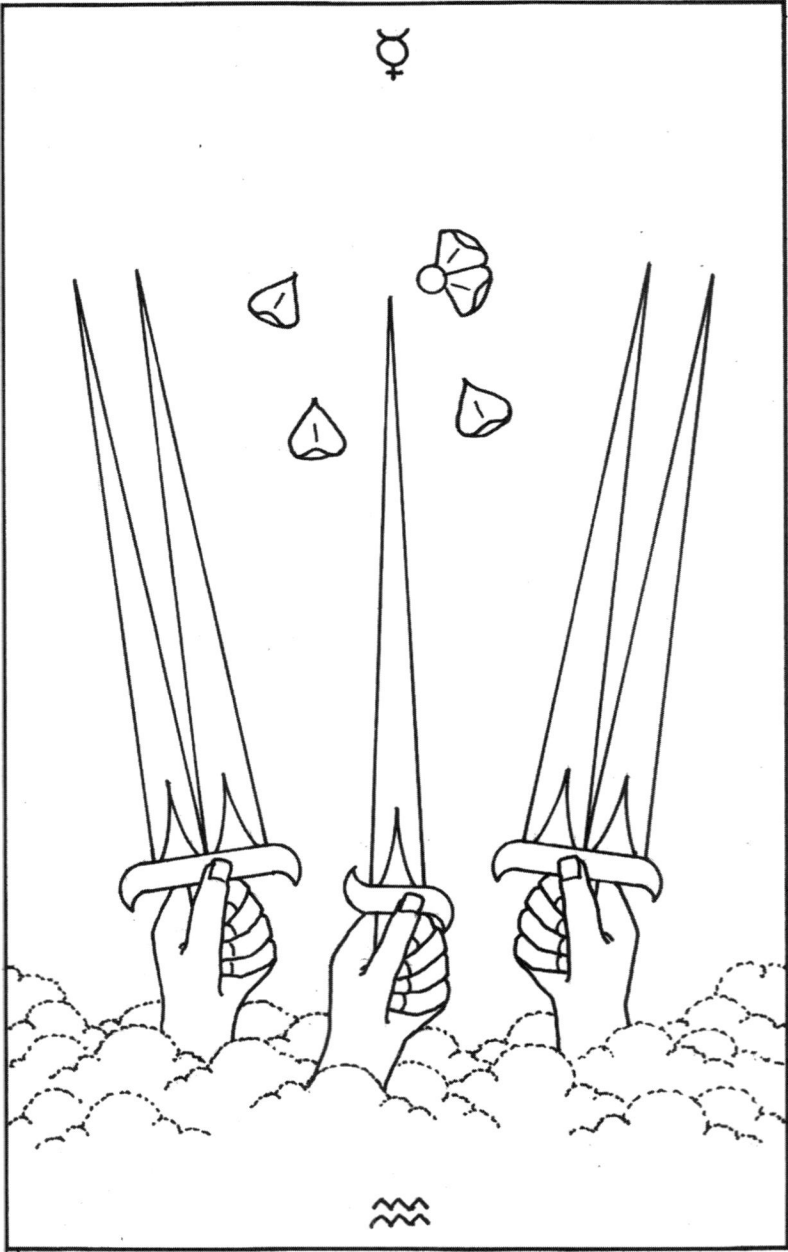

Five of Swords

Title	:	Lord of Defeat
Element	:	Air
Force	:	Vau
Alchemic	:	First Stage Multiplication
Kabbalistic World	:	Yetzirah
Sephirah	:	Geburah
Angelic Choir	:	Seraphim
Vice/Virtue	:	Virtue is completed task; Vice is failure
Planet of Sephirah	:	Mars
Angels	:	Anaiel; Chaamiah
Astrological	:	Venus in Aquarius, zero–ten degrees
Colours	:	Swords Turquoise White; Background Soft Lilac Grey; Shading, Astrological and other symbols complementaries to above; Rays, clouds translucent Bright Scarlet; Rose petals and Hands White

The Five of Swords shows that the additional Sword from the previous card has, in fact, shattered the rose and split apart the locked swords through the application of too much force. The disunity has equal forces of two swords on each side, with a central disrupting sword. This force was necessary to break the locked stalemate of the previous swords.

The falling petals and clouds lowered again to the bottom of the card show that again the wings of the white eagle have been clipped. The clouds are higher, however, which appears to show more moisture as strength is restored and the Mercury is united with the Sun and Moon for transmutation. This is the first stage of multiplication which is an operation of the Great Work where the 'Powder of Projection' is multiplied. To do this the operation must be repeated many times but each time with more perfected matters, but even in this a reduction of time occurs. It is said that *every solution is made according to expediency and that every matter which dissolves the Moon dissolves also the Sun*. This reduction is the first stage as explained above.

When observing this card you will see the negative influences shown as the two outer hands. The initial or central sword represents truth. As such, this has shattered the framework around it resulting in a new framework to be established.

The Angelic Choir of angels of Geburah of Yetzirah is called the Seraphim (Fiery Serpents). These angels are strongly karmic in their designation and help to make us understand the necessity of trial through Fire so that Love and the acceptance of the Light will eventually come to us. It is the acceptance of karmic debt that must be repaid that these angels excel in and they teach us revenge is destructive and should only be repaid with love.

The Virtue of Geburah is the energy to complete what we have set out to do, in spite of the obstacles placed in our path. This shows building or rebuilding and brings out competitiveness as old values are exchanged for new ones. It is very much learning by experience. The Vice of Geburah is shown by the triumph of Geburah's destructive powers. It is the 'would-be conqueror' being conquered. The destructive force of one's own nature being turned back on one.

The first angel governing this card is Anaiel 'Lord of Hosts, Virtues' and the second is Chaamiah who is titled 'Hope'. Both concepts are restriction with a hope of potential development.

The Sephirotic Planetary Influence is Mars in an Air Element. This tends to bring out a dynamic intellectual capacity. It can blunt Mars's force to a certain extent but the Airy framework can turn to severe criticism if one is not careful. Any form of communication with Mars in this position will lack tact and shows problems in this area.

Venus in Aquarius characterises avoidance of relationships; emotions governing higher reasoning. The love of independence shows that any close relationship will not last, if it gets started. Variety here is the spice of life and this shows an ever-changing state. Eccentricity is also shown as it exemplifies those who make their own rules in society and will not follow any one else. It is the essence of the soldier or mistress of fortune. One's needs are usually fulfilled through groups and friends, however, a high standard is expected of others and often leads to disappointment.

Divination

Geburah of Vau—power of the Word. Around one there are constant arguments and disagreements and before long people will try and drag you into their problems and even provide you with a set of enemies. It is time to stay neutral and keep away from disagreements. Defeat, loss, malice, spite and slander, evil-speaking, questions not being answered, failure after effort, anxiety, trouble, aspects which are malicious, slandering, lying, spiteful; someone or something blunders into a situation without considering the consequences. In relationships this card usually depicts loss of love, disappointment, or just fear of defeat, but something that is retrievable. Depression can cloud one's thinking; no sympathy shown from others; a negative outlook. In material matters there is apprehension about investments and security; loss of money; mishandling of matters. Loss of job, or just feeling one's work does not fulfil one's needs and quitting. Sickness in health, usually brought on psychosomatically.

Six of Swords

Title	:	Lord of Earned Success
Element	:	Air
Force	:	Vau
Alchemic	:	Second Stage Multiplication
Kabbalistic World	:	Yetzirah
Sephirah	:	Tiphareth
Angelic Choir	:	Malachim
Vice/Virtue	:	Virtue is Devotion to the Great Work; Vice Egotistical Price
Planet of Sephirah	:	Sun
Angels	:	Rehael; Yeizael
Astrological	:	Mercury in Aquarius, twenty–thirty degrees
Colours	:	Swords Soft Reddish Grey; Background Soft Lilac Grey; Complementary colours to background and swords for shading, astrological and other symbols; Clouds and star Shell Pink of Tiphareth; Rose and Hands White

In the Six of Swords the former balance of the Four of Swords has been restored but on a stronger footing. All six Swords now support and are bound by the Rose, which is the symbol of the goal. Three swords joined to one handle in a hand is a trident. So, here we have two tridents. As they are raised above the centre of the card supporting the rose, these allude to our lower consciousness being raised into the realm and consciousness of the higher consciousness and uniting to form a bond of realisation. The Trident is power, threefold, and an emblem of the Gods and known as the thunderbolt of heaven which imparts realisations through its announcements. The pattern formed by the crossing tridents is a cross within a square. The triple force creates a counterbalancing affect. The rose therein brings forth the Rosicrucian concept of the 'Rosy Cross' indicating 'cosmic truth'. Alchemically, the clouds risen again show the white eagle flying, but not quite, as the clouds still touch the bottom and are joining in the bottom centre, therefore the eagle is still earthbound. In this you will see the consciousness still being bound to the lower as it experiences higher realisations. Second Stage Multiplication is where the Peacock's tail emerges with the appearance of glorious colours, which announce a success of the work. Hence the title of this card being 'Lord of Earned Success'. There is union of minds, higher and lower, of form and matter, intellect and intuition, thus all forms of thought are illuminated.

Yetzirah of Tiphareth is the angelic Choir called the Malachim ('Kings' or 'Controllers'), and these are analogous to the Order of Virtues. These angels give reinforcement to those who need it, especially in matters of war and health. These angels form the esoteric study patterns that become available to those who undergo the Tiphareth experience. Their duty is to make these study frameworks available and to help strengthen the Will to succeed in those aspirants that they choose to help on the path of the Great Work.

The Virtue of Tiphareth is Devotion to the Great Work, which relates to the commitment they form when they enter this level. It is strict adherence to making sacrifices so that one can continue with the discipline needed in the search for the hidden mysteries. The Vice of this Sephiroth is Egotistical pride. It is the inability to cope with the problems that go with the responsibility of attaining this level. It is Ego inflation at its worst and can cause a shutdown of one's ability.

The first angel governing this card is Rehael, who is titled 'Swift to Condone' and the second is Yeizael, who is titled 'Making Joyful as Wine'. The two associations show negativeness dampening a celebration or happy event.

The Planetary association is the Sun in an Air Element and relates to the framework of intellectual stimulation in any group or structure that is dedicated to an ideal. It shows almost no limitations on how far one can go and is very auspicious.

Mercury in Aquarius characterises teaching and scientific development. Aquarius relates to the scientific mind, an ability to tap into a humanistically universal understanding, and to tap into aspects of the archetypal realms of consciousness. Mercury in this Sign shows ease in understanding the hidden meanings in mystical and occult subjects as well as an inclination towards travel. Awareness of self and life expands through group contacts and friendships. A merging of ideas and minds is essential for these characters. They are often spokespersons for groups or causes.

Divination

Tiphareth of Vau—harmony in thought. This is a time where nothing will come easy for the enquirer but when it does, it comes in bucketfuls. Success through hard work and effort; labour; journey by water; shows success but through careful calculation lest too much force will shatter the Rose. Success after anxiety and trouble; difficulty in dealing with people initially is indicated but success comes later after energy expenditure. A good time to make plans and money; good for travel, group activities, conferences, gatherings; uniqueness in families; stabilizing love relationships; competition or speculation through strategy; work promotions; partnership support; successful business agreements and contracts; popularity. Study; the metaphysical sciences may be explored; otherwise, general academic study. Co-operation through organizations; intercommunication; humanistic concerns.

If ill-dignified then selfishness and conceit, lack of patience and applied effort, things attempted only half-heartedly.

Seven of Swords

Title	:	Lord of Unstable Effort
Element	:	Air
Force	:	Vau
Alchemic	:	Third Stage Multiplication
Kabbalistic World	:	Yetzirah
Sephirah	:	Netzach
Angelic Choir	:	Elohim
Vice/Virtue	:	Virtue is Unselfishness; Vice is Greed
Planet of Sephirah	:	Venus
Angels	:	Kehihael; Mikhael
Astrological	:	Moon in Aquarius, twenty–thirty degrees
Colours	:	Swords very cold pale blue; background soft lilac grey; shading, astrological symbols, rose stalk and leaves complementary colours to swords and background; clouds are Grapefruit in colour; Hands and Rose White

The Seven of Swords introduces an additional Sword. The detente situation in the previous card is now at its limit and is, to a certain extent, unstable with the introduction of the neutral force. Both sets of Swords agree to give the Rose to the neutral force for safe-keeping but this force is an interim one only.

This is not a negative card, but more one of neutrality. With the two tridents representing the threefold power twice over, and alluding to above and below, there is still power and connection of the lower with the higher. The seventh sword holding the rose threatens to unbalance the situation and as it comes from below with the rose on the lower part of the shaft, it shows that spirit has descended closer to matter.

The thickened clouds imply a lot of heat added to the great waters (elixir). Socrates says:

> When the heat penetrates, it makes subtle all earthly things, that are of service to the matter, but come to no final form while it is acting on the matter.

With the Moon in Aquarius being the astrological association of this card, the moon modifies the heat by its coldness and here the Distillation occurs seven times to separate the destructible moisture. Alchemically you also see the Swan appearing out of Cauda Pavonis (third stage Multiplication). We have Cygnus, the Swan, flying in midheaven. The swan of eternity, flying in time and space, is the symbol of life itself, the cleansing, purifying 'living waters' of Aquarius. The Swan, however, has not yet matured, alluding to instability due to maturity. Symbolically the Swan represents transformation and change.

Yetzirah of Netzach is the angelic Choir called the Elohim ('Divine ones'). The Elohim provide man with a glimpse of what he can attain if he so desires. This glimpse is through the Archetypal concept, supplied by Tiphareth, through the process of reflection. The general title of this choir is Princes or Principalities. Occult teachings state that the Elohim are spirits capable of giving treasure and riches and they and their dependents serve in all operations, being a mass composed of different orders. Their additional functions are to inspire religious thought and action and raise the level of the motional consciousness so that the energies of Tiphareth will be clearer on the next step up the Tree.

The Virtue of Netzach is Unselfishness. It relates to the individual who ascends the Tree and must leave behind all his or her worldly desires as Tiphareth is entered. It is the concept of personal sacrifice. The Vice of Netzach is Greed and shows a strong pull from the material side. This is the concept of the pleasure-seeker with little or no regard for the feelings of others. The Greed makes the individual a slave to his or her own passions.

The first angel governing this card is Kehihael, who is titled 'Triune' and the second is Mikhael, who is titled 'Who is like unto Him'. Both show the threefold action of things in order to balance them correctly.

The Planetary Sephirotic energy is Venus in an Air Element. This relates to money and influence made through the media, via the arts. Any form of communication will be positive and propel the individual into areas of success. There is also a strong affinity to religious groups. Travelling is strongly indicated with financial and spiritual rewards as a result.

The Moon in Aquarius characterises the unconventional, the eccentric, and occult pursuits. It also shows independent thought and direction. There is a tendency to be social yet aloof at the same time. There are strong tendencies to go with one's intuitive instincts before thinking things through, plus extreme sensitivity to occult influences—such as channelling. It is the time for the unconventional. These people can be very emotional, but with an uncanny way of reasoning out their emotions. Security can be sought through groups or friends. As they have very open minds, they can be very impressionable and very humanistic.

Divination

Netzach of Vau—inspired thought. This card relates to the concept of playing a waiting game; letting people come to you when they are ready and not before. Freedom of choice is important. Changeableness, emotional impulsiveness and sensitivity; a need to utilize all talents; partial success, yielding when victory is within grasp; over-emphasis on the future rather than the present; feelings of inadequacy; affrontment and insolence, spying on others, betrayal of confidences; inconsistent effort. In most situations the inference is that it is too early to act, so wait. Creativity is focused through children whether of mind, soul or flesh. A need to gain security; feeling insecure. Workload increases, feeling a situation is futile. The advice of this card is persistence, to remain positive and aware so that current delays are only temporary. Indecisiveness; intrusion. On a more evolved level this card shows unfolding of spirituality, a time of allowing change and preparation for greater work to come.

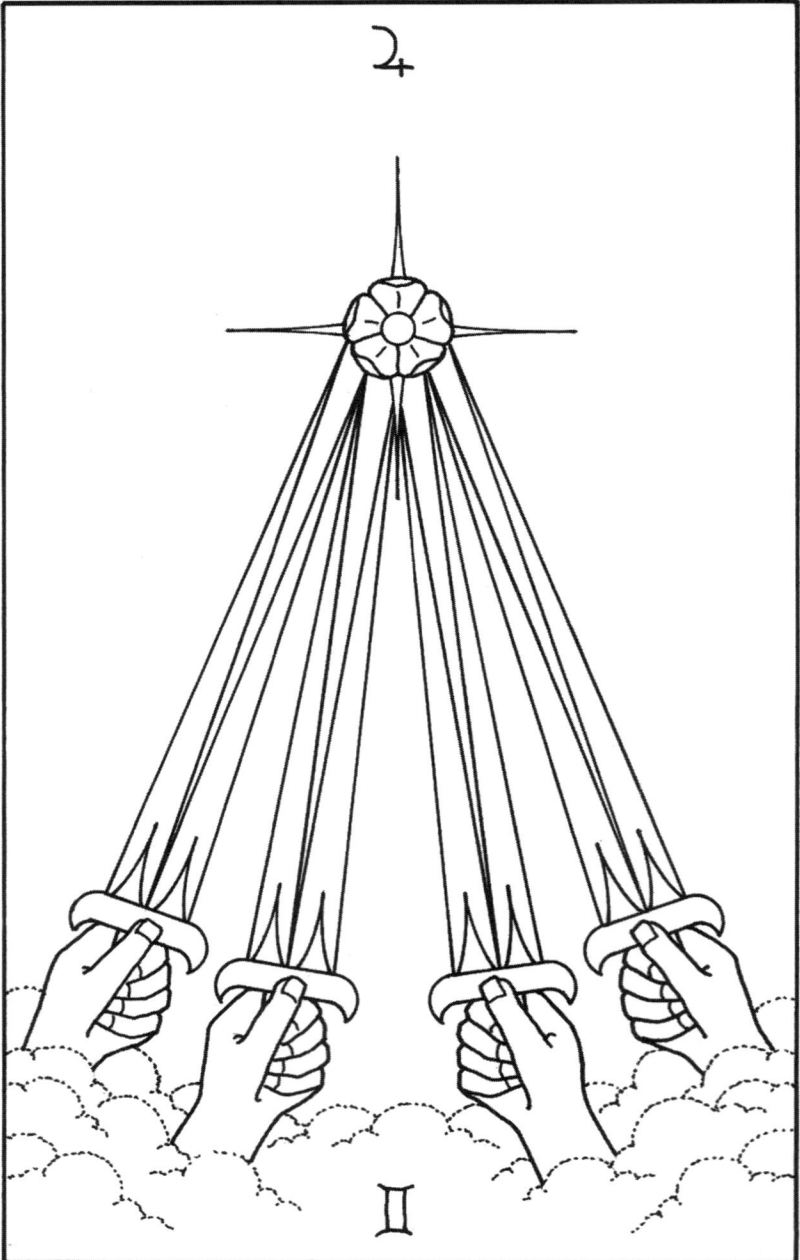

Eight of Swords

Title	:	Lord of Shortened Force
Element	:	Air
Force	:	Vau
Alchemic	:	First Stage Separation
Kabbalistic World	:	Yetzirah
Sephirah	:	Hod
Angelic Choir	:	Beni-Elohim
Vice/Virtue	:	Virtue is Truthfulness; Vice is Self-deception and deceit
Planet of Sephirah	:	Mercury
Angels	:	Vamibael; Iahael
Astrological	:	Jupiter in Gemini, zero–ten degrees
Colours	:	Blue Violet Swords; Cinnamon Brown background; shading, astrological symbols complementary colours to the swords and background; clouds and star translucent Garnet Red; White Hand and Rose

The eight swords balance the rose. If too much force or pressure is applied to the rose it will shatter. However, it is not shattered nor pierced, therefore is only restricted in movement, hence the name 'Lord of Shortened Force'.

This is a very difficult alchemical stage where much care must take place in the operation. In the first stage of Separation a constant temperature and pressure must be maintained so that only the pure and subtle shall separate from the impure and gross. This is 'Separatio

Elementorum'. The pure is imprisoned by the impure and is through careful operation released. The Golden Treatise of Hermes says:

> *Take the flying volatile and drown it flying and divide and separate it from its rust, which yet holds it in death; draw it forth and repel it from itself, that it may live and answer thee, not by flying away into the regions above, but by truly forbearing to fly. For if thou shalt deliver it out of its straightness, after this imprisonment and in the days known to thee shalt by reason have ruled it, then will it become a suitable companion unto thee and by it thou wilt become to be a conquering lord, with it adorned.*

Yetzirah of Hod is the angelic Choir called the Beni-Elohim ('Sons of God'). Their function is to divert the powers of Light and Darkness to an intellectual framework so that each can be adequately grasped. They help provide this distinction also through our thought processes and archetypal imagery. As a result, they sow the seeds to understanding on any magical or hermetic philosophy that we can adapt to. Also they give us the motivational impetus to balance up the intellectual approach.

The Virtue of Hod is Truthfulness. When one enters Hod one's intellectual framework gradually works together in a balanced relationship with the Truth. The Truth comes from the communicative aspect of Hod's nature. The Vice of Hod is Self-deception and Deceit. This is brought about through Ego inflation, due to emotive responses of the Water Element, which makes us lose our sense of perception, especially through our mental imagery. The Psyche here is being cornered and will send out false responses to the personality resulting in Self-deception.

The first angel governing this card is Vamibael, who is titled 'The Name which is over All' and the second is Iahael, who is titled 'Supreme Essence'. Both concepts display an all-encompassing force which wishes to be identified with its essence.

The Sephirotic Planetary association is Mercury in an Air Element. The main theme is one of communication and feedback from it. The whole concept is based almost entirely on an intellectual framework and a lack of any emotive responses, which can be both good and bad, depending on the situation. It is calculation at its best.

Jupiter in Gemini can relate to intellectual activity that is not tested practically. The whole combination is extremely versatile and shows a great deal of changeability and emphasis on the lower mind. Also those with this combination may lack practical experience in matters; they are often stimulated to intellectual pursuit. In matters of communication those with Jupiter in Gemini may talk too much on associating factors, but take too long to get to the point on any matter. Their energies expand too far and often never complete anything. This is often an aversion to restriction. On the whole this combination is very auspicious but when seen through the framework of the pictorial aspect of this card the expanding force is restricted somewhat until a great deal of pressure is built up, shown by the six swords restricting the rose. Too much force applied to too small an area.

Divination

Hod of Vau—the intellect. In this situation, as the rose has not been shattered, one manages to cope with the mental pressure, but only just. It is a time where people around you are very demanding and there is no free time. Too much attention to the whole at the expense of the detail and everyone wanting something all at the same time. While this force is not overwhelming it cries out for personal attention. Restriction of the mind, where one feels bound to a particular thought pattern or life situation; inability to see clearly; refusal to see. Plans may be interfered with; financial difficulties and adverse circumstances restrict one; obstacles in all directions. In relationships people do not see eye to eye on matters; emotional obligations cause restriction to one's freedom; relationships can become bondages. Difficulty in freedom of expression. On a lighter note, the ordeals depicted by this card cause one to draw on inner powers and inner truth in order to release oneself from such restrictions. If ill-dignified it is malice, pettiness and domineering qualities; division of ideas; conflict and interference; prosecution; capture; imprisonment; restriction. The only way the forces that this card represents can be handled is with patience and a sense of order.

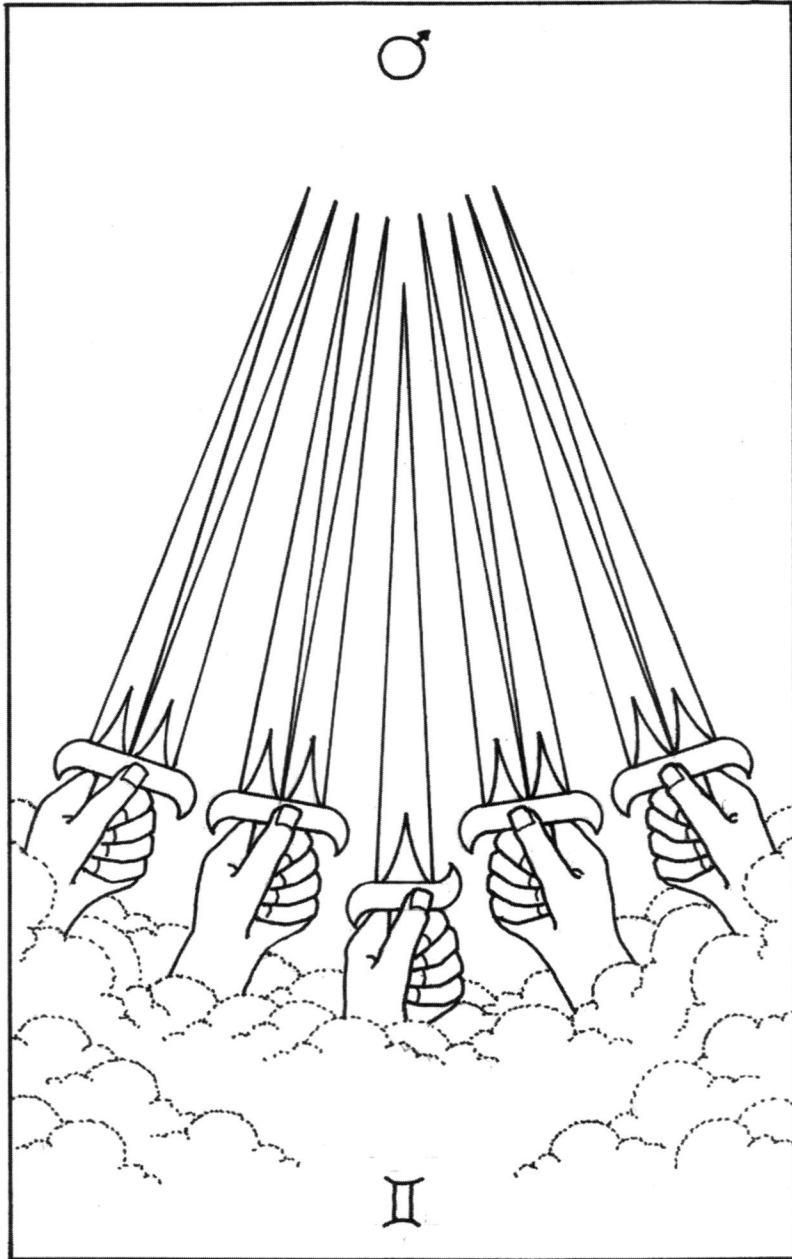

Nine of Swords

Title	:	Lord of Despair and Cruelty
Element	:	Air
Force	:	Vau
Alchemic	:	Second Stage Separation
Kabbalistic World	:	Yetzirah
Sephirah	:	Yesod
Angelic Choir	:	Ashim
Vice/Virtue	:	Virtue is Independence; Vice is Subservience
Planet of Sephirah	:	Moon
Angels	:	Nghaneauel; Mochaiel
Astrological	:	Mars in Gemini, ten–twenty degrees
Colours	:	Scarlet Swords; Cinnamon Brown background; shading and astrological symbols complementaries to swords and background; Clouds translucent very dark violet blue; Hands White

The Nine of Swords has the rose omitted. This has been destroyed by too much pressure (shown as a concentrated build up in the previous card) and the Swords now have a lack of direction. They eventually turn inward towards each other. The central sword strikes up from the centre depicting severe disruption in contrast to the previous card's control. The unconscious strikes back and without the rose, there is no illumination from the Spirit. This is absence of the higher mind. With the lower mind only in control, there becomes a lack of discipline to thought and blind energy, without motive or reasoning. It is disruptive to the soul and repetitive as it struggles to survive the only way it knows.

Alchemically the second stage of Separation alludes to the 'Fire of the Stone'. Furthermore, from the Golden Treatise of Hermes:

> *Extract from the ray its shadow and impurity by which the clouds hang over it, defile and keep away the light; since by means of its construction and fiery redness, it is burned. Take, my son, this redness, corrupted with the water, which is as a live coal holding the fire, which if thou shalt withdraw so often until the redness is made pure, then it will associate with thee, by whom it was cherished and in whom it rests.*

It is also the 'red lion' who must drink his own blood once he is discovered terrestrial. This further alludes to the Last Supper, where Christ ate his own flesh and drank his own blood (symbolically). The meaning behind this may be that one must return to the unconscious beginnings to recognise and accept the true self.

Yesod of Yetzirah is the angelic Choir called the Ashim (Fiery Ones). Their function is to make ground on each day by preparing the subconscious through dreams at night. To a certain extent they help one form the creativity needed for day to day activity and also work on planting seeds of ideas for long-term growth projects. These angels do not create, but put things in such a manner that the energy and direction they give is more easily understood. They function through the Mental Plane and are considered conductors and arrangers of the conversion of the energies from the higher self in more tangible terms.

The Virtue of Yesod is Independence and it is here that one learns to compromise with the dual polarity of the two pillars of the Tree. As a result of the duality, an intermediate concept is formed which could be ascribed to Independence or the first stage of manifestation. The Vice of Yesod is Subservience and shows a lack of motivation and a state where one has to be guided constantly.

The first angel to govern this card is Nghaneauel, who is titled 'Rejoicing', while the second is Mochaiel who is titled 'Vivifying'. Both concepts relate to a celebration due to a type of birth or rebirth. The implication is that through hard times a new lease on life develops.

The Sephirotic Planetary association is the Moon in an Air Element. This is an ever-changing situation and shows a stimulation of intellectual pursuits. There is very much a lack of substance here and people will tend to grasp at theories rather than the practical considerations.

Mars in Gemini characterizes one who manifests nervous energy, rapid thought, skill in the communications field. This also relates to an expression of energy on the mental level with the influence of Mars being anything but steady. Its impact in Gemini is usually through speech or writing and shows a critical flavour in its composition. Mars does enhance the communication skills but if uncontrolled can be a rambling scenario with no fixed point of reference. One can expect trouble in areas of travel or communication with Mars's scattering effect on Gemini. One's vitality and power has to reaffirmed. Mental pressure on self or others, playing power games with another.

Divination

Yesod of Vau—merging intuition and thought. By turning inward the swords, by analogy, relate to the probing of the mind. Mental cruelty that is self-inflicted is one of the meanings of this card as also is too much pressure from study or work. It is also despair, cruelty, pitilessness, malice, suffering, loss and misery, lying, dishonesty and slander. In love matters one partner inflicts mental cruelty on the other. In other cases a person may be so confused their mind cannot settle on any clarity. Relationships can be painful, disputes arise, impatience. Travel is not advised as a scattering of energy occurs; there could be injury. Discord in family matters; pressure from all directions. In health matters there may be nerve damage, psychological stress and trauma, or just stress in general. Pain through miscarriage or abortion. Work issues provide a lot of pressure but no recognition. Difficulty putting ideas together; inability to study; examination stress; a feeling of 'I am going out of my mind'. Aggressiveness and contempt. Mystic or spiritual pursuits must not be continued until one is able to still one's mind. The Two of Swords is the antidote to this card.

Ten of Swords

Title	:	Lord of Ruin
Element	:	Air
Force	:	Vau
Alchemic	:	Third Stage Separation
Kabbalistic World	:	Yetzirah
Sephirah	:	Malkuth
Angelic Choir	:	Kerubim
Vice/Virtue	:	Virtue is Discrimination; Vice is Scepticism
Planet of Sephirah	:	Earth
Angels	:	Damabaiah; Mengel
Astrological	:	Sun in Gemini, twenty–thirty degrees
Colours	:	Rich Amber Swords; Cinnamon Brown Background; shading and astrological symbols complementaries to swords and background; clouds translucent tertiaries, flecked with glowing gold; hands White

The Ten of Swords goes a step further than the previous card for the swords now turn toward each other into separate warring forces, since the rose is not present to reveal some sort of Spiritual goal. The six hands however, show some form of balance and equilibrium beneath. The two central swords are in combat, holding a concentrated force turned inward which could go on for eternity unless a transformation and separation takes place. If it does not, destruction occurs, hence the name 'Lord of Ruin'.

Alchemically we have here the third stage of Separation—*Separatio Per Abscessum*. Soul and Spirit has been separated from the Body and later, when purified, will be infused back into the Body. As you see, it is the Body's material Soul which must be separated and transformed into something much higher; thus a conversion from its own materiality. The White Eagle, then, has flown.

Malkuth of Yetzirah is the angelic choir Kerubim ('Whence I shall be led'). These angels are considered to be the higher echelons of the four Elemental states. Though they are not elementals by nature their function is to direct them and all elementals take their orders from this angelic choir. They take the energy of the elements and set them in motion. Folklore has it that the Kerubim were in fact once elemental by nature but graduated from the boundaries to take higher office when their spirits were transmuted to that of Light.

The Virtue of Malkuth is Discrimination and this is the process where we are able to discern the good from the bad, the positive from the negative. Because Malkuth is a world where there are numerous overlaps of other dimensions, Discrimination is needed so that we have a sense of our own reality. The Vice of Malkuth is Scepticism (of other existences) where the Ego takes over and one cannot accept anything until proven at a Malkuthian level. There is little thought or dedication to the spiritual content of man or even in the Earth for that matter. By closing off like this to the dictates of our Higher Selves, we deny the Self the right to dedicate anything for a higher purpose.

The first angel governing this card is Damabaiah, who is titled 'Fountain of Wisdom' and the second is Mengel, who is titled 'Nourishing All'. Both concepts allude to growth and nourishment.

The Sephirotic Planetary association here is aligned with the geocentric view of the Earth being the centre of our Universe. Within this concept there are both positive and negative traits. The Positive trait is that Earth is accepted as a living planet to respect and merge with. The negative aspect is where the Earth is exploited for maximum gain and no thought is given to the later consequences.

The Sun in Gemini characterizes dualism and adaptability. This meaning is not negative at all but when it is expressed through the framework of the card it becomes self-defeating and destructive. It has a total reliance on the mental faculties while ignoring the practical within a practical environment. This shows a leaning towards an impulsive nature for as soon as plans do not work, then another set of plans are draughted up. Oral skills at communication are important here and show inspirational qualities. The Sun in Gemini typifies as a Sun Sign, however, in association with this card, the more negative traits are emphasised.

Divination

Malkuth of Vau shows the ending of a matter, disruption before plans are completed. Complete and utter disruption; ruination of all plans; this force was conceived to ruin others; strong will; compulsiveness; pride; lack of stillness of thought; insanity; no concern for others; injury; lack of logic or reasoning; false hopes; mental anguish; loss of mental and psychological control; hardship; rifts; sadness; tears; deceit; divorced from reality. On a lighter level the Ten of Swords can just be showing a stressful time and with good cards surrounding, a time that can be easily handled. In relationships one can have one's soul laid bare; be rejected; boosting one's ego at the expense of others. In work issues the work environment can be a battleground. Others' views confuse and stress one. Too much pressure from all levels. Aspirations are not fulfilled; contracts cause a sense of imprisonment; a situation is deadlocked; no mercy. The thought pattern appears to be 'if I can't have it then I will destroy it'. Brainwashing; obstacles in travel; public debates not going in one's favour. This card is the opposite of the Ace of Swords, therefore the Ace of Swords is its antidote.

Ace of Disks

Title	:	Root Powers of the Earth
Element	:	Earth
Force	:	Heh final
Alchemic	:	Aurum Aurae
Kabbalistic Worlds	:	Assiah
Sephirah	:	Kether
Magical Weapon	:	Fylfot Cross
Grade	:	10 = 1 Ipissimus
Planet of Sepirah	:	Neptune
Archangel	:	Auriel
Myth	:	Rod of Aaron
God form	:	Ptah
Mineral	:	Diamond
Plant	:	Passion Flower
Colours	:	Clouds, hand, roses, stars and central circle of disk and winged disk, brilliant white rayed gold; second and fourth circles of disk, rose branch and leaves, primary green; Black for third and outer rim of circles, of disk and for shading on rosebush; Maltese Cross and Kerubic Cross are Red; Background of card translucent red with rays of white coming through

Kether of Heh Final is the last stage of growth manifesting in a new cycle or era. The central Disk in this card has four concentric circles showing the four Elemental Divisions of Malkuth fuelled by a fifth, as the innermost white circle and representing spirit. This works through the balanced framework of the Four Rivers of Paradise, which are represented by a red Greek cross. The Four White roses around the circle are placed so that they form the outline of a square showing the balance of spirit and matter. The symmetry is a cross within a circle within a square. The roses symbolize both heaven and earth, life and death. Alchemically they are the Work and the Rebirth of the Spiritual. The twelve subdivisions of white relates to the twelve astrological divisions and their effect on matter, especially through the seasons. The eight leaves on the Tree show the regenerative concept of nature (the four corporeal and four incorporeal elements). The four roses and the eight leaves add up to twelve and stand for the twelve-rayed Star. The White Winged Maltese Cross shows spiritual growth of matter through the Solar influence, as applied to man. As Man is master of his own destiny the hand thus grasps the branch on which the Disk sits.

This card can also be linked to the biblical story of the Rod of Aaron. As a rod of power it represented the subjective spiritual mind which operates on a higher mental sub-plane and ministers to the Causal body development. Putting together all the symbology of the Ace of Disks it points to the Eternal Synthesis, the great whole of the visible Universe, the realisation of counter-balanced power.

There are three rosebuds on the branch of the Ace of Disks, which relate to the Triad, the Unmanifested Trinity and alchemically to Salt, Sulphur and Mercury. When these three alchemical principles are united after purification they become an entire and perfect body. In the *Praxis Spagyrica Philosophical* it says:

> *Accordingly God brought forth nature by way of a natural union and birth, so it can work, sustain and produce itself. Through mutual assistance it can now bring forth everything decreed by a heavenly influence and impression upon it. It will show itself through material manifestation, substance and being, out of whose mixture arise the elements as water, air and earth. Within the three lies hidden the fourth element of fire. Through the coction of fire is brought about a soul, a spirit and a body. Through this union we will find them as Mercury, Sulphur and Salt. These three, when united, represent a perfect and entire body no matter under what form. Everything in the world is separated into three, namely: Animalia, vegetabilia and mineralia.*

The alchemical stage of this card is *Aurum Aurae*—Golden Aura. It is said that the 'Sun and Gold' have a 'special correspondence and a peculiar attractive power and love together, because the Sun hath wrought the Gold through the three principles, … but hath its original and beginning from the heavenly and golden loadstone/As a branch is now held out of the clouds, the great waters have now been transmuted into Earth, therefore now we have the mists over the land and the preparation of also, the First Matter'.

The Egyptian God-form associated here is Ptah, Father of the Gods (which reinforces his link through Kether),who was self-created and built up his own body. Ptah was a God whose head supported the sky and his feet rested on the earth. This also gives a distinct parallel with Metatron and Sandalphon as placed in the Tree of Life. Ptah's seat of worship was Memphis and he was a God of Wealth, Vegetation and of the Master Builders. One of his important functions was to build Halls of Learning.

The symbolic manifestation of Kether is typified by the Fylfot or Swastika. This symbol has been the basis for many religions, Christian, Hindu, Buddhist and is also inherent in the religions of the American Indians, to name but a few. This universal symbol is also linked very firmly with the solar wheel and while it is shown stationary, its function is one of movement. When moving, the four bent arms of the Swastika form the four concentric circles on the Disk. Other associations are the Crown and the point (first point of reference or beginning).

Kether of Assiah is the Rosicrucian Grade of Ipissimus ('he who is most himself') shown by the characters 10 = 1. Some of those who reach this highest level of attainment with the Rosicrucian system, become heads of various Orders using either a visible or invisible guidance. They become a very pure channel for the higher powers to work through. It must be pointed out that they are still of Assiah and must obey its rules. Some of those who attain this level do not work through groups at all. They are spurred on to new areas of development which they pioneer, through many mediums, to reach others of similar vibrational level (Rays) and help them in their struggle to work through the various 'sheaths' of Assiah.

The Sephirotic Planetary association is Neptune in an Earth Element. This shows growth on the material plane where the emotive issues are looked at in more practical terms and bringing together ideals and expressing them in a way we can understand. It is a good down-to-earth analogy with Neptune in an Earth Element and will help us to understand the large amount of changes that are about to take place in our life.

In the Mineral Kingdom, associated with Kether, is the Diamond. By virtue of its shape it relates to the seventh chakra, which is situated on the top of the head and the sixth chakra which is called the Brow chakra. One of its functions on the subtle energy level is to remove blockages and negativity, by removing negative thought forms, helping the body detoxify itself and working at clarity of thought.

In the Plant Kingdom, associated with Kether, is the Passion Flower. This flower works primarily on both the Crown and Brow chakras and its function, like the diamond, is to release negativity. One interesting side function of this is clearing the chakras so that channelling can occur, for this plant has the ability to tap into any type of religious or quasi-religious energy. It helps to readjust one's spiritual awareness without the negative pitfalls and odd behavioural patterns that sometimes accompany any spiritual quest. This plant helps combine the high spiritual nature with that of the earth and integrates the two, producing a type of harmony.

As the 'Root of the Powers of Earth' the Ace of Disks is the Earth element with the Sun and Moon united, but mainly the Lunar, cold, passive and feminine nature. With fire it is warm, with air it is dry and with water it is heavy, cold and damp. The earth element is symbolic of material and concrete forms, matter, the physical body, our operation in daily life throughout the five senses; structure, form, life in its most material form, nourishment.

Divination

This is the final state, the material but still in its infancy as things have not yet had a chance to develop to full potential; new a state of development, whether it be career or home; moves here are not yet seen that will propel the querent forward resulting in material gain; a new jobs appearing and also the successful completion of a sale where a large amount of money changes hands. Health turns better after a period of illness; sureness in outcomes of new projects; positive outlook; promises of better things to come; receiving the fruits of one's efforts; gain of material goods; pleasant relationships; gatherings; education developing; readiness to enlarge one's field of activity; buildings; new home; property; house plans are drawn up; negotiations get under way; new beginnings in all matters. Potential success; profit and fulfilment. Marriage; joining of couples; contracts; partnerships. Spiritual matters are confined to the material world and level of understanding through symbology. Rejuvenation. In a negative perspective the Ace of Disks can portray not enough knowledge or structure to develop to full potential what is required; rigidity in beliefs.

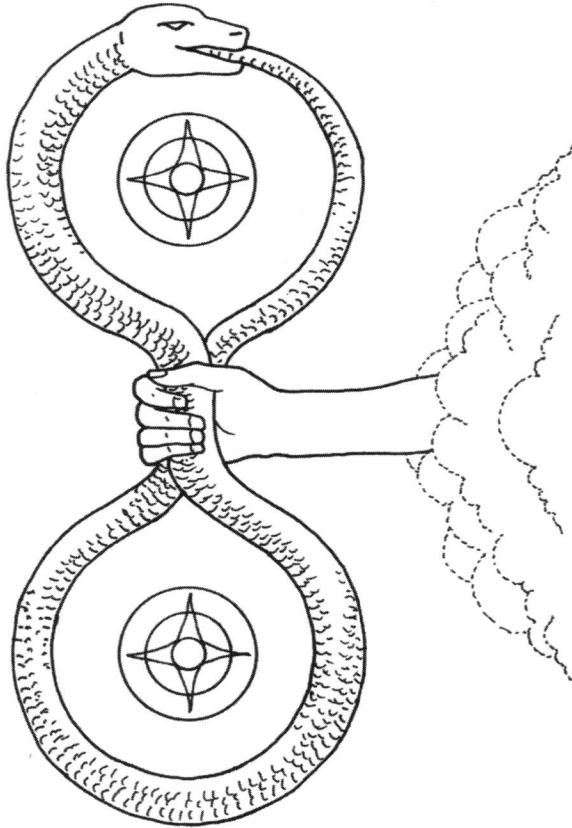

Two of Disks

Title	:	Lord of Harmonious Change
Element	:	Earth
Force	:	Heh final
Alchemic	:	First Stage Exaltation
Kabbalistic World	:	Assiah
Sephirah	:	Chokmah
Magical Weapon	:	Inner Robe of Glory
Grade	:	9 = 2 Magus
Planet of Sephirah	:	Zodiac (Uranus)
Angels	:	Lekabel; Vesheriah
Mineral	:	Turquoise
Plant	:	Amaranthus
Astrological	:	Jupiter in Capricorn, zero–ten degrees
Colours	:	Hand White; Clouds and stars White flecked with red, blue and Yellow; Disks Cool Blue rayed Yellow; Background Dark Greenish Brown; shading, astrological symbols, Snake, all complementary colours to the above

The Two of Disks has a green and gold serpent in the act of self-fertilisation which is needed for the roses which contain the seeds for growing. As yet there is no framework or bush for them to attach themselves to as it has not itself had the chance to grow. The shape of the serpent is the symbol of the figure eight, which is also called the Lemniscate or symbol of infinity. It is also the Western equivalent of the Ying/Yang symbolism of Chinese Taoism. This whole concept is supported by a hand that projects from the cloud representing the Sephirah of Chokmah.

The Magical Weapon or symbol of Chokmah is the 'Inner Robe of Glory'. This is the full awareness of the subtle bodies and energy centres. It is the inner kernel of the Soul being revealed to the devotee through experience and meditation. Dion Fortune summed this up in the following passage:

> It is the male force that implants the fecundating spark in the passive ovum on all planes and transforms its inert latency into active upbuilding growth and evolution … Force embodied in form and form ensouled in force.

This gets to the essence of what this card represents and is extremely complex, make no mistake about it. The Snake encircling the Disks shows a symbol of the dual circuit formed in the joining of the Etheric bodies during copulation. It is a symbol of the elemental marriage on a purely etheric level. There are other associations here as well, the Phallus, Tower and its geometric symbol of the straight line which has emerged from the point in Kether.

Alchemically this card is also the first stage of Exaltation and can allude to the salts of metals at the stage of their magistery during the whitening stage. The snake is often symbolized as Mercurius and called the 'fiery wheel of existence' when shaped in the figure eight. This figure has also stood for the alchemical symbols of Sal Alkali, Sal Gemma, White Vitriol and Tutia. Also, from these symbols one can have the pure fluid metal (zinc) that is itself generated from the three fluid primals and crystallised within salt.

Chokmah of Assiah is the Rosicrucian grade of Magus (9 = 2). True insight is revealed for the Magus and Wisdom results. It is a grade where individuals start to feel their power and many who attain this level have the ability to transcend many aspects of nature, associated with the elements. It is also a point where the karmic influences in this life have been recognised and are worked on, so that no more Karmic debt is incurred. There is also an understanding of past life influences and the Magus now understands what he or she must avoid and must embrace in spiritual pursuits.

The first angel governing this card is Lekabel, who is titled 'Teacher' and the second is Vesheriah, who is titled 'Upright'. Both concepts show that one teaches by example if they are to succeed.

The Planetary Sephirotic influence is Uranus in an Earth Element. The vastness of Uranus' electrical nature is now bogged down in the element. Sudden changes in one's financial and material status is shown. What one has today one may not be able to retain tomorrow. The earth framework has brought the quickness and erratic pattern of Uranus to a slow steady pace and very much is resolved on a more settled level.

Jupiter in Capricorn characterises change through re-adjustment where a complete revamping of self-image, takes place for the better. These people are concerned with becoming more than they are, therefore are full of goals and objectives and always look ahead. Because Jupiter is in its Fall in Capricorn, it weakens Capricorn's individualized energy and opens up the prospect of giving freely to others. The Capricorn influences re-enforce good financial considerations with Jupiter in this position. There is a strong desire for power and social status and wide travel. The changes occurring with Jupiter in this position, however, will be done through a conservative framework. Quite often success is obtained in foreign lands; there is power and brilliance with leadership qualities.

The Mineral association of Chokmah is Turquoise. Its function is to align and balance all the chakras so that a union with the Higher Self is made possible. It is also a healing stone and energy enhancer and its focus is to galvanise the body into repairing itself by focusing its healing power in the various subtle bodies. It is an excellent stone to use in any form of meditation and brings one closer to one's spiritual goals. Wisdom and understanding of one's earthly nature with the higher is more readily accepted with the energies from this stone.

The Plant association of Chokmah is Amaranthus. This plant works mainly on the Crown and Base chakras in an indirect way to stimulate the third chakra into taking a more aggressive role in the body. Its function is that of a 'revealer' for it brings forth wisdom from the Higher Self so that when a difficult task is performed in the physical, why the task has to be accomplished is thoroughly understood. This is accomplished by the increased manifestation of one's psychic abilities and the enhancement of our intuitive faculties in making us more aware.

White Vitriol is also known as Zinc Sulphate. Vitriol is also known as the Salts of Metals and Alkali is vitriol that has been mined. The formation of the material form in the mineral and vegetable kingdom takes place when Zinc is made solid by imbibing it in Sal Alkali (glass salt). Sal Gemma is a sparkling salt and known as a metaline salt.

Divination

Chokmah of Heh Final represents a pleasant change, a visit to friends. Increased realisation; constructive force towards creation; harmony of change, both gain and loss; a location change, whether it be work, home, health or going away from things, but ultimately for the better. Financial gain; return trip; a good business move; the wheel of commerce; reshaping of law; constant movement; finding new friends; a move for the better; industry; happy and healthy environment; gain or loss in investments, depending on surrounding cards; adjustments made when disrupted; changes within employment; stimulating interaction between people; social gaiety; improvement in relationships; alliances; adjustments to education; returning from where you started; journeys connecting business interests. If ill-aspected this card is unreliable, foolish, inconsistent and argumentative and shows a financial loss; unable to communicate clearly; suspicion.

Three of Disks

Title	:	Lord of Material Works
Element	:	Earth
Force	:	Heh final
Alchemic	:	Second Stage Exaltation
Kabbalistic World	:	Assiah
Sephirah	:	Binah
Magical Weapon	:	Outer Robe of Concealment
Grade	:	8 = 3 Magister Templi
Planet of Sephirah	:	Saturn
Angels	:	Yechuiah; Lehahaiah
Mineral	:	Star Sapphire
Plant	:	Witch Hazel
Astrological	:	Mars in Capricorn, ten–twenty degrees
Colours	:	Disks Poppy Scarlet rayed Amber; Background Dark Greenish Brown; Hand and Rosebuds White; Stars on disks, clouds, Grey flecked Pink; zodiac symbols, branch and leaves complementary colours to the disks and background

The three Disks are in the shape of an upward-pointing triangle, the geometric shape analogous to Binah. With the third Disk being added, fertilisation has occurred and been successful. As such, two new rosebuds are growing from the rosebush showing an infant state of development. Also, this is the first card to actually show the rosebush which has just been formed. This is the Supernal above the Abyss on the Tree of Life; the unmanifested being complete before it gives manifestation to the next triad below it. The rosebush also is shaped in the Papal cross alluding to concealed mysteries, which is also emphasised by the unopened rosebuds.

Alchemically the Three of Disks is second stage Exaltation. Additionally, the image depicted in this card is an upward-pointing triangle with a straight line dividing it from the apex through to the bottom, giving the symbol of *Sal Alkali*, representing the 'Oil of the Philosophers'. Another name for this is 'Salt of Wisdom'. We now draw a line where the branches of the rosebush spread out to the right and left. This is a line just above the apex of the triangle, giving the symbol of Cauda, which is Latin for 'tail of an animal'. If you will refer back to the Two of Disks, you will see how the Serpent swallows its tail. This is again depicted here and is alchemically referred to as self-fertilization. Another symbol comes from the images in the Three of Disks, which is the cross with a small circle on the top of the vertical line and on each end of the horizontal line (formed by the disks). This is a symbol for Vitriol, known as 'the true self', emphasizing the true essence of the stone being formed through rectification.

The Rosicrucian grade of Binah is the Magister Templi or Master of the Temple and is signified by the numbers 8 = 3. The actual significance of this grade is reflected in the title. Especially the term Master, which relates to having mastered a certain level. In this instance it is the Second Order and the Abyss that has to be mastered before one can transcend to the 8 = 3 which is the first level of the Third Order. The Third Order is one that transcends physical structures and is the plane where masters meet as equals. Those who reach this level must in reality look after, augment and change where necessary, the Second Order.

Binah of Assiah, the Magical Weapon or symbol is the Outer Robe of Concealment. This whole concept opens the door to many layers of meaning. Crowley directly related this to the Yoni and the principles inherent in Tantra. Dion Fortune was not so forthright though she also hinted at this direction, especially in the concept of fertility. This involves the sexual beatification of the coupling that lights the individual to ecstatic bliss and to heightened sensitivity of the senses. In the Two of Disks we dealt with the esoteric significance of sexual coupling and in this instance we have the physical and psychological implications of it, fertility being one such option. Taken in a much wider context it relates to the occult Outer Orders functioning under the direction of their inner counterparts. The term Outer Robe of Concealment can also show the outward expression of physical manifestation.

The first angel governing this card is Yechuiah, who is titled 'Knower of All Things' and the second is Lehahaiah, who is titled 'Merciful'. Both concepts relate to the gaining and sharing of knowledge that may help others.

The Sephirotic Planetary association is Saturn in an Earth Element. This is possibly the best position for Saturn to be in, for it shows most of the changes that are to come about are not visible at first and when results do come, they come as a great surprise. This is a very slow-moving situation but it does purport power and fame, only after great difficulty. Nothing will flow and everything positive that comes will be like extracting teeth, but it will come, in time.

Mars in Capricorn characterises a materialistic outlook with the drive and framework to make good at what one is working at. The Martian energy for dynamics is self-evident here and being Exalted in Capricorn shows a successful conclusion to whatever one applies oneself to. The tremendous drive often defeats others who simply give up. Not only drive but good strategy is also apparent with Mars in this Sign along with the label of the hard taskmaster.

Mars in Capricorn shows results by getting one's hands dirty. Any theory of applied Higher states of awareness has to be worked through on the practical level. This character is very ambitious, assertive, powerful and strong. Career and future is shaped.

The physical manifestation of Binah, in the Mineral Kingdom is the Star Sapphire. It aligns and opens all the seven chakras so that a higher state of awareness is reached and experienced on a conscious level. It increases one's psychic abilities and helps augment the Etheric body (by releasing the much needed energy that lies dormant in the chakras) which in turn directs the physical into a better state of health and attunement with people and things around the individual. So that nothing negative can occur while all this balancing is going on, this stone also stabilises the emotions.

The Plant Kingdom associated with Binah is shown by Witch Hazel. This plant works all the chakras and especially concentrates on enabling us to see ourselves in a very detached manner, so that we have the ability to let go all the negative patterns that we have kept up and are keeping us from being in tune with ourselves. This brings about a greater awareness of our true spiritual path and brings forth the necessary contact with the Higher Self so that one can be guided more directly on the path best open to us.

Divination

Binah of Heh Final relates to business, paid employment, commercial transaction. The foundation, or groundwork, has been laid before being built on; building up, erecting, creation and realisation, increase in the material side of things; productivity; fertility; growth; constructive ideas and actions; commercial transactions; financial and physical on a minor level; a hard worker; effort to self-educate and develop skills; craftsmen; builders; mechanics; physical labour; short journeys by road; property issues; sporting activities; body building; marriage may be worked at successfully; a working relationship within a partnership; investments work towards growth; recognition for work; earning esteem and honour; material in focus; sceptic; workaholic; politics; action speaks louder.

If ill-aspected then it shows selfishness, a narrow, prejudiced viewpoint, possibly trying to develop a situation before it has stabilised enough; aggravation between people; quarrels; discontent; encountering jealous, negative reactions from others; over-work.

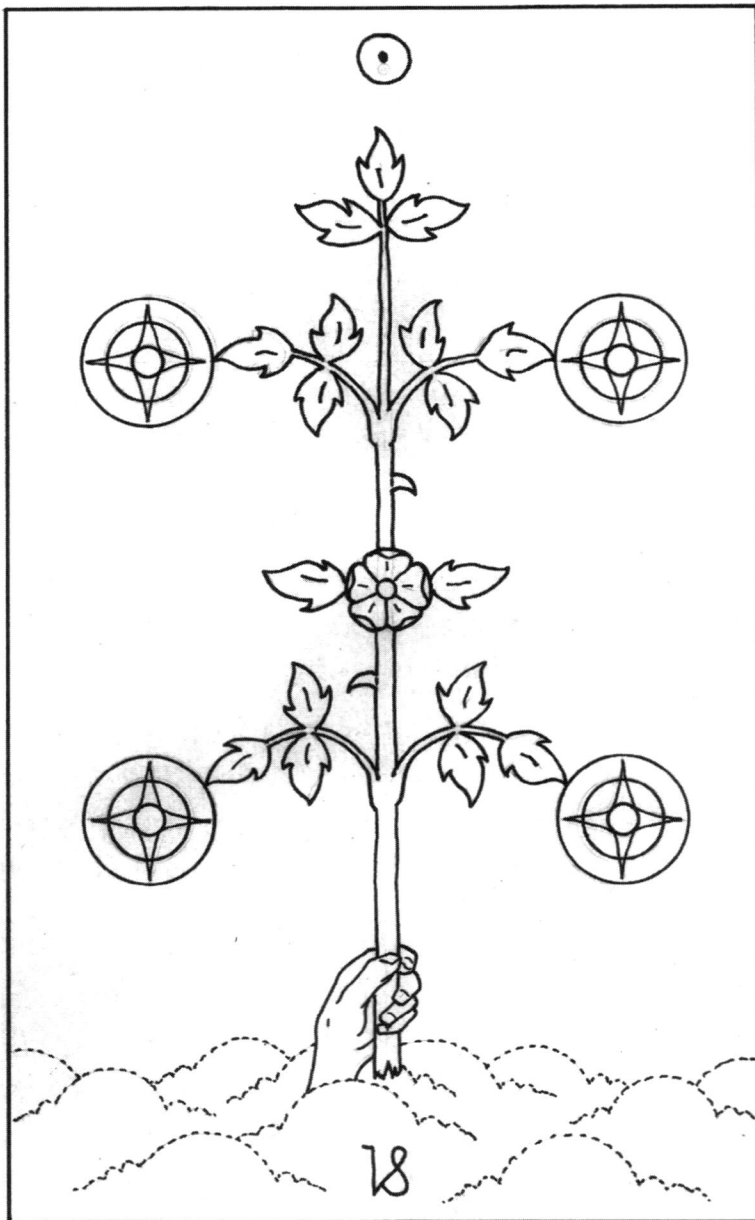

Four of Disks

Title	:	Lord of Earthly Power
Element	:	Earth
Force	:	Heh final
Alchemic	:	Third stage Exaltation
Kabbalistic World	:	Assiah
Sephirah	:	Chesed
Magical Weapon	:	Wand (Sceptre/Crook)
Grade	:	7 = 4 Adeptus Exemptus
Planet of Sephirah	:	Jupiter
Angels	:	Keveqaiah; Mendiel
Mineral	:	Ruby
Plant	:	Pomegranate
Astrological	:	Sun in Capricorn, twenty–thirty degrees
Colours	:	Deep Melon Yellow Disks; Pale Bluish Grey background; White hand and rose; complementary colours for the shading, rosebush and leaves and astrological signs; stars on disks and clouds Deep Azure, flecked Yellow

The Four of Disks has an extra Disk to the previous card but also shows a loss, for only one of the two rosebuds in the Three of Disks survived. As a result, it has bloomed fully and there are no other flowers to take and share in the vital essence that feeds it through the rosebush. The rosebush has grown around the rose and it is now placed in the centre of the entire bush and, in fact, to a certain extent controls the growth and structure of the bush itself due to its unique solar position, as a central force. The Disks around it form a square and are placed in juxtaposition to each other so that their weight will not interfere with the growth of the rose. The four sides of the square represent the four elements showing manifestation on the physical plane. With the Rose in the centre the symbol of a circle within a square is also formed, characterising a soul within the elements, therefore a divine guiding force and mastery within the physical plane.

Alchemically the Four of Disks is third stage Exaltation. This is the stage of purity and the Fire within:

> *The celestial fire which flows to us on the earth from the Sun is not such a fire as there is in Heaven, neither is it like that which exists upon the earth, but that celestial fire within is cold and congealed and it is the body of the Sun. Wherefore the Sun can in no way be overcome by our fire. This only happens, that it is liquefied, like snow or ice, by that same celestial Sun. Fire, therefore has not the power of burning fire, because the Sun is fire, which, dissolved in Heaven, is coagulated within us.*

Looking at the image of the card one can see the alchemical symbol for the word 'month'. This is the square formed by the disks with a line drawn from each corner to the rose and is also known as the 'material quintessence'. Therefore a time is applied to the alchemical processes. With the vertical line through the middle of the square Vitriol as perfected sulphur in its reddening stage is symbolized. Another symbol represented here is calcined Tartar representing the magistery of whitening during calcination (perfect restoration). The circle within the square formed by the rose and disks is a symbol for Cinnabar. It has been said, 'Where you see the presence of Cinnabar, gold or silver is not far off'.

The Rosicrucian Grade of Chesed is called Adeptus Exemptus or Exempt Adept and is shown by the numbers 7 = 4. The exemption referred to here is freedom from the restriction of the former grades. The Adept has now reached a level where Self development is paramount which will overshadow any previous preconceptions of what the Second Order expects of one who reaches this level. The function of the Exempt Adept is to formulate new links into frontier states of awareness and occultism (yet still retaining the essence of what has been taught as Rosicrucian philosophy). Here the limitations are lifted and one sees things as a fully-fledged Adept.

Chesed of Assiah, the Magical Weapon associated here, is the Wand, Sceptre or Crook. The entire concept is one of a symbol of Power by rulership or Divine right. In the Golden Dawn context this is exemplified by the Wand of the Praemonstrator, the Officer in the Neophyte grade who is associated with Chesed. This wand works through the power of Netzach as its base, which is the base of the Pillar of Mercy. The wand in fact denotes power tempered with Mercy. The wand here though, is not that of the lone wielder but that of a person who has control and power over a large group or organisation.

The first angel governing this card is Keveqaiah, who is titled 'To be Rejoiced in', and the second is Mendiel, who is titled 'Honourable'. Both of these titles together show accomplishment to be proud of and done so honestly and honourably.

The Planetary Sephirotic association is Jupiter in an earth Element. This is a very fortunate situation and shows success and an expansion of business projects. It is independence and financial success but it also shows part of that success being curtailed by the limited framework it has to work through. This indicates that a time of change is imminent as the drive of Jupiter must now push the earth element to its limitations.

The Sun in Capricorn characterises growth through experiencing material development. It is a creative energy at its best. There is also a caution here too, for this creative side cannot have the outlet it needs which results in a spiralling of vital energy. The Capricorn energy helps push this in the best direction by continually bringing forth newer goals. For individuals with the Sun in Capricorn there may be a tendency to be too self-centred in their approach to things, if they are not careful. Endurance, power and great ambition are indicated here.

The Mineral Kingdom association to Chesed is in the form of the Ruby. It works mainly through the Heart chakra and balances it to the point that it eases anger and jealously and makes people less fanatical in emotional and spiritual pursuits. When this centre is balanced, others will look towards such a person to guide them in some way. This person will then be thrust into the limelight in some positive way. The Ruby is also a fine tuner of our emotional content and presents a more strengthened and stabilised outlook where our emotions and passions are concerned.

The Plant Kingdom associated to Chesed is the Pomegranate. This works through the Heart chakra and its function is to integrate our emotions so that when unified they present a stronger and more stable personality and physical body. When individuals are stuck in an emotional niche so that they are unable to understand why life is dealing them bad cards, so to speak, Pomegranate will bring them out of their limited outlook and strengthen their resolve by bringing in more maturity.

Divination

Chesed of Heh relates to gain of money and material possessions, and influence. This card is assured material gain, success and control; achievement after hard work, although the situation must be worked at to maintain this; financial security; solid foundation in education; sound and lasting relationships; property; buildings; boundaries established to environment and ideas; endurance and strong life force; contained self-hood; successful business management; air-tight contracts; power; security within a job; strong constitution and health; maintenance of status quo; hard and capable worker; proficiency; standing one's ground; supporting partner; fortified against one's enemies; potential growth; safe ground; establishments. If ill-dignified it shows success that leads to nothing; prejudiced; covetousness; suspicion and discontent; preoccupation with career can interfere with love matters; self-preoccupation; cramping of life style; self-imposed restrictions; over-powerful parent.

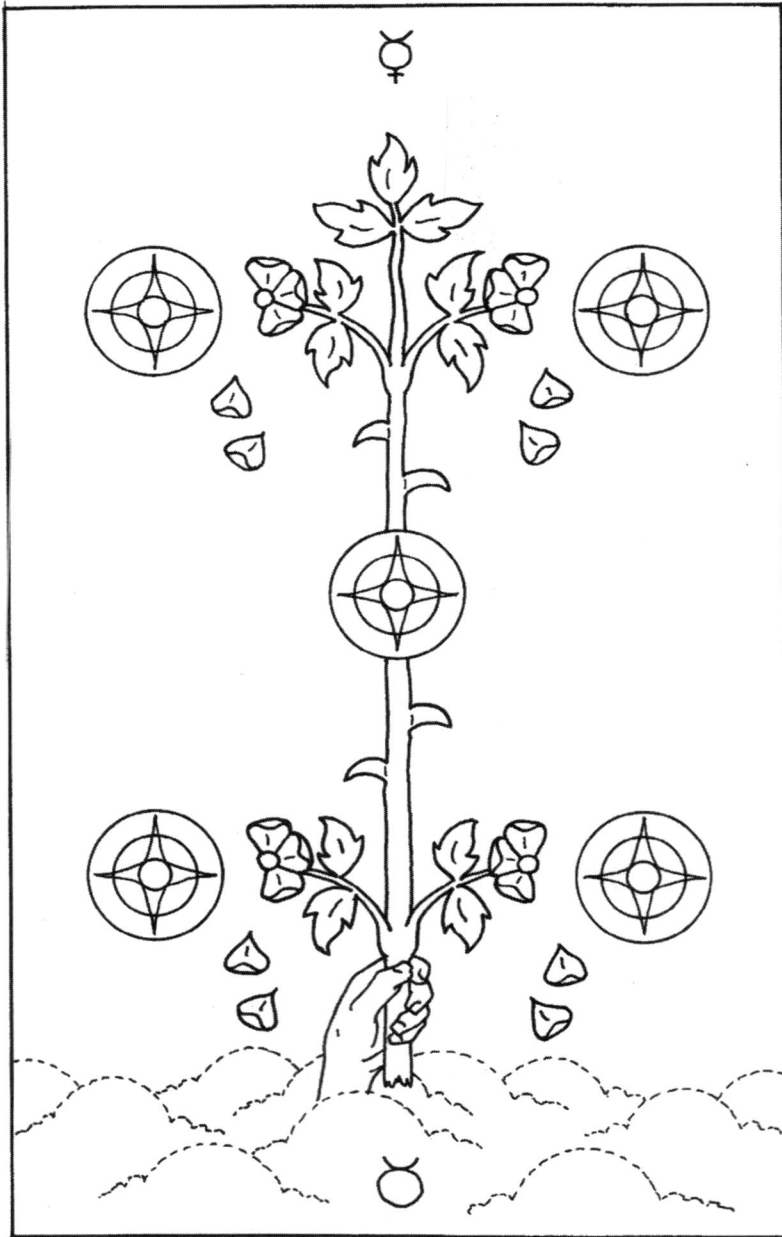

Five of Disks

Title	:	Lord of Material Trouble
Element	:	Earth
Force	:	Heh final
Alchemic	:	First Stage Dissolution
Kabbalistic World	:	Assiah
Sephirah	:	Geburah
Magical Weapon	:	Sword, Spear, Scourge
Grade	:	6 = 5 Adeptus Major
Planet of Sephirah	:	Mars
Angels	:	Mibahaih; Puial
Mineral	:	Citrine Quartz
Plant	:	Thyme
Astrological	:	Mercury in Taurus, zero–ten degrees
Colours	:	Disks Grey Indigo rayed Violet; Background Rich Red Brown; Clouds and stars on each disk Red, flecked with Black; Hand and Roses White; shading, rosebush and leaves, astrological signs complementary colours to the disks and background

The Five of Disks pictures a rosebush too heavily ladened with an extra Disk, which creates problems as there is not enough vitality in the rosebush to support five Disks. This is borne out by the petals of the roses falling from lack of nourishment. The upper and lower disks form, as in the Four of Disks, the square still representing the four elements and manifestation on the physical plane. With the Disks in the centre replacing the Rose from the previous card, we still have a circle within a square. However, being a disk, it is the material element of us, therefore the divine force from the previous card has been replaced by the subconscious as our guiding force. For Jung, the unconscious is 'the fly in the ointment'. The crystal clarity which we now seek is now clouded.

The alchemical symbolism from the image of this card is very similar to the Four of Disks, however, more tainted in form where some impurity must be removed. Alchemically this is the first stage of Dissolution. Dissolution is a method by which time and nature come into account, as you will see by the image of five disks producing a symbol of the material quintessence and yet as the central image is a disk and not a rose, the quintessence has not yet been extracted. It is the slow separation of matter or a body into component parts, by a liquid. From 'Treatise on The Great Art' by Dom Antoine-Joseph Pernety:

> *The putrefaction of the Matter in the Vase is then the principle and the cause of the colours which are manifested and the first permanent one which must appear is the black colour. ... This colour signifies then putrefaction and degeneration which ensues and which is given to us by the Dissolution of our perfect Body. The following words indicate that Flamel speaks of the second operation and not of the first: 'This Dissolution comes from the external heat, which aids and the interior dignity and sharp, wonderful power of the poison of our Mercury, which resolves into pure dust, even into impalpable powder, whatever resists it. Thus the heat acting on and against the Humid Radical, metallic viscous and oleaginous, produces the blackness of the Matter. It is that black veil with which the ships of Theseus returned victorious from Crete and which caused the death of his father. Thus it is necessary that the father should die, in order that from the ashes of this phoenix another should rise and that the son should be king.'*

The Rosicrucian Grade associated with Geburah is Adeptus Major and is signified by the numbers 6 = 5. The Adept here is at a point where the practical aspects of his or her art and knowledge have been tested and found to be exceptional. It is a time of a great deal of experimentation into the very limits of practical magic and a study of the Astral planes.

Geburah of Assiah is the Elemental Weapon, of which there is more than one. The most important is that of the Sword; it is a symbol of guarding as well as justice and enforcement. Its alchemical counterpart is that of the symbol of penetration. To wield the sword great force, strength and sense of purpose are needed and Geburah is one Sephirah that has all of these qualities. The Spear, also associated here, brings forth phallic representations of strength, but also the ability to attack an enemy from a distance. Another weapon is the scourge which relates to punishment and is the extreme side of Geburah's nature.

The first angel governing this card is Mibahaih, who is titled 'Eternal' and the second is Puial, who is titled 'Supporting all Things'. Both aspects come together in showing an everlasting commitment. Both titles of these angels are actually quite fortunate ones showing everlasting commitment. The card however modifies these so that the positive force is simply overworked in a framework that cannot support it. This is yet another reason why the drawing of what the card represents should be understood rather fully than simply using the astrological aspects for its meaning.

The Planetary Sephirotic association is Mars in an Earth element. This is not a very good position, for all the energy of Mars is curtailed or brought to a stop in the density of earth. The result of this produces a smothering effect where the fiery power behind it self-destructs. It shows opposition to expansion and indicates that one's ambitions are greater than one's abilities.

Mercury in Taurus characterises someone who focuses on material matters, details and the parts rather than the whole. Sometimes there is a stubbornness here to accept the reality of any situation. There is no originality but a persistent streak that pays off to those who want financial success. They have good minds and are able to deal with the material world well and do have the ability to go beyond their social limitations, providing they are able to see beyond these limitations. These people can be curious about the nature of the physical world and a sense of security will be found through material application and learning how practical/mechanical things work.

The Mineral Kingdom associated with Geburah is Citrine Quartz. This works mainly on the Base, Heart and Throat Chakras. Its esoteric influence alleviates self-destructive qualities. It is also an amplifier of thought forms and produces a better contact with the higher self through the alignment of all the subtle bodies. This brings hope and more self-esteem and promotes the body's healing abilities. Any form of anger can be channelled to a more useful purpose with the use of this crystal.

The Plant Kingdom association here is the Thyme. It stimulates the emotions so that things happen. It works directly on the Heart and Abdominal chakras, the two chakras that represent the last of the lower chakras and the first of the upper. This herb creates a bridging effect and one may gravitate towards a group situation so that all pent-up emotions can be released in a safe and directed manner. Thyme performs the functions of energy transference from the physical to the mental and as such strengthens our Will Power in sorting out our life.

Divination

Geburah of Heh Final is loss of profession, loss of money and anxiety. The whole situation relates to loss of money due to overspending, bad health due to overworking, a lack of cohesion with people around you and worry. Responsibilities; need for survival; poverty; adversities; preoccupation over material matters and one's problems in life; marriage for money; endurance during a struggle; mental negativity; lack of nourishment to one's needs; searching for success; reshaping conditions; labour; developing security. In relationships there is coldness; poor communication; worry and burden of responsibility; inability to see from another's view; discord; and insecure in one's self-esteem. Trouble in working environment or unemployment; anxiety about one's future; confusion as to direction; too many petty details to deal with causing clouding-over of the mind; worry over health. Class differentiation; religious dogma; difficulty during travel.

Six of Disks

Title	:	Lord of Material Success
Element	:	Earth
Force	:	Heh final
Alchemic	:	Second Stage Dissolution
Kabbalistic World	:	Assiah
Sephirah	:	Tiphareth
Magical Weapon	:	Lamen of the Rose Cross
Grade	:	5 = 6 Adeptus Minor
Planet of Sephirah	:	Sun
Angels	:	Nemamaiah; Yeileel
Mineral	:	Rose Quartz
Plant	:	Hemp Agrimony
Astrological	:	Moon in Taurus, ten–twenty degrees
Colours	:	Disks Silver rayed Sky Blue; Background Rich Red Brown; Hand, Rose, RoseBuds White; Clouds, stars on disks Straw Yellow; Rosebush, leaves, astrological symbols, shading are complementary colours to disks and background

The Six of Disks has a blooming rosebush which is influenced by the Path of Gimel on the Tree of Life, with its Lunar influence, pouring through very strong emanations from Kether into Tiphareth. Three Disks on either side of the Tree show balance and dependability. The six rosebuds and six roses in bloom make twelve, alluding to cycles of life, the twelve zodiac signs, where the six disks are the six planets, excluding the Sun which is the card itself. Through each month the Sun travels through the twelve zodiac signs, influencing the cycles of the earth, so here the Six of Disks with its placement in Tiphareth brings seasonal growth, life and nourishment.

Alchemically it is the second stage dissolution, but the shadow/blackness described by the Five of Disks has flown away leaving a hidden magistery. The decay of the former card has now reached a state of remission. What is left of the dead matter has been removed and the remaining matter left is now purified. This in turn will go through another form and a change before the next level is reached and the hidden magistery is revealed. In each Work the alchemist must dissolve the body with the spirit. Albertus Magnus said:

> *The beginning of the work is a perfect solution; and all those that we teach is nothing else but to dissolve and recongeal the spirit, to make the fixed volatile and the volatile fixed, until the total nature is perfected by the reiteration, both in its Solar and Lunar storm.*

The Rosicrucian Grade of Adeptus Minor is that of the fledgling Adept and is shown by the numbers 5 = 6. It is the ending of the theory of Elemental magic and stepping into the realm of High Magic. There are two elements in this grade that have to be mastered. The first is the theoretical study of High Magic and the second is to be able to perform it well on a practical level. It is the stepping stone on the road to the Adept. Generally speaking, the Adeptus Minor will still be working with High Magic on a certain level, but the upper echelons are for the next level of 6 = 5. This is also the first real exposure to the Rosicrucian concept and before the powers of Light deliver their additional knowledge, one must grapple with the basics of High Magic.

The Magical Weapon of Tiphareth is the Lamen of the Rose Cross. Basically the Rose Cross acts as a Lamen and protects the heart centre during any form of High Magic by placing an astral seal of the Second Order. This shows to any negative influence, that the Adept is protected by the power of the whole Second Order. It also helps direct the Adept to bring down the Light correctly when doing practical work. Its function is a power source from which to tap into the Rosicrucian Order so that anyone who wears the Rose Cross and is initiated into the Second Order, will never have to stand alone.

The first angel governing this card is Nemamaiah, who is titled 'Loveable' and the second is Yeileel, who is titled 'Hearer of Cries'. These two concepts show love and affection expressed through the bounty of materialism bestowed on someone who needs it.

The Planetary Sephirotic association is the Sun in an Earth Element. This means slow and gentle growth in a project and one is forced to wait patiently. This is the foundation of the evolutionary process where one must work through trial and tribulation, learning by one's mistakes on the way. It is a time to be mindful of the direction one is going in and not to rush into things too quickly.

The Moon in Taurus represents Spring, new growth and abundance. This also gives emotional security and it is very important to stabilise the influence of the Moon in this Sign. There are strong life-long friendships formed with the Moon in Taurus. The Moon shows the hidden side of one's nature while Taurus's consistent nature relates to the search for the hidden knowledge taking over an entire lifetime. Identity and power is seen through material possessions; accumulation of wealth is important.

The Mineral Kingdom associated with Tiphareth is Rose Quartz. This crystal stimulates the Heart and Throat Chakras and eases anger and frustration by giving one a sense of self-worth. It also helps any form of creativity and self-expression and allows the individual to channel these energies into a more productive output. It helps circulate the Chi or life Force throughout the body which results in tissue regeneration and particularly circulatory problems.

The Vegetable Kingdom associated here is Hemp Agrimony. This plant relates directly to the Heart Chakra and teaches one to be in harmony with one's surroundings. It brings about a type of rebirth where one becomes more attuned to universal laws which govern us and our planet. The individual's sense of values is stimulated by this plant so that the present incarnation will be accepted more readily, whether one has only a short time left or a lengthy period.

Divination

Tiphareth of Heh Final is success in material things. The card relates to gain in material undertakings, power and influence, authority over people; a powerful personality; donations; working for the common good for all; gifts; attractive proposition; emotional and financial security; growth in any matter; success in career and relationships; enlarging one's field of activity; benevolence; close family ties; building improvements in life and material possessions, in home and environment; gaining financially through a sale; sports and arts patronized; awards won; small wins in gambling; spiritual centres can also turn profits; fruitfulness regarding children; earned rest and recreation; raise in wages; help and encouragement; occupations where there is service to others; public fundraising schemes; social climbers; lost objects found; inheritance; rejuvenation. If ill-dignified then it shows those who are purse-proud, insolent or prodigal; threats to one's prosperity; losing face and respectability; bribery.

Seven of Disks

Title	:	Lord of Success Unfulfilled
Element	:	Earth
Force	:	Heh final
Alchemic	:	Third Stage Dissolution
Kabbalistic World	:	Assiah
Sephirah	:	Netzach
Magical Weapon	:	Lamp and Girdle
Grade	:	4 = 7 Philosophus
Planet of Sephirah	:	Venus
Angels	:	Herachael; Metzrael
Mineral	:	Copper
Plant	:	Elecampane
Astrological	:	Saturn in Taurus, twenty–thirty degrees
Colours	:	Disks Black rayed Blue; Background Rich Red Brown; Stars on disks and Clouds Light Green flecked Amber; Hand and RoseBuds White; complementary colours for shading, Rosebush and leaves, astrological symbols

With the formation of the seventh Disk, the rosebush has enough strength to produce buds, but not enough as yet to mature them. However, the fact that the buds are on the upper levels shows promise for the future. So the meaning here is that something is shown as started but not yet finished. Since there are no buds on the lower level of the bush no material result has arisen. The whole outline of the Disks here resembles the Geomantic Figure of Rubeus which is a very negative figure and we are told in the Golden Dawn Geomantic papers that Rubeus is 'Evil in all that is good and Good in all that is Evil'. The symbols formed by the disk positions are a rectangle below a triangle which points down. This symbolises, along with the rosebuds on the upper part of the bush, power descending into matter. At this point this power can be used for good or evil, but the tendency is to the latter as there are no rosebuds on the lower branches, therefore spirit has not entered fully into matter.

Alchemically this is the third stage of Dissolution, which is where a change has again taken place in the work where it is newly white, but it has not yet fully reached purity and the corruption beneath must still be separated. Yet to understand Dissolution in this card, which is also known as solution, the following quotation from the second gate in 'The Twelve Gates' should be considered:

> But yet, thou understandeth not utterly, the very secret of philosopher's dissolution. ... For I tell thee truly without delusion, Our solution is cause of our congealation. For the dissolution on one side corporal, Causeth congealation on the other side spiritual. And we dissolve into water which wetteth no hand, for when the earth is integrally incinerate, then is the water congealed, this understand; For the elements be so concatenate, that when the body from this first form be altered, a new form is induced immediately, for nothing is without form utterly. ... The more thine earth and the less thy water be, the rather and better solution shall thou see.

The Rosicrucian Grade of Netzach is called the Philosophus and is represented by the numbers 4 = 7. This represents the Fiery aspects of one's nature being fused and cemented together hence the dual aspects of both Fire and Earth are applied to this Sephirah. It is a time of consolidation where all the elements are now working together within the individual and this brings additional polarity and balance to the personality. For here the Philosophus must relate to others from the emotive response and to do this requires a great deal of balance and dependability. The Philosophus has perfected his or herself by being familiar with the practical areas of elemental magic both in theory and practice along with a certain degree of control over the Fire Element.

The Magical Symbols of Netzach are the Lamp and Girdle. The Girdle relates to the girdle of Venus on which all the symbols of the zodiac appeared, which in turn shows the completed cycle. It gives beauty and elegance and 'rekindles extinguished flames'. The Lamp also relates to the reflected light of the Sun in Tiphareth which lights the way for Venus, in her guise as Mother Nature, for all to follow in her footsteps and be in harmony with her.

The first angel governing this card is Herachael, who is titled 'Permeating all things' and the second is Metzrael, who is titled 'Raising up the oppressed'. Both these concepts allude to overthrowing things that tend to restrict, something allied to the forty-ninth hexagram of the I Ching, 'Revolution'.

The Planetary Sephirotic Association is the position of that of Venus in an Earth Element. This symbolises material success and support in matters financial but shows problems in relationships where one cannot get out of the situation one is in. The Earth element will also bring delays, both emotional and material and nothing will happen in a hurry. The whole thing is a very drawn out process.

Saturn in Taurus portrays a very heavy situation where little or zero growth is shown. It does however give almost unlimited endurance and reliability. There is a strong need to be financially secure to offset a deep emotional need for security. Stubbornness and a need for deep habit-forming patterns show up here. The rigidity here can be used for one's benefit but it also shows a lack of interest in taking a chance. Limitations and tests are implied as these people are often unsure of their own worth. They often have to prove themselves through their outer material success.

The Mineral Kingdom associated with Netzach is the metal Copper. It aligns the five lower chakras and works at opening the Heart Chakra in particular. Its effect on the physical body is anti-inflammatory. The subtle effect it produces is self acceptance with one's lot and a better understanding of how one relates to others, especially in sexual relationships. It does this by aligning the spiritual and mental natures so that some forms of self-gratification, at the expense of our higher natures, will be averted.

The Vegetable Kingdom associated here is Elecampane. The properties that this plant promotes within the individual is a love of self and an appreciation for form, synthesis, beauty and any form of adornment. It has the ability to make individuals see themselves clearly without the outer protection of the Ego. In fact, it tries to transform the Ego into being more spiritually attuned. It gives off an inner beauty and promotes self-esteem. People put their trust in the energies of this herb and those you take can bathe in this aspect of its function.

Divination

Netzach of Heh Final is unprofitable speculation and employment. This alludes to promises of success unfulfilled, loss of hope and promise; disappointment, misery, deception and lies; heavy expenditure; loss of money; lack of resources or foresight; illness; run-down health; throat problems; loss through business dealings; failed relationships; depression; limitations being defined; unfinished education; no support or backing; indebtedness; obligations; direct negative karmic issues; creative blockages. On the positive side, the Seven of Disks will show a definite effort to finish what was started; although a lot of external enthusiasm, little inner power; a serious disposition; finished karma; a hard worker; discipline; self-containment; assimilating life's experiences.

Eight of Disks

Title	:	Lord of Prudence
Element	:	Earth
Force	:	Heh final
Alchemic	:	First Stage Congelation
Kabbalistic World	:	Assiah
Sephirah	:	Hod
Magical Weapon	:	Grade Sashes
Grade	:	3 = 8 Practicus
Planet of Sephirah	:	Mercury
Angels	:	Akaiah; Kehethel
Mineral	:	Amethyst Quartz
Plant	:	Peppermint
Astrological	:	Sun in Virgo, zero–ten degrees
Colours	:	Disks Amber Yellow rayed Red; Background Livid Indigo; Stars on disks and Clouds Reddish Golden; Hand and Roses White; complementary colours for shading, Rosebush and leaves and astrological symbols

The Eight of Disks has four Roses on the lower half of the rosebush, indicating that a material result has been achieved, but is not totally completed as the roses do not grow on the upper parts of the rosebush. This is something that will not last and exists only on its own efforts although it does have support from the spirit. This is a time between the seed being sown and harvest time. If the weeds are not removed the crop will be strangled, therefore, with Prudence one must act to assist the growth of what one starts. The Stella Matutina changed this so that it had four roses on the top of the rosebush instead of the bottom, the idea being that it was a continuation of the previous card which had rosebuds on the top part of the bush. Though this was done for continuity in the Stella Matutina I have found that in divination the original version as given in the Golden Dawn papers is far more accurate. Roses on the top of the bush show growth in the higher worlds and none in the lower or material and is definitely not the influence of this card. The figure is shaped like that of the Geomantic figure of Populus which is 'Sometimes good and sometimes bad; good with good and evil with evil'. It also depicts a gathering.

Alchemically the Eight of Disks is first stage Congelation, which is where the aqueousness of a substance is reduced in consistency towards a solidification:

> Seeing that the Matter assumed a sound consistency; that it no longer flowed, it has formed their congelation, their Indurations; this is why they have said that the entire Magisterium consists in naturally dissolving and coagulating. This same Matter congealed and hardened so that it will no longer dissolve in water, has called them to say, that it was necessary to dry and fix it.

The Rosicrucian grade associated with Hod is that of Practicus and given the numbers 3 = 8. This is the Water element. The planetary association of Mercury applies the intellect to the sephirah, while the Water element as a grade implies that, at this stage, the intellect and emotions are experienced equally and the adept is to learn to integrate in balance the emotions with the intellect, uplifting them into the realms of higher reasoning and compassion.

The Magical symbol of Hod is the Office of the ancient mystery schools. This was a symbol of rank, but also it acts as a definite magical amulet. In the case of the Golden Dawn this was, in part, represented by the Grade Sashes of the Order, both Outer and Inner Orders. It is not a Lamen but something more visible attached to the Order which one belongs to as a whole. Its function is both to attract and repel certain powers utilised in magical ritual by awakening in the wearer the association with the various powers he or she can call on, if the need arises.

The first angel governing this card is Akaiah, who is titled 'Long Suffering' and the second is Kehethel, who is titled 'Adorable'. When combined these concepts show something very loveable or beneficent that is long-suffering because it cannot get away from what it is doing and make any advancement until the necessary lesson is learned.

Planetary Sephirotic association is Mercury in an Earth Element. Here mind is applied to physical ability bringing forth a practical outlook and dexterity, craft and skill. The earth element can weigh down the light, liquid energies of Mercury, however, causing a slowing of pace of any matter.

The Sun in Virgo characterises one with a good business sense and a great deal of versatility in any physical pursuit. It shows strong recuperative powers. The Sun in this sign brings a strong accord with nature and the ability to live in harmony with it. These people have a compulsive need always to be productive and keep busy. They worry excessively and can fritter away time in too many pursuits. Stress is a problem which can affect health.

The Mineral Kingdom association of Hod is Amethyst Quartz. This activates the Brow, Base and Throat Chakras. It is a thought amplifier and helps people integrate their thinking process by allowing more clarity of their thought patterns. This gem also strengthens the will and helps break negative habits. It also helps accept love given to the individual. On a more physical level it helps those whose immune systems (through the Endocrine glands) have collapsed or are under a great deal of stress.

The Plant Kingdom associated here is Peppermint. This plant works mainly on the Third Chakra but also has the ability to align all of the chakras. It acts as a cleansing effect for the subtle energies. It works mainly with Mercury and helps the individual function on the Mental level. It shows us how to help others and alleviate our own fears by tapping into ourselves and producing greater levels of energy. This in turn helps us in determining karmic patterns and lessons that have to be learned in this life.

Divination

Hod of Heh Final relates to skill, prudence, cunning. Hard work; productivity; movement of property; farming; gardening; building; improvement of health; growth in relationships or partnerships; fertility; growing family; monetary gain in small sums; growing business; everything working slowly in with the times; long-term projects; partial success but more work still to be done; sharing with family and friends; attuning with nature; welfare; developing skills; average living; great effort in all matters; co-operatives and work groups; unfinished preparations; small attainable goals; conscientiousness; eventually reaping the fruits of one's labours. Negatively, it shows one marking time and not getting anywhere, no fulfilment, over-careful in detail at the expense of the whole; it portends meanness, avariciousness, hoarding, lack of enterprise.

Nine of Disks

Title	:	Lord of Material Gain
Element	:	Earth
Force	:	Heh final
Alchemic	:	Second Stage Congelation
Kabbalistic World	:	Assiah
Sephirah	:	Yesod
Magical Weapons	:	Perfumes and Sandals
Grade	:	2 = 9 Theoricus
Planet of Sephirah	:	Moon
Angels	:	Hazeyal, Eldiah
Mineral	:	Moonstone
Plant	:	Blackberry
Astrological	:	Venus in Virgo, ten–twenty degrees
Colours	:	Disks Cerise rayed Turquoise; Background Livid Indigo; Stars on disks and Clouds Citrine flecked Azure; Hand and Roses White; complementary colours for shading, Rosebush and leaves, astrological symbols

The Nine of Disks shows white roses coming from all Disks. Unlike the previous card there are now four roses on the top counterbalancing those on the lower part of the bush. The extra Disk from the previous card has in fact opened up a channel so that the upper and lower parts of the bush are now unobstructed. In fact the channel for communication between these two areas is so good that the two additional buds shown beside the central Disk give even more potential for development. Eighteen leaves on the rosebush connect this card to the major arcana, the Moon. Also, eighteen is the multiplication of nine, the number of this card and also reduces to nine.

This card with all the roses coming from the Disks is yet another reason why the Stella Matutina opted to change the previous card as they thought that the growth on the lower disks was a next step to natural development. In this context they were correct but their reasoning on the previous card was still aesthetically faulty.

The clouds lie like morning dew over the land, from which nourishment is drawn by the rosebush. Alchemically the Nine of Disks is second stage congelation which is the final stage before the completion of the work. A chymical marriage has occurred and a final transformation of the vital spirit takes place. The Nine of Disks is the culmination of all the other operations and preparation for the final transformation. 1 Corinthians 15: 42–49 explains this by saying:

It is sown in corruption; it is raised in corruption. It is raised in glory. It is sown in weakness; it is raised in power. It is sown in natural body; it is raised in spiritual body. There is a natural body and there is a spiritual body. And so it is written. The first man Adam was made a living soul; the last Adam was made a quickening spirit. Howbeit that was not first which is spiritual, but that which is natural; and afterward that which is spiritual. The first man of the earth, earthy. The second man is the lord from heaven. As is the earthy, such are they also that are earthy. And as is the heavenly, such are they also that are heavenly. And as we have borne the image of the earthy, we shall also bear the image of the heavenly.

The Rosicrucian Grade for Yesod is Theoricus and is designated by the number 2 = 9. This is the elemental grade of Air and is under the Luna influence. The Theoricus will be aroused psychically by certain elemental currents or tides that flow through the earth. In his or herself, he or she will be aware of how these changes affect the physical body through energy surges. It shows emotional stimuli which draws forth the life essence through the vital areas of the subconscious. This is brought about by subliminal imprinting of certain symbols (through ritual) onto the subtle bodies.

The Magical Weapons of Yesod are Perfumes and Sandals. Winged Sandals are often attributed to Mercury and Hermes though in Yesod they take on a whole new meaning. The Moon is often referred to as 'the Goddess of Golden or Brazen Sandals', which relates to the Moon moving across the night sky. Perfumes are associated with the element of Air and their link to Yesod bears this out.

The first angel governing this card is Hazeyal, who is titled 'Merciful' and the second is Eldiah, who is titled 'Profitable'. Both these concepts together show profit being bestowed mercifully to those who need it.

The Sephirotic Planetary association is the Moon in an Earth Element. The emotions are now trapped in the physical plane and things are expressed through pleasure of the body and material possessions. Things are done for the sense of self-gratification rather than for the betterment of self. One can be easily ruled by the emotions, with the Moon in this position, and any action will probably stem from this area before any other faculty is utilised.

Venus in Virgo represents material gain, mainly concentrating on a career situation. Here we have the formation of high or critical standards, analysis of emotions and sincere gestures. Feelings of inferior sexuality or social standing are covered up by a very cold exterior which sometimes prevents possible relationships from occurring. Work and intellectual pursuits are engaged so that close contact with other people can be avoided. There are attractions to material comforts and the beautiful things in life. Wealth is generally acquired through the effort of employees. The key to Venus in Virgo is the power to analyse; to see the whole and the individual parts that make up the whole.

The Mineral Kingdom association of Yesod is Moonstone which has the tendency to bring the spiritual side of one's nature in harmony with the other areas of one's life. It helps increase one's psychic awareness and brings out hidden thought forms that have remained in the unconscious for a great deal of time. By doing this it makes one face up to the reality of the situation without affecting the spiritual messages the Higher Self sends us. Also it helps align the Astral and Emotional bodies.

The Plant Kingdom associated here is Blackberry. This governs mainly the third chakra. Blackberry helps in the area of love and patience, especially if they are tied to religious pursuits. It gives strength to the conscious mind and helps one accept those of like mind around you. It is used as a travelling Talisman in Astral work and helps keep emotional balance. It helps us walk our own spiritual path and at the same time blocks any outside interference so that we can reach our true spiritual goals.

Divination

Yesod of Heh Final means inheritance, general increase of material goods. Success especially through channels of communication. This is complete realisation of material gain, achievement and inheritance; realisation of the development and richness of life; self-indulgence; material comfort; practical achievement; strong life-force; dreams turned into reality; trophies; winning; successful business venture; increase of responsibility; firm stand under a challenge. In matters personal and relationships there is friendly advice; talk and relaxation; company of friends and family; sex appeal; opening up to people and receiving a response; family and children; outdoor activities. In other matters, property obtained; horticulture; agriculture; farming; sport; creative arts; enjoyment of life; gainful employment; wage rise; applying one's talents; insurance; financial advisor. If ill-aspected then covetousness and theft are indicated; critics; taking advantage of one's prominence; gambling others' money, or one's own; corruption.

Ten of Disks

Title	:	Lord of Wealth
Element	:	Earth
Force	:	Heh final
Alchemic	:	Third Stage Congelation
Kabbalistic World	:	Assiah
Sephirah	:	Malkuth
Magical Weapon	:	Magical Circle and Triangle
Grade	:	1 = 10 Zelator
Planet of Sephirah	:	Earth and the four elements
Angels	:	Leviah, Hihaiah
Mineral	:	Antinomy
Plant	:	Fennel
Astrological	:	Mercury in Virgo, twenty–thirty degrees
Colours	:	Disks Grey Indigo rayed Violet; Background Livid Indigo; Stars on disks and Clouds Black rayed with Yellow; Hand and Roses White; complementary colours for shading, Rosebush and leaves, astrological symbols

The Ten of Disks depicts the rosebush at its best giving its maximum number of roses and Disks. The shape relates to a perfect mirror image of both upper and lower worlds where everything is working in harmony. The final conjunction of these worlds brings a completed work. There being no more leaves sprouting from the top of the rosebush shows that no more growth is required. The five upper disks are the four incorporeal elements plus spirit and the five lower disks are the four corporeal elements plus spirit within the corporeal and are equally balanced in their perfected and completed form in Assiah; Aron's Rod, from the Ace of Disks, has reached its full power and bloom.

Alchemically we have the final stage of Congelation, but it can also allude to the 'completed work', the 'Philosopher's Stone'. From another perspective this card is the 'Crowned Lion' or 'Crowned King' where the Matter is spiritualized. From this Multiplication and Projection take place. At the last operation there is the union of the Philosophic Stone, which is said to be finally cemented with its component parts agreeing rather than repelling (i.e., four elements in harmony). Khunrath states that the Stone is the universal medium of restoration and preservation and that its own equilibrating virtue will expel suffering and any disease mentally, emotionally or physically. The Stone contains the Azoth, which also reduces bodies to their First matter and then reanimates these bodies with the 'Universal Form', hence the term turning matter into Gold, Crystals into Gems, etc. However, travelling the Tarot from another direction, the Ten of Disks is the First Matter.

There are two Rosicrucian grades associated with Malkuth. The first one is the Neophyte grade, designated by the numbers 0 = 0. This is an initiation process to the whole of the Tree before one can enter Malkuth proper. It is a bridging process that introduces the Neophyte to the energies of the Tree, from the perspective of the Order. The second Grade is the Zelator, 'Serious student', shown by the numbers 1 = 10. Malkuth relates to the Element of Earth and the Zelator must now start to study the Lower magic of the Tree, in terms of symbology and group ritual. It is the point where one starts to feel the energies of the Tree and to make some ground in realizing the associations of the Tree. Here the wealth of the Tree is available to the Zelator, if he or she progresses up the Tree. The door has opened and the first step has been taken.

The Magical Image of Malkuth is the Magical Circle and Triangle. This is the symbol of trapping the elemental powers and making them do our biding. The Circle protects us, through the density of the Earth Element and the triangle holds the spirit of what we wish to utilise. The whole concept is where the introduction of ritual can boost our powers where we can control the energies of different dimensions.

The first angel governing this card is Leviah, who is titled 'To be Exalted' and the second is Hihaiah, who is titled 'Refuge'. Together these show that a haven or refuge is reached when one has reached the very pinnacle of one's journey, the Philosopher's Stone.

Mercury in Virgo relates to financial success due to intellectual stimulation. It also relates to taking chances for intellectual stimulation. There are indications of success through writing and study. An orderly environment is needed with Mercury in this Sign and it bodes well for any type of research. Knowledge will be acquired during everyday activities and the importance of maintaining healthy mind and body is stressed. Environmental issues are very important and the power of the mind over matter also holds great importance. Negatively applied, Mercury in Virgo will characterize gossip, slander, frittering away energies and wealth.

The Mineral Kingdom association of Malkuth is the metal Antinomy. This metal is the one used by alchemists to make the Philosopher's Stone with its all curative powers. It brings a sense of equilibrium to the self by restoring the link between the Mental, Physical and Spiritual bodies. It is considered the one true metal of alchemy and has become even more popular with alchemists than gold in its use.

The Plant Kingdom associated here is Fennel. This stimulates the first three chakras. It helps to ground the individual to earth states of awareness, especially healing and earth magic in general. It helps attune one to the earth's energy vortex and makes those energies available to those who seek them. During any form of healing this plant will help link up to the patient and remove any negative blockages. It belongs to love, through the earth energies to all its creatures for when taking this herb we are linked directly to them.

Divination

Malkuth of Heh Final is riches and wealth. This shows completion of material gain and fortune but nothing beyond, as one is at the very pinnacle of success, the *Summum Bonum*. This is not only monetary wealth but wealth of mind, presence of being, possessions and spirit. Your body is your temple, therefore it must be looked after by whatever natural means one can use. Material prosperity through estates, inheritance, accumulation. Reunions, small gatherings, celebrations; property; buildings; land; heavy responsibility; security. In relationships romantic affairs may bring material gain; success in a relationship; children; money and position through a partner. In career and employment, bonuses; successful career; wage rise; good job offer; harmony in one's working environment; powerful contacts; professionalism; honour; achievements. Health matters show rejuvenation; good health; natural healing methods; exercise and good nutrition. If ill-dignified then sloth, old age, loss of wealth, or excessive need, dullness of the mind.

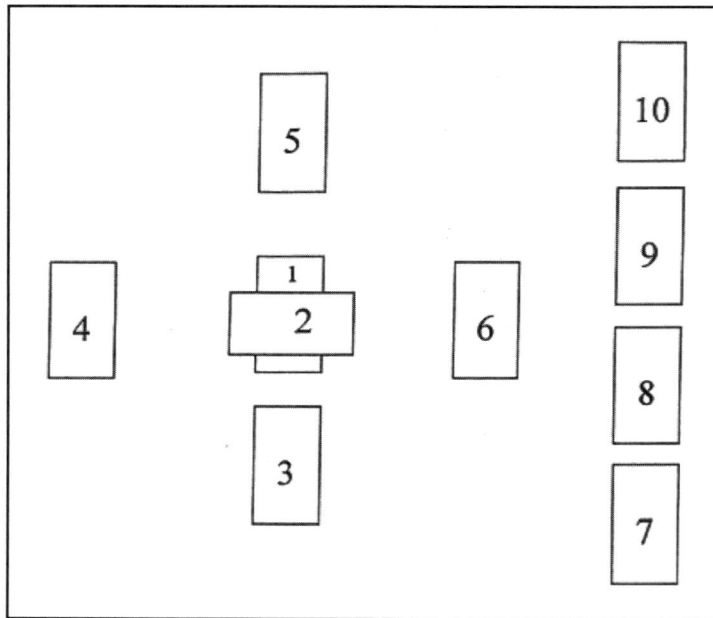

Divination and the Tarot

'To divine' is defined in Webster's Dictionary as to foretell and to predict. The word 'divine' is defined as 'pertaining to God, holy and something that is excellent in its highest degree'. It is interesting to have the same word representing two seemingly different meanings. Divination is the act of divining and Divining is the act of a diviner or augur. Now, the word, 'Augury' is defined as 'the art or practice of foretelling events by signs or omens … divination'. It seems here that there are two types of divination and yet the root of these methods pertains to the Divine, the holy and connected to God. Divination, then, can perhaps be termed as something which is guided by the Divine Light. But let us look at this a little more. Most diviners look into events of the past, present and future. Not just the future. From our own experiences with Tarot readings, the diviner can also look into the state of the querent's consciousness, mental, emotional and spiritual state, past and present and probability of the future.

Many ask us, how are you able to see into this time span. To understand this, you must be able to see the Universe as a whole and realize that dividing the Universe up into parts is always arbitrary, something of a convention. Everything in the Universe is part of each other, from large objects to sub-atomic particles. Once you understand this, you can understand how the past, present and future can be read. Try to imagine three holograms, one of the past, one of the present and one of the future. Then look at the future hologram and divide that up into many more holograms of probabilities of the future. This is basically what the reader is looking into. The past and present are as they have been acted out, but the future is only a probability.

When a person sits in front of you for a reading, the future you will see is only the probable course of direction into which that person has already placed themselves, and to where the momentum of where they are now flows. The next day, week, month or year from the reading you gave might see the person change that course of probability with their own conscious direction of their life. 'How then can one see a true future?' Quite simply put, the reader just does, as there is a psychic link-up between the two people, activated by the willingness of the querent to receive information and the 'intent' of the diviner. The main probability forecasted is usually the one that the querent follows, consciously or unconsciously. When there are crossroads, where the querent may make a personal decision to change his or her course of direction, these usually show up in the cards. This is where the diviner can be misled and read only one direction instead of seeing crossroads for what they are. Turning points in a person's life are where the querent alone must choose which path to walk. The diviner can only give an idea to the querent as to what each path will be like, although this is at times extremely difficult when there are many possibilities.

The Tarot then, does not show fate. For you have free choice as to how you run your life and once you are told what might be coming up you have more conscious control over it. After all, 'we make our own reality'. A tarot reading done properly can show an individual how to take their life into their own hands. A good tarot reader will always place an individual's power back into their hands to make their own decisions.

A method I use to help push my perceptions into the future for a person is to get them to also think of the time frame that we are looking into. I ask them to scan their minds over the time frame as if looking over a calendar, not to think of what they are doing, as that will influence the reading, but to just think of 'time'. This adjusts their auric vibrations which helps me looking forward in time.

During readings, a reader will quite often find additional questions directed from the querent, that are not fully answered by the laid out cards. A simple method of answering without disturbing your spread is to cut (divide) cards from the deck (like cutting the deck into two piles) while you or your querent concentrate on the question. With this method you obtain straight answers, even a 'yes' or a 'no' with a positive card for 'yes' and a negative card for 'no'. The in-between cards, such as the Fool, Judgement and Justice would depict that the matter is not decided yet. The card read from a cut is the bottom card from the first cut (the pile you remove from the deck).

Some people have difficulty concentrating on specific questions and find their minds flicking from one subject to another. This is quite easy to detect psychically as you will feel a shift in consciousness to a sense of confusion. If you find this happens, usually the card the person cuts will reflect their own state of mind, or provide a dual answer. This is where you must ask them, what they are wanting to know. Then you can cut the cards for them on each issue of dual thought, to clarify. Try to word your questions or the querent's questions, clearly and specifically, rather than in broad terms. In that way a clear answer can be extracted from the spread. Quite often I have been asked 'What about my Love life?' Can you imagine the multiple answers a few cards cut or laid out could give one on this very general question! Firstly, there is no time direction to the question: past, present or future! You would do best to establish whether the person is currently involved or not. Then, you could word the question about that relationship, or on one that is coming up. A simple way of finding out if a person will be involved, if your spread does not imply it, is to concentrate on a question to that effect and cut the cards. A 'yes' or 'no' answer will provide it.

Never, except in certain instances, use the terms 'will I', 'should I' or 'can I', as the cards will come up, saying in the case of the later 'of course she can', but that does not necessarily mean it will be successful. In the case of 'should' or 'will', the cards very often come up pointing out that it is the individual's decision. You are better off asking 'If', I/the querent, go in this direction how will matters turn out? Where you say 'this direction', you and/or the querent are actually visualising it. Do not ever take the responsibility of telling a person that they 'will' or 'should' do something as their actions are their responsibility. Split your questions up into options, probabilities; never let a querent use an 'and/or' question, as the answer will be confused.

Divination is a serious thing, so direct your querent to be sensible in their questions. Do not use divination for fun or mere curiosity for yourself or others. Avoid using the cards in parties and under the influence of alcohol. Try not to do readings for those people who are just out to test you or the validity of the cards. This blocks the 'light' as it is not a sincere intent directed by the person. Our higher selves cannot be fooled.

When doing readings for yourself, or having them done for you, you must open your mind to the utmost and absolute truth within your own being, as your higher self cannot be deluded by any intellectual cover-up. Excuses of 'covering up' are a refusal to face or see the truth. The truth must be listened to and accepted. If you don't like your answers, draw another card asking your higher self to advise you, via the card drawn, as to what you can do to deal with or improve your situation. Avoid assumptions of what the card 'could' be meaning, after a clear meaning has already been given. This can also be an avoidance of the truth—a tactic which the ego plays quite well.

If you are the reader, do not be led into these tactics of truth-avoidance by your querent. Quite often a querent's thought patterns can lead you into saying what they want to hear and not what is true. A querent's confusion can act as static interference to your psychic channelling of information. Thought patterns and vibrations from people can act like radio waves. A person's fear of the truth can short-circuit your own psychic insight into the future for the required information. Mental and psychic training to be able to still your mind from all interfering thoughts, will help considerably. A diviner must be free of his or her own emotions and prejudices to give a free and unbiased reading.

You may ask, how does one know what a card is really talking about. The answer is gut instinct and also by virtue of a controlled card spread, where each card is placed in a position that represents something. The meditation chapter in this book will aid you in learning to perceive clairvoyant meanings of the cards. The previous chapters will give you the mental knowledge and understanding for each card. What is important, is that you use both your clairvoyance and mental knowledge. You first perceive clairvoyantly, then you translate it mentally to speech, also incorporating the intellectual knowledge where applicable. Some readers use one or the other, but we find a combination of both is most successful.

It is up to each individual tarot reader as to the method of setting up a reading. However, we have suggested a small step by step method below. You will see that the diviner shuffles the cards. We have found this better, as a lot of people do not know how to shuffle and thereby damage the cards in the process. You may also find them all over the floor, if another shuffles them. Shuffling the cards yourself will not prevent a good reading. All you have to do while shuffling is call on Divine guidance, link up with your higher self and have your higher self link with the querent's higher self, then concentrate on the question/purpose of the reading. Shuffle until you feel you have linked up (you may feel a sensation in your fingers). The querent's input is their cut of the cards.

When divining for someone else, take the cards from them with your left hand while you are receiving the vibrations that they have put into the cards. Get them to cut the cards with their right hand, as that is the hand that sends the vibrations.

A simple (non-ritual) method for reading cards:

a. Sit East of your cards (and querent).
b. Still your mind from stress and interfering thoughts, breathe deeply.
c. Make a small prayer for Divine help and blessings. Draw the Light to surround you and fill you. This is your protection.
d. Concentrate on your querent's questions while shuffling the cards. The querent can shuffle the cards if they prefer though it is better that you do it as your mind will be more focused.
e. After shuffling, place the cards in front of you. The querent cuts once, creating two piles (or twice to three piles—you have a choice) cutting left to right with their right hand.
f. You take the left pile(s) and (sequentially) place on top of the right pile, with your left hand and then deal the cards.

When looking into a person's life with the cards, try not to link up with their astral/emotional subtle bodies alone. You should view the whole of the entity you are reading, working from your Crown, Ajna and Alta Major chakras. In some cases you may find dealing with people throws your own chakras and subtle bodies out of alignment. A gem remedy combination of Rutilated Quartz and Herkimer Diamond can help you keep these aligned. Some people are also empathic and absorb emotional and health problems from other people. This can leave you feeling quite unwell after doing readings. A flower essence combination of Walnut, Pink Yarrow, Fennel and Euphorbia is very helpful, or any one of these. These will help protect you and strengthen you from the emotional and other states of your clients.

In the earlier Golden Dawn temples there were two forms of Divination. The first was the short answer to a question and the second is a very long-winded version that was usually done with complete ceremonial ritual and would take up to four hours to complete. This latter method was usually revealed in the Inner Order and will be discussed in the following chapter.

Tarot cards were given out in the Golden Dawn in the Outer Order grades, usually at the level of 4 = 7 (Philosophus) in some temples and the Portal in others. These days, in some temples however, Temple members are learning the Tarot from Neophyte grade. Since the Inner Order method of ritual could not be revealed until the postulant entered the Inner Order, the very popular Celtic Cross or Gypsy method was taught, so that the aspiring Adepti could at least get the feel of doing divinatory work with the cards. The following Golden Dawn lecture on the gypsy method is very close to that which A.E. Waite published in his book on the Tarot around 1910, though our copy is dated 1896, long before Waite ever heard of the Golden Dawn. I do not think that this method was invented by the Order (though history may prove me wrong) but adapted from some earlier work, possibly that of Vaillant or some other earlier researcher.

Gypsy method of tarot divination

This mode of tarot Divination is the most suitable for rapidly obtaining an answer to a definite question.

The Diviner selects a card to represent the person or matter about which he inquires. This card is called the Significator and should he wish to ascertain something in connection with himself, he takes the one which corresponds with his personal description. A Knight represents a man of Forty years and upwards. A King represents any male under that age.

A Queen is a woman over Forty years of age and upwards, who has children and is of mature appearance.

A Princess is a woman under that age who has not had children. The Four Court Cards:

The Wands represent very fair people with yellow or auburn hair, fair complexion and blue eyes.

The Cups show people with light brown or dull hair with grey or blue eyes.

The Swords show people with hazel or grey eyes, dark brown hair and dull complexions.

The Disks show people with very dark brown hair or black hair, dark eyes and sallow or swarthy complexions.

You can be guided on occasion by the known temperament of a person. One who is exceedingly dark may be energetic and would be better represented by a Sword card than a Disk. On the other hand a very fair subject who is indolent and lethargic should be referred to Cups in place of Wands. If it is a matter about which an inquiry is to be made, the Significator should be a Trump or small card which bears a relationship to the matter. Suppose that the question is 'Will a lawsuit be necessary?' In this case, take the Trump Card 'Justice' as the Significator since it has reference to legal matters. But if the Question is 'Shall I be successful in a lawsuit?' one of the Court Card representing yourself should be selected. Subsequently consecutive divinations can be performed to ascertain the course of the process itself and its result to each of the parties concerned.

Having selected the Significator, place it on the table face upwards, then shuffle well and thoroughly the rest of the cards, cutting three times after each shuffle. Lastly, keeping the face of the cards downwards, turn up the top or front card of the pack and cross the Significator with it and say:

1. This card covers him.
   This card gives the influence which is affecting the person or matter of the enquiry generally, the atmosphere in which the Ether current moves. Turn up the second card and say:
2. This crosses him.
   It shows the nature of the obstacles on the matter. If this is a favourable card, the opposing forces will not be serious, or it may indicate that something good in itself will be productive of good in this particular connection. Turn up the third card and say:

3. This crowns him.

   It represents first, the Querent's aims or ideals in the matter. And second, the best that can be achieved under the circumstances but that which has not yet been made actuality. Turn up the fourth card, place it below the Significator and say:

4. This is beneath him.

   It shows the foundation or basis of the matter, that which has already passed into actuality and which the Significator has made his own. Turn up the fifth card and say:

5. This is behind him.

   It gives the influence that has just passed or is passing away. If the Significator is a Trump Card, or a card that cannot be said to face either way, the diviner must decide beforehand which side of the Significator he will take as facing. Usually this fifth card is placed on the right-hand side of the Significator, as it will be found that most of the Court Cards are looking towards the left. Turn up the sixth card, place it on the side the Significator is facing and say:

6. This is before him.

   It shows the influence that is coming into action and will operate in the near future. The next four cards are turned up in succession and placed in a line by the side of the others which are in the form of a cross.

7. This is himself.

   This signifies the person himself or else the thing enquired about and shows its position or attitude on the matter.

8. The eighth card represents his house.

   This is his environment and the tendencies at work there which have an effect on the matter, for instance, his position in life, the influence of immediate friends and so forth.

9. This card gives his hopes and fears in the matter.

10. The tenth card is the final result.

Additional to the above Golden Dawn method, there are several ways one can choose a significator:

1. By visual appearance of the querent. This can be matched with a Court Card.
2. By the apparent psychological/personality state of the querent, which again can be matched with a Court Card.
3. By a person's Sun sign (zodiac sign). Each Court Card rules from twenty degrees of one sign to twenty degrees of another:

   January 11 to February 9 would be the Prince of Swords

   February 9 to March 11 would be the Knight of Cups

   March 11 to April 10 would be the Queen of Wands

   April 10 to May 11 would be the Prince of Disks

   May 11 to June 11 would be the Knight of Swords

   June 11 to July 13 would be the Queen of Cups

   July 13 to August 13 would be the Prince of Wands

August 13 to September 13 would be the Knight of Disks

September 13 to October 14 would be the Queen of Swords

October 14 to November 13 would be the Prince of Cups

November 13 to December 13 would be the Knight of Wands

December 13 to January 11 would be the Queen of Disks

For the Princesses, you would match the querent up more archetypically. They usually represent a young woman or girl that has not had a child.

4. By knowledge of a person's astrological horoscope. Convert the Sun sign and rising sign (ascendant) to the elements. For example if the querent had a Leo sun sign and an Aries rising sign, the Knight of Wands would be the significator. The reason for this is that the Knight of Wands is the Fiery part of Fire and Leo and Aries are both Fire signs.

Combinations applicable to each Court Card

Knight of Wands: Sun sign and ascendant combinations of Fire signs, e.g., Aries, Leo or Sagittarius.

Queen of Wands: A Fire sun sign, either Aries, Leo, or Sagittarius and a Water Ascendant, either Cancer, Scorpio or Pisces.

Prince of Wands: A Fire sun sign (as above) and an Air Ascendant, either Gemini, Libra, or Aquarius.

Princess of Wands: A Fire sun sign (as above) and an Earth ascendant, either Taurus, Capricorn, or Virgo.

Knight of Cups: Water sun sign, either Cancer, Scorpio, or Pisces and a Fire ascendant, either Aries, Leo, or Sagittarius.

Queen of Cups: Water sun sign and Water ascendant, zodiac signs as above.

Prince of Cups: Water sun sign as above and Air ascendant. (The signs applied to the elements are listed above now so they will not be repeated below.)

Princess of Cups: Water sun sign and Earth ascendant.

Knight of Swords: Air sun sign and Fire ascendant.

Queen of Swords: Air sun sign and Water ascendant.

Prince of Swords: Air sun sign and Air ascendant.

Princess of Swords: Air sun sign and Earth ascendant.

Knight of Disks: Earth sun sign and Fire ascendant.

Queen of Disks: Earth sun sign and Water ascendant.

Prince of Disks: Earth sun sign and Air ascendant.

Princess of Disks: Earth sun sign and Earth ascendant.

Of course, with this method, the sex of the person makes no difference to what card acts as their significator.

We have included below some additional divination methods. Each one has its own merit, but we have found the Horoscope spread quite excellent for divination, giving the diviner ample room to be quite specific to the querent as to what is happening in his or her life. This is due to each card being placed in a position that represents an area of life and that card is discussed in that context. If you refer back to the chapters on the cards you will see some mention about how those cards operate in different subjects (areas of life). This will be very helpful when coming to understand the Horoscope spread. The Horoscope spread below is a different version from other published methods, which we have developed over a period of years.

Horoscope spread

The order of laying out the cards follows the order of the quadruplicities of astrology; cardinal, fixed then mutable in relation to the signs of the zodiac and angular, succedent and cadent in relation to the astrological houses. The twelve cards in the circle are positioned in the astrological houses which are numbered as below.

The central card, card thirteen, is likened to the Sun, as it moves through the signs over the houses. The term 'houses' is just referring to a division which contains an area of activity in life. I have modified the meanings of the houses to apply to a Tarot reading and these areas of life associated with each house are:

House 1: Where the querent is coming from, state of mind and how he or she is dealing with life. Physical vitality.
House 2: How the querent is managing their money, possessions and self, e.g., self-confidence/esteem.
House 3: Short journeys, close friends, brothers and sisters, studies, writing.
House 4: Home environment, real estate, parental/family relationships.

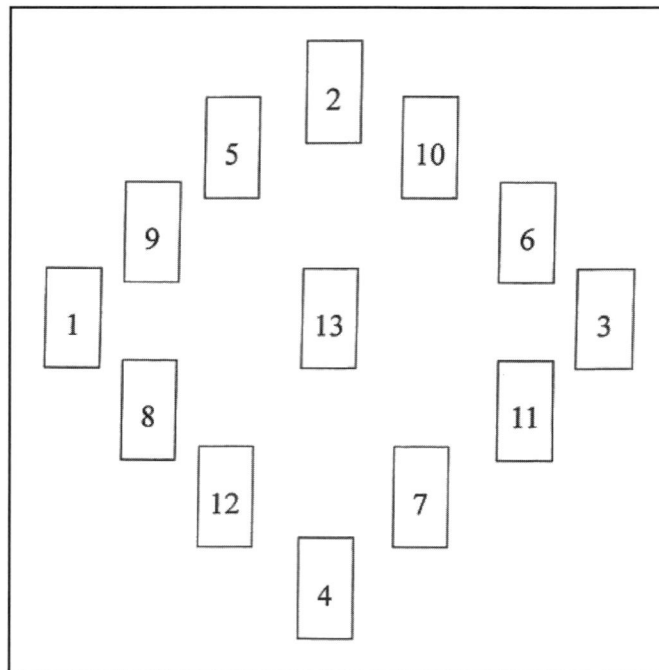

House 5: Love/romance matters, sometimes speculation and gambling, children, recreation.

House 6: Work environment and work relationships, personal health affected therefrom.

House 7: Marriage, partnerships, social activities, contracts, partner.

House 8: Money coming to you (or going from you). In some cases legal matters, matters of transformation.

House 9: Long journeys, studies, education, relatives, higher aspirations, writing, publishing.

House 10: Goals and career; where you are heading.

House 11: Friends in group situations, creative interests, sports, clubs etc., reaction to personal affairs.

House 12: One's psychological state, health, response to life (work) conditions, enemies.

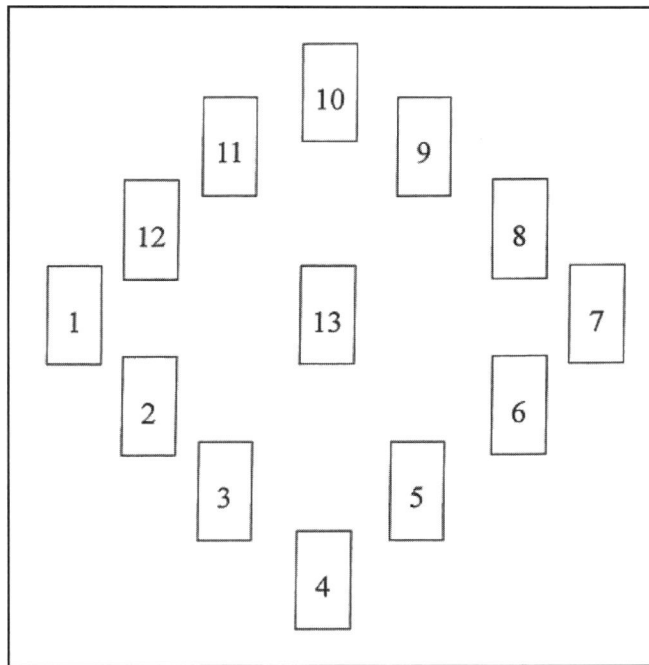

In reading the horoscope spread, you do not necessarily work from house 1 to 12 individually. Instead you should pair the opposite houses to each position, so that you can view the influencing factors to any matter and also include the central card as an influence. Pair the card on house 1 with house 7, house 2 with house 8, 3 with 9, 4 with 10, 5 with 11, 6 with 12. This way you will read the subject matters in the paired houses together. For example, house 9 is the influencing factor to house 3 and house 3 is the influencing factor to house 9 issues.

There are also combinations of three or more houses to get a further understanding of subjects. For example:

Health matters are seen in a combination of houses 1, 6 and 12.

Love matters and marriage issues are a combination of houses 5, 11, 7 and 1. The card in house 5 would be the condition of the relationship. House 1 is how the querent feels about it, House 7 is the actions or thoughts of the partner or where the partnership is going. House 11 contributes to the other three houses in meaning, or shows the outside pressures. Or, Houses 1 and 7 will show one relationship either being entered or just leaving depending on the lay of the cards and houses 11 and 5 will show another relationship either being entered or leaving. Sometimes a Court Card is in the centre too which could represent one or the other of the persons involved in the relationship playing a key role, or it could be a third party. Only your intuition, experience and clairvoyance will tell you which is which. Or, you could cut the cards with direct questions to find out who is who. For work and career issues a combination of houses 6, 12 and 10, sometimes house 4. For personal life and home issues houses 4, 3 and 5 and sometimes including houses 2 and 1 to show how the querent is handling these issues.

To know if a person is shifting house, usually a card in house 4 shows this, for example the Ace of Disks. But, this can be backed up by houses 2, 8, 3 and sometimes 9. Why? Well, cards on houses 2 and 8 may show the financial change taking place, which usually goes with a shift and a change of possessions. Cards on houses 3 and 9 usually show the travelling from one place to another, and the movement of and settling in property. When a person actually relocates, the signs of this show sometimes right throughout the spread; for example, a card indicating relocation such as the Ace of Swords, or the Death card, sitting in houses 1 or 4. A new job will also be shown in houses 10 and 6 and the shift as aforementioned.

Artistic or creative activities can show up by a card describing such in any area of life, either as recreation (houses 5 and 11), through work, home or just as a personal self-expression (houses 1 or 3). Spiritual matters are shown through houses 12, 1, 4 or 8. Usually, however, a separate reading is done for this matter.

We have not overlooked the central card, as this is very important in a reading. When pairing cards in different house positions the central card acts, most of the time, as a balancing factor as to where matters are heading either positive or negative. Where it is not used, is when you intuitively feel it does not apply to a particular situation. If, out of a combination of cards the majority (including) the central card show a positive outcome, then that is what you will read. If the outcome is still positive, but the central card is a negative one, then there will be underlying issues, or a struggle to contend with. So, the central card will add or deduct in points towards a positive or negative result. The central card can sometimes represent what one has been through and shows the past clouding the present, even though positive cards in the houses may show matters improving. This central card is quite often the result ahead, but now and again it represents the past, or sometimes is a representation of both. This is also where your clairvoyance, or intuition comes into use, to decipher how to use the central card in any given reading. Read it in context with every combination of cards, unless you intuit it otherwise.

Sometimes, even though you may have concentrated on the future when shuffling and laying out your cards, they talk of the past or present. This is because the querent's auric emanations may be strongly fixed in the past or present, on issues not yet released. Quite often a spread will show a little of each, past, present and future. If this happens, you either didn't concentrate on a specific time span, or, there are matters necessary to talk of to the person to help them release the past.

To determine what happens after you have established the story of the reading, ask the querent whether certain things are happening now, or have recently happened. If those issues have taken place, cut more cards for the future and place them over the House 9 of the past. Then continue your reading. If the querent does not relate to the events you initially spoke of, then it is usually something coming up in the future. The querent does not know the future and this should be pointed out to the querent, otherwise he or she will think you have the wrong information.

With the horoscope spread you will find you can be quite specific as to what is happening in the different areas of life. To add to this detail, after reading the whole circle, ask the querent if they have any questions on 'specific' matters. Point out that you can give straight answers to straight questions, simply by cutting the cards (the cut card gives the answer). This is where the querent may ask some straight questions such as 'if I take this job, will I be happy in it?' But, most of the time the person will give a vague question which you will have to reword into something specific. For example 'what about my career?', 'what's going to happen there?'. In actual fact, you would have already answered that with the main horoscope spread, so you must guide the querent to be more specific in what they want to know. Direct your thoughts clearly and you will get a straight answer from the cards.

Sometimes, you may need to cut two or more cards on the same question. When you do this you rephrase the question so that you can hit the subject at different angles to get a more holistic picture. Again, the querent is not going to know how to ask questions of the cards, so you must establish what that person is really wanting to know so that you can phrase the questions properly.

Quite often some people want to ask delicate questions that they cannot voice outright due to their need for privacy. Give them the opportunity to get their answers for themselves. Explain that they only need visualize the question in their minds and cut the cards themselves. You look at the cut card and interpret it for them with a positive or negative response. Sometimes a description of the card is needed which the querent must apply to their question and interpret it themselves. This works quite well if the querent is able to focus his or her thoughts. Advise them, however, on how not to ask questions as discussed earlier, as most people will ask 'Will I do this?' 'Will' must be their choice and even if the answer was yes, tomorrow the person may change their mind. Sometimes a question like that can be answered, but be sure to state 'in all probability this may happen, but you have the choice', rather than emphatically say 'it will happen'. If the person is at a crossroads and has choices to make, isolate each choice and cut cards for each direction, to see which way life will go if she or he chose that direction. This is an area it is best to instruct the querent to do, as they can best visualize the vague or exact directions they are perceiving.

Example of a horoscope spread

The following is a transcription of a tape recording of a reading. The querent requested a general forecast into the next six months. This querent is a regular client therefore some issues may not be fully identified by the cards laid out. 'R' will represent the Reader and 'Q' will represent the Querent. Any comment in brackets is an added note for your assistance when reading this example.

Reader shuffles the cards scanning six months into the future for the querent while the querent also concentrates on the six months ahead. Querent cuts cards then Reader gathers them up and deals out the Horoscope spread.

R: This appears to be quite a good spread. The next six months look as if there are some good issues ahead. However, just to clarify I'm not picking up what you have recently done, have you already been through some restructuring in your personal life? Because the Tower in the middle shows some disruption and restructure going on and the Universe card actually shows you stepping through a new threshold for yourself and looking at new potentials for yourself.

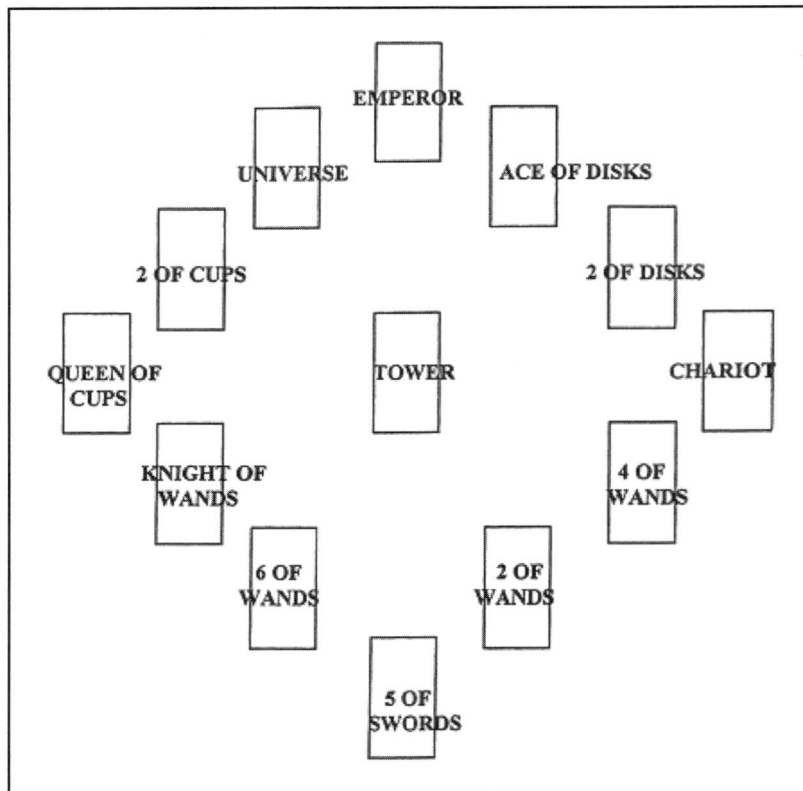

Q: Yes, that fits.

R: And so it is very much, perhaps a restructure of your psyche and the way you are seeing things as well.

Q: Yes.

R: This also may have an effect on your personal relationship side of things. Have you felt your relationships have been going through some renewal and change?

Q: You mean in general, all my relationships? Yes it has.

R: Yes, this would be more talking about overall relationships. You seem to be seeing people through new eyes and those who are negative in your life, you seem to be letting go and throwing out.

Q: Yes. I am.

R: You are not, sort of, letting them have a bad effect on you?

Q: I am definitely trying. I just wanted to come and check with this reading that I am moving in the right direction.

R: I would say so, you have the Emperor card sitting up in the tenth house, showing that you are moving in the right direction. You are taking a significant stand for yourself as far as your beliefs and where you want to head. Now, career-wise, I see you are wanting to create a lot of achievement with that card up there. But, you are also finishing off a phase for yourself because you have the completion card and the love card in the sixth and twelfth positions and the Emperor card in its position show a combination of looking at where you are at. You will be thinking okay, I'm finishing off my time here, effecting what I am doing.

Q: (Nodding in agreement.)

R: In other words, doing a damn good job, basically, for yourself. You enjoy yourself, but there is a next stage coming up.

Q: Yes.

R: Where if it is not a job change, it will be actually an advancement for you. But it still comes back to the issue of decision-making about family and things like that. It's still there in the overall structure of this spread, for example the Two of Wands in the fifth house. Does this relate to you still?

Q: Yes.

R: It's not an issue that's gone out of your life still, it is still there.

Q: The family one do you mean?

R: Having a child!

Q: Yes, that is another thing I wanted to find out from you. I'm going back to the surgeon to see what we will do next, because they have found out why I can't conceive. I was conceiving, but not …

R: Not actually carrying through, it was terminating itself all the time. That would make sense then looking at the Tower in the centre, showing shocks on that level, but also the awareness now of the problem. But it was obviously something you weren't aware of at the time. With the combination of the Universe card, the Two of Wands, the Chariot and Queen of Cups shows you looking at new ways to achieve your goals when it comes to children, your love relationship, etc. (Chariot in seventh house and Two of Wands in fifth house), and so, that was why I felt you were finding yourself on new ground there.

Q: Yes, that's right.

R: With the Chariot there (seventh house), you and your partner appear to be looking on to new potentials to where you are heading. But, there are problems, however. You have the Five of Swords in the position of home issues and environment and it does show a lot of depression coming through at times. Do you find that you get depressed a lot?

Q: Yes, I think that is part of it, because as you said, I am trying to release the past, but it's pretty tenacious.

R: Hum! Yes, it does hold on, doesn't it? And yet with the Love card (Two of Cups) sitting in the twelfth position, you have actually got a situation where your psyche is coming into more harmony. The duality of yourself is coming into more harmony with your inner and outer self.

Q: Yes.

R: And so, I really think you are actually doing wonderful work here. It is just that you have to shock yourself into it at times, because you have the Tower card in the middle which shows that you will always have to create a shock and awakening for yourself. This will bring in more awareness, but sometimes it is not nice when it happens.

Q: Yes!

R: I see a house shift here in the cards, are you both expecting to shift?

Q: We have shifted just recently.

R: With the Ace of Disks in the ninth house, the Six of Wands in the third house and the Chariot card in the seventh, shows a new situation being created, travelling to a new situation and establishing yourself (Ace of Disks) there. It is actually a good move shown by this combination of cards. Are you happy with your move?

Q: Oh, wonderful!

R: The victory card shows this feeling of success there. With the Knight of Wands in the second house and the Two of Disks sitting up in the eighth position—these are positions of money matters—it shows a change. A quick change when it happened, where you were at possession-wise, property-wise, because the Two of Disks may represent property here. It shows a change of finances also and it is an improvement in the longer term, but in the shorter term shown by the Knight of Wands, I would say the money would be going out of your hands as fast as it comes in.

Q: Yes, that is about right. Now, if you can go back to the baby thing, I probably will need another operation, I just wanted to check out—uh, I'm pretty sure it is going to come right–I wondered whether you had any idea of time or …

R: Okay, with the Judgement card I cut in the beginning of the reading just to check on what was coming through and whether the reading was really about you, it was showing that you were entering into a point of crossroads of decisions, or waiting on decisions.

Q: Yes.

R: And, so it is hard to actually give a timing on a situation, when it is decisions of other people and not just you. But, I will go into that and see what we will come up with, okay (At this point the reader concentrated on a series of questions and cut the cards. Positive cards gave the reader a 'yes' to her directed questions and negative cards gave a 'no').

This year! It is August at the moment and it appears to certainly be before Christmas.

Q: Is that the operation or the baby?

R: I was focusing on the operation. It should be reasonably successful.

Q: Yes that is good.

R: But is still indecisive at present (High Priestess) as to whether they will give you the operation or try another form of treatment. Because I see, they are tending, by the looks of it to take the attitude of, we will wait and see.

Q: I haven't seen the surgeons yet, but that would explain it and it would be better in a way.

R: This will make sense then if your doctor is waiting for the surgeon's answer. Of course it is wait and see.

However, it does look promising, the whole situation and in past readings I have done for you I have always seen that you were going to have a child.

Q: Yes, I am now pretty sure that is going to happen. Last time I came I checked out certain relationships with people. Am I still going on the right lines with these people?

R: Just concentrate on that question and cut the cards. (Querent cuts.) You have cut the Princess of Wands. The answer is yes and no. Were you thinking of many people or just one?

Q: I was thinking of two.

R: That is probably why I got a double feeling from that card, even though generally the card would not mean that.

It is a good card in its own right, it is going ahead wilfully in the direction you should and the result will be positive. So in a way, your answer is yes. But now cut one card per person.

Q: I'll ask whether I'm dealing with them in the right way. (Querent makes cut concentrating on one person.)

R: The Five of Wands says no, there are a few problems coming through with this person. Is there another angle you can look at this? As the path you seem to be taking with this person is a harder road.

Q: Yes, I'm probably not thinking clearly about it.

R: Focus on how you have been dealing with one of those people and in your mind concentrate on the question, while you cut the cards, 'Is this the right way to deal with this person?'

Q: (Querent does this and a positive card came up.)

R: Answer is yes. Do you want to check on the other person?

Q: No that is the leading person.

R: Okay. Does that cover everything for you.

Q: Yes that is good actually. Just one more! I want to check out if the spiritual side of my life is going well–I think it is?

R: Just concentrate on that and cut the cards. (Querent does this.) The Princess of Swords comes up here. I would say yes to your concentrated question, but I would say that the material restrictions of existence tend to frustrate you. You seem to have also a strong, firm hold on the ground and not let yourself fly a little more spiritually. So you may be holding yourself back by holding on to the past or old pedestals. But you have the ability to allow it to all work for you, shown by that card.

Q: Just keep working on it? Thanks. That was excellent, thank you.

The yes/no spread

Method 1: A very simple way of finding a straight yes or no answer is to cut the cards once. The card at the bottom of the first cut will, by virtue of its positive or negative meaning, give a yes or no. If the card is neither positive or negative, like Justice, Judgement, High Priestess, Temperance, the answer may be that the querent themselves is still to choose, or it's an issue not defined as destiny yet due to many other influencing factors.

Method 2: Lay the cards out in the following order:

Cards 1 and 2 represent the past issues leading up to the present. Card 3 is the present and cards 4 and 5 the resulting factors. If cards 4, 5 and one or two of the others are negative, the results are likely to be a No. If cards 4 and 5 are positive the results are likely to be Yes, even if the present and past show negative cards.

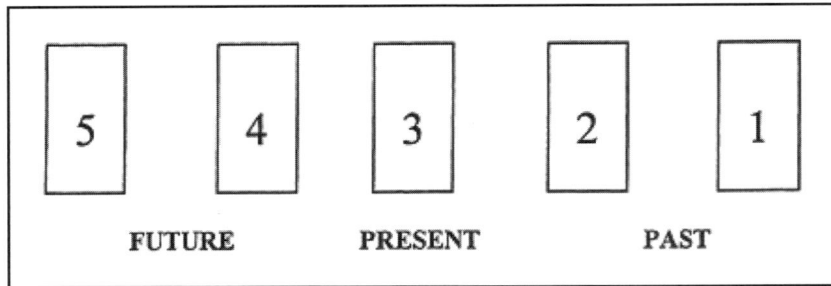

The hexagram spread

This is an excellent little spread for quick and concise answers to any question that requires a short and concise answer.

Card 1: Past actions which influence the present.
Card 2: Present conditions and issues.
Card 3: Near future events.
Card 4: Underlying influences, hopes or fears.
Card 5: Environmental factors influencing.
Card 6: Any opposing factors.
Card 7: End result (taking into account the influence of cards one to six).

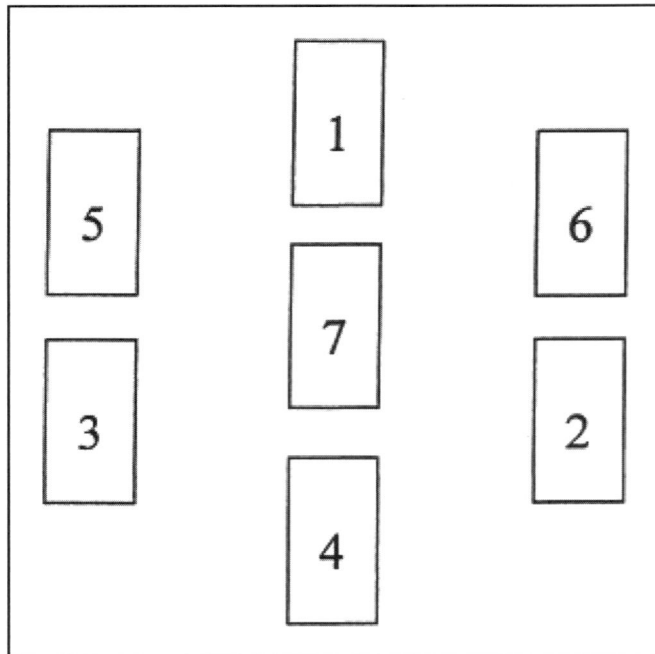

Three sevens spread

The Three Sevens Spread is for short readings which need to discuss past, present and future. Bottom Row represents the past, Middle Row represents present circumstances, Top Row represents future. When reading, read the cards marked 'KEY' with the adjoining cards, right and left, blended into the interpretation, the right-hand side what is more obvious, the left side the unobvious.

21	20	19	18 KEY	17	16	15	FUTURE
14	13	12	11 KEY	10	9	8	PRESENT
7	6	5	4 KEY	3	2	1	PAST

Method 1: Can be used for relationships. Decide on a significator (a Court Card representing you or another). Select only the Court Cards out of your deck, shuffle them and deal them out after cutting. You will see who is coming towards you and who is leaving you by the direction the people in the Court Cards are facing in relation to the significator card. If the significator does not come up, try again. Variations of this method can be used to suit whatever question you ask.

Method 2: Using the whole deck. Concentrate on your question, shuffle, cut and deal seven cards in the order numbered above. The whole spread can be read in the terms of what is coming up in the near future with Card 1 being the present influence.

Diamond spread

This spread is for short-answer questions such as, 'What is my destiny?', or 'Where am I heading in life?', spiritually or otherwise. However, such questions are usually too profound for a short answer and the cross and triangle spread or the horoscope spread may prove a better method. Nevertheless, the Diamond Spread will give a quick, although general, answer.

Fan the cards face-down across the table and have the querent choose five cards from the whole deck. Lay the cards in the order they are given to you, as below:

```
        3
1       5       2
        4
```

1 = past achievements or subconscious conditioning.
2 = the present and tools you now have to work with. What you must deal with now.
3 = where you are heading, the next goal or factor to deal with.
4 = what your new cycle will start with after you have accomplished Card 3.
5 = resulting factor.

General relationship spread

Steps

1. Separate the sixteen Court Cards out of your deck, into a separate pile.
2. Choose a Significator representing the querent.
3. Shuffle the pile of Court Cards and deal eight cards in a horseshoe shape, right to left and, if the significator appears in the eight dealt cards, proceed to step four. If not, then take up the cards, reshuffle, concentrating your question and deal again. If the significator does not turn up, abandon the reading until another time. These cards will be the people involved.
4. Return the rest of the Court Cards to the main deck and shuffle. Have the querent cut the deck once. Place the bottom pile on top of the cut pile and deal from the top of the pack one card under each of the eight dealt cards, dealing from right to left. This second row of cards will show the issues involving the querent's relationships with each person represented in the Court Cards. These issues can be what sort of communication the querent will have with these people. The card under the significator's card will show how the querent feels or reacts.

Personal relationship spread

The purpose of this spread is to see how a current or proposed relationship with a known person will go with the querent.

1. Choose a significator card representing the querent. Choose a significator card representing the person inquired about. If there is more than one person inquired about, choose significators for them all.
2. Lay the querent's card down in the centre of your table. Place the card representing the person(s) inquired about to the:
   Left of the querent if a past relationship;

Right of the querent if a future relationship;
Below the querent if a present relationship;
Above the querent if a wished or possible relationship.

3. (a) Shuffle the rest of the deck and fan it out on the table face-down away from the cards already laid.

(b) The querent selects each card per person enquired about with a mentally focused question. For example: 'How will this relationship with X proceed over the next Y?' Whatever the querent's intent, help him or her to voice a clear question that demands an answer which will satisfy their need to know.

(c) Place the chosen cards over the significator card(s) representing the individual(s) focused on. These cards should provide an answer. If not, have the querent choose another card with a further question and lay it over the respective card(s).

Triangle and cross spread

The Triangle above the Cross is a symbol used in the Philosophus ceremony of the Golden Dawn. It is an image of Him who was unfolded in the Light. The Triangle is the Triune Light. A use of this spread is to see the balance of the higher and lower states of yourself by viewing the state of your subtle bodies. The positions of the cards for this, would then be:

1 = my Spirit Body
2 = my Casual Body
3 = my Higher Mental Body
4 = my Lower Mental Body
5 = my Astral/Emotional Body
6 = my Etheric Body
7 = my Physical Body

Another way of using this spread is for more basic questions. The positions would then be as follows:

1 = What is above (what guides).
2 = What gives assistance.
3 = Present reality to the situation.
4 = How you see the present and how you handle it.
5 = What is below, wishes, hopes, desires.
6 = Near future, what is coming next.
7 = Resulting factor.

Brief meanings

Majority of Cards of a Particular Suit:
Wands—Energy, quarrelling, opposition.

Cups—Pleasure and merriment.
Swords—Trouble, sadness, sometimes sickness and even death.
Disks—Business, money, possessions.
Trumps—Force of considerable strength, but beyond enquirer's control.
Court Cards—Society, meeting with many people.
Aces—Strength generally. Aces are always strong cards.

Majority of Cards of Similar Type—Different Suits:
4 Aces—Great Power and Force.
3 Aces—Riches and success.
4 Knights—Great swiftness and rapidity.
3 Knights—Unexpected meetings. Knights generally show news.
4 Queens—Authority and influence.
3 Queens—Powerful and influential friends.
4 Kings—Meetings with the Great.
3 Kings—Rank and honour.
4 Princesses—New Ideas and plans.
3 Princesses—Society of the Young.
4 Tens—Anxiety and responsibility.
3 Tens—Buying, selling, commercial transactions.
4 Nines—Added responsibility.
3 Nines—Much correspondence.
4 Eights—Much news.
3 Eights—Much journeying.
4 Sevens—Disappointments.
3 Sevens—Treaties and compacts.
4 Sixes—Pleasure.
3 Sixes—Gain and success.
4 Fives—Order and regularity.
3 Fives—Quarrels, fights.
4 Fours—Rest and peace.
3 Fours—Industry.
4 Threes—Resolution, determination.
3 Threes—Deceit.
4 Twos—Conference and conversations.
3 Twos—Reorganisation and recommencement of a thing.

Brief Meanings of Each Minor Arcana Card Generally:

Wands

Ace—Symbolises force, strength and planning of matter according to its nature.
Two—Influence over another, dominion.

Three—Establishing one's independence.
Four—Settlement, arrangement complete.
Five—Quarrelling, fighting.
Six—Gain and success.
Seven—Opposition, sometimes courage with it.
Eight—Hasty communication, letter or message.
Nine—Strength, power, health, energy.
Ten—Cruelty, malice towards others. Overbearing strength. Revenge and injustice.

Cups

Ace—Fertility, productiveness, beauty, pleasure and happiness.
Two—Marriage, love, pleasure, warmth.
Three—Plenty, hospitality, celebration.
Four—Receiving pleasures or kindness from others, yet some discomfort with it.
Five—Disappointment in love, Marriage break-up, Unkindness from friends.
Six—Wish, happiness, success, enjoyment.
Seven—Lying, deceit, promises unfulfilled, illusion, deception. Error, slight success but not enough energy to retain it.
Eight—Success abandoned, decline of interest in a thing.
Nine—Complete success, pleasure and happiness, wishes fulfilled.
Ten—Matters settled in accordance with one's wishes. Complete good fortune.

Swords

Ace—Strength through trial and tribulation, mental stimulation and planning.
Two—Quarrel resolved, peace restored.
Three—Unhappiness, sorrow, parting due to interference.
Four—Convalescence, recovery, getting away from it all.
Five—Defeat, loss, malice, slander and gossip.
Six—Labour, work, journey by water.
Seven—Untrustworthy, journey by land.
Eight—Narrow, restricted, petty, possible prison if extreme.
Nine—Dullness, suffering, malice, cruelty, pain.
Ten—Ruin, death, failure, disaster.

Disks

Ace—Material gain, power but in initial stages only. Labour and work about to begin.
Two—Change for the better, including location.
Three—Business, paid employment. Laying a firm foundation.
Four—Gain, power and influence, stability.
Five—Health and financial problems due to over-stimulation of both areas.

Six—Success in the material.
Seven—Unprofitable speculations, employment hassles. Work undertaken without payment.
Eight—Skill, prudence and cunning.
Nine—Inheritance, increase of money.
Ten—Riches and wealth.

The Court Cards are to be treated as individuals and their respective elemental framework shows their action within it.

On the Signification of the cards:
A card is strong or weak, well-dignified, according to the cards which are next to it on either side. Cards of the same suit on either side strengthen it greatly either for good or evil, according to their nature. Cards of the suit answering to its contrary element, on either side, weaken it greatly for good or evil. Air and Earth are contraries as are also Fire and Water. Air is friendly with Water and Fire, and Fire with Air and Earth.

If the card of the suit of Wands falls between a Cup and a Sword, the Sword modifies and connects the wand with the Cup, so that it is not weakened by its vicinity, but is modified by the influence of both cards; therefore fairly strong. But if a card passes between two which are naturally contrary, it is not affected by either much, as a Wand between a Sword and a Disk, which latter, being Air and Earth, are contrary and therefore weaken each other.

Pairing cards together in a reading:
On pairing the cards each is to be taken as of equal force with the other. If of opposite elements they mutually weaken each other. If at the end of the pairing of the cards in a pack, one card remains over, it signifies the partial result of that particular part of the Divination only. If an evil card and others good then it would modify the good.

If it be the Significator or the Enquirer, or of another person, it would show that matters would much depend on the line of action taken by the person represented. The reason of this importance of the single card is that it is alone and not modified. If two cards are the end, instead of a single one, they are not of so much importance.

Ceremonial ritual and divination

Within the Golden Dawn there is a long method of Divination. This was done with full ceremonial and ritual format and would take many hours to do properly. This method was only used by those in the Golden Dawn's Inner Order. There are a number of people in Golden Dawn temples both past and present who simply use the full divination process of 'Opening the Key' (as given below) without any ritual at all, which shows a fundamental lack of knowledge of its full function. The full ritual process allows not only the diviner to see the process of the questioning slowly unfathomed, but also enables one to see what Astral forces are working for and against them during the reading. This knowledge gives additional ability for seeing the various currents or emanations of energy patterns, how to deal with them, when to use them, when not to use them and how to charter a course through them if needed. The full faculty of clairvoyance is used here through the correct invocations.

To those of you not familiar with this method we would suggest you get used to doing the full formulae a couple of times, without the ritual, until the whole process is familiar to you then adapt the ritual formulae to it and try and do a reading exercising the ritual faculty. For those not interested in ritual, however, within the 'Opening of the Key' there are five good methods of divining, which can be used individually at any given time as readings in themselves. I would also stress that the 'Opening of the Key' method is utilised only for major, important events in one's life.

The basic following steps are taken from the Golden Dawn's Z2 document on Divination which was based on the various steps of the Neophyte ceremony of the Order. There is often confusion over this document. What it does, is simply apply common sense to any form of divination by making sure that all angles are covered before you begin. I would also point out that in the Z2 method there are additions to the basic outline of 'Opening of the Key' which relate more specifically to the ritual process itself.

Using the guidelines of the formulae, below, write your own ritual format for your divination when performing the Opening of the Key or any other ritual divination you wish to perform. Generally the adept would wear a white robe when performing any work in this manner and would have for use his or her own magical implements and props. For those who have no magical implements and have not prepared them in the Golden Dawn manner, as given in Regardie's book, 'The Golden Dawn', we have included the chapter entitled 'Scrying, Travelling in the Spirit Vision, Ritual and the Tarot', which contains a quick method of blessing one's magical implements, together with suggestions of what you can use.

Z2 formulae of divination

A—Form of Divination. (The tarot cards are placed on the altar or table on which the divination is about to be done.)

B—The Diviner. (One should be wearing the Rose Cross to establish the link with the Inner Order of the Golden Dawn.)

C—Forces acting on Divination. (A planetary flashing tablet with the symbol of the planet that relates to the question to be placed on the altar. On the reverse side of this tablet should be the symbol that the question comes under—whether Wand, Cup, Sword or Disk.)

D—The Subject of the Divination. (The subject of the question should be written down and placed on the table.)

E—The preparation of all things necessary and the right understanding of the process so as to formulate a connecting link between the process employed and the macrocosm. (The Banishing Ritual of the Pentagram, then purify and consecrate your work-space, circumambulation.)

F—The Invocation of the Higher; arrangement of the scheme of divination and initiation of the forces thereof. (Invoke the Middle Pillar formula and the LVX Signs, plus do the DWB-Divine White Brilliance invocation.)

G—The First entry into the Matter. First assertion of limits and correspondences beginning a working. (Invoke the Angel HUA to give you guidance in obtaining correct answers to the question.)

H—The actual careful formulation of the question demanded; and consideration of all its corre-spondences and their classification. (Read out the question aloud, and focus on the question requesting guidance from the Higher to guide you in seeing the truth.)

I—Announcing aloud that all correspondences taken are correct and perfect, the Diviner places his hand upon the instrument of Divination. Standing at the east of the Altar, he prepares to invoke the forces in the Divination. (One is to have the Elemental Weapon present that relates to the structure of the question. It is then taken up and raised above the head and the Colour of the Sephirah, relating to the question, is then soaked into the auric body of the Adept, while the name of the Sephirah is vibrated.)

J—Solemn invocation of the necessary spiritual forces to aid the Diviner in the Divination. Then let him say: 'Arise before me clear as a mirror, O magical vision requisite for the accomplish-ment of this Divination'. (The name of the Archangel which rules the element you are work-ing with in relation to the type of question you are asking is then vibrated, then the planetary name of the Angel.)

K—Accurately define the term of the question, putting down clearly in writing what is already known, what is suspected or implied and what is sought to be known. Ensure that you verify in the beginning of the judgement that part which is already known.

L—Next let the Diviner formulate clearly under two groups or headings:
(a) The arguments for.
(b) The arguments against the success of the subject for divination, so as to be able to draw a preliminary conclusion there from either side. (This involves shuffling, cutting and examining the deck and selecting a Significator and performing the First Operation, 'Opening of the Key'.)

M—First formulation of a conclusive judgement from the premises already obtained.

N—Same as Section L. (This relates to performing the Second Operation.)

O—Formulation of a second judgement, this time of the further developments arising from those indicated in the previous process of judgement, which was preliminary to this opera-tion. (Reading the Second Operation.)

P—The Comparison of the first preliminary judgement with a second judgement develop-ing there from, so as to enable the Diviner to form an idea of the probable action of forces beyond the actual plane, by the invocation of an angelic figure consonant to the process. And in this matter take care not to mislead the judgement through the action of thine own preconceived ideas, but only relying after due tests, on the indication afforded thee by the angelic form. And know, unless the form be of an angelic nature its indication will not be reliable, seeing, that if it be an element, it will be below the plane desired. (Basically, this relates to the use of Astral vision or clairvoyance when viewing the results of the two previ-ous spreads.)

Q—The Diviner now completely and thoroughly formulates his whole judgement as well as for the immediate future as for the development thereof, taking into account the knowledge and indications given him by the angelic form.

R—Having this result before him let the Diviner now formulate a fresh divination process, based on the conclusion at which he has arrived, so as to form a basis for a further working. (The Third Operation is then undertaken.)

S—Formulate the sides for and against a fresh judgement and deduce the conclusion from the fresh operation.

T—The Diviner then compares carefully the whole, judgement and decisions arrived at with their conclusions and delivers now plainly a succinct and consecutive judgement thereon. (This is the fourth Operation.)

U—The Diviner gives advice to the consultant as to what he shall make of the judgement.

V—The Diviner formulates clearly with what forces it may be necessary to work in order to combat the Evil, or fix the Good, promised by the Divination. (This is the fifth Operation.)

W—Lastly, remember that unto thee a divination shall be as a sacred work of the Divine magic of Light and not to be performed to pander unto thy curiosity regarding the secrets of another. And if by this means thou shalt arrive at a knowledge of another's secrets, thou shalt respect and not betray them.

You would finish off the ritual divination with a thanks to the guiding forces, a purification and consecration ritual, a license to depart and finally the banishing ritual of the Pentagram.

Opening of the key

This method of Tarot divination is called 'Opening of the Key' and is done in five operations all of which relate to the actions of the Tarot on the Celestial Sphere and the actions of the Convoluted Forces on them:

(a) First operation shows the actions or influences of the Aces through the Four Worlds.
(b) The Second operation shows the actions of the twelve houses of the zodiac.
(c) The Third operation shows the influences of the Signs of the Zodiac.
(d) The Fourth operation shows the influences of the thirty-six decanates of the Minor Arcana.
(e) The Fifth operation shows the rule of the Sephiroth over the Celestial Heavens.

At this point we are now able to see the overall extent of this Golden Dawn system and especially the celestial Sphere which is very important for the tides or influences of the entire Macrocosm. In Aleister Crowley's 'Book of Thoth' and Paul Foster Case's book on 'Tarot', both one-time Golden Dawn initiates, this method is given with no explanations as to its origin. In the last chapter in Case's book on Tarot Divination is almost a direct quotation from the Golden Dawn papers though no acknowledgement of their authorship or origin is given.

The method

Step 1.   Make a decision of what Significator you are going to use.

Step 2.   Hold the pack in the left hand and one of the Magical Weapons in the right and invoke over the cards:

In the Divine name of HUA who art set over the operations of the Secret Wisdom. Lay thine hand invisibly on these consecrated cards of art, that thereby I may obtain true knowledge of hidden things, to the glory of thy ineffable Name. Amen.

Step 3. Shuffle the Cards well. If the Diviner does this he must concentrate on the person enquiring. If the Querent prefers not to do this, he must then concentrate on the Question in hand.

First Operation—The Opening of the Question

1. The Querent cuts the cards in half (while concentrating on the question) with the right hand and placing the second half of the deck to the left of the original facing down, with space between each pile. The original pile, is then cut in half again and the cut pile is placed in the middle of the first two piles. The pile on the far left is cut in half and placed on the far right. So we now have four separate piles about the same size. These represent the forces of YHVH but the Order is the same as that of the Hebrew letters, that is from right to left, the Pile representing the Yod force being on the extreme right.
2. The Diviner turns over all piles and reads the cards facing up on the top of each pile. The Y pile represents the Fire Element and matters pertaining to action, energy, inspiration etc., so the card read will be a description of that part of the person's current situation or purpose in being there for a reading. The H pile is representing Water and shows the emotions, relationships, joyous or sad happenings and will be read as described above. The V pile is Air and represents communications, mental activities, etc. The H(Final) pile is Earth and represents the querent's material and physical world. A majority of particular cards will show the main issue involved. The Four Piles are searched for the Significator and when found it signifies the elemental framework from which the answer will come.
3. The Diviner takes the pile which has the Significator in it and fans it out from right to left in the form of a horseshoe shape.
4. (a) Groupings:
    Note the majority of a suit, numbers, Court and Trumps.
    (b) Counting:
    Count from the Significator, from the direction it is facing. If the figure or card is a direct facing one then count to your left. The card you finish at in your counting is also the next number you count from and is also the card you read. Knights, Kings, Queens, count 4. Princesses, count 7. Aces count 11. For the Pip Cards, the number they represent. Planetary Trumps count 9. Elemental Trumps count 3. Zodiac Trumps count 12. Make a story for these cards, as it is the beginning of the affair.
    (c) Pairing:
    Pair the cards on either side of the Significator, then those outside them and so on. Make up another story, filling in details which are omitted in the first.

Second Operation—The further development of the matter

1. Querent shuffles cards and places them face downwards on the table.
2. Diviner deals cards into twelve packs which form a complete circle, for the twelve astrological houses of the heavens.

3. Look for the Significator in the pack that relates to the astrological house whose meaning relates to the framework of the original question. If Significator is not there then look for it in a pack representing some similar astrological house. If the Significator is in a house that in no way represents the question then abandon the reading and try again a few hours later.
4. Spread out in the horseshoe shape and count the pile containing the Significator and count and pair as before.

Third Operation—Continuing development of question

1. Shuffle as before.
2. Diviner then deals out twelve packs as before only this time they represent the Signs and not the Houses of the Zodiac. The first pack representing Aries, the first Sign, and the next, Taurus, the second, and so on.
3. The particular Sign and house that the Significator falls under is noted and this will govern this stage of the development of the Question.
4. This pack is then spread out in the form of a horseshoe and the counting and pairing process of the previous operations is continued.

Fourth Operation—Penultimate development of Question

1. Shuffle, etc., as before.
2. Take Significator from pack and place face upwards in the centre of the table.
3. Let the thirty-six cards following him form a ring around the table with the nine o'clock position as the start, going counter clockwise.
4. Count and pair as before—the first card with the thirty-sixth, etc.

Fifth Operation—Final result

1. Shuffle, etc., as before.
2. Diviner places ten cards in the form of the Ten Sephiroth of the Tree of Life then continues to deal out the rest of the cards in similar manner until all are dealt.
3. Look for Significator and the pack it is in as the influence of this Sephirah will colour the whole reading.
4. Take the pack the Significator is in and pair as before and count, etc. in horseshoe spread.
5. Merge all stories together and you should then have a very detailed description of the event.

Example of opening of the key

This form is especially applicable to Divination concerning the ordinary material events of daily life.

It is a mode of placing the cards based upon the scheme of the dominion of the Tarot Symbols. The more rigidly correct and in harmony with the scheme of the Universe is any form of Divination, so much the more is it likely to yield a correct and reliable answer to the enquirer. For then and then only, is there a firm link, bond or union, established between it and the occult forces of Nature. The moment the correct correspondences of the symbols employed ceases to be observed, the link between them and the inner Occult Forces is strained and in some cases broken. For this cause, therefore, is it that will sometimes yield a true and sometimes a false answer and at other times a partly true and partly false, because the correspondences are either not rigidly observed or else made use of by an ignorant and uninitiated person.

There are a number of reasons for this, for each person will attempt to Divine from his or her own perspective. Some people prefer Divining directly form their Etheric Body, others use the Astral or Emotional bodies and some the Mental Body while a very rare few will Divine straight from the Causal Body. In each of these bodies there are seven chakras and when the Diviner uses one of the subtle bodies, he or she will use a certain chakra or combination of chakras to bring the information across. This all depends on the psychic makeup of the individual. In order to keep the link pure the Golden Dawn Adept will put on his insignia, costume, or grade badge and make directly over the pack any Invoking Hexagram or Pentagram, either with the hand alone, or with any of the Four Elemental weapons present and/or Lotus Wand (a full explanation of these are given in Regardie's 'Golden Dawn' Volumes) and possibly may use some elemental force to help in the Divination. The Consecrated Elemental weapons help hold and balance the link to the Subtle Body and chakras utilised, for this is necessary due to the long period of time needed to complete the reading (it can take from anything from two to four hours to complete it). Working without the implements for this length of time on, for example, say the Etheric body can be extremely exhausting and the Elemental Weapons help to keep one's concentration fixed for that long length of time it takes to finishing the reading.

For those of you who do not possess the Elemental weapons and have no desire to make them, yet want to try this method out we suggest the use of the Hebrew letters of the Holy Name YHVH placed on the table in front of you. Apart from this there are certain flower essences and Gem Elixirs that work just as effectively, Yarrow flower essence being one such example. A good method for the beginner, of finding out which subtle bodies and chakras are being utilised for Divination is to dowse this out with a pendulum then consult the lists of elixirs published in the books 'Flower Essences and Vibrational Healing' and 'Gem Elixirs and Vibrational Healing (Vol. 1 and 2)' by Gurudas.

We have given an abridged version of the original Order example (by Mathers) of this Divination reading, because it has so many hidden meanings in the instruction and to try and rewrite another reading with all the associated details would not make any sense when the original is good enough. The influence of the surrounding cards, the way certain cards face, the influence from the Elemental viewpoint (of the surrounding cards) is of paramount importance here. One of the few failings that this reading has, is that it does not give a time scale for when all this is to happen and that is possibly one of the few changes we would suggest when each operation is accomplished. The instruction here is complex and the ability to be able to do a reading as per this paper, is a necessary part of the Adeptus Minor training in many Golden Dawn temples.

Example spread

Supposing that a Young man asks the Question 'Shall I succeed in my present affairs?' His complexion is fair and his Hair light brown. The Diviner takes the King of Cups for Significator (had he been an older man he would have selected the Knight of Cups) which matches the appearance of the individual. It should be pointed out here that the Court Cards can give personality profiles (which do not always match the physical appearance) as well and since the Enquirer is unlikely to know the personality of the Diviner, it is best to use the cards based on the appearance of the Enquirer only. Now the Enquirer can either shuffle the pack his or herself, while concentrating on the Question or get the Diviner to do it for them. We have always found it helpful to use a mental image of the Enquirer's face over the cards while saying the question out loud, which helps one to focus more. If one is asking the question on his or her own behalf then only the question will be focused on while shuffling.

The Enquirer is then instructed to cut the deck in half and to place the uppermost half well to the right and then to cut each portion in half again which gives a total of four portions of cards.

Whoever cuts, cuts to his own right. These four portions are now turned upwards. The Ten of Wands is strong as it comes under the presidency of YOD which governs the Wands and Fire. The Six of Swords is moderately strong as it comes under the presidency of the HEH which rules Cups and Water. The Four of Disks is weak (because it is a contrary element) and comes under the Presidency of VAU which rules Swords and Air. The Chariot is strong (as Cancer–a Watery Sign) because it is in the place of HEH (final) which rules Disks and Earth (Earth and Water being compatible elements).

The Diviner reads these four cards as a preliminary thus:

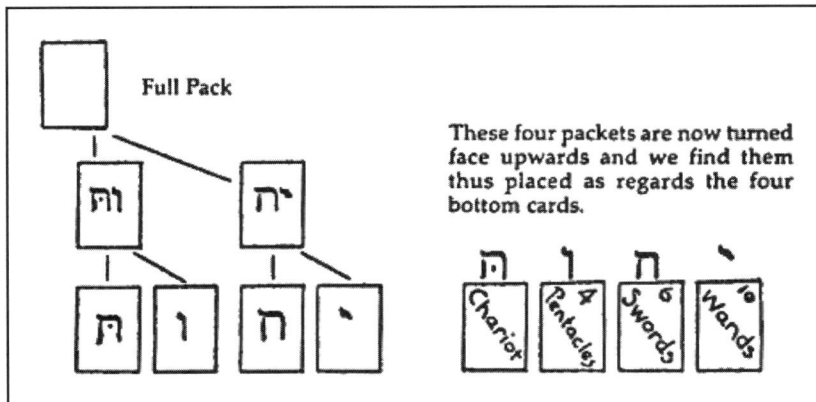

'The Enquirer works very hard and gains but little money, yet matters are beginning to improve'.

This is because the Ten of Wands shows cruelty, harshness, etc.; the Six of Swords, labour and work; the Four of Disks, gain of money; and the Chariot, success.

The Diviner then examines the Four Packets to find in which the significator is. It proves to be in one in which the Six of Swords is the bottom card. This is in the place answering to the Letter HEH, which represents pleasure and rules the Cups. This is so far a good omen, as it shows society and merriment. This pack of cards is retained for reading, the others are put aside as having no direct influence on the question. Let us suppose that the retained pack contains twenty cards and that they are in the order described below. The Diviner spreads them out in the form of a horseshoe.

The suit of Cups is distinctly in the majority: pleasure, visiting friends, love-making, etc. There are three Knaves (Princesses) which indicate society of the young, from which the Diviner reads that the enquirer is fond of young people and of flirting, etc. There being no other set of three or four cards of a sort, the Diviner proceeds to read by counting from the Significator, whose face is turning towards the Nine of Wands.

The counting therefore proceeds in the direction of the arrow, thus: 4 from the King of Cups, Ten of Disks. 10 from this, Eight of Cups. 8 from this, Wheel of Fortune. 9 from this, Knave of Wands, 7 from this, Ten of Cups. 10 from this, Five of Wands. 5 from this, Knight of Wands. 4 from this, Ace of Disks. 5 from this, Ten of Cups. And as this card has already been taken, this form of reading finishes here.

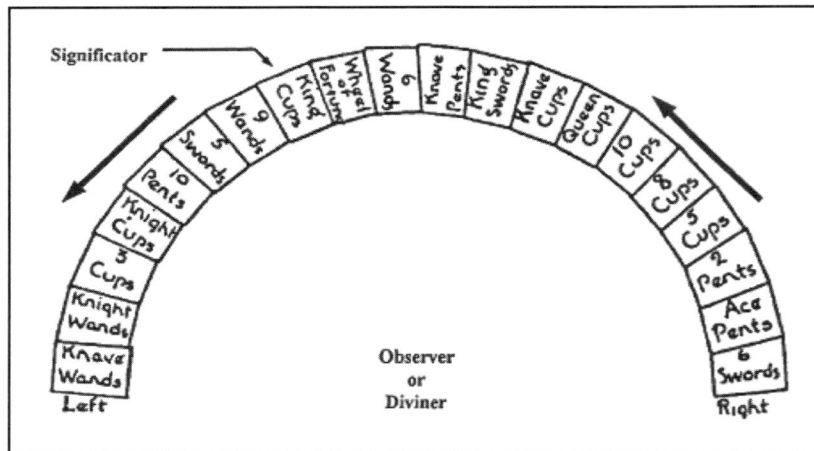

In this reading as hereafter explained, each card is modified by the card on either side of it; if it be an end card, such as the Six of Swords, in this case it is modified not only by the card next to it, Ace of Disks but also by the card at the opposite end, Knave of Wands.

If these cards are of a contrary element to the card itself, they very much weaken and neutralise its force, but if the contrary element is only in one card and the other is of a connecting nature, it does not much matter. This is explained later among the tabulated rules. The King of Cups is between the Nine of Wands and the Wheel of Fortune, both of which cards are of a fiery nature and therefore contrary to the Cups, which is Water and therefore it shows the Enquirer is rather lacking in perseverance and energy. Ten of Disks, 'His business will prosper', Eight of Cups, 'but yet he will lose interest in it, owing to his love of pleasure and society' (shown by the Eight of Cups having the suit each side of it). Wheel of Fortune, 'and through his Fortune changing for the better.' Knave of Wands (Knight of Wands on one side and Six of Swords on the other), 'He yet is anxious through falling in love with a graceful and sprightly girl with chestnut hair and fair complexion whom he has recently met' (shown by the Knight of Wands turned contrary to the course of the reading). Ten of Cups, 'His suit is at first favourably received', Five of Swords, 'but some slanderous reports and mischief making' (not altogether without foundation) 'come to her knowledge'. Ace of Disks, 'though his increasing prosperity in business', Ten of Cups, 'had lead her to regard him with favour'.

The Diviner now pairs the cards from opposite ends of the Horseshoe, thus:

This part of the reading is quite remarkable for here a second level now becomes apparent which adds newer dimensions to the reading.

(Knave of Wands/Six of Swords)

'She is anxious about this'.

(Knight of Wands/Ace of Disks)

'And he begins to neglect his business which is fairly good'.

(Three of Cups/Two of Disks)

'And instead throws aside his business for pleasure'.

(Knight of Cups/Five of Disks)

'The consequence of this is that the engagement between them is broken off, shown by the Knight being turned in the opposite direction'.

(Ten of Disks/Eight of Cups)

'Still his business does fairly well though he is losing interest in it'.

(Five of Swords/Ten of Cups)

'The matter is subject of much gossip'.

(Nine of Wands/Queen of Cups)—These two cards are of contrary suits and therefore of little importance, however the prime cause of this gossip is the Queen of Cups—a fair middle-aged woman.

'Among their acquaintances'.

(King of Cups/Knave of Cups)

'He moreover, begins to pay attention to another girl of not quite so fair complexion.'

(Wheel of Fortune/King of Swords)

Who, however, prefers a dark man, who is much admired by the fair sex.

Shown by his being next to two Knaves and a Queen.

(Six of Wands/Knave of Disks)

'But he has already gained the affections of a girl with dark brown eyes and hair.' (This description is obtained by mixing the effect of Wands with Disks.) This concludes the reading of the First Operation.

SECOND OPERATION

(Further developments of the Matter)

The Enquirer again carefully shuffles the cards and places the pack on the table face downwards, but is not to cut them. The Diviner now takes the pack and deals it round, card by card, in twelve packets, face downwards in rotation (Deal and read in order of the Astrological Houses against the direction of the Sun.) So that the first packet answering the ascendant will consist of the first, thirteenth, twenty-fifth, thirty-seventh, forty-ninth, sixty-first, seventy-third cards, as shown and so on.

This Operation is under the presidency of the Court Cards, whose dominion in the celestial heavens falls immediately between that of the four Knaves (Princesses) and that of the Keys answering to the twelve Signs of the Zodiac. It represents the twelve Astrological Houses of heaven, as shown. Without altering the relative order of the packets, or of the cards in the packets, the Diviner examines each in succession, till he finds the one which contains the Significator. This he retains for reading, noting carefully to which astrological house it corresponds, then gathers up the other packets and puts them aside, as they are not of any further use in the operation.

As before, the Diviner, reads the packet containing the Significator, by spreading them out in the form of horseshoe, first reading them by counting the cards in order from the significator in the direction in which the face of the figure on the card is turned and next by pairing the cards together from the opposite ends of the horseshoe. It is hardly likely that in so small a packet there will be either three or four cards of a sort, but if there be, the Diviner takes note of same and also observes which suit predominates. We now return to the examples commenced in the previous section.

We will suppose the Enquirer to have shuffled the cards correctly, while thinking of his present affairs and that the Diviner has dealt them round into twelve packets. The packet containing the Significator is contained in the Ascendant and it contains the following cards in the order given.

This mode of reading shows that the Significator is in the Ascendant and it will principally relate to the Enquirer's manner of living at this point. The Significator in this case, is right way up, whereas in the previous reading it was inverted, and is looking towards the Nine of Swords, the direction in which the reading proceeds, counting thus: 4 from the King of Cups, Knave of Disks; 7 from this, the Sun; 9 from this, Knave of Disks; 7 from this, the Sun, where the reading ends.

King of Cups/Knave of Disks: 'The Enquirer is unhappy' (looking to Nine of Swords) 'and makes the acquaintance of the girl with the dark hair and blue eyes with whom the dark young man (his rival) is in love. (She is artistic and well-mannered and hopes to carry out her wishes, i.e. to many the dark man, with whom the fair girl, to whom the Enquirer has transferred his affection, is now in love.) For she is beginning to be apprehensive regarding her success, and is jealous in consequence'.

Playing the cards from the opposite end of the horseshoe the Diviner proceeds:
(King of Cups/Nine of Swords)
'The Enquirer is anxious and his health begins to suffer.'
(Eight of Disks/Sun)
'But hopes ultimately to succeed through skilful action in the matter.'
(Four of Swords/Knave of Disks)
'He therefore endeavours to make a friend of the dark girl.'
(Temperance)
'As he expects to realise his wishes by her means in the end.' (This is shown by the card being single in the end.)

THIRD OPERATION
(Continuing the development of the question)
The Enquirer again carefully shuffles the cards, while thinking earnestly of her affairs. The pack is not cut. The Diviner deals out the cards into twelve packets in precisely the same manner

of the Second Operation. Only instead of being referred to the twelve Astrological Houses, these twelve packets are under the presidency of the twelve keys of the Tarot—attributed to the twelve Signs of the Zodiac. The first packet, Emperor—Aries, the second Hierophant—Taurus, the third the Lovers—Gemini and so on. As before the Diviner selects a packet which containers the Significator for the reading and rejects the rest. He notes the meaning of the Key answering the Sign of the Zodiac, under which the packet falls. He spreads the cards out in the form of a horseshoe, exactly as before. I now continue the example before commenced:

We will suppose that the packet containing the King of Cups is that whose position answers to the Hierophant—Taurus and consists of the following cards as arranged in the diagram. The Hierophant and a majority of the Keys in this packet, being Keys alike, show that the forces at present at work are ceasing to be under the control of the Enquirer. The reading proceeds as to the usual order of counting, as follows: King of Cups/Two of Wands, Magician/Queen of Wands, Universe/Tower, then Two of Wands again. (The reading would then proceed by the pairing of the cards as usual.)

(King of Cups/Two of Wands)

'Though anxious concerning several matters, he (Enquirer) is beginning to succeed better by this line of action.'

(Magician/Queen of wands)

'Which seems to be quite the best, But the older woman (who previously made mischief and was represented by the Queen of Cups in the first Operation) who is artful and a gossip.'

(Universe/Tower/Two of Wands)

'Again injures the matter because she wishes to get an influence over the enquirer herself.'

(Pairing the cards, the Diviner proceeds)

(Two of Wands/Tower)

'Her influence cunningly exercised, brings about a complete disruption of the whole matter.'

(Universe/Magician)

'The entire matter becomes invested with trickery and glamour.'

(Queen of Cups/King of Wands)

'As she herself pays him a good deal of attention and sympathy.'

(Two of Disks)

'Which furthers her plans by bringing about a friendship between them.'

FOURTH OPERATION

(Further developments of the Question)

As before, the Enquirer is instructed to shuffle the pack and place it on the table, but not to cut it.

The Diviner takes the pack, turns it face upwards and goes through it, being careful not to disarrange the order of the cards, till he finds the Significator; at this point he cuts the pack, that is to say, he takes the Significator and the cards which had been beneath it and places them on the top of the remainder, turning the whole face downwards again, ready for dealing out.

The consequence of this operation is that the Significator becomes the top card of the pack (bottom really; face on the table). The Diviner takes off the Significator, places it face down on the middle of the table then lays out the following thirty-six cards (relating to the thirty-six decanates of the Zodiac) in the form of a circle around it, face upwards, which shows a further development of the question. These are dealt round in the order and direction as dealing with the twelve packets in the two previous operations.

The reading proceeds by the same law of counting, but instead of counting from the Significator itself, it begins from the first card of the thirty-six and always goes in the direction of the dealing. The suit which is in the majority and the circumstances of either three or four cards of a sort being found in the thirty-six Decanates are also noted. When the reading by counting is finished the cards are paired together: first/thirty-first; second/thirty-fifth; third/thirty-fourth and so on, placed in order successively upon the Significator. Our example continues.

We will suppose the Enquirer to have shuffled the pack and that the Diviner takes it in his hands and in turning it up finds the bottom card to be Temperance. On going through it he comes to the Significator, thus:

He therefore takes the cards from the King of Cups to Temperance included and places them above (or behind) the Five of Disks, being careful not to disturb their relative order. This has really the effect of cutting the pack between the Queen of Wands and the King of Cups when he again turns them face downwards ready for dealing, the King of Cups will necessarily be the top card and the Queen of wands the bottom card; Temperance being immediately above the Five of Disks, the former top card. The Diviner takes the top card, the Significator and places it upwards in the centre and then deals round in succession thirty-six cards, face upwards in the order shown in the above diagram. Let us suppose them to be thus arranged. The reading always proceeds in the same direction as the dealing in this form of operation, commencing the counting from the first card dealt.

We have here twelve out of twenty-two keys; Seven of Wands; Seven of Cups; Five of Swords; Six of Disks; total thirty-seven including Significator. The preponderance of the Keys represent 'Influences beyond the control of the Enquirer'. There are four Princes (Kings)—'Meetings with influential persons', and four Eights, 'Much news and correspondence'.

The counting proceeds as follows from the first card dealt. King of Cups—Six of Cups—Five of Disks—Hermit—Four of Cups—Fortitude—Four of Swords—Seven of Cups—Justice—Five of Cups—King of Swords—Emperor—Six of Cups again.

(King of Cups/Six of Cups)

'The Enquirer's love of pleasure going.'

(Five of Disks)

'Brings about loss of money and business' (by overspending in the first place).

(Hermit)

'And he is forced to be more prudent'.

(Four of Cups)

'And not go into the society of others so much, which has already brought him anxiety' (shown by Four of Cups between Two of Wands, contrary element weakening the effect of this card).

(Fortitude)

'He works more closely'. (The individual here works at shoring up his own interests by seeing people independently and doing a bit of lobbying behind the scenes, with positive results.)

(Four of Swords)

'And begins to get better' (due to the help of an old friend whom he has not seen for some time).

(Seven of Cups)

'Yet he has not sufficient energy in his nature to stick with the work for long.'

(Justice)

'The retributive effect of this is'

(Five of Cups)

'that he loses his friends.'

(King of Wands)

'And his former rival who, though rather a vain man, is energetic and hard-working.'

(Emperor/Six of Cups)

'replaces him in popularity and esteem.'

Pairing them now the Diviner proceeds.

(King of Cups/Death/Six of Cups)

'The Enquirer loses his pleasure in consequence.'

(Four of Swords/Seven of Cups)

'And becomes less energetic even than before and more anxious for pleasure-going than ever.'

(Moon/Chariot)

'Yielding to the temptation of idleness and vanity by means of fraud.'

(Eight of Swords/Ace of Disks)

'He embezzles the money of his employer and sees prison staring at him in the face.'

(Eight of Cups/Temperance)

'The result of this is the loss of good name'.

(Three of Disks/Five of Disks)

'And his situation of trust.'

(Ten of wands/Two of Cups)

'His former friends and admirers turn a cold shoulder towards him.'

(Foolish Man/Justice)

'And the result of his folly is that he is arrested and brought before a court of Law.'

(Seven of Wands/Hierophant)

'The decision is adverse.'

(Judgement/Hermit)

'And Judgement very justly given against him.'

(Emperor/King of Wands)

'But his Employer, though stern, is a kind-hearted man.'

(Two of Swords/Nine of Swords)

'He offers to take him back and overlook the past.'

(Star/Fortitude)

'As he hopes that this will have proved a lesson to him.'

(King of Swords/CEng of Disks)

'And points out to him that his former rival'

(Three of Wands/Eight of Disks)

'though perhaps vain, was yet, a hard-working and good man of business.'
(Four of Cups/Ten of Swords)
'The Enquirer in consequence of this determines to completely give up his former mode of life which had brought him to the brink of ruin and becomes a steady man.'
(Eight of Wands/Six of Wands)
'After this he suddenly receives a hasty message that gives him much pleasure.'
(Three of Cups/Nine of Disks)
'Stating that owing to the loss of a relative he is the inheritor of a legacy'. (We must confess that the meaning of the cards in this set, especially the Three of Cups, has nothing to do with a loss of a relative and we can only assume that Mathers was working from a high clairvoyant level of the situation.)

This concludes the Fourth Operation.

It is always necessary for the Diviner to employ his intuition in reading and sometimes he will have to clairvoyantly go through the card of doubtful signification. Thus in the reading given it is only the circumstance of the Moon, Chariot, Eight of Swords, and Ace of Disks being followed by other confirmative cards which justifies such an evil meaning for them.

FIFTH OPERATION
Conclusion of the matter.

The cards are to be again carefully shuffled by the Enquirer but not cut. The Diviner then takes the pack and deals it card by card in rotation into ten, answering to the Tree of Life. This refers to the rule of the ten Sephiroth in the Celestial Heavens. This being done, the Diviner selects the packets containing the Significator for reading, noting carefully under which Sephirah it falls and taking this as a general indication in the matter. This packet is then spread out in a horseshoe form and read in the usual way, counting from the Significator and this time in the direction in which the face of the figure looks. The cards are finally paired together as in the previous Operation. This completes the Mode of Divination called 'the Opening of the Key'. We now give the conclusion of the example'.

We will suppose that the cards have been shuffled and dealt in the following manner into Ten packets answering to the Sephiroth in the Tree of Life: seven

The packet containing the Significator falls under Binah, containing the third, thirteenth, twenty-third, thirty-third, forty-third, fifty-third, sixty-third and seventy-third cards dealt. The is an argument of sadness and trial. The cards are spread as show below. There are a number of variations on this spread. One such is to Divide the Tree into the Three Pillars. The Pillar of Severity on the left-hand side of the Tree shows the negative influences. The right-hand Pillar of Mercy shows the positive outlook, while the central Pillar shows the Outcome. Malkuth represents the Material result while Kether the Spiritual. Yesod is events leading up to the result and will also show the mental state where applicable. Tiphareth is the central focusing point for the whole reading.

The counting proceeds as follows: King of Cups–Star–Judgement–King of Cups again. Evil cards are in the majority, another argument of loss and trouble.
(King of Cups/Star/Judgement)

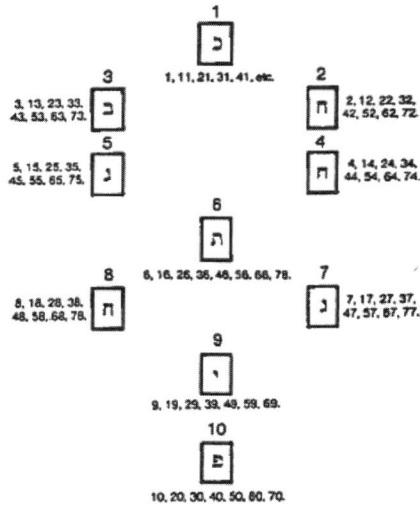

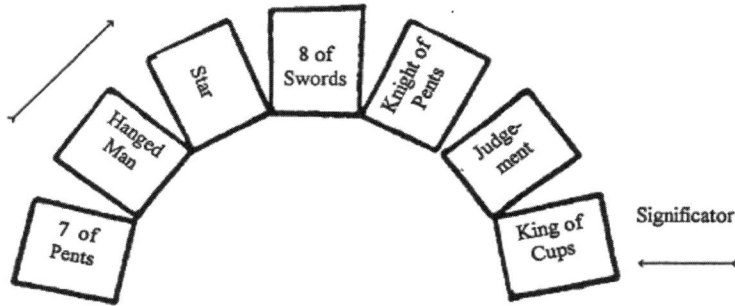

'He has hopes of thus re-establishing his fortunes and that a favourable result will ensure for him.'

The Diviner then pairs them.

(King of Cups/Seven of Disks)

'He plunges therefore into speculation by which he loses heavily (Seven of Disks is near Hanged Man).'

(Knave of Cups/Hanged Man)

'His love affair comes to nothing.'

(Star/Judgement)

'All his expectations are disappointed.'

(Knight of Disks/Eight of Swords)

'And his life for a time is arduous, petty and uninteresting.'

(The coming of the trouble is here shown by the Knight of Disks looking against the direction of the reading. If it were turned the other way it would show that his troubles were quitting him and matters would improve.)

This completes the Operation and shows the general development and results in question.

An alternative method of divination ritual

The following is an alternative and shorter method of using ritual with a Tarot spread. We have included this as many would not have the time or inclination to perform the full ritualistic version of the Z2 formula with the Opening of the Key. With the following method you can apply any sort of card spread you wish, merely by inserting it in the appropriate spot, using the ceremony below as a standard formula.

Set up your work space by placing your seat in the centre of your work space and facing West. Your altar is placed in front of you with your Tarot deck laid on top. On your altar you may also wish to have: incense, a wine glass of consecrated water, a white candle, a magical dagger or Sword (beside you, at your right hand), and your Lotus Wand. If you have no Lotus Wand, your sword or dagger will suffice. Place a writing pad (magical journal of Tarot workings) and pen beside you, with matches to light the incense and candle.

1. Light your candle and incense.
2. Holding your Lotus Wand by the black band, walk deosil (clockwise) to the North East. Raise the Lotus Wand above you and say:

HEKAS HEKAS ESTE BEBELOI
   Return deosil to the East of the Altar, lay down Lotus Wand and pick up your magical Sword.

3. Facing East, perform Lesser Banishing Pentagram Ritual.
4. Lay Sword down by your Altar, pick up your cup of holy water and walking to the East of your working circle, stand facing east and hold up your cup and form a cross with your movement. Then dip your fingers in and touch the air in front of you, beneath where you formed the cross, three times in the form of a triangle pointing up. This is the image of the cross above the triangle. Walk to the South and again form the image of the cross above the triangle and repeat in the West and the North, finishing East. Raise the cup up facing East and say:

'I PURIFY WITH WATER'

5. Walk deosil to West of your altar, put down your cup in its position and pick up your incense. Continue deosil to East and with the incense perform the cross above the triangle symbol. You touch the air before you with the incense by waving motions to form this image. This is repeated in the South, West then North of your circle, then return East. Facing east raise the incense up and say:

'I CONSECRATE WITH FIRE'

6. Return to your seat and place your incense down. Pick up your Lotus Wand. Circumambulate deosil around the space thrice, holding Lotus Wand by White Band.

7. Vibrations and visualizations:
   (a) Begin to pranic five breathe deeply.
   (b) Vibrate the angelic name 'HUA'.
   (c) Call down your Divine White Brilliance (with the vibration of the LVX formula and 'I.A.O', if you are a Golden Dawn initiate, or some other method of drawing down the power that is familiar to you) raising your arms up.
   (d) Linking yourself with your higher self, call on Divine guidance to perform the reading.
   (e) Looking at your Tarot Deck, link your sphere of sensation (aura) to feel an empathy.
      1. Sitting East of your card symbolizes you come from the Light.
      2. *Hekas Hekas Este Bebeloi* means something like 'get out, get out, all who do not belong'.
      3. While doing this imagine a wall of astral waters surrounding and protecting you.
      4. While doing this you imagine a wall of fire within your wall of water protecting your working space. Focus on the deck and the Querent (if there is one, or yourself if the reading is for you).
8. Formulate your question, shuffle and cut the cards and perform your divination reading. Make any notes, or better still make a tape-recording of it.
9. Repeat the purification and consecration as shown above. Thank your higher self and the attending Angel.
10. Reverse circumambulate three times around circle with Lotus Wand.
11. Perform Banishing Pentagram ritual with your magical Sword. Extinguish your candle and record any necessary notes.

Tarot and meditation

Meditation on the Tarot can cover a great many methods. The following chapter, 'Scrying, Travelling in the Spirit Vision, Ritual and the Tarot' covers quite a few methods of active Tarot meditation. However, we will address here the art of meditation and passive Tarot meditation.

The essential meaning of meditation is a disciplined mind technique that is used to achieve a chosen or heightened state of consciousness. In doing this the meditator will cause a prolonged concentration of a particular thought form toward a particular focus point. This focus point can be almost anything, however, the most common would be a mantra, mandala, yantra, prayer or object of spirituality, crystal, rock, visual image, etc. In this book however, we will be discussing the use of Tarot cards as focal points for meditation.

Intent and purpose is essential, therefore, reasons for meditating on the Tarot as described in this chapter, the previous chapters and the next chapters are:

To gain deeper insight into the card itself;

To gain deeper insight into aspects of your own subconscious;

To balance the imbalances you find in yourself by using the archetypal energies of the cards;

To gain deeper insight into Life;

To align your subtle bodies so that you are tuned in to your spiritual source; Prayer and Invocation is the effort to utilise your conscious faculties and attune them with the Higher Self.

To obtain information

The steps taken before focusing on a Tarot card are:

(a) Place yourself in a relaxed position in a quiet uninterrupted place and begin deep abdominal rhythmic breathing. Relax your body by starting a tense and relax process with your muscles, working from the tip of your toes, gradually up to the top of your head. Breathe in when tensing and breathe out when relaxing, imagining all the tension floating away. Now place your thumb and third finger of the same hand against your nostrils. Breathe in up to the count of four (through the left nostril) hold for the count of eight and expire the breath through the right nostril for the count of eight. While closing the left nostril with the thumb, breath in up to the count of four and repeat the process again with the other nostril until three complete cycles have been accomplished.

(b) Quieten your emotions, (sit back from your self and observe your emotions rather than take part in them, then lift your thoughts away from them).
Still your thoughts (again lift your consciousness into an observation state from your thoughts. Watch them wash past you but do not follow them or get lost in them, then slowly focus a state of stillness to a single point in front of you).
You may need to practice steps (a) and (b) many times over a period of weeks, before you are able to continue with the following steps.

(c) Your conscious mind and awareness is then narrowed down to the focal point, which will be a chosen tarot card. When you do this your subconscious mind can be bypassed and your superconscious mind will become activated. This opens you to your own 'mind-mirror' where a calm, detached, inward and outward awareness occurs.

(d) Watch the picture of the card and let the image impress itself on your 'mind-mirror'. Close your eyes and observe the scene in front of you, absorbing the information/knowledge/ insights that flow from your meditation.

(e) At this point you may put your 'meditation-in-motion' by vibrating an invocation or affirmation of the particular card, written by yourself, or as given below.
Or, by moving into a rhythmic dance and chant (this can be done when applied to certain types of music), moving around in a circle, but not in such a way that you become dizzy. The purpose for either of these two methods would be to experience a spiritual elevation, or raising your ego-self to a higher dimension so that you can identify with the card. In some cases there is a floating and identification with the Universe.
In some cases you may wish to finish your meditations at step (d) and skip step (e) going straight to step (f).

(f) To come out of your meditation you replace yourself to your initial position (if you danced). Return the image of the card from your mind-mirror to the card before you. Continue your rhythmic breathing and concentration, withdrawing yourself from your experience by again becoming an observer. Watch the thoughts and emotions flow past until you only focus on one blank point in front of you, stilling your thoughts and emotions while repeating the breathing exercises given above. Open your eyes and relax. Have something to eat and drink.

Another form of passive meditation is using the tarot cards as talismans to attract or repel. This is simply by leaving a card or cards pertaining to your need, on a table or wall, where they can be seen by you each day. As often as possible you use (through mental projection) the image of the combination of cards you are using, as a power source to attract or repel what you desire. This same method can be used actively also, as described below.

For an active magical meditation chose three cards and a significator that represent the purpose for your meditation. Place the propelling/directing card at the apex of a triangle. Place the cards that will support the subject at the other two points of the triangle and the significator card in the centre. If you want to make it more ritualistic this can all be done under temple conditions with candles and incense, etc. With the apex of the triangle pointing in the direction you intend, vibrate your invocations and purpose, projecting your thoughts using the power from the images of the cards. You may use a photo of the object or person you are meditating on, by placing the photo at the apex of the triangle, or in the centre. Position depends on purpose. A crystal can also be used, placed at the base of the triangle between the two base cards.

'Dialogue' with the cards is another form of meditation. This is where you hold a conversation with your inner self, using the cards as answers from your inner self. While you are holding your inner conversation, cut the deck, or choose cards from the deck and turn them over to view. The chosen cards are the responses to your thoughts.

The following examples show various Invocations associated to the Trumps. We would suggest that after some experience has been gained with these then readers could write their own particular Invocations for the Keys.

Tarot invocations

Fool

> I stand before the dawn of Creation
> The Golden Rays of the Mystic dawn fall upon my Body
> I reach out to the Tree of Knowledge
> My body becomes as pliable as a child
> The Cloak of Divine Innocence falls upon me
> I keep my darker Self on a lease
> The Blossoms unravel their petals before me
> As the new dawn approaches I am as reborn!
> From my seat of Wisdom I behold the Crown of Glory within my grasp,
> I humble myself as I step towards it
> And receive the Light, LUX of my Soul!
> The Blossoms shake up the Tree
> From the lowest to the Highest
> As the penetrating Light permeates my being
> I become the whirling Cross of Aleph as it envelops me
> It takes me up to the Crown of Glory
> I unite with the Light of Lights, Soul of my Soul!

The Universe unfolds before me as I merge with Time itself as the Golden Dawn breaks within me.

The Magician

I stand in contemplation before the Altar of the Universe
The Caduceus upon my breast opens up the Knowledge before me,
My weapons of wonder stand before me
My whole being throbs with the desire of the task
I humble myself before the greatness of my masters
I become one with the Universe as my Silent Invocation begins,
I am about to wield the weapons of wonder and the heavens open up before me,
My seat is Understanding the forces of Creation
My goal is the Power and the Glory
My Will is Mighty and of the Gods
The Elements cower before me as I make them do my bidding,
The Forces of Light and Darkness are at my command,
But Light is my beacon and darkness flees before me,
This battle I have won!

High Priestess

As I reach out with the Cup, beyond the Veil
My head turns towards the Secret Wisdom
I invoke the untapped emptiness of my Soul
My Cup is empty and I wish to share it
Come Forth my Higher Genius into the veiled mist
Come forth my mentor beyond the Abyss
Come forth my Spirit of the Moon
By the Silver Light of Diana's Brazen Sandals see Eternity beyond me
I am the bearer of the Grail that is yet untouched by human lips
I am the Guardian of the Abyss
Through me the Crown of Immortality can be obtained
This relates to the Chakras starting to open.
My head is illumined by its Brightness and my feet are adorned with its Beauty

Empress

I sit upon the Throne of Power
The Ankh of Life against my womb
The Spirit above about to descend
The Crown above me supports my whims

Wisdom and Understanding are my strengths
I am Mother of the Spring
Growth is my direction,
I am doorway of Life and Love,
Gaea Mother of us all
Richness and Bounty are my legacy
Health to all who embrace my ways,
Mother nature is my creed
I share my wealth to those you ask
My Royal decree is to live life full
For this I give my full support
The Girdle of Venus enforces my ways,
and entices those who seek me out,
blush upon my generous gifts,
I am Empress of the Earth!

Emperor

I am Power and Control,
My Aries nature will survive,
I am the nature of the ram,
I am the window as I see beyond,
For I think and so I am,
My rod of power is wielded right
My virile nature helps keep tight,
my domain is what I make,
Though royal and strong I give and take,
My feet are Beauty and my Crown is Wisdom,
Both fear and love me, for I am in command,
I sit upon the Throne of Might,
for all the world to see and judge,
I am the power and the glory,
I am the pedestal of future man,
to look in wonder at the result of my commands,
I am the Emperor whom you seek!

Hierophant

I am Strength and Dogma and slow to move,
My Taurean nature will not give in,
I give comfort to those who seek me,
My feet are Mercy and my Crown is Wisdom,

Its triple nature gives me support,
The staff of Vau is at my command,
to help in those who seek me not,
I am slow to anger and slow to strike,
All men fear me when I move,
For my judgement comes from above this plane,
My Throne is formed from the Higher Powers,
Their decree is my command!
I work in secret for all mankind
The darkened forces flee before me,
For I am Just above all else,
I will guide the Aspirant through the Sacred Mysteries,
I am the Visible of the Invisible,
For I make conformity in Chaos,
I am the Hierophant, Priest of all!

Lovers

I am chained to the rock of dogma, feted and alone,
I seek release from my torment as I am here through no fault of mine,
Fear grips me as I wait for him who has come to devour my soul,
My heart is heavy with anticipation as the fates approach me,
I see the monster before me rise from the depths,
My heart is in anguish as I cry out in terror,
In the sky above I seek my rescuer,
The sun on his shield blinds with its brilliance,
His sword rises to protect me from harm,
The hero of the Gorgon battles now comes to my aid,
My heart goes to him who helps me,
His battle with the monster is great,
A champion named Perseus wins the day,
We are united body and soul as a constellation in the sky,
I am favoured of the Gods, immortality is my price,
For we are the Lovers and communion reigns!

Chariot

I formulate the Astral vehicle around me,
As I gaze upon the Heavens I wish to be there,
My Will is my guide to the regions above,
The horses of balance will not lead me astray,
The Higher Aspiration of Soul draws me forever upwards,
The wheels of the Mercabah spin around me,

The Severity of my Will supports my climb to Understanding.
My Mind flies upwards and the darkened clouds flee away,
The Light above me is my beacon,
For I am the Charioteer!
New boundaries open up to me,
I will fight for my rights and the rights of others,
The Light of Kether is my inspiration,
Go ye steeds of the Stars and lead my way to Victory!

Strength

I stand before the stronger twin,
The Green and Red Lion together at last,
I draw Strength from the Superior force to feed my Spirit,
All who come into contact liquefy before me,
My might is the unseen ability to absorb any who come to me,
The flowers I hold show the freshness of growth,
I sap the energy of all those who wish to conquer me.
With every new conquest I grow stronger,
I move in slowness with my wits for protection,
I am Strength, Leo in the Sky and am undefeated.

Hermit

I sacrifice much to achieve my purpose,
I am the herald of the Light of a new Era,
With my Lamp I bring Light to the darkened Souls,
My pedestal is Beauty and my Crown is Mercy,
Travel is my way of life,
I reject the material in search of the Spiritual,
I am the right hand of the Crown and Glory,
My staff of Righteousness is my support,
The beams of my Lamp guide my search,
I have Yehovah's mandate to make my quest,
I give spiritual comfort to those that seek it,
For I am Hermit! wanderer in search of lost Souls.

The Wheel of Fortune

I hold souls in balance, for good or evil,
As I turn the Karma is my guide,
Who will win and who will lose,
That depends on the Souls' actions past,

Though life allows the return to the source,
To live life badly means the wheel spins again,
The Sphinx above is the watcher of my actions,
The ape below will tilt the balance,
I reflect on life while on the Wheel,
It spins in space while my lives revolve,
For I am the Wheel of destiny,
With Mercy above and Victory below I cannot fail in my task,
The fates weave before me as I give impetus to Life!

Justice

I sit on the throne of Justice in the Hall of Maat,
The scales I hold show the balance of power,
The sword I hold is for Justice or retribution,
Those who come to me seek my favour,
My footstool is Beauty and my Crown is Severity.
I can be Kind or Severe with those brought before me,
'As ye Sow, so shall ye reap' is by command,
I will have no tricks within my domain,
For innocence I will protect,
For Evil I will slay,
For I am Justice by right of command,
I am the Law to protect us all.

Hanged Man

I am in the cover of darkened water,
My head is immersed in a sea of dreams,
I struggle for survival against the odds,
I seek the Light through Inner Struggle,
As I float in the cove of Mem,
My hands are bound as I confront my Dreams,
My feet are tied and I cannot run from myself
reflection and rebirth are my attributes,
I search for the Baptism of my soul,
My feet are in Severity and my head in Splendour,
I am the Bark of Osiris on the River of Life,
What is above shall show below,
I am purged of thoughts that do not become me,
I am forced to confront my place in life,
I am the Hanged Man and it is Enlightenment I seek!

Death

I am the slayer of the temporary state,
No one escapes my daily wrath,
The harvest I reap is Life itself,
No one escapes my deadly blade,
My spirit soars above the material,
I come to all when least expected,
Prepare for me now while there is still a chance,
Redemption comes to those who fear me,
My soft footsteps are seldom heard,
Life beyond me is that of the Spirit,
The material world is my domain,
I am Death and people cower before me,
prepare for the journey beyond the dreams,
new doorways open for the believers,
A transition state is what I am!

Temperance

I am the Transformer of Water and Fire,
With my Cups of balance I do mix the brew,
Through the Seven Stages does it pass between,
I give Strength to the weak and take from the Strong,
My pedestal is Foundation and my Head is Beauty,
I am the Sun and the Moon of what you seek,
I stand between the two antagonists,
I cleave to the safety of the middle ground,
I am stability in motion,
For I am the Middle Pillar of the Tree,
And I am Temperance, Alchemist of all!

The Devil

I am he who was here when the Earth was formed,
I am Nature and let the World be formed of me,
Prince of the Garden and of Forbidden delights,
I will blind you with my gifts when asked,
My feet are Splendour while my head is in Beauty,
I live life to the full and regret not of my actions,
For I am the Tempter of Nations and all succumb to me,
I am strength in matter for all who want,
I control the Elements who cower before me,

I am Desire itself for those who covet me,
Hear my sermon and divide your riches for no one escapes me,
I work in darkness and refute the Light,
Matter and weakness are my allies,
I am the Diablos—the Adversary of all who oppose me!

The Tower

I stand in solitude and am immovable in my ways,
My beliefs become shattered with the Almighty Power of the Unknown,
I am forced to change my ways and purify my thoughts and directions,
Negative thoughts are purged from my being by the Holy Fire,
On my right is the perfected framework for my beliefs,
On my left are the Qlippothic elements who will try to change me,
I have changed from necessity to a purified state,
First the Blackening, then the whitening,
I seek refuge from the Holy Fire that flashes from the Universe,
I am the perfected vessel with impurities removed,
I am the Tower of Kings now perfected from the Light.

Star

The Heavenly crystals light up the sky above me,
The Light of Sothis bathes me in its Splendour.
I kneel before the River of Life and mix the Blessed Waters,
The Seven Stars above me are within me.
For as it is above it is below,
My feet are the Foundation while my head is in Victory,
The Tree of Life and of Knowledge stand each side of me,
Each jug I pour into the River of Life comes from the Tree of Knowledge of Good and Evil
and the Tree of Life,
The essence of my Soul is above me and guides me in my work,
As the waters from the River of Life nourish the Trees on its banks
So do I give back the essence to that which has sustained them,
I am a Star both above and below!

The Moon

I am the embryo of my being,
The water is the womb which sustains me as I seek nourishment from above,
For me this is the Path of hardship,

The Moon above is my guide as I slowly crawl towards development,

Her glare is now blood red,

The dogs bay at her endlessly,

She Lights my path and protects me from my enemies,

I slowly leave the water and cleave to the Middle Path,

The Watchtowers to my left and right are reminders of my true direction,

The Lunar dew descends upon me, giving me nourishment, unseen by those who watch,

My Evolution has begun as responsibilities are brought to bear,

I am the Seeker of the Path, Child of the Lunar Light!

The Sun

I rise up towards the brightness of the Light,

I am a twin soul that breaks beyond the boundaries,

The middle path to light is embraced

This draws me upwards towards the essence above,

Through the veil of promise I glide as my true nature is revealed,

The sun's rays bring down their nourishment which I bathe in

The reflected glory of Light, Warmth and Love.

Give me your power!

Give me your protection, so that I may abide by your wisdom.

Judgement

I see my lives before me as I am purified with water

I break free of the earth and am purified by fire,

Through these lives I break free of the body as the spirit of Shin beckons me from above,

The angels blasts his notes as I leave this world.

Above me are the fiery serpents who mix with the rays of promise

The judgement of the most high is upon me and I must rise to the occasion,

The fiery triangle sits above me for the purification of the soul

I stand before the judgement and await the gates of paradise or the fires of hell.

The Universe

I stand before the Portal of the Universe itself,

I bare myself before the Stars which are my guides,

I merge myself in the protection of the Venusians Earth, the Sheath of my Soul,

The Twelve Constellations show all my natures, for I have reversed them all,

For each Incarnation has affected me greatly.

Beyond are the Four Angels of the Presence who guard the Portals of the Universe,

My feet are in the earth of Malkuth while my head is in the Lunar Light,

> I control the Aeythers that surround the earth,
> The wands I hold show my balanced nature, yet I am on an ever-changing pedestal,
> For I am the Universe, controller of all!

Included below are two very successful methods which we tested out during a series of workshops we gave on the Tarot. These are methods which we devised ourselves, therefore, if there is any similarity to any other published material, we can only put it down to synchronicity.

Your personal tree of power

This is a method one can use to view oneself, in life or in a present situation, from a spiritual, mental, emotional and material viewpoint. It can help you to realize your priorities and gain focus at whatever level you can work at.

Prepare your space for meditation and light Sage incense and a white candle. You will need your deck of cards, a pad and a pen.

1. (a) Choose ten realistic goals or accomplishments you want to achieve by the end of the year (or some other chosen time span) and write these down in a list.
    (b) Choose ten Tarot cards from your deck that represent each of these goals and write each card's name beside your goal.
    (c) Separate these chosen cards from your deck and lay the deck aside.

2. Shuffle your chosen cards and lay them out from one to ten in the pattern shown below in the form of the Kabbalistic Tree of Life:

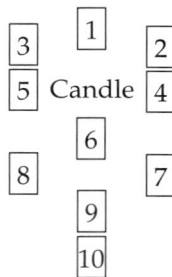

```
        [1]
  [3]         [2]
  [5]  Candle  [4]
        [6]
  [8]         [7]
        [9]
       [10]
```

3. Each goal which you wrote down on your pad, as represented by a chosen card, will now be governed by a Sephirah on the Tree. Write the Sephiroth numbers, as above, on your list, beside each listed card, which is associated with it by virtue of its placement.
    The action of each Sephirah will govern the way in which you should approach your goal and the priority order in which you should deal with them, that is, from ten to one. The names of the Sephiroth and their actions under the condition of this spread are:

1 = Kether: It is considered that this is the unattainable, the concealed; power given by the Light and of the Spirit. Therefore cards placed in this position would represent goals that must be approached from a purely spiritual point of view and seen as long-term works towards perfect completion.

2 = Chokmah: Its virtue is devotion and its function, wisdom; a state of spiritual experience and vision, attainable through the path of Mercy, peace, love, unity and equilibrium; cosmic catabolist, releasing of latent energy. Cards placed here also represent goals to be approached from a spiritual point of view and seen as long-term works towards evolution. Matters must be left to be manifested as stimulus.

3 = Binah: Understanding and foundation of primordial wisdom; vision of sorrow and virtue of silence. This is the third position requiring a spiritual view when looking at goals. One must leave this goal inactive and contemplate in silence. It is a good time to conceive something in the abstract and first form the understanding of one's true needs and motives.

4 = Chesed: Contains the blessings of the Divine, Mercy, Love, Majesty. Your approach to the goal represented here should be in organising and preserving that which has already been attained in preparation for the next stage. Formulate the ideas and bring the abstract into concretion.

5 = Geburah: Strength and Severity, Justice and Power. Goals represented by cards in this sphere are now ready to be put into active and aggressive action, however, their priority is still not that great, so action may be spasmodic. These goals will not be achieved without encountering some strife or struggle.

6 = Tiphareth: Sacrifice, vision of harmony of things, devotion and mysteries. This is the centre and goals represented here have a habit of having everything else revolve around them. However, some form of transformation and/or sacrifice must be made to achieve this goal. Temptation to procrastinate is strengthened by the lure of comfort and perhaps the search for too much harmony.

7 = Netzach: Victory, vision of beauty triumphant, experience of opposites, illusion; life force of nature. Here goals are fourth in order of priority and are in danger of being illusory. This position shows partial manifestation of goals; something which needs to become more specialized and the density of thought-forms must be sorted through to win clarity. Therefore contemplation of faith is stronger than contemplation of intellect.

8 = Hod: Absolute and perfect intelligence; vision of splendour; the independent Will, working objectively. Goals represented here are planned out and activated intellectually. This is the third position of priority which may already be in action. Mental blocks and inhibitions must be cleared for the dynamic energy of higher planes to pass through and guide one's work. Intellectual attainment.

9 = Yesod: Foundation of the Universe, Independence or Idleness, purification of emanations. Here goals must be concretely proved and corrected in their design and representations. All operations are carried out and are successful as they improve on existing conditions. This position is second in priority order. It must be realised that it is not form that contains life, but life that contains form.

10 = Malkuth: Kingdom, sphere of the elements, the Gate. The first goal of priority will sit here. This is Manifestation of a goal, Success or Ruin, Wealth or Oppression. Here you must act and concentrate on completion. It is achieved stability, discipline and mastering of lessons, if you want success.

The following ritualistic meditation is optional. It is likened to god-form assumption, except you assume the image of your vision in the attempt to help it manifest.

Meditate over your Tree of Power, vibrate an affirmation and/or invocation for each goal (drawn from the card), affirming your intent to achieve that goal and your realization of the manner in which you must approach it. Immerse yourself in the visual picture of each visualised success.

Example:

Mrs Xs Tree of Power for 1992.

List of goals	Associated cards	Spheres
Safety of travel next week	Chariot	Seventh
Lecture Successfully	Hierophant	Tenth
Heal myself	Sun	Second
Write proposed project	Six Swords	Fifth
Success with ongoing studies and assignments	Magus	First
Diet properly	Three Cups	Sixth
Exercise regularly	Three disks	Third
Continue art work	Temperance	Ninth
Make business a success	Ten Disks	Eighth

Mrs X's first priority on her list, was to travel a distance to a place and lecture. This was going to take several days so she had concern as to success and safety. With the Chariot, representing this priority and placed on Netzach, it shows that the trip would be pleasant and quite social. Its priority of importance was dealt out to be not strong as it was three spheres away from sphere ten, which brings to the querent's attention what would be of first priority. This shows her she need not pay too much attention to any dangers of the trip as it would be safe. The Hierophant turned up in Malkuth which showed the actual lecture was to be the first issue of concentration. The answer to this goal, was success. The Hierophant is ruled by Taurus, an Earth sign and sits in an earth sphere, showing an affinity for the element Mrs X would find herself in.

Mrs X reported that the trip went safely and she hardly noticed the miles go by. On returning she had a passenger, making the trip sociable. The lecture ran smoothly and successfully and was well received.

The next goal Mrs X listed was to heal herself. The Sun sits in Chokmah, showing she has a long way to go before healing and must draw on her powers of wisdom and heal through spiritual means. The next goal was a proposed project and the Six of Swords appeared in Geburah. This showed a need to aggressively apply herself and her intellect. The order of priority was not serious, so she could relax and not get uptight when other commitments took her away from her work. Her goal to continue successfully with her assignments ended up in Kether. Wow! The Magus sitting in Kether! She is certainly on the right path here and must focus 'on-going' with a spiritual purpose and not look at what her studies will bring to her materially.

To diet properly is represented by the Three of Cups and is in Tiphareth. Here she must centrally focus this issue at the centre of her life and be consistent. She must also focus her diet for soul nourishment as well; a central and important thing she must not overlook, but also perform in a relaxed manner as its priority is not urgent, just essential. The Three of Disks was chosen for exercise and was laid on Binah. Interesting! I don't think she will achieve this in a regular and consistent manner. In fact she may even take a break from serious exercise. Binah is advising her that there is something she must understand about her compulsive need (Three of Disks) to work-out and re-evaluate her priorities to spiritual rather than to physical. Balance, perhaps!

The next goal was to continue her art work. Temperance is placed on Yesod and perhaps shows a next-in-line focus (No. 2), but I feel this is 'in her dreams. rather than physically manifesting much this year. Last but not least, on her list is the Ten of Disks for successful business. Well, you can see what she wants, money. Landing on Hod sets it forward to third place in priority (or happening) and developing through intellectual and communicative application. Mrs X reported that she made her living as a consultant and recently business has picked up.

In summary, viewing the variety of questions asked, you can see this person is channelling her energies not only into physical/material matters, but into mental/spiritual matters. Therefore a balance is appearing in the make-up of Mrs X. Where the cards and goals lie on the Tree emphasises how the querent should use her personal power. You would have seen that the types of cards the querent chose represented her state of mind and intent towards her goals. These cards sitting in different spheres on the tree were then activated according to their energies and affinities to the spheres.

Your personal wheel of power

For this method you will need a copy of your own horoscope (Natal Chart) calculated by an astrologer or computer. Have it done using an 'Equal House' method. You will also need an understanding of what symbols are on your chart so that you can view what planet is in what zodiac sign and what zodiac sign sits on the cusp of what house. Have your astrologer point this out to you. The houses (pie divisions) in your chart should be numbered from 1–12 in an ant-clockwise direction, starting from the left mid-horizontal point, which is your Ascendant. The zodiac symbol drawn to your Ascendant is your 'Rising Sign.' In this exercise we will be ignoring the actual degrees of the Signs and Planets. By now you will be aware that each major arcana card has an Astrological attribution, as do the Minor Arcana also.

Steps

1. First sort the major Arcana from your deck, dividing them into piles of Zodiac and planetary attributions.
2. Choose a Court Card from the deck which represents yourself.
3. Place the zodiac cards in a circle of twelve positions, just like the houses in your natal chart and in the order of the zodiac positions in your chart. For example, if you have Pisces rising, you would place the card the 'Moon' in the first House position; Emperor in the second House; Hierophant in the third House; Lovers in the fourth House; Chariot in the fifth House; Strength in the sixth House; Hermit in the seventh House; Justice in the eighth House; Death in the ninth House; Temperance in the tenth House; Devil in the eleventh House and the Star in the twelveth House.

Place your Court Card in the central hub of the wheel you have created. Some of you will find that your natal Chart shows a Planet in a different House from the zodiac card position in your wheel. Still, place the Planet card over the Zodiac card (Sign) in which the planet is found, even if it is a different house. Observe the combination in your meditations, then also meditate on the planet card under the House influence in which it is found in your natal Chart. Example:

4. First stage meditation: Mediate on the wheel as a whole. This is your Wheel of Power. Draw from its energies. When you meditate on a card you can draw on the archetypal energy of it, which can bring out or control and understand those qualities within yourself. Meditate on the individual cards in the Houses, their meanings in those Houses (see Horoscope spread in the chapter on Divination). Then meditate on the combinations of cards, that is, the card opposite each card and their influences thereon. These oppositions should be an awakening influence at best, or a conflicting one at worst. The cards on either side of a card and their influences will unlock further meanings. The third card to each side of a card will show the challenges to that card. The fourth card to each side of a card may show its harmony. With this technique you can get to know yourself more deeply. View the positive and negative of each card and reflect on yourself; how you have been operating these energies in your life. Then start working on yourself in your meditations to strengthen the positive qualities (see step 7).
5. Now take the planetary cards and place them partially over or beside the cards in the Houses. Your natal Chart shows where the planets should sit.

For example, if you had Jupiter in Leo and Pluto in Leo, both cards would be placed beside the Strength card. If you have Neptune in Libra, you would place the Hanged Man beside the Justice Card. Example:

6. Second Stage Meditation: Repeat First Stage meditation, but this time, include the merging energies of the cards representing the Planets with the cards of the Zodiac.
7. To build the positive qualities, choose another card from your deck out of the Minor Arcana, which represents those qualities. Place that card over the card you are meditating on. Include

this additional card in your meditation, merging its positive energy into the vibrations of the other cards and draw this into yourself.

8. For personal insights into yourself:

(a) First record on a sheet of paper, or in your magical diary, all of the cards and their positions in your Wheel of Power and any notes you want to make for yourself about them.

(b) Then gather up the whole deck. Shuffle and cut into three piles with a question in mind such as 'Where am I at now in my Life?' Place the three piles into one (bottom pile to middle) then that pile over the top of the third pile.

(c) Lay out a new horoscope spread as per the spread described in the Divination chapter. Now compare the cards with those recorded in your Wheel of Power spread. The new horoscope spread will show what influences are currently influencing you. The influences can be positive or negative in respect to their meanings when compared to the cards in the Wheel of Power spread. This may help you in dealing with current situations.

(d) Repeat your meditations as described above.

(e) With each area you want to improve on, cut a card from the deck with the question in mind 'How can I deal with this situation to improve matters?' This is how you go about dealing with problems on a conscious level. Do not be discouraged if the cards, when cut, turn up a negative card, as with every card here, there is an opposite alternative. For example, if you cut the Five of Cups, this would suggest that you must deal with your fear of disappointment.

9. Another method of meditation in your Wheel of Power spread is to choose a minor arcana card that has astrological symbols that represent your Planetary positions in Signs. Place these cards in their respective positions on your Wheel and continue meditations towards 'Self Knowledge'.

For example, if you had a Moon in Aquarius, you would take the Seven of Swords and place it beside the Star. Moon in Capricorn would be placed beside the Devil.

Dreaming and the tarot

Study of the significance of dreams has been with us in one form or another since man's existence on this planet. However, it is not until recent times that Jungian psychotherapy has tried to take dream analysis out of the Shamanistic field and into the scientific arena. Dreams are extremely important, in the sense that they show the deep undercurrent of emotive responses. Jung considered that dreams related to dammed-up subconscious patterns of thought coming through in archetypal plays. These show us what we refuse to deal with on an conscious level. The archetypal imagery of dreams and the tarot are extremely interrelated.

When looking at the study of dreams one can show hidden fears that work beneath the surface of the mind. With the concept of dream analysis, as combined with the use of the Tarot, we, start to get into the arena of dream control, with the eventual concept of the conscious controlling the sub-conscious. While the psychological approach to dream control is relevant, we are going to try and look at dreams also within the esoteric confines of Subtle Body anatomy as well. Dreaming can be classed into the following categories:

1. Creative dreaming.
2. Group dreaming.
3. Precognitive dreaming.
4. Telepathic or out of body dreaming.
5. Lucid dreaming.
6. Awareness dreaming.

Before we go further into dream analysis, the first thing we must be able to do is to remember the dreams themselves. The way to do this, is on the exact moment of waking, immediately start recalling your dreams of the previous night. Write them down in full in a notebook.

The main category that we will be dealing with in this chapter is creative dreaming. By this, we mean that we revert back to a previously chosen dream and try and change it. This will mean going back into the particular state or level of the subconscious that we were in when we had the original dream. Our dream state is controlled by our Astral Body and Lower Mental Bodies. The Astral Body is the Body that has a vast storehouse of archetypal imagery and is the filtration Body of past, present and future events in the Astral plane. It is the effect of the interplay of desire and of sentient response upon the self at the centre, and the resultant effect in that body is experienced as pleasure and pain.

Tarot dreaming is part of the Creative dreaming aspect, which some call Redreaming. It relates to accepting the archetypal imagery of the keys as latent symbols within us and accessing those symbols. The Tarot gives us a doorway into the subconscious (especially the Astral and Mental Bodies) where we contact and explore dissociated states of consciousness and bring them to the surface of the conscious mind. The whole concept is a fact of integration within the self with the use of the Tarot Keys as a doorway to access that part of the self to which the dream related. Take for example a frightening dream that keeps reoccurring. You would access it in creative dream recall by using a card as the doorway to that part of your subconscious. The dream would be recreated right up to the frightening point, then, while in control, you would re-enact the scene, but in such a way as to resolve the fear and danger. Then you would find out what was on the other side of that fear.

In the methodology of dreams and visionary work with the tarot, correct interpretation is essential. There are a number of approaches to this. One method is to examine every set of symbols seen within the dream or vision and compare with the symbols of the cards. The other is to view the main theme of the vision which was the main point of attention and choose a Tarot card that is related. Even through our visionary work with the tarot, there is a framework of restriction in interpretation. What revolves around the dream is the symbolism of our personal ideals and this is, in effect, the primary motivating force for our visionary work and need for interpretation.

Example of an Re-enactment of a Dream

Tarot card used: 'Judgement' from the Golden Dawn Tarot.

The adept scrying this card was receiving a particular dream at intervals over a period of months during 1983. She would always wake up at the point when she was being attacked by snakes. Each time she had the dream she was able to travel a bit further into it, but asked us how she could resolve the dream on a conscious level. When she came to us about the dream, she was at a stage in her grade work where she was doing practical alchemy. The following is an abridged version of the re-enacted dream.

First entry through the card Judgement I met a black wall. Could not go through so returned and attempted again. Second attempt was successful. Once on the other side I was aware of the snakes around an Angel. This was different to my dream as there I kept falling into a pit of snakes who were always trying to bite me which they did not as I was super fast. But here, in this working, the snakes were uninterested in me. I walked through them into the dark passage from my dream. It was made of large stone blocks. This took me into a large stone temple, dimly lit by torches, columns around the sides and a walking area around the sides and a great rectangle pit in the middle. Just like an indoor swimming pool. Wide steps into it and again wide steps at the other end of the rectangle (all grey stone). (The scene was later recognised as a previous dream where I would always walk along the left side of the walking area, found a door then returned due to a python guarding it.)

In the middle again was a very large cauldron upon a fire with some alchemic mixture in it bubbling away. This time I walking down the steps, straight through the middle of the pit, circumambulated the cauldron three times and continued straight along the middle to the steps on the other side. As I ascended the steps, the cauldron overflowed and filled the pit half full with grey-black liquid. I ascended the steps and came to a rectangular stone entrance showing a more brightly-lit passage beyond. The walls had hieroglyphs painted thereon, Egyptian-like drawings and colourings. A demon-like figure flashed at me to prevent my entry. I went straight through. It was illusion. I continued along a passage (still moving East), for some distance and was met by a gigantic, hissing python. Here, I saw it for an illusion and moved straight through unharmed, keeping a straight course. I was again challenged by the python reappearing in front of me. I repeated my action going straight through. I had no fear and I saw them as illusions thrown up by my subconscious.

Then I stopped. Turned South towards a hidden doorway. It opened, but before I entered a grey haired, off-white robed elderly man appeared and pushed in front to enter first. I stood back in courtesy. When I stepped through he was at my side. He went to lead forward, so I challenged him for his name and purpose and made the 5 = 6 signs. He returned the signs … I asked his name and it was given in two syllables, Go-ol phonetically, Gaiol more correctly. He moved in and I followed. There was no other direction to go for this passage was the same as the other. We came to a large chamber, the same as the first chamber. This time dimmer in lighting. There was an audience around the walls amongst which my guide disappeared.

I kept a straight line of focus to my front and yet saw all that was around me. There was the Pit again, pitch black. There was a band no wider than my foot stretching from me across the middle to the other side. In the middle the band widened into a cube then narrowed again. There appeared an image opposite, ceremoniously dressed in a black and gold, body-fitting gown with jewelled and gold adornments. She wore an adorned headdress that appeared Egyptian in design with gold and jewels hanging down each side of her head. I tight-rope walked the band. The figure opposite imitated my actions covering the same distance as I. As we got closer the image became more visible and the clothing appeared different. Now a woman dressed in white Egyptian dress to knees; elaborately dressed in jewellery and high gold headgear which was shaped like two peaks on each side of a hump. She had black straight hair and lots of makeup.

We met in the middle and were to merge as one. This I instantly knew, as she was me and I was her. When merged the black band disappeared leaving us in the cube as one. The pit lightened to show the cauldron (I was back from where I had entered), into which I was lowered, submerged into the bubbling syrup-like black-grey mixture. I rose again with my appearance the same as the woman. I was submerged again and then rose returning myself as plain old me again. I instinctively grabbed into the air and the python appeared in my hand. I submerged with it. Came up again without the python, then ascended onto a cube and was lowered to the floor (now clear of liquid) facing the direction in which I was heading (which was originally the door and steps through which I'd entered earlier). I strode forward through the pit, down the middle, up the steps to the door of the original entrance, through the dark passage and out through the card.

As you can see from the above working, a transmutation took place. The adept reported a much more balanced state of mind and freedom from certain fears in her life. With such dream workings, as shown above, you may find a lot will happen that appears to be out of your control. However, it is all within your own sub-conscious, so you do have control.

Scrying, travelling in the spirit vision, ritual and the tarot

Once I (CZ) was approached by an acquaintance who asked me how he could project himself to scry or astral travel. As he had no occult training in such things I had to start with the basics, but left out any explanation of trainings that a Golden Dawn adept would have. The information given to him, however, I felt was adequate; it involved techniques successfully used by many other people. A few weeks later he came back quite exasperated. 'Nothing works' he said. 'I sit for ages, even light candles and incense and nothing works!' On further questioning him about his methods and experiences I found he was not able to still his mind from interfering thoughts and outside noises. So I gave more explanation of the basic steps in meditation to create a more 'still state' leaving one's mind more receptive. A week later he again claimed failure. Again I questioned him, wanting to help him in his quest. I found he was over-analyzing everything he was doing and perceiving. He also had no 'Purpose', nothing to focus on in his exercise, there-fore no 'Will and Intent'.

Without Intent your Will cannot activate and without Focus, your Will has no direction. In addition, you must not be afraid to let your imagination loose, for to scry in the spirit vision you will have to teach yourself to creatively visualize and hold images in your mind's eye and be able to transform those images at Will. These are the kind of things a Golden Dawn initiate learns as he or she works through the Outer Order grades to the Inner Order.

Firstly however, you must learn to meditate, which is discussed in the previous chapter. Scrying in the Spirit Vision is a clairvoyant perception of what you see. It is vision in the mind's eye and there is not too much difference between this and meditation. In fact, nowadays, there is a therapeutic method called 'Alchemic Hypnotherapy', which is not much different from what is discussed here. Some of its practitioners delude themselves in thinking this is a new therapy, however, it is as old as the world itself; just a new name.

Travelling in the Spirit Vision is Astral Travel. This is where you actually enter the scene, or dimension, that you are viewing and have an influence on that dimension. A ray of yourself travels to the place you are viewing.

In both cases the adept must take the role as the observer, the sightseer. The exercises described below, however, can be used for both methods and it is up to the practitioner to choose what level they want to work on. We will be using the term 'Scrying' to refer to both techniques.

For any work on these levels, a person must be in a state of mental calm and clarity, in an undisturbed place and in a relaxed, comfortable position, with loose clothes. Any attempts to work with the cards on an astral level will not succeed and would not be safe if your mind is in a state of anxiety, fear, anger, etc. Therefore, before you start any working, some form of meditation must take place to relax yourself and put your anxieties, worries and daily memories temporarily out of your mind.

The object in scrying is multifold and involves testing your senses on a number of different planes to advance your ability in clairvoyance and other such work. When an Adept reaches the rank of 5 = 6 in the Golden Dawn, which is the Inner Order, the R.R. et A.C., these two forms of exercises with meditation would be taught, using the Tarot cards as doorways. The main focus would be to do path-workings. 'Path-workings' is a term used to refer to climbing the Tree of Life. If you refer back to the earlier chapters on the Kabbalah, you will see how the Tarot cards are associated with the Kabbalistic Tree of Life.

What the Adept would be required to do is, starting with the thirty-second Path and the card entitled 'the World', scry this card and Path and record the experience. The intention is that a more comprehensive understanding is obtained on more than one level, not only the lower mental but on the emotional, astral and higher mental levels of comprehension. The Adept would then scry the thirty-first Path and its associated card, then the thirtieth Path and so on, going in reverse numerical order to Path 11.

Now these Paths lead to Sephiroth, which is another aspect the Adept may attempt to scry. In scrying the Sephiroth the Adept would also incorporate the minor arcana. For example in scrying Malkuth the Adept would also study and scry the Ten of Wands, the Ten of Cups, Ten of Swords and Ten of Disks.

Some Adepts also like to descend the tree by the Lightening Flash which is as follows: Paths 11, 14, 19, 22, 24, 27, 30 and 32. Travelling the Tree up or down is in the World of Assiah at the initial attempt. If the Adept wanted to experience the other worlds, he would have to use Will and Intent to focus into those worlds and travel the Tree again. It is very rare for a trainee Adept to jump a world and not wise to do so during the process of balanced development.

Apart from scrying the Tree the Adept may want to also Travel it in the Spirit Vision. Mathers considered that over-doing this type of work was a very real danger and suggested that it be done no more than once a week at the most. But some people can easily handle twice a week. Gauge yourself. If you experience side-effects such as sensitivity to sound, reacting negatively to others, vertigo, ego-projection, or detachment from daily reality, then take a rest from scrying work until matters return to normal. Do not be an egotist and think you are better than anyone else and put yourself under more than you can handle. Be gentle with your psyche.

It is interesting for the reader to note, that the order of the paths followed up to Tiphareth, are the same order the Adept went through the Outer Order before entering 5 = 6. There is certainly 'method' and 'purpose' in the approach used by the Golden Dawn.

Techniques of scrying a tarot card

Before any special working, informal or formal, some effort should be made to provide a space to work in by clearing negative energies from that space and from yourself. Imagining a golden psychic circle surrounding you and reinforced by the banishing pentagram ritual should be sufficient. Your own body cleanliness is also important. When following the ritual method, a ritual bath or shower and anointing would be helpful. An informal method would be to build up the image of the Tarot Key in your mind's eye, then mentally project your vision through that image as if it were a doorway and you were passing through a holographic image. You then step into (in your mind's eye) a landscape, or scene. (If you were Travelling in the Spirit Vision you would also send a ray of light from your Heart Chakra after drawing the power of the Divine Light through your Crown Chakra and circulating it throughout your body. You then follow that ray of light with your consciousness, to its end through the doorway, then form an embodied image of your astral self, maintaining a silver thread of connection to your physical form.) Then you would mentally call for a guide and wait for some form of movement in your direction, animal or human.

The entity that comes towards you may be your guide through the world you have just entered. You then test it with a symbol; for example, place the image of the Banner of the West in its path. If it walks through that image, the entity means you no harm and has come to you. You ask it (with projected thoughts) if it will guide you and what its name is. The entity will communicate in the same way. So off you both walk, fly or swim (however you feel inclined to travel in that realm) and observe what there is to be seen and shown by the guide. Do not hesitate in your thinking or picturing else psychosomatic effects will be produced.

When you have had enough, return to the entrance-way that you had previously created, the same way you travelled through the vision, except by the reverse path (like a movie being run backwards). This is a mental reversal of the scenes you saw. Give your thanks and farewell to your guide and step backwards through the holographic image of the Tarot card, drawing your consciousness to your physical form. (For those astral travelling, you must also draw your ray of light back with your consciousness, so that nothing of yourself is left in that other world.)

Mentally close the door and dissolve the Tarot card image. Record your vision in detail, then have something to eat and drink (a very important thing to do to help bring you back to earth).

To summarize the above:

Scrying in the spirit vision (astral)

1. Select in Macrocosm a certain symbol. It must be balanced with the correct colour, shape and imagery of its correlations.
2. Send a thought ray from your spiritual consciousness (illuminated by Higher Will) into the part of the Sphere of Sensation (astral form) of the symbol selected. (This can be called a magical mirror of microcosm.)
3. Concentrate entire focused consciousness on the symbol and follow this ray of reflection out into the various higher planes that one wishes to explore.
4. Return by reversing points 3, 2 and 1 above. Close astral door, dissolve vision.

All images of guides that approach you in your visions must be tested so that you do not travel with a false guide and end up having a bad trip, or worse still getting lost in your vision. If, once tested, the entity does not pass the test, or grows angry, dismiss it and dissolve it. Then send out your call for your real guide. It is your vision, after all, and you can dismiss any part of it. YOU are in control. If you do not feel in control, pull yourself out of your vision, close the door and try another time when you are more able, or when you have someone who can help you through it, like a member of your temple with experience.

You can test the proposed guide with grade signs, using the sign of your own grade. For those not in a Golden Dawn Temple and without grade signs, you can prepare your own symbols of recognition that the guide must return to you to prove it is of truth and honesty. Or, as suggested, the Banner of the West.

There are also symbols you can visually project on to your picture to create certain visual effects. These are Hebrew letters:

Tau—to remove a memory (imagined picture) of what you see so that the real scene can form
Kaph—to construct a stronger vision
Peh—to express impatience and hurry the guide or elements of the vision along; or anger to combat any aggressive element or entity in the vision
Resh—to counter delusions of haughtiness, vanity
Daleth—to express pleasure or remove image causing intellectual vanity
Beth—to cause banishment of delusion and lying
Gimel—to control wandering thoughts

It is very easy to see only what your memory and imagination invokes, so try not to force an image of the scene once you have passed through the door. Let the events unfold naturally. Granted, you will also be experiencing aspects of your own psyche (inner world). Only experience will give you the necessary discriminative powers to know what is another dimension and what is your own inner realm. Therefore, test yourself and retest yourself, so there is little doubt left to your perceptions.

We have often seen people believing with such blind faith that they would even fight with their beliefs through denial, claiming that what they had seen in an astral working was a true external contact. From the evidence of their transcripts, I would have to disagree. So, do please have the humility to perhaps admit there may be an error and recheck all 'workings'. This can be done by two people individually and at different times doing a working on the same card without letting the other know what the results were until both have finished a transcript. Then compare them and discuss the variances and similarities.

The Formal Method is more ritualistic in approach. Magical implements may be used and Holy Names, Angels and ritual symbols. We have provided a method below which you can implement for yourself. This is not a compulsory method, or the only way. You can break it down to parts and simplify/intensify it to your own magical training. If you are not a practising magician you may not have the magical elemental weapons. Instead you can replace them for substitutes such as a red candle for the fire element, a rose or incense for the air element, salt or a stone for the earth element and a glass for the water element. Just be sure to bless and cleanse any item you use.

For an altar you may have your own consecrated altar, but any surface cleaned and blessed can be used. Anyone can bless an object. You only need to believe in yourself and have faith that there is a higher power which you can call down. Those of you who are familiar with ritual can do a purification and consecration over the object with your blessing. Those who are not ritualists may only need to project the thought of purification and consecration by water and fire respectively.

To bless your magical implement

1. Wash the object if it is washable, e.g., incense and salt cannot be washed so ensure they are virgin (new from a packet).
2. Do a purification and consecration ritual over the object (optional).
3. Quieten your mind and visualize a white light coming down from above your head into the top of your head and filling your body while vibrating 'EHEIEH' (Eh-he-yay). This is the Divine Light.
4. Imagine that Light surrounds you and the object you are blessing.
5. If you can lift the object, hold it up high in front of you. If it can't be lifted hold your hands above it and say: 'In the name of YEHESHUAHI call on ADONI to bless this ... (name of object) for my magical use'.
6. Pause for a moment imagining the powers of the Divine Light fill your object. Form a seal of protection around the object (golden ring). Then place it down on your altar, or wrap it in a clean, preferably white, cloth.

If you do not have a Lotus Wand as required below, use creative visualization. Your right hand, index finger and thumb can be Wand enough. The same can be used for a magical sword, or you can use your dagger as a substitute. The type of incense you use will depend on what Tarot card you are using. Use an incense which has an affinity with the astrological association of the card.

Ritual for scrying the tarot

Set up your work space by placing your seat in the centre of your work space and facing West. Your altar is placed in front of you. On your altar place your elemental implements: Dagger and Incense in the East, Candle and Wand in the South, Glass/Cup in the West with your cup of blessed water. Your Tarot card which you will be scrying (or travelling) in the centre. The Magical Sword should be lying upright beside you or on the altar alongside the Lotus Wand. A writing pad (magical journal of Tarot workings) and pen will be beside you, with matches and snuffer.

1. Light your candle and incense.
2. Holding your Lotus Wand by the black band, walk deosil to the North East. Sitting East of your card symbolizes you come from the Light. Raise the Lotus Wand above you and say:

'Hekas Hekas Este Bebeloi'

Return deosil to the East of the Altar, lay down the Lotus Wand and pick up your magical Sword.

3. Facing East perform the Lesser Banishing Pentagram Ritual.
4. Lay Sword down by your Altar, pick up your cup of holy water and walking to the East of your working circle, stand facing east and hold up your cup and form a cross with your movement. Then dip your fingers in and touch the air in front of you beneath where you formed the cross, three times in the form of a triangle pointing upwards. This is the image of the cross above the triangle. Walk to the South and again form the image of the cross above the triangle and repeat in the West and the North, finishing East. Raise the cup upwards, facing East, and say:

'I Purify with Water'

5. Walk deosil to West of your altar, put down your cup in its position and pick up your incense. Continue deosil to East and with the incense perform the cross above the triangle symbol. You touch the air before you with the incense by waving motions to form this image. This is repeated in the South, West then North of your circle, then return East. Facing east raise the incense up and say:

'I Consecrate with Fire'

6. Return to your seat and place your incense down. Pick up your Lotus Wand. Circumambulate deosil around the space thrice, holding Lotus Wand by White Band.
7. Vibrations and visualizations:
   (a) Begin to pranic breathe deeply.
   (b) Vibrate the Title of the Card concerned for the number of times of the number of the Key.
   (c) Vibrate the Angel's name that is associated with the card concerned.
   (d) Draw the Sigil of the Angel while holding the white band of your Lotus Wand and vibrate the Angel's name.
   (e) Looking at your Tarot card, link your sphere of sensation (aura) to feel an empathy with the card while building up an image of that card in your mind. Closing your eyes hold that image and observe it growing. (Do not complicate the moment by focusing on detail). Watch the image grow until it is as large as a doorway directly in front of you. Now visualize yourself stepping by, rending the Veil.
   (f) Stand on the threshold, on the other side of the door and vibrate the Angel's name again through pulsing out your thought. In this realm you communicate telepathically. Then pulse the request for a guide and wait. A guide in some form should arrive. (If the guide does not arrive, pulse again. If after three calls nothing happens, back out by the card, close the door and try another day.)
   (g) Test your guide with your chosen symbol or grade sign and expect the sign returned. If your guide is true, obtain its name and request to be shown this realm you are now in. Go with the guide by mentally visualizing yourself moving through the scenes that unfold in front of you.
   (h) When you tire or feel it is time to stop, request the guide to return you to the door. Do so by back-tracking the path and scenes you went through.
   (i) Thank the guide and back yourself through the door of the card reversing the Rending of the Veil.
   (j) Close the door by dissolving the image of the card in front of you.

8. Repeat the purification and consecration as shown above.
9. Reverse circumambulate three times around circle with Lotus Wand.
10. Perform Banishing Pentagram ritual with your magical Sword. Dowse your candle and record your vision.

If you are exhausted, or if the vision persists, perform the signs of Horus and Harpocrates to return lost energy to you. If there is any great difficulty getting back, imagine returning to earth (after flying through the air) and picturing country, city and home. Also eating and drinking after recording your vision helps to ground you.

The following visionary work is an example of how one perceives when projecting through a Tarot Key. The first vision is of the Key, The Fool. We have selected a vision of this particular card because of all the Golden Dawn Keys, this is the most complex. Generally most work on the Keys usually starts from the last, The Universe, and one then works one's way through to the Fool. If you feel more work is needed, then simply start the whole process all over again. What you see one day will not always be shown again, if the vision is repeated. The object here is to find out more about the Keys with every repeated vision. One ex-member of Whare Ra has projected into a specific Trump hundreds of times over a twenty-five year period and has built up an enormous file of visions of that card, which is constantly being reviewed. When the vision is complete we would suggest you wait for a day or so, then do an analysis on the vision in terms of what you think you have gained from it and what you think it has taught you about the Key itself. No matter what the Golden Dawn associations of the Keys are, the real meaning of this type of work is how it affects you personally and this is where constant recording of your visions is a great help in plotting the various gains you make over the years.

Vision of the fool

As I stepped through the doorway unto a grassy plain. The Sun was in the North East and it was very hot. I called for the guide and it came in the form of a bird–a small grey/white pigeon type. Once I gave the Grade Signs the bird changed shape into a woman with wings who then returned the signs I made. I noticed a bright yellow hue emitted from her and she was bubbling with happiness and enthusiasm and on her forehead I noticed an upward-pointing triangle encircled. She also had a wand and she did an invocation and we stepped through yet another doorway.

This time I found myself on a sandy beach with an island in the background. My guide was still with me and she points to the sea and tells me that this is Chaos–the unrevealed–full of unconscious content, for behind the image of the Fool lies the great eternal sea. The sea, like the unconscious should never be rushed at; it must be approached carefully so that one can harvest its products. The islands in the background, emerging out of the sea are conscious thoughts set above the unconscious. The whole imagery of the Fool is control of the unconscious, represented by the sea as I see it now.

The guide goes on to tell me that Uranus is merely empathy, as is the Hebrew letter Aleph. She also says that the youthful child is the Spirit Mercurius and is also like quicksilver and has as many functions as the sea itself. I was then told that if I wished to harvest the products of my mind I was going to have to build a bridge from island to island and map these out, and also build a safe boat to travel (the boat was the bridge referred to) to travel over the unconscious mind.

She points to the heavens and stresses the importance of astrological timing and again refers to the sea and the fishermen on it. No one goes out in a storm but if you are caught up in one you must learn to weather it and not use certain levels of the unconscious at inopportune times. I asked her about the wolf in the card which I did not see near me. She then points again to the sea and says that the wolf is its greyness, the unconscious wave. The Child is a liquid Mercurius with the wolf as the hidden agent—hence its dark colouring. When the sun shines on the sea you then see silver but when the storm clouds cover the sun you see darkness for these are the same but different, just like the mind.

By harvesting at the correct time the sea will provide many benefits and the greyness will not hurt you. Advance and try and harvest during the storm and the greyness of the ocean will sweep you away. I then asked about the Tree within the card and she said that the Tree is the molecule or structure in much the same way as a reef is in the depths of the ocean. The sea supplies organisms to the structure to grow and change, stabilise and die, just like the process of birth, death and rebirth. The Tree in the card is a structure that could be altered by the child and the wolf over a period of time to suit their own needs, just as a child can chop a tree down the wolf can use its branches as a lair. Each has its own functions. In essence, the Tree within the card is one's own personal growth structure that is constantly changing—a flux just like the blossoms on the tree; each only exists for a moment in time, then it is renewed in different areas of the tree, as so must your structure change and develop with it. I then asked about the brightness of the oak (in my colouring of this Key the oak is extremely bright, reflecting back its light onto the child). She says that the reflection of the sun causes this but not in physical terms, as the brightness emitting from the outer structure of the Tree is its pulsation rate. It is the basic pulse of life itself and the child stands bathed in it as the sun nourishes all things.

She says that the entire Key is a card that represents human manifestations of the soul—nothing outward but everything internal; it is spirit, the hidden aspiration of the self not yet manifested.

I ask her whether there is more symbology and she shows me another representation of a boat in the form of a lunar crescent and informs me that it is the Moon moving on the waters, reflecting; it is not tangible—an image of things not yet to be. I then left.

As one can see, there is a wealth of information in this vision and with each journey more information is imparted and one is able to understand more of what the Key represents. Over the years multiple journeys into this particular card have been done and as one's perception alters then more is learned. The real key, we feel, in this type of work, is not the symbolism but how it alters with each vision. Gradually one can draw power from certain aspects of Tarot symbolism. A vision can also be recreated if one feels that one has not studied an area enough. To an extent, this type of work is timeless.

Quite often music is also an added stimulus in working out one's perceptions through visionary Tarot work. With the Fool, for example, Pat often uses the Bolero as its timing seems to fit this card which he has renamed the 'Awakening' to fit more in line with its Uranian concepts. Out of all the Golden Dawn papers we have read, only one lecture by Felkin (dated 1898) showed an experiment with music and visionary work, but he was very much aware of the shamanistic approach from his missionary travels. Many of today's pioneers into frontier states of awareness also use music as a form of mystic stimulus. There is, for example, 'Tarot Suite' by Mike Batt who has tried to work on mystic lines. Ultimately though, it is up to the individual to choose the music of his or her own choice to help stimulate the Tarot Vision. This is a concept used since the 1960s, and pioneers in this area such as author Neville Drury, have worked in this field for a number of years.

Another example of visionary work by another Adept is with Key 18.

Vision of the card the moon

I entered through the card as a doorway and emerged on a bank. I crawled at first like the crayfish in the card, then stood up in my full astral form. The dogs moved closer to each side of me, their forms larger than myself. I vibrated the Archangel's name 'Gabriel' and called for a guide. Gliding along the central path ahead of me came a lavender-hooded and robed figure on a donkey. As it dismounted, the donkey turned into a turtle and dived into the water, disappearing. Signs were exchanged as well as names, however, I will use the term 'Guide' for this record. The guide tended to stand slightly to the right of me.

We transformed into doves and flew the middle path, past the dogs who jumped slightly. My guide was on my right for the whole trip. We flew between the towers. A dark image was on the top of each tower with long sticks—there was a movement from both. We flew on towards the hills. The path between the hills became a swift river at the bottom of a mountainous gorge. There was a path high up on each side of the gorge. We flew the middle path, on and on, towards the cloud and four yods, past the mountains to a plateau where the roads on each side joined in the middle as one road. We landed and changed to our own forms. We sat in the middle of the road and talked.

I asked about the moon and its phases. I cannot remember exact words now, which were quite elegant, but it went something like this: The power of the moon is through the sun—reflection—it also reflects the stars. But the moon has its own specific vibrations and way of reflecting which alludes to its individual power. As the moon grows, the power is stronger. Regarding the balsamic moon, you have no reflection of light, only the stars are felt. Here you have no interference of energies to reach the stars in any working. This is a time of great power in the earth, from the earth and nature, undirected forces. ...

We retransformed into doves and continued, flying through the cloud and Yods, towards the moon, then through the image of the moon. All this time the landscape was night. We flew into a triangular chamber from its apex. It was the symbol of water. On each side were softly clothed people in white. Walking forward to me was one in white whose flowing clothes changed to black and her hair changed to black. She was a very handsome and confident woman. But, her manner was sharp—a hint of sarcasm and ruthlessness. I asked who she was. The answer was that she was my psychic power—combined with my negative tendencies—when we merge she will be of the middle path, and my inner powers will be tapped and I will be able to empower my negativity, transforming it. We merged and my appearance became an image of a tall, mentally powerful woman. Guide and I continued as doves out of the chamber still following the middle path, which is now of stagnant water and dead lilies. But, as we flew over the water it became a fresh stream and the lilies became alive. We arrived at a giant lily and landed. I was told what this was about, but alas, now recording this I have forgotten. We continued in our own images on foot along the path, now dry land. The landscape is now golden—an amber light. Images began appearing and disappearing on each side (which seemed to me from TV programmes). Guide told me not to misunderstand, although the appearance may be trickery, it is showing the power of the mind.

I came face to face with an elaborately dressed man—smooth of face, turban and white and soft green colours of jewelled clothes. It turned out to be a false ego, glamour, etc. I dissolved the figure and a spider reappeared. I dissolved the spider image. We continued walking and we came to a red room. By this stage I was tiring in my vision and my mind had played trickery. So we turned back and travelled the same way we had come. During the return my mind wandered off the path a few times so I had to Will myself back. No problem. Guide and I bid farewell at the door. I stepped through, closed the door. I remember a bit about the Lotus now. Healing power. I was given a cup of drops of liquid from the Lotus. I first offered it to the guide who drank, then I drank.

Here are two examples of an abridged version of a vision:

Vision of the wheel of fortune

On entry the Wheel opened up in the middle with spokes splaying outward. I entered. I found three parallel paths, one of gold (right), one of poverty (left) and a central one. A guide came dressed in white veil-like clothes, clad close to his body and covering a youthful face. We exchanged signs and names. He said he was Caph. We walked a short way along the middle path and I asked the secret of the card. Caph said: to know—to predict—to know and recognise the seeds of change and act accordingly at the right time—not to resist. After further conversation and exchanging of understanding we returned to the entrance, made our goodbyes and I returned.

Short, precise and a sharing of understanding which only the adept experiencing the vision would have had. In this case no landscape was described. Apparently this was not as important to the adept, compared to the conversation. Every person sees things differently, according to their own psyche and interests. They will also record their visions differently. For example, the first vision above showed a person very articulate and with a good memory of conversation. The other visions, however, showed people who were less able to remember detail and conversations, or were less concerned with detail in conversation and would rather 'see'. In some cases the practitioner may be tired or just unable at the time to hold a vision for a long period, therefore some records of scrying sessions will be short.

Vision of the card the world

Through the door I see below me a bright star. I leapt to the middle of it then raised my arms in the form of a cross. Rose up a ray of light to another entrance. Through this there was a landscape, barren and a winding road. I vibrated the name and called for a guide. From the distance galloped a man on a brown horse. He arrived in front of me. The man was big but lean, wrinkled face, indigo clothes, green girdle with sword hanging from it. The horse's equipment was fancy, like the knights of old. Before I could get any answers, he swung me up behind him. I pulled myself away and leapt back down, demanding his name and the signs. His name was Cassiel and the signs were given. I asked him to show me the workings of the plane (he seemed in so much of a rush and everything thereon went very fast).

At this point I was again placed behind him on the horse, which then turned a white colour. We sped along the road to a wreath of haze. In the middle of the haze I saw a beautiful landscape of trees and a road leading through it. Cassiel said it was the path to Yesod. We did not enter but continued in a different direction. I was shown construction of a pyramid building, but when I put my hand on it my hand went through. Then I saw a mud pool and asked what was that. He said the quintessence. He said I was not yet ready to see its true appearance. We went to the top of the mountain and absorbed the warm rays of the sun, watching the light descending.

We returned the way we came, back to the entrance. I asked Cassiel what his job was here. He said he was the angel of Saturn and so obliged to show me this realm. Also he said he was 'in my mind one'! We made our farewells and departed.

Introduction to the celestial tarot

Within the Golden Dawn's grade of Zelator Adeptus Minor and Theoricus Adeptus Minor, there were three fundamental lectures that related to the abstract Tarot that have caused a great deal of confusion both within and without the Order. In 1983, we had the opportunity of discussing these Golden Dawn lectures with Israel Regardie and while we differed in opinions on how the system worked we both conceded that it was extremely technical in detail. When we first discussed the idea of doing this section of the Tarot book with other Adepti in the New Zealand Order we originally thought of simply repeating the 'Mathers-cum-Westcott' arrangement of the papers. It was pointed out to us that a repetition of these papers would make some of the readers feel cheated since these have been available for some years. What was needed was a fresh approach involving a little more simplicity than the way the original papers were written, which was for the experienced Golden Dawn Adept. On discussing these papers with members of the Whare Ra temple we eventually decided to go along with the concept of rewriting some of the original Golden Dawn Tarot papers. Since the main purpose of this Book is the Golden Dawn Tarot we have taken the liberty of pruning the original papers somewhat in this section. For a full explanation to be given would involve too many sub-systems, and I think here is not the place for that. With the newer explanations we have tried to produce some form of simplicity that the Order papers did not have. Whether or not we have succeeded will be up to the reader to judge.

Without doubt Mathers was brilliant, but in the Celestial Sphere section of the original papers he was guilty of playing intellectual mind games and obscuring his purpose. What he is trying to show, by use of analogy with the Tarot, is a function of a whole system of influence, which to discuss fully would take a book in itself. It is very easy to get side-tracked by this section and dazzle oneself with Kabbalistic dexterity, or make it an astronomer's delight or nightmare, whichever one perceives it to be. We have tried to stick to the concept of the Tarot as the central theme, for that is our frame of reference. This section should not be considered a rewrite of the Mathers papers on the Star Maps but a rewrite of certain sections of them: other parts will be explained further in other books. We intend to be dealing with the Tarot aspect of the four Golden Dawn papers:

1. Tree of Life Projected on a Solid Sphere.
2. The Operation and Rule of the Tree of Life in the Celestial Heavens as if Projected on a Solid Sphere.
3. Law of the Convoluted revolution of the Forces symbolised by the Four Aces round the Northern Pole.
4. Schemphamphoresh.

It is inevitable that there will be some repetition of the original Golden Dawn papers, especially the descriptions of the constellations applied to the Tarot which really need no improvement upon and are straightforward enough. In the first paper though we feel we have explained more easily why Mathers concentrated on the Star Regulus. We have chosen to rewrite the second paper by Westcott, expanding on some of the original descriptions. For the third paper a great deal needs to be explained in more simplistic terms and thus has been reworked along the original lines. This is the paper attributed to the Theoricus Adeptus Minor Grade and possibly one of the most difficult of Golden Dawn theology to master. We would also point out that what is given here is only the tip of the iceberg concerning its use in the other sub-systems, and this is where the real theory begins.

Almost twenty years ago when we both first attempted to study the Convoluted Forces paper, its basic meaning eluded us for years, for the key to its use is simplicity. When we first attempted to rewrite this paper we had more headaches that one could imagine in trying to sort it out. Israel Regardie admitted to us that after fifty years of studying it, he had not fathomed it.

For a while Israel Regardie (as we did for a number of years) considered the Enochian theory to be the Order's crown and glory of teaching. We have, however, found that this, along with other systems, fits into the 'Celestial Sphere'. There are so many hidden directions that this paper gives in so many other areas, it would be better suited as a book in itself and, as such, it is beyond the scope of this Tarot book to discuss them all. The fourth paper ties in the use of the planetary system to the Minor Arcana and the celestial sphere. It took us a number of years to appreciate the full intricacy of this Tarot-constellation system until we used it with other systems within the Golden Dawn, such as Enochiana, Natal Astrology and Auric work, to name but three. Gradually things became a lot clearer. I have decided to amalgamate the four papers under one heading of the Celestial Sphere, as there is a great deal of cross-referencing between the papers which tends to confuse things, unless one is very familiar with all three. It was Chris Zalewski who over the years re-drew the Golden Dawn Star maps into some intelligible form which corresponded with the descriptions of the cards from the old Whare Ra papers which we received and which were very badly drawn to say the least.

Celestial tarot

The principle method of studying the Zodiac of both the Northern and Southern Hemisphere is to imagine the Earth is as a sphere within a huge celestial sphere. Upon this larger sphere are the various signs and constellations of the zodiac which has as its Equator the path of the Sun as it journeys through the heavens as seen from the Earth. The path of the Sun is called the Ecliptic. In the Golden Dawn teachings this huge hollow sphere is called the Macrocosm, or Greater Universe, but when reduced onto the Earth, it becomes the Microcosm, and when further reduced on man, it becomes the spherical energy field generated by man himself. This is called the Sphere of Sensation and is, of course, related to the Hermetic Axiom of:

> *That which is below is as that which is above and that which is above is as that which is below, for the performances of the Miracles of the one thing.*

The Golden Dawn then broke up this huge celestial canopy of stars into various sections which they attributed to the rule of the Tarot for they considered that the Tarot cards themselves could also be applied to govern sections of it. The first major division of note is the lower sphere of the Southern Hemisphere related to the twelve major constellations that applied to the zodiac signs. These are further broken down in the next lower quadrant to encompass the cards of the Minor Arcana as applied astrologically. The celestial canopy as seen from the Northern Hemisphere is then divided up into a further twelve divisions, omitting the Princesses, which were attributed to the four divisions of the lower quadrant and were made analogous with the Four Aces.

Instead of measuring the zodiac from zero degrees Aries, the Golden Dawn considered that the point of reference should be zero degrees Leo as measured from the Star Regulus, the 'Heart of the Lion'. This brought the procession of the Zodiac back in line with the Precession of the Equinoxes. This also applies to the Tarot as well, for Mathers says:

> The Tarot method of reckoning from the Star named Regulus has, it will be seen, the effect of making the Signs and the Constellations coincide.

Regulus was, of course, one of the principle stars of the heavens and was said to have ruled them, according to the ancient Babylonian system of astrology. As a star it had many names such as Sharru in Babylonia, Maghi in India, Miyan in Persia and Heen Yuen in China. It was also one of the Four Guardians of Heaven or Royal Stars of Persian astrology/astronomy, for both sciences were then considered as one. At this point we start to see the system from which Mathers had developed his system of the zodiac, for the Four Royal stars of Persian astronomy were (according to Flammarion): Fomalhaut (Aquarius), Regulus (Leo), Alderbaran (Taurus) and Antares (Scorpio). These divisions are of prime importance for they form the main points of reference, as is the Kabbalistic sephirah of Tiphareth when the Tree of Life is also applied on the celestial Sphere (which will be discussed later).

As to exactly why Regulus was chosen by the Golden Dawn as the point of reference to start the zodiac from, or rather rectify it, is complex. It was the star that Hipparchos said revealed to him the precession of the Equinoxes. Regulus was near the point of division where the Summer Solstice starts (when the constellations and signs coincided) and, as such, was the Yod force or initial impetus of the Fiery Summer. While this entire system that Mathers utilised may appear esoteric, the American psychic Edgar Cayce also concurred that the 'Babylonia-Persian system of Astrology' was the one that rectified the Signs and the Constellations and not that of the ancient Egyptian or Indian systems, which were later conceived. Cayce also stated in his readings that the same laws that govern the physical plane also govern the planets, stars and constellations, which coincides with the principles of the Macrocosm and the Microcosm. Since Cayce's track record in psychic archaeology is well-documented and well-proven to date, it appears that Mathers created or re-created this ancient system of astrology and, like Cayce, tapped into some vital etheric current, by developing the Golden Dawn system.

On viewing the Tarot as applied to the Celestial Sphere, you will notice that the planetary and zodiac arrangement is not that of orthodox astrology. The slower-moving outer planets are omitted. The planets are arranged in a way that was taken from the Hebrew Schemphamphoresh document. Its basis is Exodus 14: 19–21, from which seventy-two angelic names are formed, two of which are attributed to each card of the thirty-six Pip Cards of the Minor Arcana (excluding Aces). Since this book primarily deals with the Tarot, we will confine its discussion to that framework. We would also point out that although Mathers changed the starting point of this document from Aries to Leo, he retained the original order of the names from Aries. This has caused some confusion to some occult scholars as to exactly which angelic name was applied to which Tarot card. One will also note that with seven planets and thirty-six decanates of the zodiac an even planetary division to the decanates is not possible, so Mars rules over an extra decanate, joining Aries and Pisces, the Alpha et Omega of the old zodiac.

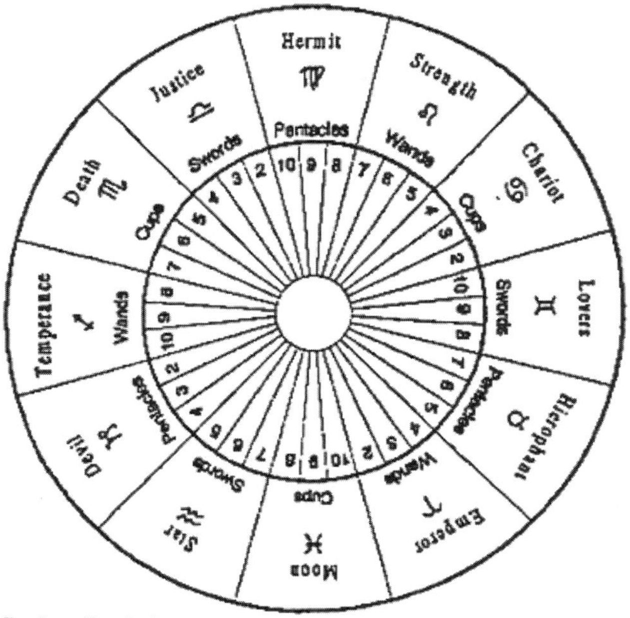

Southern Hemisphere

Northern Hemisphere

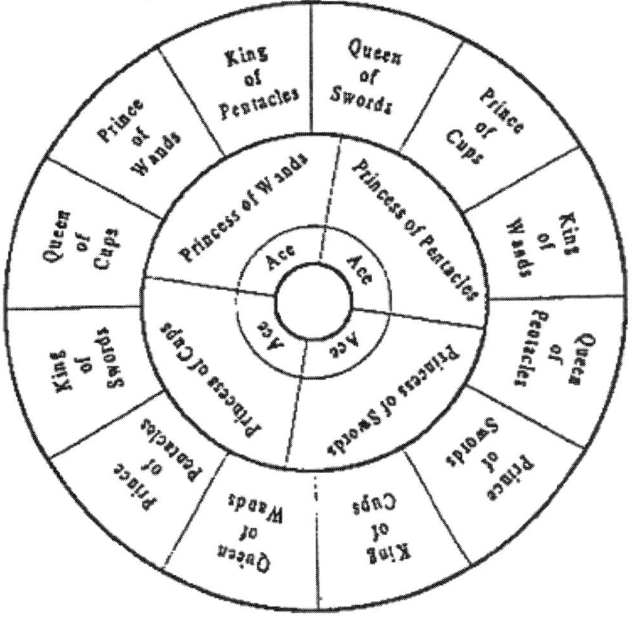

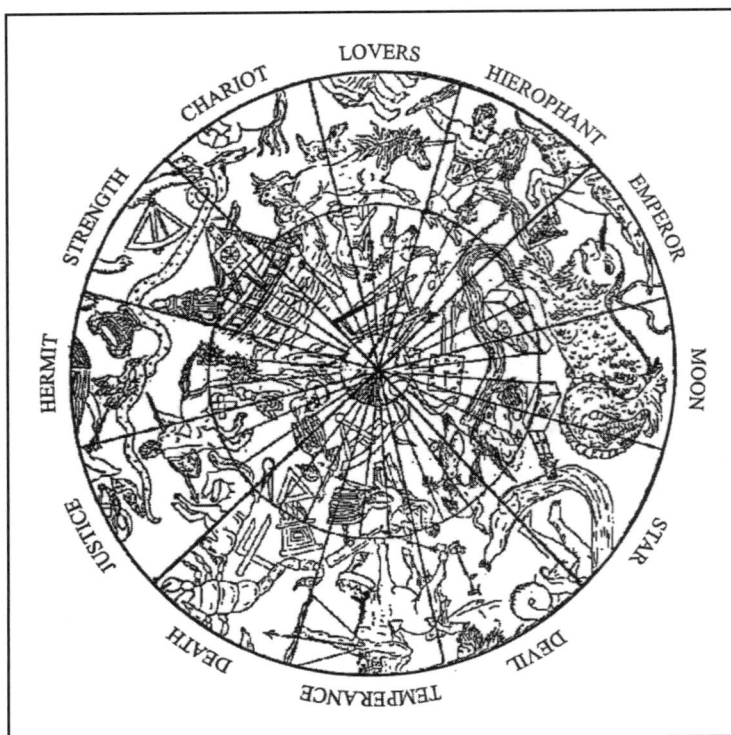

I would also point out that there appears to be a basic and uncorrected error in some of the Golden Dawn Tarot papers. This is the allocation of the zodiac degrees to the cards of the Minor Arcana. The Zodiac starts at zero degrees (the heart of the King Star, Regulus)–not one degree, Leo, as can be found in the original documents. Subsequently, after every thirty degrees, each incoming sign then starts at zero degrees.

Tarot star maps

When the Tarot is directly applied to the Celestial Sphere of the Zodiac the Four Princesses rule the Heavens from the North Pole of the Zodiac to the forty-five degrees of Latitude North of the Ecliptic. These form the thrones or bases on which the Four Aces sit over them and who rule the central Sphere analogous to Kether. The Four Knights, four Queens and four Princes rule the Celestial Heavens from forty-five degrees, North Latitude, down to the Ecliptic. The twelve Tarot Keys attributed to the Twelve Signs of the zodiac rule the Celestial Heavens from the Ecliptic to forty-five degrees of South latitude. The thirty-six smaller Pip Cards (omitting the Aces) rule the Celestial Heavens from forty-five degrees South of the Ecliptic to the South Pole, or Malkuth.

The Four Aces then revolve around Kether (forty-five degrees Longitude) and their framework of reference is through their support cards, the Princesses, with each Ace relating strongly to the corresponding Princess of the same suit. The order given for the following Tarot associations are so that they emanate from Kether across the Heavens until they meet again at Malkuth in the lower Sphere covering the Southern Heavens. The numbering system below is not sequential but shows the cards by way of generation. The Trumps associated to the planets are not given here for they are titled 'Lords who Wander' and, as such, are said to move across the heavens, having no fixed abode. The influence of them though is felt when describing the Minor Arcana or Pip Cards so their appearance in this Celestial Sphere is through the influence of a Sign. (Mathers originally meant this list to be the backbone of some future systems he was developing for his Inner Order Grades above the Zelator Adeptus Minor. A careful study of all the astrological mythology associated to each card will reveal more meanings to its functions.)

1. **Ace of Wands:** This forms part of the tail of Draco, forefeet of Ursa Major, tail of Ursa Major and of the Northern Dog of Canis Venatici.
2. **Ace of Cups:** Head of Draco, body and legs of Hercules.
3. **Ace of Swords:** Body of Draco. Right arm of Orpheus, head and body of Lacerta. Body of Cygnus.
4. **Ace of Disks:** Body of Draco. Legs of Cepheus. Tail of Ursa Minor and the Pole Star. Legs of Cassiopeia. Head and neck of Camelopardalis.
8. **Princess of Wands:** Rules from North Pole to forty-five degrees and from zero degrees of Cancer to thirty degrees of Virgo, the end of Virgo. The throne of the Ace of Wands extends forty-five degrees from twenty-two degrees of cancer to seven degrees to thirty degrees of Virgo within the limits of forty-five degrees Latitude.
    Star Group of the above: Tail of Draco. Head and forepart of Ursa Minor, left arm and part of the head and chest of Bootes. The greater part of the Northernmost Dog of Canis Venatici. Tail and back of Ursa Major (also called the Seven Ploughing Oxen, Wains Constellation, Seven Rishis, Seven Bright Ones who follow their Lord, etc.)
12. **Princess of Cups:** Rules from the North Pole to forty-five degrees of Latitude and from zero degrees of Libra to thirty degrees of Sagittarius in Longitude. The Throne of the Ace embraces from twenty-two degrees to 301 of Libra to seven to 301 of Sagittarius within the above limits of Latitude.
    Star Group: Head of Draco. Left arm body and legs of Hercules, part of the head, right shoulder and club of Bootes.
16. **Princess of Swords:** Rules from the North Pole to forty-five degrees Latitude and from zero degrees of Capricorn to thirty degrees of Pisces Longitude. The Throne of the Ace extends from twenty-two to thirty degrees of Capricorn to seven degrees to thirty degrees of Pisces as before.
    Star Group: Body of Draco, part of Lyra. Head, body and right arm of Cepheus, the King and Father of Andromeda, the whole of Cygnus, head and body of Lacerta, back and part of head of Vulpecula the Fox.
20. **Princess of Disks:** Rules from the North Pole to forty-five degrees Latitude and from zero degrees of Aries to thirty degrees of Gemini Longitude. The Throne of the Ace embraces twenty-two to thirty degrees of Gemini within the Latitude as above.

Star group: Body of Draco, legs and part of right arm and Sceptre of Cepheus, tail and hindquarters of Ursa Minor, with the Pole Star of our Earth, head and neck of Camelopardalis (Giraffe), a body and right arm, throne and legs of Cassiopeia, the Queen of Cepheus and Mother of Andromeda, head of Ursa Major.

7. **King of Wands:** Rules from Ecliptic to forty-five degrees North latitude and from twenty degrees Cancer to twenty degrees Leo in Longitude.

   Star Group: Head, body and tail of Leo, body and tail of Leo Minor, hindquarters and legs of Ursa Major, head and forequarters of Southern Dog of Canis Venatici.

17. **Knight of Disks:** Rules from the Ecliptic to forty-five degrees North Latitude and from twenty degrees of Leo to twenty degrees of Virgo.

    Star Group: Head and body of Virgo, left arm of Bootes, hair of Berenice. Body and hindquarters of Southern Dog of Canes Venatici, hindfeet of Northern dog of Canis Venatici.

14. **Queen of Swords:** Rules from the Ecliptic to forty-five degrees and from twenty degrees of Virgo to twenty degrees of Libra.

    Star Group: Right leg of Virgo, body and right arm and right leg of Bootes. Beam and part of scales of Libra.

11. **King of Cups:** Rules from the Ecliptic to forty-five degrees and from twenty degrees of Libra to twenty degrees Scorpio.

    Star Group: Part of the scales of Libra, left claws of Scorpio, body and legs of Ophiucus, the holder of the Serpent. Front half of Serpent's head, right arm and club of Hercules.

5. **Knight of Wands:** Rules from the Ecliptic to forty-five degrees North latitude and from twenty degrees of Scorpio to twenty degrees Sagittarius.

   Star Group: Top of head and bow of Sagittarius, head and right arm of Ophiucus, near half of Serpent.

18. **Queen of Disks:** Rules from the Ecliptic to forty-five degrees North Latitude and from twenty degrees of Sagittarius to twenty degrees of Capricorn.

    Star Group: Top of head, neck and horns of Capricorn, left hand of Aquarius, the man who carries the water, the whole of Aquila, the Eagle, the greater part of Delphinus, whole of Sagittarius, the Arrow, forefeet and body of Vulpecula the Fox and the tail of the Cygnet which he seizes.

16. **King of Swords.** Rules from Ecliptic to forty-five degrees North latitude and from twenty degrees of Capricorn to twenty degrees of Aquarius.

    Star Group: Tail of Capricornus, head and body of Aquarius, head and forelegs of Pegasus, the winged horse who sprang from the blood of Medusa, near the sources of the ocean, the whole of Equilaus, the lesser horse, part of head of Dolphin, tail and hindquarters of Vulpecula, part of the wing of Cygnus, the swan, part of the head of Pisces.

9. **Knight of Cups:** Rules from the Ecliptic to forty-five degrees of North latitude and from twenty degrees Aquarius to twenty degrees Pisces.

   Star Group: The body and tail of one of the Pisces and part of the band. Body and wings of Pegasus, head and arms of Andromeda, chained to the rock of Lacerta.

6. **Queen of Wands:** Rules from the Ecliptic to forty-five degrees North Latitude and from twenty degrees of Pisces to twenty degrees of Aries.

Star Group: The other fish and part of Band of Pisces, head and back of Aries, body and legs of Andromeda, the Triangle, hand and left arm of Cassiopea, winged instep of Aries.

19. **King of Disks:** Rules from the Ecliptic to forty-five degrees North Latitude and twenty degrees of Aries to twenty degrees of Taurus.
    Star Group: Tail of Aries, one horn and shoulder and back of Taurus, whole of Perseus and head of Medusa, hindquarters and legs of Camelpardalis, left leg of Auriga, Charioteer and part of Capella, the she-goat that bears kids in her arms.

13. **Knight of Swords:** Rules from the Ecliptic to forty-five degrees North latitude from twenty degrees Taurus to twenty degrees Gemini in Longitude.
    Star Group: Head and Body of Caster, one of the Gemini, greater part of Auriga and Capella, head and forepart of Lynx, forefeet of Camelopardalis.

10. **Queen of Cups:** Rules from Ecliptic to forty-five degrees North latitude and from twenty degrees Gemini to twenty degrees of Cancer in Longitude.
    Star Group: Head and Body of Pollux, the other of the Gemini; greater part of Cancer, the crab; face of Leo; head and face of Ursa Major.

The following twelve keys govern the celestial heavens
from the ecliptic to forty-five degrees south latitude

65. **Fortitude:** Rules the whole of Leo, from the point of Regulus or Cor Leonis.
    Star Group: The forelegs and hindfeet of Leo, greater part of the Sextans and of Crater, the cups, part of the body of Hydra, the great Water Serpent, greater part of Antila Pneumatica, the Air-Pump, greater part of Pisces Nautica, a small part of the ship Argo.

66. **Hermit:** Rules the whole of Virgo.
    Star Group: Left arm, hand and arm of Virgo and her ear of corn; part of the body of Hydra, Corvus, the Crow, part of the Crater, tail and right hand of Centaurus, the man-horse, small part of the Air-Pump and of Argo.

68. **Justice:** Rules the whole of Libra.
    Star Group: Part of the South Scale of Libra, tail of Hydra, head, body, arms and forefeet of Centaurus and the legs, body and tail of Lupus, the Wolf, which he is killing. Right Claw of Scorpio.

70. **Death:** Rules the whole of Scorpio.
    Star Group: Body and tail of Scorpio, head and neck of Lupus, the whole of Ara, the altar, two feet of Ophiucus, point of arrow of Sagittarius, part of Norma, the Mason's square.

71. **Temperance:** Rules the whole of Sagittarius.
    Star Group: The whole of Sagittarius, the Archer, except right hind leg, the tail, the crown of the head, extreme points of Bow and Arrow, Corona Australis, Telescope, Pavo, the Peacock.

72. **Devil:** Rules the whole of Capricorn.
    Star Group: The whole lower half of Capricornicus, the he-goat, part of Pisces Australis, Southern Fish, Microscope, part of Grus, the Crane. Part of Indus.

74. **The Star:** Rules the whole of Aquarius.
    Star Group: Legs of Aquarius and the issuant water head of Piscis Australis, part of Grus, part of Phoenix, part of Apparatus Sculptorum, part of Cetus.

75. **The Moon:** Rules the whole of Pisces.
    Star Group: The connecting band of Pisces, the body of Cetus, the sea Monster to which Andromeda was exposed, part of the Apparatus Sculptorum. Part of Phoenix, part of Fornax.
61. **The Emperor:** Rules the whole of Aries.
    Star Group: Legs of Aries, part of the Body of Taurus, head and fore-part of Cetus, part of Fornax and of Eridanus.
62. **The Hierophant:** Rules the whole of Taurus.
    Star Group: Head and forepart of Taurus the Bull. The Bull sent by Neptune to frighten the horses of Sol and those of Hippolytus. The greater part of Orion the Giant and hunter. The beginning of the River Eridanus unto which Phaeton was hurled when attempting to drive the horses of the Sun, greater part of Lepus, the Hare.
63. **The Lovers:** Rules the whole of Gemini.
    Star Group: Legs of Castor and Pollux, the Gemini, Canis Minor, a small part of Cancer. The whole of Monoceros the Unicorn, except the hindquarters. Head and forepart of Canis Major, the Greater Dog.
64. **The Chariot:** Rules the whole of Cancer up to Regulus in Leo.
    Star Group: One claw and part of the body of Cancer, forepaws of Leo, head and part of Hydra, part of Sextans, a part of Pisces Nautica, hind legs and tail of Monoceros, part of the mast, rigging and prow of the ship Argo.

The keys below of the minor arcana rule the decans from 45 degrees
south of the ecliptic to malkuth at the south pole

21. **Five of Wands:** Zero–ten degrees of Saturn in Leo.
    Star Group: Part of Argo and Pisces Volcun.
22. **Six of Wands:** Ten to twenty degrees of Jupiter in Leo.
    Star Group: Part of Argo and Pisces Volcun.
23. **Seven of Wands:** Twenty–thirty degrees of Mars in Leo.
    Star Group: Part of Argo and Pisces Volcun.
24. **Eight of Disks:** Zero–ten degrees of Sun in Virgo.
    Star Group: Part of Argo and Pisces Volcun.
25. **Nine of Disks:** Ten–twenty degrees of Venus in Virgo.
    Star Group: Hind feet of Centauri, part of Pisces Volcun.
16. **Ten of Disks:** Ten–twenty degrees of Mercury in Virgo.
    Star Group; Hind legs of Centauri, part of Chameleon.
27. **Two of Swords:** Zero–ten degrees of Moon in Libra.
    Star Group: Hind legs of Centauri, part of Crux, Musea and Chameleon.
28. **Three of Swords:** Ten–twenty degrees of Saturn in Libra.
    Star Group: Part of Crux, Musea and Chameleon.
29. **Four of Swords:** Twenty–thirty degrees of Jupiter in Libra.
    Star Group: Part of Musea, Circinus, Compasses and Chameleon.
30. **Five of Cups:** Zero–Ten degrees of Mars in Scorpio.
    Star Group: Part of Circinus, Chameleon and of Triangulum Australia

31. **Six of Cups:** Ten–twenty degrees of Sun in Scorpio.
    Star Group: Part of Triangulum Australis, Apus the swallow and Octano.
32. **Seven of Cups:** twenty–thirty degrees of Venus in Scorpio.
    Star Group: Part of Pavo, Apus and Octano.
33. **Eight of Wands:** Zero–ten degrees of Mercury in Sagittarius.
    Star Group: Part of Pavo, Apus and Octano.
34. **Nine of Wands:** Ten–twenty degrees of the Moon in Sagittarius.
    Star Group: Part of Pavo, Apus and Octano.
35. **Ten of Wands:** Twenty–thirty degrees of Saturn in Sagittarius.
    Star Group: Part of Pavo, Hydra, Watersnake.
36. **Two of Disks:** zero–ten degrees of Jupiter in Capricorn.
    Star Group: Part of Pavo and Hydra.
37. **Three of Disks:** Ten–twenty degrees of Mars in Capricorn.
    Star Group: Part of Tucana and Hydra.
38. **Four of Disks:** Twenty–thirty degrees of the Sun in Capricorn.
    Star Group: Part of Tucana and Phoenix.
39. **Five of Swords:** Zero–ten degrees of Venus in Aquarius.
    Star Group: Part of Phoenix, end of Eridanus.
40. **Six of Swords:** Ten–twenty degrees of Mercury in Aquarius.
    Star Group: Part of Hydrus, Reticulus, Rhombus.
41. **Seven of Swords:** Twenty–thirty degrees of the Moon in Aquarius.
    Star Group: Parts of Phoenix, Hydra, Reticulum, Eridanus.
42. **Eight of Cups:** Zero–ten degrees of Saturn in Pisces.
    Star Group: Part of Phoenix, Eridanus, Reticulum.
43. **Nine of Cups:** Ten–twenty degrees of Jupiter in Pisces.
    Star Group: Part of Phoenix, Eridanus, Reticulum.
44. **Ten of Cups:** Twenty–thirty degrees of Mars in Pisces.
    Star Group: Part of Phoenix, Dorado, Reticulum.
45. **Two of Wands:** Zero–ten degrees of Mars in Aries.
    Star Group: Part of Phoenix and Dorado.
46. **Three of Wands:** Ten–twenty degrees of the Sun in Aries.
    Star Group: Part of Coelum Sculptori and Dorado.
47. **Four of Wands:** Twenty–thirty degrees of Venus in Aries.
    Star Group: Part of Coelum Sculptori.
48. **Five of Disks:** Zero–ten degrees of Mercury in Taurus.
    Star Group: Part of Eridanus, Columba, Naochi, Dorado, Equilaus, Pictoris.
49. **Six of Disks:** Ten–twenty degrees of the Moon in Taurus.
    Star Group: Forepart of Lepus, Tail and Wing of Columba, part of Equilaus.
50. **Seven of Disks:** Twenty–thirty degrees of Saturn in Taurus.
    Star Group: Part of Equilaus and Lepus, Body of Columba.
51. **Eight of Swords:** Zero–ten degrees of Jupiter in Gemini.
    Star Group: Feet of Canis Major, Prow of Argo, part of Equilaus Pictoris.
52. **Nine of Swords:** Ten–twenty degrees of Mars in Gemini.
    Star Group: Legs of Canis Major, Part of Prow of Argo.

53. **Ten of Swords:** Twenty–thirty degrees of the Sun in Gemini.
    Star Group: Hindquarters of Canis Major, part of Prow of Argo.
54. **Two of Cups:** Zero–ten degrees of Venus in Cancer.
    Star Group: Prow of Argo and Tail of Canis Major.
55. **Three of Cups:** Ten–twenty degrees of Mercury in Cancer.
    Star Group: Prow of Argo.
56. **Four of Cups:** Twenty–thirty degrees of Moon in Cancer.
    Star Group: Prow of Argo.

Tree of life on the celestial sphere

When viewing the Sphere of the Celestial Heaven with the Tree of Life superimposed upon it, the central uppermost point corresponds to the Sephirah of Kether and the lower to Malkuth. At this point you will see that there are now two of each Sephirah and four of others and this scheme will also refer to the Paths joining them as well, the exception being Kether and Malkuth, the top and bottom of the central axis. The tarot association here is completely different due to the fact it works on another plane, that of the Kabbalah and this point must not be confused with the general association with the Star Maps. It would pay the reader to do a thorough study of the Tarot associations with both the Sephiroth and constellations, as far as their influences go, for there is yet another hidden formula in this. There are a total of twenty-two Sephiroth and seventy-two Paths on the Celestial Sphere, which is highly significant in itself.

Kether: Will govern a radius of ten degrees around the central axis point.

Star Group: This will encircle the whole of Ursa Minor with the exception of the tail and three of the loops of Draco.

Tarot Association: Four Aces.

Chokmah (a) and (b): Will be sixty degrees North Latitude with a ten degree radius.

Star Group (a): The left hand, arm and part of Head of Bootes and touching the right foot of Hercules.

Tarot Association (a): Knights of Wands and Swords. Two of Wands and Swords.

Star Group (b): The head and shoulder of Cepheus and Lacerta.

Tarot Association (b): Knights of Cups and Disks. Two of Cups and Disks.

Binah (a) and (b): Both have a ten degree radius and within the sixty degrees of North Latitude.

Star Group (a): Includes Pole Star, head of Camelopardalis, tip of the tail of Draco.

Tarot Association (a): Queens of Cups and Disks. Three of Cups and Disks.

Star Group (b): Lyra and left knee of Hercules.

Tarot Association (b): Queens of Wands and Swords. Three of Wands and Swords.

Chesed (a) and (b): Thirty degrees North Latitude with a ten degree radius.

Star Group (a): Part of Coma Berenices, of Bootes and of Virgo.

Tarot Association (a): Four of Wands and Swords.

Star Group (b): Part of Andromeda and Pegasus.

Tarot Associations (b): Four of Cups and Disks.

Geburah (a) and (b): Thirty degrees of North Latitude and ten degree radius.

Star Group (a): The right wing of Aquila and tail of Serpens.

Tarot Association (a): Five of Wands and Swords.

Star Group (b): Part of Hound and Telescope.

Tarot Associations (b): Five of Cups and Disks.

Tiphareth now has four Sephiroth allocated to it and therefore each Sephiroth will relate only to one suit of cards instead of two. The size of the Four Tiphareth Sephiroth is in fact the same size as Yesod in the Southern Hemisphere. The small size of Tiphareth relates to the fact that it is a reflection of the hidden Tiphareth centre on the Axis of the Sphere and since it is on the Ecliptic is the furthermost point from it. Each of these points will have to be measured from zero degrees Leo, which Mathers associated to Regulus and related to zero degrees of all the Fixed Signs.

Tiphareth (a–d): On the line of the Ecliptic. Five degree radius with 2.5 degrees in Northern Hemisphere and 2.5 degrees in Southern Hemisphere.

Tarot Associations (a): Six of Wands and King of Wands.

Star (a): Regulus—Zero degrees Leo.

Tarot Associations (b): Six of Cups and King of Cups.

Star (b): Zero degrees Scorpio.

Tarot Association (c): Six of Swords and King of Swords.

Star (c): Zero degrees Aquarius.

Tarot Association (d): Six of Disks and King of Disks.

Star (d): Zero degrees Taurus

Netzach (a–b): Thirty degrees of South Latitude with a ten degree radius.

Star Group (a): The Unicorn and the head of Canis Major.

Tarot Association (a): Seven of Cups and Disks.

Star Group (b): Pavo, the Telescope, Corona Austrina and feet of Sagittarius.

Tarot Association (b): Seven of Wands and Swords.

Hod (a–b): Thirty degrees of South Latitude with a ten degrees radius.

Star Group (a): Part of Cetus and Fornax.

Tarot Association (a): Eight of Wands and Swords.

Star Group (b): Part of the loop of Hydra and the tip of Corvus.

Tarot Association (b): Eight of Cups and Disks.

Yesod (a–d): Sixty degrees South Latitude.

Stars (a): Directly below Leo on the Middle Pillar-part of the rigging and hull of Argo.

Tarot association (a): Nine of Wands.

Stars (b): Musca.

Tarot Association (b): Nine of Cups.

Stars (c): Tucana.

Tarot Association (c): Nine of Swords.

Stars (d): Caelum—Engraving Tool.

Tarot Association (d): Nine of Disks.

Malkuth: Ten degrees of South Latitude.

Stars: Mensa, Pictor, Volans, Dorado.

Tarot Association. The Ten of Wands, Cups, Swords and Disks; The Four Princesses of the above suits.

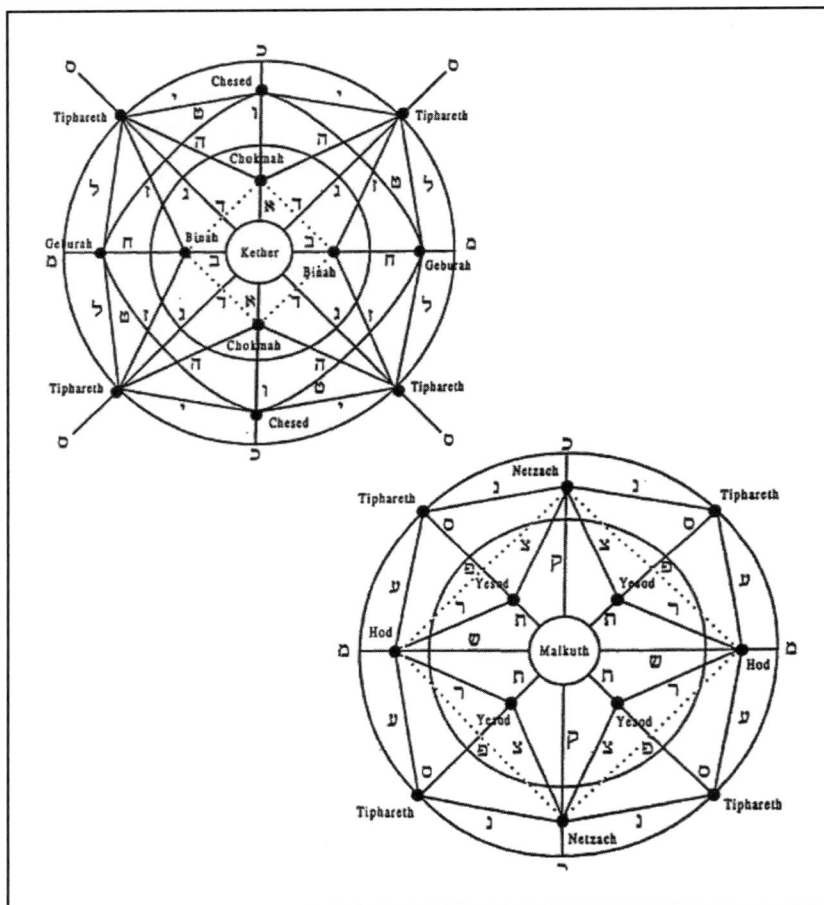

The various paths cutting across the Celestial Sphere and linking the Sephiroth are also associated with the Trumps. The whole concept of this association can also be applied to the Sphere of the Earth and brings to light interesting conclusions as to what card from both the Major and Minor Arcana cover countries and shows forth varying degrees of influence. Since this work is very complex and detailed I have omitted this portion as it in fact goes way beyond the scope of reference of this book and it relies very heavily on other sub-systems of the Golden Dawn.

Convoluted forces

Creeping Dragon Formulae. The World of Yetzirah—Earthy Part of Malkuth.

This particular section deals with the movement of the Aces around the North Pole and shows how their influence extends to the Ecliptic and how the Southern Hemisphere seasons are generated. Mathers used here the four convolutions of the Dragon around the Polar Ecliptic as being analogous to the Four Aces and in the order of YHVH. As stated earlier each of the Aces relate to part of the main body of the Dragon though there are portions of the Upper part of the head and the lower tail which do not apply to them for the Aces cover only a ten degrees radius and the Dragon goes beyond this in size. Some maps have the Dragon with six loops and others with four. We will be concerned only with the loops inside the ten degree radius which, for the sake of argument, will be considered as four. We will be dealing mainly with the quaternary and the elemental associations to the Signs:

```
Ace of Wands  = Fire   = Aries, Leo, Sagittarius.
Ace of Cups   = Water  = Cancer, Scorpio, Pisces.
Ace of Swords = Air    = Gemini, Libra, Aquarius.
Ace of Disks  = Earth  = Taurus, Virgo, Capricorn.
```

It must also be considered that the Aces sit directly over the Princesses and that the same association with the elements also apply, but whereas the Princesses remain stationary, the Aces on top of them rotate. Simply consider an Ace as the impetus and the Princesses as the framework through which the Aces operate. It is very much like the Aces are a Yod Force, starting things off, until things start manifesting through the Princesses as the Heh (final) influence. Since each Princess is allied to an Ace of the same element, when the Aces rotate over them they are attracted by that same force or influence. Fire and Air would attract Fire and Air but repel Water and Earth, and of course the Aces would be at their strongest point when directly over the Princess of their own element.

Stations

These are the Signs of the Zodiac under the action of the Aces. The first Station actually starts with the initial boundary of the Princess of Wands in the Sign of Cancer. The table below shows the generation of each Station with the Area covered by each Princess.

Sign	Station	Dominion of Princess
Cancer	1	Wands
Leo	2	Wands
Virgo	3	Wands
Libra	4	Cups
Scorpio	5	Cups
Sagittarius	6	Cups
Capricorn	7	Swords
Aquarius	8	Swords
Pisces	9	Swords
Aries	10	Disks
Taurus	11	Disks
Gemini	12	Disks

Each Ace has what is called a Throne and these are the fixed Signs. It must be remembered that there are Four Thrones that rule over the Four quadrants which are the Four Aces whose rule is the same as that of the Princesses, as discussed earlier. Mathers called the movement of the Aces the 'Direct of Creeping Dragon Formula', because of the rolling or creeping way they work around the constellation of the Dragon, which, for the purposes of this discussion, is done in an anti-clockwise manner. Starting Point of Reference:

In order of YHVH

    Ace of Wands = On Station 2 = Leo
    Ace of Cups   = On Station 1 = Cancer
    Ace of Swords = On Station 12 = Gemini
    Ace of Disks = On Station 11 = Taurus

If we look at the tail of the constellation of Draco we find that it is directly under the sign of Leo in the Ecliptic and starting point of the Throne of the Ace and may give some indication as to its throne. Instead of the Aces next moving forwards one Throne each, we have what is called a sticking point. The Aces at this point do not move like a flat disk, but roll over each other. The Ace of Wands remains where it is, attracted by its Throne while the Ace of Cups is on top of it

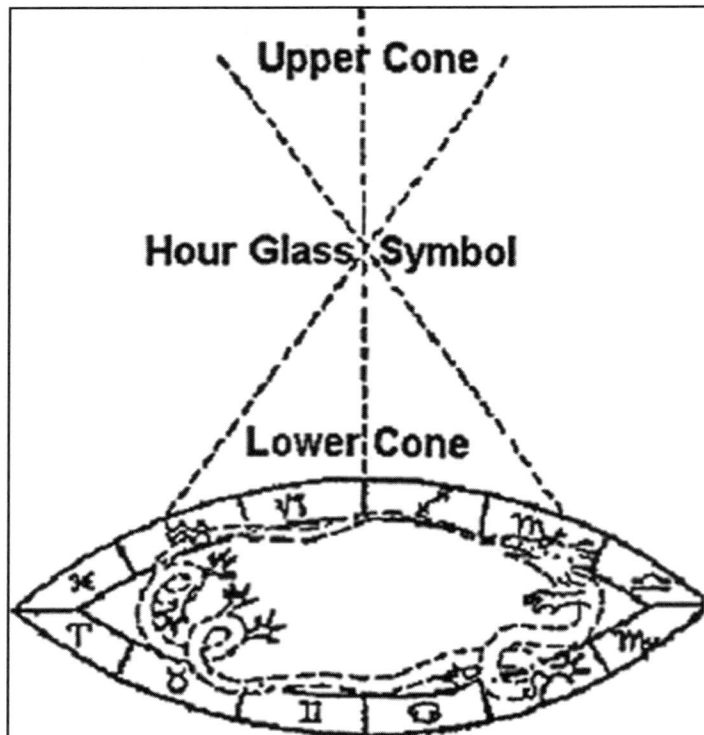

with the Ace of Swords now on **Station 1** and the Ace of Disks on **Station 12**. (The Ace of Wands in fact remains here for Five more movements of the Aces until the Ace of Disks has passed over it and is in the **Station 3**). The next movement shows that the Ace of Wands does not move while the other Aces leapfrog over yet again in the same order as before. In the next move we have the Ace of Cups on **Station 3** for it has moved off the Ace of Wands while the Ace of Swords then takes its place above the Ace of Wands and the Ace of Disks moves on to **Station 1**.

In the next movement the Ace of Cups moves to **Station 4** while the Ace of Swords moves to **Station 3** while the Ace of Wands still remains on **Station 2** with the Ace of Disks directly over it.

In the next movement the Ace of Cups goes to **Station 5** while the Ace of Swords goes to **Station 4**, the Ace of Disks to **Station 3** and the Ace of Wands remains where it is and is now free to make the next move. **Station 5** is also the seat or Throne of the Ace of Cups, for the Water Sign Scorpio attracts the Ace of Cups and holds on to it until the other Aces have moved over it. The next attracting force is the Air Sign of Aquarius, **Station 8**, which holds the Ace of Swords until the others have rolled over it. The Ace of Disks is then attracted to its Throne, the Earth Sign of Taurus, **Station 11**, and the process starts all over again. This whole concept is very much analogous to the Sun passing through the Zodiac Signs and bringing the seasons. Consider the whole Celestial Sphere as a composite of the Four Worlds with the energy of the Aces working down through the various worlds until Malkuth, in the Southern Hemisphere, is reached. As the energy of the Aces goes through the Central Axis of the Sphere and creeps slowly across the face of the Sphere, it undergoes something of a reversal at the centre of the Axis in the hidden Tiphareth centre, reflecting the energy through to Malkuth which then rotates out through the Minor Arcana to the Ecliptic, which is stimulated into operation through the operation of the Four Princesses in Malkuth.

Looped or flying dragon formulae: the world of Yetzirah. Airy part of Malkuth

The formula goes clockwise and deals with the World of Yetzirah. The Diagram below shows the heads of the Dragon on the Cardinal or the more Active Signs. Whereas in the previous formula the action was direct, here the elements have lightened and intermingled so that this Airy influence is more subtle. Now in this formulae the Throne of each dominion is not one sign, for Mathers says:

> 'Now also the Throne in each Dominion is marked in the Book T as embracing more than one third of each dominion now extended to because of the enduring effect of its force'.

What happens is that the Throne of the Ace now extends to half a sign each side of the Throne. This then shows that the expanded Throne then takes up nearly the entire domain of the Ace/Princess. The heads of each Dragon, now there are four, each with two loops representing the forces of the Ace, rest in the Cardinal Signs. The influence of the Aces has been greatly extended to cover a wider area over the globe and the actions of this force are more horizontal in nature.

Leaping or darting formulae: the world of Yetzirah. Fiery part of Malkuth

This formula shows the law of attraction and repulsion. It deals mainly with the influences of the Aces (as the Dragon), settling down only on Signs that attract it, by way of their elemental nature. Taking the coverage of the Ace of Wands, the Element of Fire, we find that the head of the Dragon rests in Aries, the point where its influence now starts. The Watery influence of Pisces rejects it, causing it to rise. It comes lower and rests lightly on Aquarius and Capricorn because the Airy and Earthy Nature do not repel the Fiery influence. It is strongly attracted by the Fire sign of Sagittarius where it rests and loops, but is yet again repelled by the Watery Scorpio, but settles lightly on the Airy Libra and more firmly on the Earthy Virgo. As it comes to rest on Leo it loops, for here the Fire Sign attracts it. It has to rise suddenly due to the antipathy of the Watery Cancer but settles yet again in the Airy Gemini and Taurus, finally looping in the Fire Sign of Aries where its tail rests. The influence of the Ace or Dragon must rise quickly after its point of attraction.

Revolving or flowing formula: world of yetzirah. Watery part of malkuth

This revolving formula can be explained simply by studying the diagram of the central wheel of the Four Aces within the Zodiac circle. The principle, as it was explained to me, was to make a cardboard cut-out of the centre diagram and roll it over the Zodiac signs in successional order. The section of the diagram of the Aces that rests on Aries is, of course, the Ace of Wands. The Ace of Disks portion will then roll on Taurus and the Ace of Swords portion will roll on Gemini. The Ace of Cups portion will then roll on Cancer, etc. The relationship to the Aces and to their Signs is, of course, an elemental one with only the portion of the Ace rolling onto a Sign of the same element.

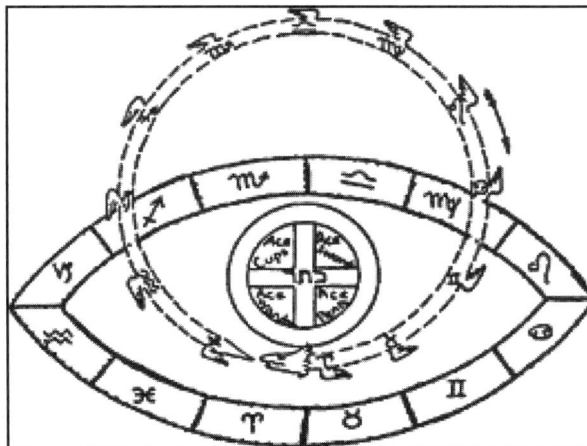